Credible and Actionable Evidence

Second Edition

*To those engaged in the continuous struggle to help create
a better future, including those whose efforts involve the pursuit of
providing rigorous and influential evaluations*

Credible and Actionable Evidence

The Foundation for Rigorous and Influential Evaluations

Second Edition

Editors

Stewart I. Donaldson
Claremont Graduate University

Christina A. Christie
University of California, Los Angeles

Melvin M. Mark
Pennsylvania State University

⑤SAGE

Los Angeles | London | New Delhi
Singapore | Washington DC

SAGE

Los Angeles | London | New Delhi
Singapore | Washington DC

FOR INFORMATION:

SAGE Publications, Inc.
2455 Teller Road
Thousand Oaks, California 91320
E-mail: order@sagepub.com

SAGE Publications Ltd.
1 Oliver's Yard
55 City Road
London EC1Y 1SP
United Kingdom

SAGE Publications India Pvt. Ltd.
B 1/I 1 Mohan Cooperative Industrial Area
Mathura Road, New Delhi 110 044
India

SAGE Publications Asia-Pacific Pte. Ltd.
3 Church Street
#10-04 Samsung Hub
Singapore 049483

Printed in the United States of America

Library of Congress Cataloging-in-Publication Data

What counts as credible evidence in applied research and evaluation practice?

Credible and actionable evidence : the foundation for rigorous and influential evaluations / edited by Stewart I. Donaldson, Claremont Graduate University, Christina A. Christie, University of California, Los Angeles, Melvin M. Mark, Pennsylvania State University. — Second edition.

pages cm

Previous edition: What counts as credible evidence in applied research and evaluation practice? Los Angeles : Sage, 2009.

Includes bibliographical references and index.

ISBN 978-1-4833-0625-4 (pbk. : alk. paper)

1. Research—Evaluation. 2. Research—Social aspects. 3. Social sciences—Methodology. 4. Evaluation research (Social action programs) 5. Educational accountability. I. Donaldson, Stewart I. (Stewart Ian) II. Christie, Christina A. III. Mark, Melvin M. IV. Title.

Q180.55.E9W53 2015
001.4'2—dc23   2014012103

This book is printed on acid-free paper.

Acquisitions Editor: Helen Salmon
Editorial Assistant: Anna Villarruel
Project Editor: Bennie Clark Allen
Copy Editor: Erin Livingston
Typesetter: C&M Digitals (P) Ltd.
Proofreader: Jeff Bryant
Indexer: Jennifer Pairan
Cover Designer: Anupama Krishnan
Marketing Manager: Nicole Elliott

SFI label applies to text stock

14 15 16 17 18 10 9 8 7 6 5 4 3 2 1

Detailed Contents

Preface

This volume addresses one of the most important and contentious issues challenging applied research and evaluation practice today: What constitutes credible and actionable evidence? We fear that history has been repeating itself of late, with the earlier quantitative–qualitative paradigm war appearing again in varied guises. These include public debates and serious professional arguments about federal research and evaluation design priorities as well as statements from several professional associations regarding the role of randomized controlled trials (RCTs) and the existence of "gold standards" for evidence. Much human capital and more than one friendship have been lost in heated disagreements about what counts as credible and actionable evidence. Lost too, we fear, have been potentially productive conversations about the varied ways in which evaluation can contribute to action and understandings that can assist in addressing important social needs.

One goal of this book was to address these thorny issues in a more positive and productive manner. We hope that collectively, the chapters in this book provide more light than heat regarding the fundamental challenge of providing credible and actionable evidence, a challenge that faces contemporary evaluators in professional practice on a day-to-day basis.

In an effort to accomplish this goal, a diverse and internationally renowned cast of evaluators were invited to participate in the Claremont Graduate University Stauffer Symposium focusing on the question, "What Counts as Credible Evidence in Applied Research and Evaluation Practice?" This illuminating and action-packed day in Claremont was experienced by more than 200 participants from a wide variety of backgrounds—evaluators, researchers, private consultants, students, faculty, and professionals from many fields. The presenters all shared their latest thinking about how to answer the question, and later, each prepared a more detailed chapter to help illuminate, from her or his vantage point, the key challenges about the nature of evidence in applied research and evaluation practice.

The result of these efforts was the first edition of this volume. It explored a broad array of issues that address the fundamental challenges of designing and executing high-quality applied research and evaluation projects. Few works have attempted to sort out these issues in a way that directly informs contemporary applied research, evaluation, and evidence-based practice. We hoped that readers would garner a new and clear understanding of the philosophical, theoretical, methodological, political, ethical, and pragmatic dimensions of gathering credible and actionable evidence to answer fundamental research and evaluation questions across diverse disciplinary boundaries and real-world contexts.

In 2012, SAGE staff conveyed interest in our development of a second edition. We consulted with each other, with many of the original authors, and with a couple of potential new authors. As a result, we decided to move forward with the new edition and to broaden its scope as reflected in a revised title, *Credible and Actionable Evidence: The Foundation for Rigorous and Influential Evaluations*. A few chapters from the first edition were dropped, given changes in the field over time. Original authors were asked to revise their chapters, taking into account new developments in the field and in their thinking as well as this somewhat broader focus. Robin Miller and Eleanor Chelimsky were each invited to contribute new chapters to the second edition.

Among the key features of this new edition are that it:

- offers authoritative statements about using credible and actionable evidence and its use toward providing rigorous and influential evaluations from leading scholars across such fields as education, psychology, health and human services, public policy, and public administration;
- covers experimental and nonexperimental methods, with experts in their use critically appraising the credibility of evidence from these varied approaches;
- provides summaries of strengths and weaknesses across the varied approaches to gathering credible and actionable evidence;
- contains diverse definitions of evidence so that students and other readers can better understand and evaluate the landscape of this highly debated topic; and
- includes a full chapter covering the major themes and the practical implications for how to best to gather credible and actionable evidence in contemporary evaluation and evidence-based practice.

In sum, then, we hope this second edition will become a valuable resource for practicing evaluators, applied researchers, students preparing for applied research and evaluation careers, scholars and teachers of evaluation and applied research methods, and other professionals interested in how to best study and evaluate programs, policies, organizations, and other initiatives designed to improve some aspect of the human condition and societal well-being.

Acknowledgments

The editors of this volume would like to express their deep gratitude to our editorial assistant, Edith Ramirez, for her wonderful dedication and excellent work on the production of this manuscript. Special thanks to the coordinator of the Claremont Graduate University Stauffer Symposium, Paul Thomas, and his fantastic group of graduate student volunteers for making the Stauffer Symposium a smashing success. We are very thankful to the chapter authors for sharing with us their best thinking and advice about credible and actionable evidence in the pursuit of rigorous and influential evaluations and for going the extra mile to make their chapters engaging and widely accessible. We sincerely appreciate the helpful reviews and suggestions for improvement provided by the reviewers of the first edition, including Larry A. Braskamp, Loyola University, Chicago; John C. Ory, University of Illinois; Melvin Hall, Northern Arizona University; Michael Schooley, Centers for Disease Control and Prevention (CDC); and pre-revision reviewers for the second edition, including Dr. Audrey J. Penner, Matthew J. Zagumny, Jennifer Fellabaum, and Christopher J. Maglio. We also extend our appreciation to the SAGE staff: Helen Salmon, acquisitions editor; Nicole Elliott, executive marketing manager; Bennie Allen, production editor; and Erin Livingston, copy editor.

Finally, this project would not have been possible without the generous gift provided by the John Stauffer Charitable Trust to the School of Social Science, Policy, & Evaluation, Claremont Graduate University. We are abundantly grateful for this essential financial support.

Stewart I. Donaldson
Claremont, California

Christina A. Christie
Los Angeles, California

Melvin M. Mark
State College, Pennsylvania

About the Editors

Stewart I. Donaldson is the professor and director of the Claremont Evaluation Center and dean of the Schools of Social Science, Policy, & Evaluation and Community & Global Health at Claremont Graduate University. Dean Donaldson continues to develop and lead one of the most extensive and rigorous graduate programs specializing in evaluation. Dr. Donaldson is currently serving as the director of the American Evaluation Association's (AEA) Graduate Education Diversity Internship (GEDI) Program and recently served a three-year term on the AEA Board. He leads the Certificate for the Advanced Study of Evaluation Program at Claremont (a distance education program for working professionals) and has taught thousands of graduate students and working professionals participating in online courses, workshops, webinars, and various other e-learning experiences. He is a Fellow of the *Western Psychological Association* and serves on the boards of the *International Positive Psychology Association* and *EvalPartners* and the editorial boards of the *American Journal of Evaluation, New Directions for Evaluation, Evaluation and Program Planning,* and the *Journal of Multidisciplinary Evaluation.* Professor Donaldson has authored or coauthored more than 200 evaluation reports, scientific journal articles, and chapters, and his recent books include *Credible and Actionable Evidence: The Foundation for Rigorous and Influential Evaluations* (this volume); *Practical Program Design and Redesign: A Theory-Driven Approach to Program Development and Developmental Evaluation* (forthcoming); *Evaluation for an Equitable Society* (forthcoming); *Theory-Driven Positive Psychology: A Culturally Responsive Scientific Approach* (forthcoming); *Emerging Practices in International Development Evaluation* (2013); *The Future of Evaluation in Society: A Tribute to Michael Scriven* (2013); *Teaching Psychology Online: Tips and Strategies for Success* (2012); *Social Psychology and Evaluation* (2011); *Advancing Validity in Outcome Evaluation: Theory and Practice* (2011); *Applied Positive Psychology: Improving Everyday Life, Health, Schools, Work, and Society* (2011); *What Counts as Credible Evidence in Applied*

Research and Evaluation Practice? (2008); *Program Theory-Driven Evaluation Science: Strategies and Applications* (2007); *Applied Psychology: New Frontiers and Rewarding Careers* (2006); and *Evaluating Social Programs and Problems: Visions for the New Millennium* (2003). Dr. Donaldson has been honored with Early Career Achievement Awards from the Western Psychological Association and the AEA. In 2013, he was honored with the AEA's Paul F. Lazarsfeld Award for sustained lifetime written contributions to advancing evaluation theory and practice and was elected president of the AEA.

Christina A. Christie is a professor and head of the Social Research Methodology Division in the Graduate School of Education and Information Studies at University of California, Los Angeles. Christie's research on evaluation practice is designed to strengthen our understanding of evaluation as a method for facilitating social change. Her theoretical scholarship intends to advance frameworks for understanding evaluation models with the goal of refining practice. She is the director of the University of California Evaluation Center, a seven-campus evaluation research center that promotes methodological advances in evaluation and supports the use of sound evidence for educational and social policy and program decision making. Her current projects include an evaluation of California's Mental Health Service Act; a large-scale place-based initiative designed to improve the education, health, and safety outcomes of children ages 0–5; and several community college remedial education initiatives. She has published widely in journals such *American Journal of Evaluation, Children and Youth Services Review, Evaluation and Program Planning, Studies in Educational Evaluation,* and *Teachers College Record.* Christie has served on the board of the AEA and is the former chair of the Theories of Evaluation Division and the Research on Evaluation Division of AEA. Currently, she is an associate editor for the *American Journal of Evaluation.*

Melvin M. Mark is professor of psychology at the Pennsylvania State University, where he also is head of the Department of Psychology. He has served as president of the AEA. He was editor of the *American Journal of Evaluation* (and is now editor emeritus). A social psychologist, Dr. Mark has wide-ranging interests related to the theory, methodology, and practice of evaluation as well as a general interest in the application of social psychology to evaluation and applied social research. Dr. Mark's awards include the AEA's Lazarsfeld Award for Contributions to Evaluation Theory. He is author of more than 125 articles and chapters in books. Among his books are *Evaluation: An Integrated Framework for Understanding, Guiding, and Improving Policies and Programs* and the coedited volumes *Social Science and Social Policy; SAGE Handbook of Evaluation; What Counts as Credible Evidence in Applied Research and Evaluation Practice; Evaluation in Action: Interviews With Expert Evaluators;* and *Social Psychology and Evaluation.*

About the Contributors

Leonard Bickman is a research professor at Vanderbilt University and Florida International University. He is coeditor of two handbooks on social research methods and the *Applied Social Research Methods* series for SAGE Publications. He is editor of *Administration and Policy in Mental Health and Mental Health Services Research*. Dr. Bickman is among an elite group of grantees who rank above the 95th percentile in the distribution of extramural National Institutes of Health (NIH) grants over the past 25 years. He is currently the principal investigator on grants from NIH, the Institute of Education Sciences, and the U.S. Department of Defense. He has received several national awards recognizing the contributions of his research, including the U.S. Health & Human Services Secretary's Award for Distinguished Service, the American Psychological Association's Public Interest Award for Distinguished Contribution to Research in Public Policy, the Education and Training in Psychology Award for Distinguished Contributions, the AEA Outstanding Evaluation Award, and Vanderbilt University's Earl Sutherland Prize for Achievement in Research. He is a past president of the AEA and the Society for the Psychological Study of Social Issues. Dr. Bickman has extensive experience in developing and successfully conducting major randomized field experiments in several substantive areas, including education, health, mental health, and criminal justice.

Eleanor Chelimsky is currently an independent consultant for evaluation policy, practice, and methodology. From 1980 to 1994, she directed the Program Evaluation and Methodology Division of the U.S. Government Accountability Office (GAO), which produced nearly 300 evaluations of government policies and programs for Congress, developed and demonstrated new methods, and disseminated information on evaluation theory and methodology worldwide. During her public service career, Chelimsky served as United States Assistant Comptroller General and as president of both the AEA and the earlier Evaluation Research Society, receiving many awards for her work. She was an economic and statistical analyst at the U.S. Mission to NATO and a research manager at the MITER Corporation and studied in Paris as a Fulbright scholar. Chelimsky has written and published extensively on evaluation and public policy.

Dreolin Fleischer received her BA from Mount Holyoke College in 2001. Before beginning graduate school, she worked as a research assistant at Goodman Research Group, Inc. (GRG), evaluating mostly educational programs, materials, and services. In 2014, she received her PhD in evaluation and applied research methods from Claremont Graduate University's (CGU) School of Social Science, Policy & Evaluation. For her master's thesis, she surveyed U.S. members of the AEA on the topic of evaluation use, and for her dissertation, she conducted an exploratory study on the "personal factor" and its relationship to instrumental evaluation use. She currently works as an associate at Slover Linett Audience Research, a firm specializing in research and evaluation for the cultural sector.

Jennifer C. Greene is a professor of educational psychology at the University of Illinois at Urbana-Champaign. She has been an evaluation scholar-practitioner for over 30 years and previously held faculty positions at the University of Rhode Island and Cornell University. Her work focuses on the intersection of social science methodology and social policy and aspires to be both methodologically innovative and socially responsible. Greene's methodological research has concentrated on advancing qualitative and mixed-methods approaches to social inquiry as well as democratic commitments in evaluation practice. She is widely sought as an expert in mixed methods and democratic approaches to evaluation that position evaluation in service of the broader public good. Greene has held leadership positions in the AEA and the American Educational Research Association. She has also provided editorial service to both communities, including a six-year position as co-editor-in-chief of *New Directions for Evaluation,* many years on the editorial board of the *American Journal of Evaluation,* and a current position as associate editor of the *Journal of Mixed Methods Research.* Her own publication record includes a coeditorship of the recent *SAGE Handbook of Program Evaluation* and authorship of *Mixed Methods in Social Inquiry.* Greene was president of the AEA in 2011.

Gary T. Henry holds the Patricia and H. Rodes Hart Chair and position of Distinguished Professor of Public Policy and Education in the Department of Leadership, Policy and Organization, Peabody College, Vanderbilt University. He also codirects the ExpERT Pre-Doctoral Fellows program within Peabody College. Professor Henry teaches the doctoral course in causal inference and a course on evaluation at Vanderbilt. He formerly held the Duncan MacRae '09 and Rebecca Kyle MacRae Distinguished Professorship of Public Policy in the Department of Public Policy and directed the Carolina Institute for

Public Policy at the University of North Carolina at Chapel Hill. Also, he is a Fellow with the Frank Porter Graham Institute for Child Development, a Fellow in the Carolina Institute for Public Policy, and a research professor in the Department of Public Policy at UNC–Chapel Hill. Henry specializes in education policy, educational evaluation, teacher quality research, and quantitative research methods. He has published extensively in top journals such as *Science, Educational Researcher, Journal of Policy Analysis and Management, Educational Evaluation and Policy Analysis, Journal of Teacher Education, Education Finance and Policy,* and *Evaluation Review.* Currently, his major educational research projects are the evaluation of the North Carolina Race to the Top initiative; the evaluation of the Achievement School District, a part of Tennessee's First to the Top initiative; and the Teacher Quality Research initiative for the University of North Carolina General Administration. Other major evaluations include North Carolina's Disadvantaged Student Supplemental Fund and Georgia's Universal Pre-K and HOPE Scholarship programs as well as school turnaround in North Carolina. Dr. Henry currently serves as panel chair for the Continuous Improvement in Education Research panel and previously served as a principal member of the Standing Committee for Systemic Reform, Institute of Education Sciences, U.S. Department of Education, and he has served on numerous advisory boards and as a consultant for several states on evaluations and longitudinal databases.

George Julnes is professor of public and international affairs at University of Baltimore and received his PhD in clinical/community psychology while working with Roland Tharp within the neo-Vygotskiian framework that emphasizes assisted performance as the way to promote human and social development. Subsequent graduate work with Larry Mohr (program evaluation) and Karl Weick (organizational sensemaking) led to the formulation of *evaluation as assisted sensemaking.* His recent work involves consulting with federal agencies on rigorous evaluation designs and developing our understanding of methodologies for assessing the value of policies and programs.

Sandra Mathison is professor of education at the University of British Columbia. Her research is in educational evaluation, and her work has focused especially on the potential and limits of evaluation to support democratic ideals and promote justice. She has conducted small- and national-scale evaluation of curriculum reforms, teacher professional development, and informal education programs. Her current research focuses on the narrowing conception of educational evaluation manifest in the standards-based and outcomes-based accountability systems. With funding from the National Science Foundation, she conducted a five-year critical ethnographic study of the effects of state-mandated testing on teaching, learning, school structure, and the practice of evaluation in public education. She is editor of the *Encyclopedia of Evaluation,* coeditor (with E. Wayne Ross) of *Defending Public Schools: The Nature and Limits of Standards-Based Reform and Assessment,* and coauthor (with Melissa Freeman) of *Researching Children's Experience.* She was editor-in-chief of *New Directions for Evaluation* and is currently coeditor of the journal, *Critical Education.* She blogs about evaluation at *E-Valuation* (http://blogs.ubc.ca/ evaluation/) and qualitative research at *The Qualitative Research Cafe* (http:// blogs.ubc.ca/qualresearch/). She also tweets about education, evaluation, and research (@SandraMathison).

Robin Lin Miller is professor of ecological-community psychology at Michigan State University, where she also serves as vice chair of the Social Science and Education Institutional Review Board. Her evaluation practice has centered on HIV prevention and care programs provided in community-based and clinical environments since the mid-1980s, with special focus on programs serving racial and sexual minority men. She was founding director of program evaluation services for New York City's Gay Men's Health Crisis, which is among the oldest AIDS-related community-based organization in the United States. Support for her evaluation work has come from CDC, the U.S. President's Emergency Plan for AIDS Relief Caribbean Regional Program, and the American Foundation for AIDS Research, among other sources. She is currently an investigator with the Adolescent Medicine Trials Network for HIV/AIDS Interventions, which is supported by the National Institute of Child Health and Human Development, National Institute on Drug Abuse, and NIH. With colleagues Jean King, Melvin Mark, and Valerie Caracelli, she leads the AEA's oral history project. Miller is former editor of the *American Journal of Evaluation* and former associate editor of *New Directions for Evaluation.* She is an elected Fellow of the Society for Community Research and Action and the American Psychological Association. Miller received the AEA's Marica Guttentag Early Career Award in 1996 and its Robert Ingle Award honoring service to the profession of evaluation in 2011.

Sharon F. Rallis is the Dwight W. Allen Distinguished Professor of Education Policy and Reform in the College of Education of the University of Massachusetts–Amherst where she teaches courses in inquiry, program evaluation, qualitative methods, and organizational theory. Her doctorate is from the Harvard Graduate School of Education. The 2005 president of the AEA, Rallis has been involved with evaluation for over three decades. She has conducted evaluations of educational, medical, and social programs, and her research and evaluation work has taken her throughout the United States and the world, including China, Canada, Afghanistan, Palestine, and Turkey. Her eleven published books, several of which have been translated into other languages, draw on her experience as a researcher and evaluator. *Learning in the Field: An Introduction to Qualitative Research* (written with Gretchen Rossman), is in its third edition and is widely used in methodology courses. Rallis has also published extensively in various evaluation journals or books and is currently editor of the *American Journal of Evaluation.*

Stephanie M. Reich, PhD, is an associate professor of education at the University of California, Irvine. Trained as a community psychologist with a focus on child development and program evaluation, Dr. Reich's research interests focus on understanding and improving the social context of children's lives. As such, her empirical investigations center on two contributors to children's socialization: parents and peers. The bulk of her work examines parent and peer interactions in early childhood, with additional research investigating peer interactions in adolescence, especially those mediated through social media. She has worked on a variety of evaluations of family-based, school-based, and medically focused interventions and is an active member of the AEA. Dr. Reich is the recipient of the Society for Community Research and Action Early Career Award, Newbrough Award for academic writing, a National Institute of Mental Health fellowship in children's mental health services research, and the Julius Seeman Award for academic and professional excellence.

Debra Rog is an associate director at Westat and president of its nonprofit arm, the Rockville Institute. Dr. Rog has more than 30 years of experience in evaluation, with a special focus on interventions addressing homelessness, poverty, and vulnerable populations. Dr. Rog is the former director of the Washington office of Vanderbilt University's Center for Evaluation and Program Improvement, where she served as principal investigator on a number of multisite research and evaluation projects in the areas of poverty, homelessness, housing for vulnerable populations, mental health, and applied research methodology. Dr. Rog's work has been supported by clients such as the Bill and Melinda Gates Foundation, Robert Wood Johnson Foundation, the Office of the Assistant Secretary for Planning and Evaluation within Health and Human Services, the Department of Housing and Urban Development, and the Substance Abuse and Mental Health Services Administration, among others. Dr. Rog has published and presented widely on mental health treatment issues, program evaluation, and methodological topics and is a recognized expert in evaluation methodology, homelessness, and mental health. She is an editor of numerous books, series, and journals. She has been active in the AEA since its inception and served as its president in 2009.

Thomas A. Schwandt is professor of the Department of Educational Psychology at the University of Illinois at Urbana-Champaign, where he also holds appointments in the Department of Educational Policy, Organization, and Leadership and the unit for criticism and interpretive theory. Schwandt's scholarship is primarily focused on the intersection of social research and practical philosophy.

He is the author of *Evaluation Practice Reconsidered* (2004), *Evaluating Holistic Rehabilitation Practice* (2004), *The Dictionary of Qualitative Inquiry* (1997, 2001, 2007); and, with Edward Halpern, *Linking Auditing and Meta-Evaluation* (1988). With his Norwegian colleague, Peder Haug, he has coedited *Evaluating Educational Reforms: Scandinavian Perspectives* (2003); with Katherine Ryan, *Exploring Evaluator Role and Identity* (2002); and with Bridget Somekh, *Knowledge Production: Research Work in Interesting Times* (2007). In addition, he has authored more than 60 papers and chapters on issues in theory of evaluation and interpretive methodologies that have appeared in a variety of books and journals. He has also given numerous keynote speeches to evaluation associations and societies in the United States and Europe. In 2002, he received the Paul F. Lazarsfeld Award from the AEA for his contributions to evaluation theory. He is editor emeritus of the *American Journal of Evaluation.*

Michael Scriven took two degrees in mathematics (University of Melbourne) and a doctorate in philosophy (Oxford University) and has an honorary doctorate in education (Melbourne). He has held positions in departments of mathematics, philosophy, psychology, history and philosophy of science, and education in Australia, New Zealand, and the United States, including 12 years at UC Berkeley; he is currently at Claremont Graduate University. He has also held research positions at the Center for Advanced Study in the Behavioral Sciences at Stanford, at Harvard, and at the National Science Foundation. His 450+ publications and 40 editorial board positions have been in 11 fields: About 90 publications are in evaluation, where he also founded an online journal (jmde.com) and a monograph series for the AEA. He has been president of the American Educational Research Association and AEA and director of the autonomous doctoral program in evaluation at Western Michigan University and is currently codirector of the Claremont Evaluation Center at Claremont Graduate University. Less conventional milestones include rowing (and winning) for Melbourne in the Australian University Head of the River Race and for Oxford in Trial Eights (1951), founding the Melbourne University Society for Parapsychology (1950), being elected a member of the Frisbee Hall of Fame, and (in Summer 2007) traveling 70,000 miles on evaluation missions to seven countries.

Part I

Introduction

1

Examining the Backbone of Contemporary Evaluation Practice

Credible and Actionable Evidence

Stewart I. Donaldson

The demand for rigorous and influential evaluations, and thus credible and actionable evidence, is at an all-time high across the globe. The most recent surge of activity has expanded well beyond the evaluation of traditional, large-scale government programs. Evaluations are now being conducted on a wide range of problems, programs, policies, practices, products, personnel, organizations, proposals, and the like across a diverse range of community, organizational, government, and international settings (Donaldson, 2013). While a systematic review of the notable developments related to evaluation practice since the first volume of this book in 2009 is beyond the scope of this chapter, I have selected a few of these developments to set the stage for this second edition.

Both the number and size of existing professional associations for practicing evaluators continue to grow rapidly. The largest national society, the American Evaluation Association (AEA), has grown to nearly 8,000 members, and the most recent annual meeting in Washington, D.C., set a new record with more than 3,500 delegates in attendance despite a U.S. government shutdown. A global grassroots movement to strengthen civil society's evaluation capacity worldwide, EvalPartners, has now identified more than 150 Voluntary Organizations of Professional Evaluators (VOPEs) boosting an aggregate total membership of more than 34,000 (Rugh & Segone, 2013). These VOPEs are not only focused on improving the supply of rigorous and influential evaluations, many are addressing the demand side by advocating for policies and systems that enable high-quality evaluation practice (Rugh & Segone, 2013). Furthermore, EvalPartners, the global movement to strengthen national evaluation capacities, announced that 2015 has been declared as the International Year of Evaluation (EvalYear; http://mymande.org/evalyear/Declaring_2015_as_the_International_Year_of_Evaluation).

This robust expansion of evaluation professional meetings and activities has been accompanied by increased opportunities for evaluation training and professional development. Recent research shows that universities across the globe are providing more evaluation degrees, certificates, courses, and professional development opportunities than ever before (LaVelle & Donaldson, in press). As the profession continues to mature, many practitioners are participating in VOPEs and annual professional meetings, engaging in professional development activities, and collaborating with one another in an effort to learn about emerging evaluation practices. Universities and VOPEs now offer evaluation practitioners a wide range of resources for improving practice, such as the latest books and journals, regular convenings, and a range of professional development opportunities, guiding principles, evaluation competencies, and evaluation standards.

In addition, there has been a rapid expansion of free online evaluation resources and professional development opportunities. For example, EvalPartners supports the My Monitoring & Evaluation project (My M&E; http://mymande.org), a website containing a massive number of evaluation resources designed to foster knowledge sharing and networking among practicing evaluators and evaluation students worldwide. This resource is a repository of free books and manuals, evaluation toolkits, webinars with leading evaluation experts, job announcements, training opportunities, and e-learning programs and certificates. The most recent free e-learning program on development evaluation had almost 13,000 participants from 172 countries (Segone & Donaldson, under review). The resources now available from the evaluation profession can greatly enhance a practitioner's ability to provide rigorous and influential evaluations. Before we begin our careful examination of the backbone of contemporary evaluation practice and credible and actionable evidence, I will briefly introduce several other important aspects of the profession of evaluation, namely evaluation theory, evaluation design and methods, and research on evaluation.

Evaluation Theory

Practitioners working in contemporary evaluation practice can benefit greatly from understanding how to use theory to enhance their practice. Donaldson and Lipsey (2006) have spelled out in some detail the different roles that different types of theory can play to improve contemporary evaluation practice. One of these theory forms is *evaluation theory*, which is largely prescriptive theory that "offers a set of rules, prescriptions, prohibitions, and guiding frameworks that specify what a good or proper evaluation is and how evaluation should be done" (Alkin, 2012). Evaluation theories are thus theories of evaluation practice that address such enduring themes as how to understand the nature of what we evaluate, how to assign value to programs and their performance, how to construct knowledge, and how to use the knowledge generated by evaluation (e.g., Alkin, 2012; Donaldson 2007; Donaldson & Scriven, 2003; Shadish, Cook, & Leviton, 1991).

In 1997, the president of the AEA, William Shadish, emphasized the vast importance of teaching practitioners how to benefit from and use evaluation theory to improve practice. His presidential address was entitled "Evaluation Theory Is Who We Are" and emphasized the following:

> All evaluators should know evaluation theory because it is central to our professional identity. It is what we talk about more than anything else, it seems to give rise to our most trenchant debates, it gives us the language we use for talking to ourselves and others, and perhaps most important, it is what makes us different from other professions. Especially in the latter regards, it is in our own self-interest to be explicit about this message, and to make evaluation theory the very core of our identity. Every profession needs a unique knowledge base. For us, evaluation theory is that knowledge base. (Shadish, 1998, p. 1)

Evaluation theories can also help us understand our quest as practitioners to gather credible and actionable evidence. They often take a stand on what counts as credible and actionable evidence in practice. However, evaluation theories today are rather diverse, and some are at odds with one another (see Mertens & Wilson, 2012). Understanding these differences between theories of practice is one way to help us understand disagreements about what counts as credible and actionable evidence.

In professional practice, it is vitally important that we are clear about our assumptions and purposes for conducting evaluation. Evaluation theory can help us make those decisions and help us understand why other evaluators might make different decisions in practice or criticize the decisions we have made about gathering credible and actionable evidence. In summary, being well-versed in contemporary theories of evaluation practice can enhance our ability to make sound choices about gathering evidence to answer key evaluation questions.

Program-theory–driven evaluation science is one of many examples of a theory of evaluation practice (Donaldson, 2007; Donaldson & Crano, 2011). This evaluation approach attempts to incorporate many of the hard-won lessons of evaluation practice over the past 30 years and to provide an evolving, integrative, and contingency-based theory of practice. Program-theory–driven evaluation science offers practitioners the following concise, three-step approach to practice:

1. Developing program impact theory

2. Formulating and prioritizing evaluation questions

3. Answering evaluation questions

Simply stated, evaluators work with stakeholders to develop a common understanding of how a program is presumed to solve the problem(s) of interest; to formulate and prioritize key evaluation questions; and then to decide how best to gather credible evidence to answer those questions within practical, time, and resource constraints.

This practical program evaluation approach is essentially method neutral within the broad domain of social science and evaluation methodology. The focus on the development of program theory and evaluation questions frees evaluators initially from having to presuppose the use of one evaluation design or another. The choice of the evaluation design and methods used to gather credible and actionable evidence is made in collaboration with the relevant stakeholders and is not solely decided by the evaluation team. The decisions about how best to go about collecting credible and actionable evidence to answer the key evaluation questions are typically thought to be contingent on the nature of the questions to be answered and the context of the setting. Stakeholders are provided with a wide range of choices for gathering credible and actionable evidence, which reinforces the idea that neither quantitative nor qualitative nor mixed-method designs are necessarily superior or applicable in every applied research and evaluation context (e.g., Chen, 1997). Whether an evaluator uses case studies, observational methods, structured or unstructured interviews, online or telephone survey research, a quasi-experiment, or a randomized controlled trial (RCT) to answer the key evaluation questions is dependent on discussions with relevant stakeholders about what would constitute credible and actionable evidence in this context and what is feasible given the practical, time, and financial constraints (Donaldson, 2007; Donaldson & Crano, 2011; Donaldson & Lipsey, 2006).

This practical approach for gathering credible and actionable evidence is highly consistent with the profession's guiding principles, evaluation standards, and other mainstream approaches to practical program evaluation (Chen, 2005; Chen, Donaldson, & Mark, 2011; Donaldson, 2007; Rossi, Lipsey, & Freeman, 2004; Weiss, 1998; Yarbrough, Shula, Hopson, & Caruthers, 2011). One of the best examples to date of program-theory–driven evaluation science in action is embodied in the Centers for Disease Control and Prevention's (2012) six-step Program Evaluation Framework. This framework is not only conceptually well developed and instructive for evaluation practitioners, it also has been widely adopted for evaluating federally funded public health programs throughout the United States. One of the six key steps in this framework is Step 4: Gather Credible Evidence. Step 4 is defined in the following way:

> Compiling information that stakeholders perceive as trustworthy and relevant for answering their questions. Such evidence can be experimental or observational, qualitative or quantitative, or it can include a mixture of methods. Adequate data might be available and easily accessed, or it might need to be defined and new data collected. Whether a body of evidence is credible to stakeholders might depend on such factors as how the questions were posed, sources of information, conditions of data collection, reliability of measurement, validity of interpretations, and quality control procedures.

Program-theory–driven evaluation science is just one of many forms of evaluation theory available today to help guide evaluation practice (see Mertens & Wilson, 2012, for a description of wide range of evaluation theories). It is summarized here to illustrate how evaluation theories offer guidance in terms of how to gather credible and actionable evidence in contemporary practice. It clearly specifies that there is not a universal answer to the question of what counts as credible and actionable evidence. Rather, it suggests the answer to this question in any particular evaluation context is contingent on the evaluation questions and choices made by the relevant stakeholders in the light of practical, time, and resource constraints. Other popular evaluation theories and approaches used to guide contemporary evaluation practice include utilization-focused evaluation (Patton, 2012), participatory evaluation (Cousins & Chouinard, 2012), empowerment evaluation (Fetterman, in press), experimental evaluation research (Bickman & Reich, Chapter 5; Henry, Chapter 4), the science of valuing (Scriven, 2013), realist evaluation (Mark, Henry, & Julnes, 2000; Pawson & Tilley, 1997), culturally responsive evaluation (Hood, Hopson, Obeidat, & Frierson, in press), feminist evaluation (Brisolara, Seigart, & SenGupta, 2014), transformative evaluation (Mertens, 2009), equity-focused evaluation (Bamberger & Segone, 2012), real-world evaluation (Bamberger, Rugh, & Mabry, 2006), values-engaged evaluation (Greene, 2005), and developmental evaluation and systems thinking (Patton, 2011), among many others (see Alkin, 2012; Mertens & Wilson, 2012).

Design and Methods

The decisions made in practice about evaluation design and methods can often be traced back to evaluation theory or at least a practitioner's assumptions and views about what constitutes good evaluation practice. Christie and Fleischer

(Chapter 2) discuss how assumptions about social inquiry and scientific paradigms seem to color views about which designs and methods provide the most credible and actionable evidence. What should be clear from the chapters in this volume is that contemporary practitioners now have a wide range of designs and methods to choose from when they are charged to gather credible and actionable evidence. The discussions throughout this volume provide more details about the strengths and limitations of these various designs and methods. These discussions illuminate ways that practitioners might use this knowledge to make informed decisions about which designs and methods to employ in practice.

Research on Evaluation

Theories of evaluation practice tend to be based more on evaluator experience than on systematic evidence of their effectiveness. That is, unlike social science theories used to help program and policy design, evaluation theories remain largely prescriptive and unverified. There has been a recent surge of interest in developing an evidence base to complement theory for guiding how best to practice evaluation (Cousins & Chouinard, 2012; Donaldson, 2007; Henry & Mark, 2003; Mark, 2003, 2007).

Although research on evaluation is an emerging area and a limited source of help for practitioners at the present time, there are now important works we can point to as exemplars for how research can improve the way we practice in the future. For example, there is a long tradition of research illuminating how to conduct evaluations so they are useful and have influence (Cousins, 2007; Cousins & Chouinard, 2012). Other recent studies examine the links between evaluation theory and practice (Alkin & Christie, 2005; Christie, 2003; Fitzpatrick, 2004), the development of evaluation practice competencies (Ghere, King, Stevahn, & Minnema, 2006), strategies for managing evaluation anxiety (Donaldson, Gooler, & Scriven, 2002) and improving the relationships between evaluators and stakeholders (Donaldson, 2001; Campbell & Mark, 2006), and the like. Furthermore, the AEA has recently supported the development of a new Topic Interest Group charged with expanding the evidence base for practice by promoting much more research on evaluation. All of these examples underscore the point that research on evaluation holds great promise for advancing our understanding of how best to practice evaluation in contemporary times in general and, more specifically, how best to gather credible and actionable evidence.

Debates About Credible and Actionable Evidence

Now that you have a brief overview of contemporary evaluation practice, it is time to focus on one the most fundamental issues facing evaluation practitioners today: How do evaluators gather credible and actionable evidence to answer the wide range of evaluation questions they face across diverse and highly variable contexts? Most would agree that the backbone of any empirical evaluation is the quality of the evidence that supports the evaluative conclusions. Throughout the history of professional evaluation, evaluation theorists, scholars, and practitioners have debated vigorously about what constitutes high-quality evaluation evidence. We will begin our journey into the depths of this fundamental issue by exploring the debates that set the stage for the first volume on *What Counts as Credible Evidence in Applied Research and Evaluation Practice?* (Donaldson, Christie, & Mark, 2009).

The Rise and Fall of the Experimenting Society

In 1969, one of the legendary figures in the history of applied research and evaluation, Donald T. Campbell, gave us great hope and set what we now call the *applied research and evaluation community* on a course for discovering a utopia he called the *Experimenting Society* (Campbell, 1991). His vision for this utopia involved rational decision making by politicians based on hardheaded tests of bold social programs designed to improve society. The hardheaded tests he envisioned were called *randomized experiments* and focused on maximizing bias control in an effort to provide unambiguous causal inferences about the effects of social reforms. This ideal society would broadly implement social reforms demonstrated to be highly effective by experimental research and evaluation, with the goal of moving at least more, if not most, of the population toward the "good life."

Some of the most important methodological breakthroughs in the history of applied research and evaluation seemed to occur during this movement toward the Experimenting Society (e.g., Campbell, 1991; Campbell & Stanley, 1963; Cook & Campbell, 1979). For example, detailed understanding of threats to validity, multiple types of validity, bias control, and the implementation of rigorous experimental and quasi-experimental designs in real-world or field settings were advanced during this era.

However, the progress and momentum of the movement were not sustained. By the early 1980s, it was clear that Campbell's vision would be crushed by the realities of programs, initiatives, and societal reforms. Shadish,

Cook, and Leviton (1991) reported that information or evidence judged to be poor by experimental scientific standards was often considered acceptable by key decision makers, including managers, politicians, and policy makers. Further, they argued that rigorous experimental evaluations did not yield credible evidence in a timely and useful manner, thus inspiring the field to develop new tools, methods, and evaluation approaches. The practice of applied research and evaluation today has moved way beyond the sole reliance on experimentation and traditional social science research methods (Donaldson, 2013; Donaldson & Crano, 2011; Donaldson & Lipsey, 2006; Donaldson & Scriven, 2003).

An Evidence-Based Global Society

Shades of Campbell's great hopes for evidence-based decision making can be seen in much of the applied research and evaluation discourse today. However, while the modern discussion remains focused on the importance of the production and use of credible and actionable evidence, it is not limited to evidence derived from experimentation. The new vision for a utopia seems to require broadening Campbell's vision from an *experimenting* to an *evidence-based* society. This ideal society would certainly include evidence from experimentation under its purview but would also include a wide range of evidence derived from other applied research and evaluation designs and approaches. Many of these newer approaches have been developed in the past two decades and no longer rely primarily on the traditional social science experimental paradigm (see Mertens & Wilson, 2012).

The promise of an evidence-based society and the accelerating demand for credible and actionable evidence has led to the recent proliferation of evidence-based discussions and applications. For example, these discussions and applications are now prevalent throughout the fields of health care and medicine (Sackett, 2000; Sackett, Rosenberg, Gray, & Haynes, 1996), mental health (Norcross, Beutler, & Levant, 2005), management (Pfeffer & Sutton, 2006), executive coaching (Stober & Grant, 2006), career development (Preskill & Donaldson, 2008), public policy (Pawson, 2006), and education (Gersten & Hitchcock, 2009) just to name a few. In fact, a cursory search on Google yields many more applications of evidence-based practice. A sample of the results of a Google search illustrates these diverse applications:

- Evidence-based medicine
- Evidence-based mental health

- Evidence-based management
- Evidence-based decision making
- Evidence-based education
- Evidence-based coaching
- Evidence-based social services
- Evidence-based policing
- Evidence-based conservation
- Evidence-based dentistry
- Evidence-based policy
- Evidence-based thinking about health care
- Evidence-based occupational therapy
- Evidence-based prevention science
- Evidence-based dermatology
- Evidence-based gambling treatment
- Evidence-based sex education
- Evidence-based needle exchange programs
- Evidence-based prices
- Evidence-based education help desk

One might even consider this interesting new phenomenon across the disciplines to be expressed in the following formula: Mom + the Flag + Warm Apple Pie = Evidence-Based Practice. Or it might be expressed as: In God We Trust—*All Others Must Have Credible Evidence*

The main point here is that the movement toward evidence-based decision making now appears highly valued across the globe, multidisciplinary in scope, and supported by an ever-increasing number of practical applications.

But wait—while there appears to be strong consensus that evidence is our "magic bullet" and a highly valued commodity in the fight against social problems, there ironically appears to be much less agreement, even heated disagreements, about what counts as credible and actionable evidence. Unfortunately, seeking truth or agreement about what constitutes credible and actionable evidence does not seem to be an easy matter in many fields. Even in periods of relative calm and consensus in the development of a discipline, innovations occur and worldviews change in ways that destabilize. We may be living in such a destabilizing period now in the profession and discipline of applied research and evaluation. That is, despite unprecedented growth and success on many fronts, the field is in considerable turmoil over its very foundation—what counts as credible and actionable evidence. Furthermore, contemporary evaluation practice rests firmly on the foundation of providing credible and actionable evidence. If that foundation is shaky or built on sand, studies wobble, sway in the wind, and ultimately provide little value and can even mislead or harm.

Recent Debates About Evidence

Before exploring this potentially destructive strife and dilemma in more detail, let's briefly look at the recent history of debates about applied research and evaluation. The great quantitative–qualitative debate captured and occupied the field throughout the late 1970s and 1980s (see Reichhardt & Rallis, 1994). This rather lengthy battle also become known as the *paradigm wars*, which seemed to quiet down a bit by the turn of the century (Mark, 2003).

In 2001, Donaldson and Scriven (2003) invited a diverse group of applied researchers and evaluators to provide their visions for a desired future. The heat generated at this symposium suggested that whatever truce or peace had been achieved remained an uneasy one (Mark, 2003). For example, Yvonna Lincoln and Donna Mertens envisioned a desirable future based on constructivist philosophy, and Mertens seemed to suggest that the traditional quantitative social science paradigm, specifically randomized experiments, was quite limited for evaluation practice (Mark, 2003). Thomas Cook responded with a description of applied research and evaluation in his world, which primarily involved randomized and quasi-experimental designs, as normative and highly valued by scientists, funders, stakeholders, and policy makers alike. Two illustrative observations by Mark (2003) highlighting differences expressed in the discussion were (1) "I have heard some quantitatively oriented evaluators disparage participatory and empowerment approaches as technically wanting and as less than evaluation," and (2) "It can, however, seem more ironic when evaluators who espouse inclusion, empowerment, and participation would like to exclude, disempower, and see no participation by evaluators who hold different views" (p. 189). While the symposium concluded with some productive discussions about embracing diversity and integration as ways to move forward, it was clear there were lingering differences and concerns about what constitutes quality applied research, evaluation, and credible evidence.

Donaldson and Christie (2005) noted that the uneasy peace seemed to revert back to overt conflict in late 2003. The trigger event occurred when the U.S. Department of Education's Institute of Education Sciences declared a rather wholesale commitment to privileging experimental and some types of quasi-experimental designs over other methods in applied research and evaluation funding competitions. At the 2003 Annual Meeting of the AEA, prominent applied researchers and evaluators discussed this event as a move back to the "Dark Ages" (Donaldson & Christie, 2005). The leadership of the AEA developed a policy statement opposing these efforts to privilege randomized controlled trials in education evaluation funding competitions:

AEA Statement:

American Evaluation Association Response to
U.S. Department of Education

Notice of Proposed Priority, Federal Register
RIN 1890-ZA00, November 4, 2003

"Scientifically Based Evaluation Methods"

The American Evaluation Association applauds the effort to promote high quality in the U.S. Secretary of Education's proposed priority for evaluating educational programs using scientifically based methods. We, too, have worked to encourage competent practice through our Guiding Principles for Evaluators (1994), Standards for Program Evaluation (1994), professional training, and annual conferences. However, we believe the proposed priority manifests fundamental misunderstandings about (1) the types of studies capable of determining causality, (2) the methods capable of achieving scientific rigor, and (3) the types of studies that support policy and program decisions. We would like to help avoid the political, ethical, and financial disaster that could well attend implementation of the proposed priority.

(1)   Studies capable of determining causality. Randomized controlled group trials (RCTs) are not the only studies capable of generating understandings of causality. In medicine, causality has been conclusively shown in some instances without RCTs, for example, in linking smoking to lung cancer and infested rats to bubonic plague. The secretary's proposal would elevate experimental over quasi-experimental, observational, single-subject, and other designs which are sometimes more feasible and equally valid.

RCTs are not always best for determining causality and can be misleading. RCTs examine a limited number of isolated factors that are neither limited nor isolated in natural settings. The complex nature of causality and the multitude of actual influences on outcomes render RCTs less capable of discovering causality than designs sensitive to local culture and conditions and open to unanticipated causal factors.

RCTs should sometimes be ruled out for reasons of ethics. For example, assigning experimental subjects to educationally inferior or medically unproven treatments, or denying control group subjects access to important instructional opportunities or critical medical intervention, is not ethically

(Continued)

(Continued)

acceptable even when RCT results might be enlightening. Such studies would not be approved by Institutional Review Boards overseeing the protection of human subjects in accordance with federal statute.

In some cases, data sources are insufficient for RCTs. Pilot, experimental, and exploratory education, health, and social programs are often small enough in scale to preclude use of RCTs as an evaluation methodology, however important it may be to examine causality prior to wider implementation.

(2) Methods capable of demonstrating scientific rigor. For at least a decade, evaluators publicly debated whether newer inquiry methods were sufficiently rigorous. This issue was settled long ago. Actual practice and many published examples demonstrate that alternative and mixed methods are rigorous and scientific. To discourage a repertoire of methods would force evaluators backward. We strongly disagree that the methodological "benefits of the proposed priority justify the costs."

(3) Studies capable of supporting appropriate policy and program decisions. We also strongly disagree that "this regulatory action does not unduly interfere with State, local, and tribal governments in the exercise of their governmental functions." As provision and support of programs are governmental functions so, too, is determining program effectiveness. Sound policy decisions benefit from data illustrating not only causality but also conditionality. Fettering evaluators with unnecessary and unreasonable constraints would deny information needed by policy-makers.

While we agree with the intent of ensuring that federally sponsored programs be "evaluated using scientifically based research . . . to determine the effectiveness of a project intervention," we do not agree that "evaluation methods using an experimental design are best for determining project effectiveness." We believe that the constraints in the proposed priority would deny use of other needed, proven, and scientifically credible evaluation methods, resulting in fruitless expenditures on some large contracts while leaving other public programs unevaluated entirely.

Donaldson and Christie (2005) documented an important response to the AEA Statement from an influential group of senior members. This group opposed the AEA Statement and did not feel they were appropriately consulted as active, long-term members of the association. Their response became known as "The Not AEA Statement."

The Not AEA Statement:

(Posted on EvalTalk, December 3, 2003; available at http://bama.ua.edu/archives/evaltalk.html)

AEA members:

The statement below has been sent to the Department of Education in response to its proposal that "scientifically based evaluation methods" for assessing the effectiveness of educational interventions be defined as randomized experiments when they are feasible and as quasi-experimental or single-subject designs when they are not.

This statement is intended to support the Department's definition and associated preference for the use of such designs for outcome evaluation when they are applicable. It is also intended to provide a counterpoint to the statement submitted by the AEA leadership as the Association's position on this matter. The generalized opposition to use of experimental and quasi-experimental methods evinced in the AEA statement is unjustified, speciously argued, and represents neither the methodological norms in the evaluation field nor the views of the large segment of the AEA membership with significant experience conducting experimental and quasi-experimental evaluations of program effects.

We encourage all AEA members to communicate their views on this matter to the Department of Education and invite you to endorse the statement below in that communication if it is more representative of your views than the official AEA statement. Comments can be sent to the Dept of Ed through Dec. 4 at comments@ed.gov with "Evaluation" in the subject line of the message.

This statement is in response to the Secretary's request for comment on the proposed priority on Scientifically Based Evaluation Methods. We offer the following observations in support of this priority.

The proposed priority identifies random assignment experimental designs as the methodological standard for what constitutes scientifically based evaluation methods for determining whether an intervention produces meaningful effects on students, teachers, parents, and others. The priority also recognizes that there are cases when random assignment is not feasible and, in such cases, identifies quasi-experimental designs and single-subject designs as alternatives that may be justified by the circumstances of particular evaluations.

This interpretation of what constitutes scientifically based evaluation strategies for assessing program effects is consistent with the presentations

(Continued)

(Continued)

in the major textbooks in evaluation and with widely recognized methodological standards in the social and medical sciences. Randomized controlled trials have been essential to understanding what works, what does not work, and what is harmful among interventions in many other areas of public policy including health and medicine, mental health, criminal justice, employment, and welfare. Furthermore, attempts to draw conclusions about intervention effects based on nonrandomized trials have often led to misleading results in these fields and there is no reason to expect this to be untrue in the social and education fields. This is demonstrated, for example, by the results of randomized trials of facilitated communication for autistic children and prison visits for juvenile offenders, which reversed the conclusions of nonexperimental studies of these interventions.

Randomized trials in the social sector are more frequent and feasible than many critics acknowledge and their number is increasing. The Campbell Collaboration of Social, Psychological, Educational, and Criminological Trials Register includes nearly 13,000 such trials, and the development of this register is still in its youth.

At the same time, we recognize that randomized trials are not feasible or ethical at times. In such circumstances, quasi-experimental or other designs may be appropriate alternatives, as the proposed priority allows. However, it has been possible to configure practical and ethical experimental designs in such complex and sensitive areas of study as pregnancy prevention programs, police handling of domestic violence, and prevention of substance abuse. It is similarly possible to design randomized trials or strong quasi-experiments to be ethical and feasible for many educational programs. In such cases, we believe the Secretary's proposed priority gives proper guidance for attaining high methodological standards and we believe the nation's children deserve to have educational programs of demonstrated effectiveness as determined by the most scientifically credible methods available.

The individuals who have signed below in support of this statement are current or former members of the American Evaluation Association (AEA). Included among us are individuals who have been closely associated with that organization since its inception and who have served as AEA presidents, board members, and journal editors. We wish to make clear that the statement submitted by AEA in response to this proposed priority does not represent our views and we regret that a statement representing the organization was proffered without prior review and comment by its members. We believe that the proposed priority will dramatically increase the amount of valid information for guiding the improvement of education throughout the nation. We appreciate the opportunity to comment on a matter of this importance and support the Department's initiative.

The subsequent exchanges about these statements on the AEA's electronic bulletin board, EvalTalk, seemed to generate much more heat than light and begged for more elaboration on the issues. As a result, Claremont Graduate University hosted and webcasted a debate for the applied research and evaluation community in 2004. The debate was between Mark Lipsey and Michael Scriven, and it attempted to sort out the issues at stake and to search for a common ground.

Donaldson and Christie (2005) concluded, somewhat surprisingly, that Lipsey and Scriven agreed that RCTs are the best method currently available for assessing program impact (causal effects of a program) and that determining program impact is a main requirement of contemporary program evaluation. However, Scriven argued that there are very few situations where RCTs can be successfully implemented in educational program evaluation and that there are now good alternative designs for determining program effects. Lipsey disagreed and remained very skeptical of Scriven's claim that sound alternative methods exist for determining program effects and challenged Scriven to provide specific examples (p. 77).

There have also been a plethora of disputes and debates about credible and actionable evidence outside of the United States. For example, the European Evaluation Society (EES, 2007) issued a statement in response to strong pressure from some interests advocating for "scientific" and "rigorous" impact of development aid, where this is defined as primarily involving RCTs:

> EES deplores one perspective currently being strongly advocated: that the best or only rigorous and scientific way of doing so is through randomised controlled trials (RCTs). In contrast, the EES supports multi-method approaches to IE [impact evaluation and assessment] and does not consider any single method such as RCTs as first choice or as the "gold standard."

This new statement briefly discusses the rationale for this perspective and lists examples of publications that consider a number of alternative approaches for establishing impact.

EES Statement:

The importance of a methodologically diverse approach to impact evaluation—specifically with respect to development aid and development interventions.

December 2007

(Continued)

(Continued)

The European Evaluation Society (EES), consistent with its mission to promote the "theory, practice and utilization of high quality evaluation," notes the current interest in improving impact evaluation and assessment (IE) with respect to development and development aid. EES however deplores one perspective currently being strongly advocated: that the best or only rigorous and scientific way of doing so is through randomised controlled trials (RCTs).

In contrast, the EES supports multi-method approaches to IE and does not consider any single method such as RCTs as first choice or as the "gold standard":

- The literature clearly documents how all methods and approaches have strengths and limitations and that there are a wide range of scientific, evidence-based, rigorous approaches to evaluation that have been used in varying contexts for assessing impact.
- IE is complex, particularly of multi-dimensional interventions such as many forms of development (e.g., capacity building, Global Budget Support, sectoral development) and consequently requires the use of a variety of different methods that can take into account rather than dismiss this inherent complexity.
- Evaluation standards and principles from across Europe and other parts of the world do not favor a specific approach or group of approaches—although they may require that the evaluator give reasons for selecting a particular evaluation design or combination.

RCTs represent one possible approach for establishing impact, that may be suitable in some situations, e.g.:

- With simple interventions where a linear relationship can be established between the intervention and an expected outcome that can be clearly defined;
- Where it is possible and where it makes sense to "control" for context and other intervening factors (e.g., where contexts are sufficiently comparable);
- When it can be anticipated that programmes under both experimental and control conditions can be expected to remain static (e.g., not attempt to make changes or improvements), often for a considerable period of time;
- Where it is possible and ethically appropriate to engage in randomization and to ensure the integrity of the differences between the experimental and control conditions.

Even in these circumstances, it would be "good practice" not to rely on one method but rather combine RCTs with other methods—and to triangulate the results obtained.

As with any other method, an RCT approach also has considerable limitations that may limit its applicability and ability to contribute to policy, e.g.:

- RCT designs are acknowledged even by many of its proponents to be weak in external validity (or generalisability), as well as in identifying the actual mechanisms that may be responsible for differences in outcomes between the experimental and control situations;
- "Scaling up," across-the-board implementation based upon the results of a limited and closely controlled pilot situation, can be appropriate for those interventions (e.g., drug trials) where the conditions of implementation would be the same as in the trial, but this is rarely the case for most socio-economic interventions where policy or program "fidelity" cannot be taken for granted;
- An RCT approach is rarely appropriate in complex situations where an outcome arises from interaction of multiple factors and interventions, and where it makes little sense to "control" for these other factors. In a development context, as for most complex policy interventions, outcomes are the result of multiple factors interacting simultaneously, rather than of a single "cause";
- RCTs are limited in their ability to deal with emergent and/or unintended and unanticipated outcomes as is increasingly recognized in complexity and systems research—many positive benefits of development interventions will often be related rather than identical to those anticipated at the policy/program design stage;
- RCTs generally are less suited than other approaches in identifying what works for whom and under what circumstances. Identifying what mechanisms lead to an identified change is particularly important given the varying contexts under which development typically takes place and is essential for making evidence-based improvements.

We also note that RCTs are based upon a successionist (sometimes referred to as "factual") model of causality that neglects the links between intervention and impact and ignores other well-understood scientific means of establishing causality, e.g.:

- Both the natural and social sciences (e.g., physics, astronomy, economics) recognize other forms of causality, such as generative (sometimes referred to as "physical") causality that involve identifying the

(Continued)

(Continued)

underlying processes that lead to a change. An important variant of generative causality is known as the modus operandi that involves tracing the "signature," where one can trace an observable chain of events that links to the impact.

- Other forms of causality recognize simultaneous and/or alternative causal strands, e.g., acknowledging that some factors may be necessary but not sufficient to bring about a given result, or that an intervention could work through one or more causal paths. In non-linear relationships, sometimes a small additional effort can serve as a "tipping point" and have a disproportionately large effect.
- Some research literature questions whether simple "causality" (vs. "contribution" or "reasonable attribution") is always the right approach, given the complexity of factors that necessarily interact in contemporary policy—many of them in specific contexts.

EES also notes that in the context of the Paris Declaration, it is appropriate for the international evaluation community to work together in supporting the enhancement of development partner capacity to undertake IE. Mandating a specific approach could undermine the spirit of the Paris Declaration and as the literature on evaluation utilization has demonstrated, limit buy-in and support for evaluation and for subsequent action.

In conclusion, EES welcomes the increased attention and funding for improving IE, provided that this takes a multi-method approach drawing from the rich diversity of existing frameworks and one that engages both the developed and developing world. We would be pleased to join with others in participating in this endeavour. (European Evaluation Society, 2007)

What Counts as Credible Evidence?

In 2006, the debate about whether RCTs should be considered the gold standard for producing credible evidence in applied research and evaluation remained front and center across the applied research landscape. At the same time, the zeitgeist of accountability and evidence-based practice was now widespread across the globe. Organizations of all types and sizes were being asked to evaluate their practices, programs, and policies at an increasing rate. While there seemed to be much support for the notion of using evidence to continually improve efficiency and effectiveness, there appeared to be growing disagreement and confusion about what constitutes sound evidence for decision making. These heated disagreements among leading lights in the field had potentially far-reaching implications for evaluation and applied research practice, for the future of the profession (e.g., there was visible disengagement, public criticisms, and resignations from the main professional associations), and for funding competitions as well as for how best to conduct and use evaluation and applied research to promote human betterment.

So in light of this state of affairs, an illustrious group of experts working in various areas of evaluation and applied research were invited to Claremont Graduate University to share their diverse perspectives on the question of "What Counts as Credible Evidence?" The ultimate goal of this symposium was to shed more light on these issues and to attempt to build bridges so that prominent leaders on both sides of the debate would stay together in a united front against the social and human ills of the 21st century. In other words, a full vetting of best ways to produce credible evidence from both an experimental and nonexperimental perspective was facilitated in the hope that the results would move us closer to a shared blueprint for an evidence-based global society.

This illuminating and action-packed day in Claremont, California, included over 200 attendees from a variety of backgrounds—academics, researchers, private consultants, students, and professionals from many fields—who enjoyed a day of stimulating presentations, intense discussion, and a display of diverse perspectives on this central issue facing the field (see webcast at www.cgu.edu/sbos). Each presenter was asked to follow up his or her presentation with a more detailed chapter for this book. In addition, George Julnes and Debra Rog were invited to contribute a chapter based on their findings from a recent project focused on informing federal policies on evaluation methodology (Julnes & Rog, 2007). The volume based on this symposium, *What Counts as Credible Evidence in Applied Research and Evaluation,* was published in 2009.

The Quest for Credible and Actionable Evidence

SAGE staff contacted us in 2012, suggesting that there was great interest in a second edition. After consulting with many of the original authors and exploring the interest of a couple of new authors, we decided to move forward with the revision and to broaden the scope to *Credible and Actionable Evidence: The Foundations for Rigorous and Influential Evaluations.* The original authors were asked to revise their chapters to take into account new developments in the field and in their thinking as well as this somewhat broader focus. Robin Miller and Eleanor Chelimsky were invited to contribute new chapters.

Our search for a deeper and more complete understanding of credible and actionable evidence begins with an analysis of the passion, paradigms, and assumptions that underlie many of the arguments and perspectives expressed throughout this book. In Chapter 2, Christina Christie and Dreolin Fleischer provide us with a rich context for understanding the nature and importance of the debates about credible and actionable evidence. Ontological, epistemological, and methodological assumptions that anchor views about the nature of credible and actionable evidence are explored. The third and final chapter in Part I is a new chapter by Robin Miller on the individual psychological processes that can affect judgments of credibility. Miller underscores that potential users often rely on various peripheral cues or heuristics to judge the credibility of evaluation evidence and that there are important factors beyond evaluation design and methods that determine if evaluation evidence is considered credible and actionable. These introductory chapters broaden the discussion and preview the positions expressed about credible and actionable evidence in the subsequent sections of the book.

Part II will explore the role of randomized experiments in producing credible and actionable evidence. Gary Henry (Chapter 4) and Leonard Bickman and Stephanie Reich (Chapter 5) explore the value of randomized controlled trials and quasi-experimental designs, while Michael Scriven (Chapter 6) questions the value they add to everyday evaluation practice. Part III explores the value of other evaluation designs and methods for producing credible and actionable evidence with chapters from Sharon Rallis (Chapter 7), Sandra Mathison (Chapter 8), and Eleanor Chelimsky (Chapter 9). Part IV provides general perspectives on credible and actionable evidence with chapters from Jennifer Greene (Chapter 10), George Julnes and Debra Rog (Chapter 11), and Thomas Schwandt (Chapter 12). Finally, Melvin Mark (Chapter 13) ends Part IV and the book with a closing chapter that reviews the central themes about credible and actionable evidence presented throughout the book and a sketch of a broader framework surrounding judgements of credibility and actionability and provides a set of recommendations for improving evaluation practice based on the framework and insights provided by the chapter authors. The chapters in this volume were written to encourage and inspire you to reflect deeply about ways to gather credible and actionable evidence in your evaluation practice and to help you provide rigorous and influential evaluations for the promotion of social betterment worldwide.

References

Alkin, M. C. (Ed.). (2012). *Evaluation roots: A wider perspective of theorists' views and influences.* Thousand Oaks, CA: SAGE.

Alkin, M. C., & Christie, C. A. (2005). Theorists' models in action [Entire issue]. *New Directions for Evaluation, 106.*

Bamberger, M. J., Rugh, J., & Mabry, L. S. (2006). *Real world evaluation: Working under budget, time, data, and political constraints.* Newbury Park, CA: SAGE.

Bamberger, M., & Segone, M. (2012). *How to design and manage equity-focused evaluations.* New York, NY: UNICEF.

Brisolara, S., Seigart, D., & SenGupta, S. (2014). *Feminist evaluation and research: Theory and practice.* New York, NY: Guildford.

Campbell, B., & Mark, M. M. (2006). Toward more effective stakeholder dialogue: Applying theories of negotiation to policy and program evaluation. *Journal of Applied Social Psychology, 36*(12), 2834–2863.

Campbell, D. T. (1991). Methods for the experimenting society. *American Journal of Evaluation, 12*(3), 223–260.

Campbell, D. T., & Stanley, J. C. (1963). *Experimental and quasi-experimental design for research.* Chicago, IL: Rand McNally.

Centers for Disease Control and Prevention. (2012). *Framework for program evaluation in public health.* MMWR, 48 (No. RR-11). CDC Evaluation Working Group.

Chen, H. T. (1997). Applying mixed methods under the framework of theory-driven evaluations. In J. Greene & V. Caracelli (Eds.), Advances in mixed methods evaluation: The challenge and benefits of integrating diverse paradigms. *New Directions for Evaluation, 74,* 61–72.

Chen, H. T. (2005). *Practical program evaluation: Assessing and improving planning, implementation, and effectiveness.* Thousand Oaks, CA: SAGE.

Chen, H. T., Donaldson, S. I., & Mark, M. M. (Eds.). (2011). Advancing validity in outcome evaluation: Theory and practice [Entire issue]. *New Directions for Evaluation, 130.*

Christie, C. A. (2003). What guides evaluation? A study of how evaluation practice maps onto evaluation theory. In C. A. Christie (Ed.), The practice–theory relationship in evaluation. *New Directions for Evaluation, 97,* 1–35.

Cook, T. D., & Campbell, D. T. (1979). *Quasi-experimentation: Design and analysis issues for field settings.* Chicago, IL: Rand McNally.

Cousins, J. B. (Ed.). (2007). Process use in theory, research, and practice [Entire issue]. *New Directions for Evaluation, 116.*

Cousins, J. B., & Chouinard, J. A. (Eds.). (2012). *Participatory evaluation up close: A integration of research-based knowledge.* Greenwich, CT: Information Age.

Donaldson, S. I. (2001). Overcoming our negative reputation: Evaluation becomes known as a helping profession. *American Journal of Evaluation, 22*(3), 355–361.

Donaldson, S. I. (2007). *Program theory–driven evaluation science: Strategies and applications.* Mahwah, NJ: Erlbaum.

Donaldson, S. I. (2013). *The future of evaluation in society: A tribute to Michael Scriven.* Greenwich, CT: Information Age.

Donaldson, S. I., & Christie, C. A. (2005). The 2004 Claremont Debate: Lipsey versus Scriven. Determining causality in program evaluation and applied research: Should experimental evidence be the gold standard? *Journal of Multidisciplinary Evaluation, 3,* 60–77.

Donaldson, S. I., Christie, C. A., & Mark, M. M. (2009). *What counts as credible evidence in applied research and evaluation practice?* Newbury Park, CA: SAGE.

Donaldson, S. I., & Crano, W. C. (2011). Theory-driven evaluation science and applied social psychology: Exploring the intersection. In M. M. Mark, S. I. Donaldson, & B. Campbell (Eds.), *Social psychology and evaluation* (pp. 141–160). New York, NY: Guilford.

Donaldson, S. I., Gooler, L. E., & Scriven, M. (2002). Strategies for managing evaluation anxiety: Toward a psychology of program evaluation. *American Journal of Evaluation, 23*(3), 261–273.

Donaldson, S. I., & Lipsey, M. W. (2006). Roles for theory in contemporary evaluation practice: Developing practice knowledge. In I. Shaw, J. C. Greene, & M. M. Mark (Eds.), *The handbook of evaluation: Policies, programs, and practices* (pp. 56–75). London, England: SAGE.

Donaldson, S. I., & Scriven, M. (Eds.). (2003). *Evaluating social programs and problems: Visions for the new millennium.* Mahwah, NJ: Erlbaum.

European Evaluation Society. (2007). *EES Statement: The importance of a methodologically diverse approach to impact evaluation—specifically with respect to development aid and development interventions.* Retrieved February 7, 2008, from http://www.europeanevaluation.org/download/?id=1969403.

Fetterman, D. (in press). *Empowerment evaluation.* Newbury Park, CA: SAGE.

Fitzpatrick, J. L. (2004). Exemplars as case studies: Reflections on the links between theory, practice, and context. *American Journal of Evaluation, 25*(4), 541–559.

Gersten, R., & Hitchcock, J. (2009). What is credible evidence in education? The role of the What Works Clearinghouse in informing the process. In S. I. Donaldson, C. A. Christie, & M. M. Mark (Eds.), *What counts as credible evidence in applied research and evaluation practice?* (pp. 78–95). Newbury Park, CA: SAGE.

Ghere, G., King, J. A., Stevahn, L., & Minnema, J. (2006). A professional development unit for reflecting on program evaluator competencies. *American Journal of Evaluation, 27*(1), 108–123.

Greene, J. (2005). A value-engaged approach for evaluating the Bunche–Da Vinci Learning Academy. In M. C. Alkin, & C. A. Christie (Eds.), Theorists' models in action, *New Directions for Evaluation, 106,* 27–45.

Henry, G. T., & Mark, M. M. (2003). Toward an agenda for research on evaluation. In C. A. Christie (Ed.), The practice–theory relationship in evaluation. *New Directions for Evaluation, 97,* 69–80.

Hood, S., Hopson, R. K., Obeidat, K., & Frierson, H. (in press). *Continuing the journey to reposition culture and cultural context in evaluation theory and practice.* Greenwich, CT: Information Age.

Julnes, G., & Rog, D. J. (Eds.). (2007). Informing federal policies on evaluation methodology: Building the evidence base for method choice in government-sponsored evaluations [Entire issue]. *New Directions for Evaluation, 113.*

LaVelle, J., & Donaldson, S. I. (in press). The state of evaluation education and training. In J. W. Altschuld & M. Engle (Eds.), Accreditation, certification, and credentialing: Whither goes the American Evaluation Association. *New Directions for Evaluation.*

Mark, M. M. (2003). Toward an integrated view of the theory and practice of program and policy evaluation. In S. I. Donaldson & M. Scriven (Eds.), *Evaluating social programs and problems: Visions for the new millennium* (pp. 183–204). Mahwah, NJ: Erlbaum.

Mark, M. M. (2007). Building a better evidence base for evaluation theory: Beyond general calls to a framework of types of research on evaluation. In N. L. Smith & P. R. Brandon (Eds.), *Fundamental issues in evaluation* (pp. 111–134). New York, NY: Guilford Press.

Mark, M. M., Henry, G. T., & Julnes, G. (2000). *Evaluation: An integrated framework for understanding, guiding, and improving policies and programs.* San Francisco, CA: Jossey-Bass.

Mertens, D. (2009). *Transformative research and evaluation.* New York, NY: Guildford.

Mertens, D. M., & Wilson, A. T. (2012). *Program evaluation theory and practice.* New York, NY: Guildford.

Norcross, J. C., Beutler, L. E., & Levant, R. F. (2005). *Evidence-based practices in mental health: Debate and dialogue on the fundamental questions.* Washington, DC: American Psychological Association.

Patton M. Q. (2011). *Developmental evaluation: Applying complexity concepts to enhance innovation and use.* New York, NY: Guildford.

Patton, M. Q. (2012). *Essentials of utilization focused evaluation.* London, England: SAGE.

Pawson, R. (2006). *Evidence-based policy: A realist perspective.* Thousand Oaks, CA: SAGE.

Pawson, R., & Tilley, N. (1997). *Realistic evaluation.* Thousand Oaks, CA: SAGE.

Pfeffer, J., & Sutton, R. I. (2006). *Hard facts, dangerous truths, and total nonsense: Profiting from evidence-based management.* Boston, MA: Harvard Business School Press.

Preskill, H., & Donaldson, S. I. (2008). Improving the evidence base for career development programs: Making use of the evaluation profession and positive psychology movement. *Advances in Developing Human Resources, 10*(1), 104–121.

Reichhardt, C. S., & Rallis, S. F. (1994). The qualitative–quantitative debate: New perspectives [Entire issue]. *New Directions for Program Evaluation, 61.*

Rossi, P. H., Lipsey, M. W., & Freeman, H. E. (2004). *Evaluation: A systematic approach* (7th ed.). Thousand Oaks, CA: SAGE.

Rugh, J., & Segone, M. (Eds.). (2013). *Voluntary organizations for professional evaluation: Learning from Africa, Americas, Asia, Australasia, Europe and Middle East.* UNICEF, IOCE and EvalPartners.

Sackett, D. L. (2000). *Evidence-based medicine: How to practice and teach EBM.* New York, NY: Churchill Livingstone.

Sackett, D. L., Rosenberg, W. M. C., Gray, J. A. M., & Haynes, R. B. (1996). Evidence-based medicine: What it is and what it isn't. *British Medical Journal, 312,* 71–72.

Scriven, M. (2013). The foundation and future of evaluation. In S. Donaldson (Ed.), *The future of evaluation in society: A tribute to Michael Scriven.* Greenwich, CT: Information Age.

Segone, M., & Donaldson, S. I. (in press). *What have we learned in using social media in the international development context? The case of My M&E, the platform of a global partnership to strengthen national evaluation capacities.* Under review.

Shadish, W. R. (1998). Evaluation theory is who we are. *American Journal of Evaluation, 19*(1), 1–19.

Shadish, W. R., Cook, T. D., & Leviton, L. C. (1991). *Foundations of program evaluation: Theories of practice.* Newbury Park, CA: SAGE.

Stober, D. R., & Grant, A. M. (2006). *Evidence-based coaching handbook: Putting best practice to work for your clients.* Hoboken, NJ: Wiley.

Weiss, C. H. (1998). *Evaluation: Methods for studying programs and policies* (2nd ed.). Upper Saddle River, NJ: Prentice Hall.

Yarbrough, D. B., Shula, L. M., Hopson, R. K., & Caruthers, F. A. (2011). *The program evaluation standards: A guide for evaluators and evaluation users.* Newbury Park, CA: SAGE.

2

Social Inquiry Paradigms as a Frame for the Debate on Credible Evidence

Christina A. Christie

Dreolin Fleischer

This book deals with the question, "What constitutes credible and actionable evidence in evaluation and applied research?" Specifically, we are concerned with the factors that influence the credibility of evidence when used to inform judgments about a practice, program, or policy. At the heart of recent discussions on the topic are policies that identify the randomized controlled trial (RCT)[1] as the *gold standard* design for generating rigorous scientific evidence of program and policy effectiveness. The identification of a particular research design as the most credible design from which decisions are made about what should and should not be considered a quality practice, program, or policy has generated a renewed interest in decision science and the use of systematic information in key decision-making contexts.

A reoccurring yet persistent debate in social science and evaluation research over how to best study social phenomena precedes the current credibility-of-evidence discussion. This debate is rooted in philosophical differences about the nature of reality and epistemological differences about what constitutes knowledge and how it is created (Patton, 2002). Thus theories of knowledge and paradigms of social inquiry have been commonly used as a frame for describing the debate—for example, *positivism versus constructivism* or, as it relates to methods, *quantitative versus qualitative*. This describes the "paradigm wars" of the past 20 years, on which the literature is extensive (e.g., Lincoln & Guba, 1985; Reichardt & Cook, 1979; Tashakkori & Teddlie, 1998).

Why has the question of credible evidence ignited such a long-standing and passionate debate among scholars? Kuhn (1970) observed that scientists preferred quantitative over qualitative data when making predictions and that hierarchy in data existed where "hard" numeric data were valued over "soft" qualitative data (Patton, 2002). Thus, by extension, identifying a type of quantitative study design as "strong" and "scientific" suggests that all others are "weaker" (if not weak) and "unscientific" and, to be sure, this is troubling to some. Scholars such as Erickson (e.g., Erickson & Gutierrez, 2002) argue that the distinction drawn between scientific (hard) and unscientific (soft) evidence based solely on the methods used to gather information is a false one and is ill conceived. On the other side, it is argued (e.g., Feuer, Towne & Shavelson, 2002) that when questions of effectiveness call for rigorous investigation, it is necessary for researchers and evaluators to offer the most reliable evidence possible, and the best method we have available to us to answer this question is the RCT. For all other questions, designs that do not require random assignment are legitimate choices.

Multiple method designs for studying programs have been offered as choices that integrate the merits of experimental and nonexperimental designs. Presumably, few would argue against this more general point. However, when asked to identify the feature of a multiple-method and mixed-methods study design that is intended to get at program impact, we find ourselves returning to the same issue of which design will offer the most credible evidence to answer the question, Did this program work? In this context, those who support the use of RCTs argue that without some measure of causality, a reliable measure of impact cannot be obtained, while those on the other side of the RCT debate tend to de-emphasize causality as the central factor in determining program impact. Thus the credible evidence debate may be less about design and methods than how each side conceptualizes *impact*.

It is fair to say that all applied researchers and evaluators would agree that there will always be limitations to evidence—in other words, that no study design is flawless. Where they disagree is on whether we can and how we should control for or intervene in an attempt to strengthen our evidence. Disagreements about whether conditions in applied studies can or should be controlled stem from and are informed by notions about truth and whether and how one can observe truth. Thus arguments about evidence, and more specifically credible evidence, call into question our basic notions of truth and science and the ways in which we perceive the world around us.

Notions of truth, and thus by extension the arguments centered on credible evidence, can be better understood when some key notions about knowledge put forth by philosophers of science are introduced. In line with how the credibility-of-evidence debate has been discussed historically, we offer a brief overview of the philosophical issues germane to a discussion about generating credible evidence in applied research and evaluation as a frame for the arguments presented by the authors in subsequent chapters of this book. The intention is not to offer comprehensive descriptions of theories of knowledge or social inquiry paradigms. This has been done well elsewhere (see, for example, Tashakkori & Teddlie, 1998). Instead, our aim is to make this and upcoming chapters more accessible for those who may be unfamiliar with some of the philosophical issues related to knowledge by introducing these topics more generally.

Framing the Credible Evidence Debate: Social Inquiry and the Paradigms

Evaluation and applied research are grounded in and are forms of social inquiry.[2] Described most generally, *social inquiry* is the systemic study of the behavior of groups of individuals in various kinds of social settings using a variety of methods. It begins with the recognition that there is a unique social dimension to human action, and the central focus of concern is, Why do people in social groups act as they do? In the Western world, inquiry along these lines has its origins in 17th- and 18th-century figures such as Hobbes, Montesquieu, and Rousseau. While these theorists systematically studied and commented on social groups, their descriptions and theories were more a product of contemplation rather than empirical investigations. Not until the mid- to late 19th century were society and social groups studied empirically through the collection and analysis of empirical data.

A subject of ongoing debate is what methods are appropriate for the study of society, social groups, and social life and whether the methodologies of the physical sciences, broadly defined, are applicable to social phenomena. Philosophers of science and social science continue to disagree on what constitutes the methods of the sciences and their potential applicability to the study of social life (Kuhn, 1970; Popper, 1963). Cutting across social science disciplines are broad philosophical and methodological questions that continue to be debated in contemporary social inquiry. Important questions include the following: What is the relationship between theory and observation? Should social scientists have a moral stance toward the individuals and groups that they study? Is this stance appropriate and would it compromise the researcher's objectivity? These and other questions form part of the theory and practice of social inquiry.

The classical social scientists made extensive use of statistics, among other data, in forming particular judgments regarding social life. Psychology introduced the experimental method, to address questions related to whether a treatment is effective in bringing about desired effects. Discussions regarding the feasibility and desirability of this methodology for the study of the social world continue to this day, prompting heated debates related to and reflective of the more general question of the applicability of the methods of the sciences to the social sciences.

Alternatively, the discipline of anthropology has given rise to ethnographies and more broadly qualitative studies of the social world. The distinction between these methods and the ones mentioned just above is sometimes couched in terms of the distinction between *explanation* and *prediction* on the one hand, and *interpretation* and *understanding* on the other. Geertz's classical essay, "Thick Description: Toward an Interpretive Theory of Culture," in *The Interpretation of Cultures* (1973) epitomizes the latter approach and in part has come to define interpretive social science where the emphasis is placed not on prediction but on meaning.

The influence of these social inquiry debates is infused in the chapters to follow. Specifically, the impacts of psychology and social experimentation are central to the arguments presented in support of the RCT. Anthropological influences such as "thick description" and observation are evidenced in the chapters in the second part, where authors argue for a more expanded view of evidence.

Informing the arguments around social inquiry is the philosophy of science, which is concerned with the assumptions, foundations, and implications of science, including the formal sciences, natural sciences, and social sciences. When examining this vast body of philosophical literature, we find scholars discussing the various ways one can think about the world around us, or the nature of reality, and the assumptions about social inquiry in terms of paradigms. The *Encyclopedia of Evaluation* (Mathison, 2005) offers the following description of a paradigm:

> Paradigm is a term used to capture a worldview or perspective that, in the case of research and evaluation, includes conceptions of methodology, purposes, assumptions, and values. . . . [A] paradigm typically consists of an ontology (the nature of reality), an epistemology (what is knowable and who can know it), and a methodology (how one can obtain knowledge). (p. 289)

Another way to think of a paradigm is as a theory of knowledge. Shadish, Cook, and Leviton (1991) explain that ontological, epistemological, and methodological assumptions make up theories of knowledge (i.e., *paradigms*). These authors define *ontology* as an assumption about the nature of reality, *epistemology* as an assumption about justifications for knowledge claims, and *methodology* as an assumption about constructing knowledge. Tashakkori and Teddlie (1998) describe these three assumptions as well as several others—for example, assumptions about the values in inquiry (*axiology*), logic (i.e., either deductive or inductive), generalizability, and causality.

Those who engage in the debate about credible evidence typically are referred to as belonging to one of two "camps": post-positivism or constructivism (and related thinking), and thus we will focus this description primarily on these paradigms. *Logical positivism* will be described first as a precursor to the aforementioned paradigms, and at the end of this section, *pragmatism* will be briefly described as one particular alternative to either the post-positivist or constructivist paradigms. Before moving into a discussion about the paradigms, we acknowledge that this kind of description as it is being offered for this book can be polarizing. Our reasons for this type of categorization are threefold. First, in order to be accessible to a wide range of readers, this introduction to the philosophy of science needs to be as straightforward and clear as possible. Second, the polarizing categorization does indeed mirror the polarizing effects of the debate on "what constitutes credible evidence." Third, these paradigms provide background and are closely related to the much-publicized quantitative–qualitative debate that transpired previously within the evaluation field. We would be remiss if we did not make it clear that the present debate concerning credible evidence encapsulates many of the issues of the quantitative–qualitative, but it is not the same debate. We acknowledge that contributors to this book do not necessarily fall plainly into either of the paradigms and that, in this chapter, we provide a simplified description of how the paradigms are typically interpreted in applied work. Nonetheless, we believe that it is a useful frame for better understanding the origins of each argument.

LOGICAL POSITIVISM

Logical positivism is linked to Comte, a 19th-century French philosopher. It wasn't until the end of World War II that the logical positivist paradigm began to lose its following. At that point, the post-positivist paradigm thinking developed and grew in popularity, particularly among the social scientists of the 1950s and 1960s. In almost a reactionary fashion, those who saw themselves as different from both positivists and post-positivists began writing about notions of relativism and constructivism. As constructivist thinking gained recognition, contention between the post-positivist and constructivist paradigms led to a fierce and ongoing debate quickly dubbed the "paradigm wars." Some considered the paradigms mutually exclusive and therefore incompatible. Others saw an opportunity for compromise and common ground, from which the pragmatist paradigm was formed.

From an ontological perspective, the logical positivist position is that there is a single reality. In other words, reality is something that can be agreed upon and observed objectively by multiple viewers. Faith in objectivity characterizes both the axiology (in this case, value free) and the epistemological position of the positivists. Thus the knower is independent of that which he or she is trying to know. As for how knowledge can best be obtained, positivists consider quantitative methods superior to all else. There are several other axioms that help to define this paradigm, such as a *rule of deductive logic*. This means moving from theory or a priori hypotheses to a narrow conclusion, with the generalizability of this conclusion being of the utmost importance. Finally, causes are linked to effects and this causal relationship is observable. Both post-positivism and constructivism grew from the positivist paradigm; however, post-positivism retained more of the positivist notions than constructivism did.

POST-POSITIVISM

Post-positivism has notable similarities to positivism. For instance, post-positivists, like positivists, believe that there is a single reality that can be studied objectively. However, the difference between the two paradigms on this point is critical, for post-positivists believe that there is no way to understand reality *in its totality*. Thus full understanding of truth can be approached but never reached. This type of realism is referred to as *critical realism*. Beyond ontology, there are other commonalities between the positivist and post-positivist paradigms. For example, most post-positivists have a strong preference for quantitative methods and deductive reasoning. However, in alignment with the notion of "approaching" truth rather than "capturing" it, post-positivists would not argue that quantitative methods or deductive reasoning should be used exclusively, just predominantly. The "approaching" truth ideal extends to views on causality as well. It is believed that causation is observable and that over time, predictors can be established, but some degree of doubt always remains associated with the conclusion. As for axiology, values and biases are noted and accounted for, yet the belief is that they can be controlled within the context of scientific inquiry.

CONSTRUCTIVISM (AND RELATED THINKING)

The constructivist ontological position argues that there are multiple realities. These multiple realities are subjective and change according to the knower, who constructs his or her own reality using past experiences and individual contexts to perceive what is known. This is referred to as *ontological relativism*. In the constructivist paradigm the "knower" and the "known" are interrelated, unlike positivist epistemology, where they are considered independent. Inductive logic is the rule, which means particular instances are used to infer broader, more general laws. Of notable distinction, inquiry is considered value bound rather than value free. It is the constructivists' position that it is better to acknowledge and consider bias than to attempt to ignore or control it. Qualitative methods are used most frequently within the constructivist paradigm because they are thought to be better suited to investigate the subjective layers of reality. Generalizability is not nearly as important as local relevance. Cause and effect are thought impossible to distinguish because relationships are bidirectional, and thus everything is impacting everything else at one time.

Related to constructivism is *social constructivism*, a sociological theory of knowledge that considers how social phenomena are not independent from the society they exist within. In other words, social phenomena cannot be divorced from their societal and cultural contexts, because the definition and meaning attributed to those phenomena are constructed by that society. To investigate social phenomena through a social constructivist lens is to consider the phenomena as others perceive them.

Also juxtaposed to post-positivism is *relativism*. Relativism, simply put, consists of a collection of viewpoints, all of which suggest that social phenomena are relative to other social phenomena and vice versa. One form of relativism is *truth relativism*; that is, there are no absolute truths. This means that truth is relative to its societal, cultural, and historical contexts. This is, of course, similar to notions of truth put forth by constructivists. Taken together, constructivist, social constructivist, and relativist thinking (which we have described under constructivism) serve to inform the arguments of those opposed to relying only on RCTs as the method for observing program impact.

PRAGMATISM

Pragmatism is not typically cited in the "paradigm wars" and is often misinterpreted to be the compromise between the two more popularly debated paradigms. True, pragmatists embrace objectivity and subjectivity as two positions on a continuum, which appears to be a truce of some kind between post-positivist and constructivist thinking. After all, there is now room for both subjectivity and objectivity to be useful at different points within an evaluation or applied research study. Another seemingly agreed-upon point is that both quantitative and qualitative methods are legitimate methods of inquiry. The decision of what method to use is based on the nature of the study question. Pragmatists also argue that deductive and inductive logic should be used in concert. Pragmatists do, however, move away from embracing equally the axioms of the post-positivist and constructivist paradigms. For example, pragmatists are more similar to post-positivists with regard to notions about external reality, with the understanding that there is no absolute truth concerning reality. More in line with constructivist thought, however, pragmatists argue that there are multiple explanations of reality, and at any given time, there is one explanation that makes the most sense. In other words, at one point in time, one explanation of reality may be considered truer than another. Pragmatists are again similar to post-positivists in that they believe causes may be linked to effects. However, pragmatists temper this thinking by providing the caveat that absolute certainty of the causation is impossible. In contrast, pragmatists are more similar to constructivists in that they do not believe inquiry is value free, and they consider their values important to the inquiry process. The pragmatist paradigm should be given attention as a paradigm unto its own.

While some argue the superiority of either post-positivism or constructivism, others have offered a rationale for a cease-fire. They reason as follows:

- Both paradigms have, in fact, been used for years.
- Many evaluators and researchers have urged using both paradigms.
- So much has been taught by both paradigms.
- Funding agencies have supported both paradigms.
- Both paradigms have influenced policy. (Tashakkori & Teddlie, 1998, p. 11)

Indeed, these points are, by most accounts, valid; however, the last two have been called into question in recent years. Certainly, over the past decade, we have witnessed a serious and concerted focus on increasing the proportion of RCTs conducted in education as well as other areas of the social and behavioral science, such as public health and social welfare. Specifically for education, the federal government announced the decree, in the form of the 2002 Education Sciences Reform Act, that the RCT is the gold standard design for research and evaluation focused on the question of program impact.

This prompted a great concern among some social scientists and educational researchers that designs from both paradigms would not be supported equally by the federal government and thus would not enjoy a balanced position in informing important policy debates and decisions related to social, behavioral, and educational programs and policies. Through the Institute of Education Sciences (IES), which has a $200 million budget (IES, 2014), it seems that the proportion of U.S. federal dollars going to RCTs has been consolidated and emphasized. There are some preliminary data, however, that show that RCTs have not taken over educational evaluation (Christie & Fleischer, 2010). Since the initiation of this most recent push for RCTs, the rhetoric has eased, in part because of the work of scholars such as Will Shadish who are studying the conditions under which quasi-experimental designs offer effect estimates that are comparable to those obtained by RCTs (Shadish, Clark, & Steiner, 2008). There has also been increased interest in understanding program variation (that is, how and why programs work and in what contexts) as researchers and funders are examining how approaches such as improvement research (for example, see Carnegie Foundation, Improvement Research: http://www.carnegiefoundation.org/improvement-research/approach) are a means for better understanding a program's impact. This more-nuanced discussion of what constitutes credible evidence in decision-making contexts is reflected in the chapters presented in the second edition of the volume.

Chapter Authors: Paradigm Positions

The purpose of this chapter is to elucidate some of the conceptual content of the chapters that follow. Regardless of whether contributors talk directly about social inquiry or the philosophy of science in their particular chapter, some theoretical work serves as a framework for their conceptual arguments. Each contributor has a history of supporting notions related to either the post-positivist or constructivist paradigm; indeed, authors were asked to contribute to this book in part because of their beliefs about truth and knowledge and social inquiry.

In each chapter, authors offer a contemporary argument about evidence. While each chapter could stand alone, taken together, they become a dialogue about what constitutes credible evidence in evaluation and applied research. Several contributors to this book offer insights and arguments about credible evidence that position them most closely with the post-positivist paradigm. A theme running through the chapters in Part II is causal inference. Both Henry and Bickman have long argued, to at least some extent, that RCTs are the best (available) method for studying causality and have pushed on many occasions for an increased presence of post-positivist thinking in our methodological discussions and applied work. For example, Bickman (coauthor of Chapter 5) conducted a large-scale RCT of a system of care designed to improve mental health outcomes for children and adolescents who were referred for mental health treatment, which he argues could only be understood well if studied using experimental methods (Fitzpatrick, Christie, & Mark, 2008). This is in line with his years of arguing for the use of RCTs to better understand mental health interventions and practice. Henry's (Chapter 4) position on the use of RCTs has intensified over time, with his more recent work, both theoretical and practical, being more focused on the exclusive use of experiments, when possible, to study educational policies, particularly related to early childhood education (e.g., Henry, Gordon, & Rickman, 2006). The authors of Chapter 11, Julnes and Rog, have edited a *New Directions for Evaluation* issue (2007) focused on scientific method choice for building an evidence base in federal evaluation studies. While Chelimsky's (Chapter 9) work has focused largely on politics use and policy-level decision making, she was trained as an economist, and her first evaluation position was as a statistician with NATO in Paris. She then returned to the United States and took a position at MIT Research Engineers (MITER), conducting evaluations of social welfare and criminal justice programs and research and development focusing on dissemination of knowledge. She is concerned with ensuring that truthful information is being using to improve social programming. Scriven, an objectivist by most accounts, critically questions RCTs as the gold standard for providing credible causal evidence. However, the alternative approach he describes focuses on gathering objective evidence for valuing programs and policies.

Other contributor's viewpoints are most closely aligned with the thinking of a constructivist paradigm. As with the more post-positivist authors, the more relativist contributors have extensive histories arguing for alternative methods and thinking about scientific evidence. For example, Greene (Chapter 10) strongly believes that inquirers' assumptions about the social world and our knowledge of it inevitably influence decisions of practice (e.g., Greene & Caracelli, 1997). She has critiqued performance measurements as inadequate measures of social program quality, as inadequate representations of program quality, and as at odds with evaluative processes that advance the ideals of deliberative democracy. Rallis (Chapter 7) has argued specifically for the use of qualitative methods in evaluation and educational research and maintains that qualitative work is not only about precision of method but is also an art (e.g., Rossman & Rallis, 2003). Mathison (Chapter 8) argues for fair and democratic evaluation of educational programs, evaluations that consider local context and values as well as the use of multiple indicators of quality and that involve diverse and often disenfranchised stakeholders (e.g., Mathison, 2007). Schwandt (Chapter 12) has published widely on constructivist, interpretivist approaches to human inquiry (e.g., Schwandt, 1994).

It is evident from these brief descriptions of our chapter authors' work how their views differ when considered through a "cloudy" (i.e., somewhat imprecise) philosophical lens.

Conclusion

For all contributors to this book, the purpose of evaluation is to promote social good. While they share this general common purpose, they differ on exactly what philosophical underpinnings should inform the strategies and proce-dures used to accomplish it. The appropriateness and validity of using RCTs as a method for pursuing social good is debated under the nuanced topic of what constitutes credible evidence. They bring to bear the methodological argu-ments surrounding this notion of credible evidence, highlight the implications of these arguments, and offer examples related to and descriptions of contexts where the relevance of the arguments can be seen.

In the chapters to follow, we will see how this debate resonates with our contributors. The authors offer us insight into the history surrounding credible evidence as well as the current debate as it has waned and swelled in importance and relevance to the field of evaluation and the practice of applied social research. Most notable, however, is that this debate has yet to fade away. We hope that you find the discussion presented here to be both stimulating and illuminating.

Notes

1. RCTs require the random assignment of individuals either to a treatment group (i.e., the group receiving the intervention or program) or to some other group that is not receiving the intervention or program. The other group can be a no-treatment control group, a waitlist control group (i.e., this group receives no intervention initially but gets the treatment after the initial study period), a treatment-as-usual comparison group (i.e., people in this group receive whatever services, if any, they would get without the experimental intervention), or an alternative treatment group (e.g., a group uniformly receiving an alternative treatment). Random assignment is argued to reduce most threats to internal validity (e.g., selection bias, maturation, history), and the use of a control or comparison group provides data to determine the relative performance of the treatment group, helping to answer the "Compared to what?" question when measuring program impact (Azzam & Christie, 2007). The defining feature of the RCT design is random assignment, where quasi-experiments do not have randomization as a feature of the study design. Quasi-experiments do not require random assignment of participants and often involve the use of a comparison group or some other kind of comparative condition (e.g., within group pre-post comparisons).
2. This description of social inquiry is summarized from Christie and Alkin (2012).

References

Azzam, T., & Christie, C. A. (2007). Using public databases to study relative program impact. *Canadian Journal of Program Evaluation, 22*(2), 57–68.

Christie, C. A., & Alkin, M. C. (2012). An evaluation theory tree. In M. C. Alkin (Ed.), *Evaluation Roots* (2nd ed., pp. 12–66). Thousand Oaks, CA: SAGE.

Christie, C. A., & Fleischer, D. (2010). Insight into evaluation practice: An analysis of evaluation studies published in North American evaluation focused journals. *American Journal of Evaluation, 31*(3), 326–346.

Erickson, F., & Gutierrez, K. (2002). Culture, rigor, and science in educational research. *Educational Researcher, 31*(8), 21–24.

Feuer, M. J., Towne, L., & Shavelson, R. J. (2002). Scientific culture and educational research. *Educational Researcher, 31*(8), 4–14.

Fitzpatrick, J., Christie, C. A., & Mark, M. (Eds.). (2008). *Evaluation in action: Interviews with expert evaluators.* Thousand Oaks, CA: SAGE.

Geertz, C. (1973). *The interpretation of cultures.* New York, NY: Basic Books.

Greene, J. C., & Caracelli, V. J. (1997). Defining and describing the paradigm issues in mixed-method evaluation. In J. G. Greene & V. J. Caracelli (Eds.), Advances in mixed-method evaluation: The challenges and benefits of integrating diverse paradigms. *New Directions for Evaluation, 74,* 5–18.

Henry, G. T., Gordon, C. C., & Rickman, D. K. (2006). Early education policy alternatives: Comparing the quality and outcomes of Head Start and state pre-kindergarten. *Educational Evaluation and Policy Analysis, 28,* 77–99.

Institute of Education Sciences. (2014, January). *About IES: Connecting research, policy and practice.* United States Department of Education. Retrieved from http://ies .ed.gov/aboutus/

Julnes, G., & Rog, D. J. (2007). Informing federal policies on evaluation methodology: Building the evidence base for method choice in government-sponsored evaluations [Entire issue]. *New Directions for Evaluation, 113.*

Kuhn, T. (1970). *The structure of scientific revolutions.* Chicago, IL: University of Chicago Press.

Lincoln, Y., & Guba, E. (1985). *Naturalistic inquiry.* Thousand Oaks, CA: SAGE.

Mathison, S. (Ed.). (2005). *Encyclopedia of evaluation.* Thousand Oaks, CA: SAGE.

Mathison, S. (2007). The accumulation of disadvantage: The role of educational testing in the school career of minority children. In B. A. Arrighi & D. J. Maume (Eds.), *Child poverty in America today: The promise of education* (pp. 66–79). New York, NY: Praeger.

Patton, M. Q. (2002). *Qualitative research and evaluation methods.* Thousand Oaks, CA: SAGE.

Popper, K. R. (1963). *Conjectures and refutations.* London, England: Routledge/Kegan Paul.

Reichardt, C. S., & Cook, T. D. (1979). *Qualitative and quantitative methods in evaluation research.* Thousand Oaks, CA: SAGE.

Rossman, G., & Rallis, S. F. (2003). *Learning in the field: An introduction to qualitative research* (2nd ed.). Thousand Oaks, CA: SAGE.

Schwandt, T. (1994). Constructivist, interpretivist approaches to human inquiry. In N. K. Denzin & Y. S. Lincoln (Eds.), *The landscape of qualitative research: Theories and issues* (pp. 221–259). Thousand Oaks, CA: SAGE.

Shadish, W. R., Clark, M. H., & Steiner, P. M. (2008). Can nonrandomized experiments yield accurate answers? A randomized experiment comparing random and nonrandom assignments. *Journal of the American Statistical Association, 103*(484), 1334–1343.

Shadish, W. R., Cook, T. D., & Leviton, L. C. L. (1991). *Foundations of program evaluation.* Newbury Park, CA: SAGE.

Tashakkori, A., & Teddlie, C. (1998). *Mixed methodology: Combining qualitative and quantitative approaches.* Thousand Oaks, CA: SAGE.

3

How People Judge the Credibility of Information

Lessons for Evaluation From Cognitive and Information Sciences

Robin Lin Miller

Professional controversies bring out the worst in academics.

Daniel Kahneman, 2011

Not long ago, I observed a planning meeting of about 30 interdisciplinary professionals working on a joint public health initiative. Each professional was part of a work team responsible for carrying out components of the initiative. As part of the meeting, each team had been asked to report to everyone on accomplishments made over the prior year. One team, which I will refer to as *Team A*, reported proudly on having, for the first time, obtained data on a large sample of people from a population about which little was known except that the population was overrepresented among HIV-infected people. Though these data were not perfect, Team A's representative noted excitedly that having these data was a critical step forward. The data assisted Team A in

AUTHOR'S NOTE: I am grateful to my colleague in the cognitive sciences, Timothy J. Pleskac, for serving as my sounding board in the development of this chapter.

identifying urgent needs and making the case that the population deserved priority attention. Team A suggested that the mere act of collecting the data sent an important political signal that this often overlooked and stigmatized population's health mattered. Collecting the data had also started the process of bolstering indigenous capacity to generate and use evidence.

Later in the meeting, Team F's representative made multiple and pointed criticisms of the quality of Team A's data. In particular, this member of Team F did not think the sampling design that Team A had used was ideal. According to the member of Team F, the sampling design Team A had used could lead to an inaccurate period prevalence* estimate. Team F's representative argued that Team A's data probably could not be relied upon. As Team F's representative went on to further explain why a probability sample was superior to a non-probability sample, the mood in the room grew visibly tense. Members of Team A interjected their disagreement, which rapidly escalated in intensity and vehemence. The tensions culminated with a member of Team A shouting at Team F's lead presenter that he found the attempt to denigrate the data (and by implication, Team A) insulting. People from other teams quickly agreed with him. Team F's representative continued making the case against the data's quality unabated until a member of Team A, shaking with fury, demanded that the member of Team F retract his remarks. Team A's members were adamant that their data could be trusted.

Who is right in their judgment of the credibility of these data, Team A or Team F? Are the members of Team A and Team F peculiar in their ability to reason, given they arrived at opposing judgments about the same data's quality? As it turns out, the interaction among members of Team A, Team F, and the other teams who joined in the fray highlight predictable individual and group differences in how people evaluate the credibility of evidence. In this chapter, I will draw on current theoretical and empirical work in cognitive and social psychology, communications, and information sciences to explore how people make judgments about the credibility of information. In doing so, I will take a larger view of credibility judgments about evidence. I will apply knowledge on human judgment and decision making to understand how people judge the credibility of evidence in the context of evaluation and why we hold steadfast to our judgments about the quality of evidence. Finally, I will suggest implications for our practice and areas for future research on how evaluators and evaluation's users assess the credibility of evidence in evaluation.

Period prevalence describes the proportion of people in a population who have a condition over a defined unit of time.

Why Do We Care About the Credibility of Evidence?

The debates on credible evidence are important for our profession because we aspire to have evaluation users act on the implications of evaluation findings (Henry & Mark, 2003; Weiss, 1988). As a consequence, we have to be concerned about how users decide that our evaluations have produced credible information and ought to be believed. Models of information, influence, and persuasion (e.g., Kelton, Fleischmann, & Wallace, 2008; Petty & Cacioppo, 1986) confirm our intuitive sense that the credibility of evidence is related to its influence. If the information generated by an evaluation can be believed, then the findings have the potential to be persuasive (Rieh & Danielson, 2007). Whether any particular evaluation can influence thinking and behavior therefore depends in part on the judgments that people make of its credibility, as credibility judgments precede processes of persuasion, influence, and use (Fleming, 2011; Mark & Henry, 2004; Rieh & Danielson, 2007).

Facets of Information's Credibility

For information and communication scientists, *credibility* typically refers to the extent to which information is perceived as believable or plausible (Tseng & Fogg, 1999; Wathen & Burkell, 2002). When users assess a piece of information, whether that information is contained within the findings of an evaluation report or in a Wikipedia article, they form a judgment about its credence. Although research on human judgment and decision making has a long history, the explosion of easy access to information on the Internet has spurred researchers to better understand how diverse information users make judgments about information's credibility and whether they do so in a manner similar to experts (Liu, 2004). Because online access to information means that people will be exposed to more information than they can reasonably process and because online information will vary in its quality and grounding in facts, the Internet has inspired resurgent interest in identifying how people determine whether information is credible and how they discern fact from fiction clothed as fact.

Despite our professional concern with grounding information in fact, research on credibility judgments tells us that facts are only a small part of how credibility judgments are made. Multiple factors besides the information's content affect credibility judgments. Peripheral features pertaining to information's appearance and who produced and received it also matter. We judge the integrity of information in the context of its peripheral aspects (Rieh & Danielson, 2007); these peripheral factors quickly become difficult for us to separate from the content of information.

INFORMATION CHARACTERISTICS

Across diverse research traditions, a core set of information characteristics has been identified as helping people decide that a piece of information is worthy of being believed. These characteristics are familiar to evaluators: Many are reflected in the American Evaluation Association's Guiding Principles (American Evaluation Association [AEA], 2004) and in well-known performance standards such as the Joint Committee Standards (Joint Committee on Standards for Educational Evaluation, 2011) and the Organisation for Economic Co-Operation and Development (OECD) Development Assistance Committee (DAC) Standards (OECD DAC Network on Evaluation, 2010). For example, people's belief that a piece of information is *accurate* or free from errors of fact helps them to conclude that the information is worth believing (Savolainen, 2011). For evaluators, getting the facts right is an obvious priority. The accuracy of a variety of methods for generating evidence about causal effects has received substantial attention in the evaluation literature's debates on credible evidence, including the prior and current edition of this text, because accuracy is such an important characteristic of information. However, other characteristics of information besides accuracy are salient in how people judge credibility, including whether information is current or obsolete, fair or imbalanced, and impartial or biased (Rieh & Danielson, 2007). Leading evaluation theories stress the need for evaluations to produce evidence that is impartial and fair (Chelimsky, 1998; House & Howe, 1999; Scriven, 1980; Weiss, 1998). Information that is viewed as free from error, up-to-date, balanced, and unbiased is most likely to be perceived as credible by a variety of information users (Kelton et al., 2008; Savolainen, 2011).

Validity of the methods used to produce the information has also received substantial research attention in studies of information users. Studies on perceived validity are commonly conducted on samples of people who engage in scholarly activities (such as students) and those who possess advanced information skills. For example, studies have found that scholars and students look for the presence of citations and indicators of a peer-review process to determine if the methods used to produce information are legitimate (Hilligoss & Rieh, 2008; Liu, 2004; Rieh & Hilligoss, 2008). College students are more likely to look for indicators of validity such as citations to decide whether information is probably accurate than are high school students (Hilligoss & Rieh, 2008; Julien & Barker, 2009; Walraven, Brandgruwel, & Boshuizen, 2009), reflecting college students' emerging expertise in scholarly practices and their developing information skills. In turn, graduate students use more indicators of validity than do novice undergraduates (Brandgruwel, Wopereis, & Vermetten, 2005). Even though senior students' judgments about validity may involve more sophistication than junior students, each level of student may reach a similar conclusion on the credibility of particular information because validity is only one among several characteristics that students may take into account.

Relevance to the specific informational needs a user has, *usefulness* of the information in solving a problem, *novelty* of the information, and *importance* of the information have also been identified in the literature as characteristics of information that people use to assess credibility (Liu, 2004; Savolainen, 2011). Though relevance, utility, novelty, and importance may be considered in assessing information, these aspects of information also pertain to judging helpfulness for a given purpose and influence peoples' willingness to attend to information and act as a consequence of it. In other words, when people encounter information that is not pertinent to what they are seeking to learn and does not add to what they believe they already know about a topic, they may not be motivated to focus closely on the information (Weiss & Bucuvalas, 1980). These features of the information-seeking context may make particular information more or less salient to an information user in addition to affecting credibility judgments. These features of context may also moderate whether features such as accuracy and validity—features of evaluations that we attribute to methodological quality—are given close consideration (Weiss & Bucuvalas, 1980).

The empirical research on credibility judgments highlights important conclusions for evaluators about the characteristics of information. A single piece of information may not possess any combination of the aforementioned characteristics in a consistent fashion (Savolainen, 2011). That is, information can be well regarded on one facet and poorly regarded on another; for instance, information may be simultaneously accurate, impartial, obsolete, and irrelevant. Just as evaluators have methods for ranking, weighting, and summing information about programs, users must have some means for arriving at conclusions about the credibility of information in light of potential inconsistencies in aspects of quality.

PERIPHERAL CUES ABOUT INFORMATION

Kelton and colleagues (Kelton et al., 2008) and Lucassen and Schraagen (2011) point out that although credibility and trust are not synonymous, trusting information is interpersonal insofar as trust characterizes a relationship between an information recipient and an information producer. High levels of trust reflect information recipients' favorable expectations of and confidence in information producers (McKnight, Choudhury, & Kacmar, 2002). Characteristics of the individuals who produce information and of information recipients therefore play a significant role in how credibility judgments are formed. So does the appearance and composition of information.

SOURCES OF INFORMATION

People use peripheral cues about who produced information to form credibility judgments. Though the credibility of information can be assessed independently of the trustworthiness of its source, source characteristics may be of particular importance when an information recipient has limited capability or motivation to assess information for its credibility. People may form a preliminary expectation of credibility based on source characteristics, which will then bias them toward looking for evidence to confirm their expectations (Slater & Rouner, 1996). When trust of a particular information source has already developed, people may allow it to stand in for a thorough and critical assessment of information. Moreover, trust in a source can blunt the impact of having produced poor-quality information on information recipients' credibility judgments (Slater & Rouner, 1996). In face-to-face interactions, source characteristics exert especially strong influence on recipients' perceptions of information credibility.

Four primary characteristics of information's source affect credibility judgments (Tseng & Fogg, 1999). A source's *presumed credibility* refers to the extent to which a source conforms to the stereotype of a trustworthy provider of information. A well-respected university press and a peer-reviewed journal of a major professional association like one of the world's many evaluation societies are examples of information sources that would be presumed to be credible sources of information on evaluation. These sources fit the stereotype of credible information outlets.

Reputed credibility refers to having titles (e.g., Professor, Inspector General, Senior Evaluation Specialist) and affiliations (e.g., Stanford University, United States Government Accountability Office, Rand Corporation) that indicate an information users' trust in the source should be well-placed. Credibility may be extended to particular individuals because they are associated with institutions and occupy roles that have a reputation for credibility, regardless of the individual's earned level of credibility or the credibility of information they produce on any given occasion (Rieh, 2002; Rieh & Danielson, 2007).

Surface credibility refers to having the outward appearance of credibility (Hilligoss & Rieh, 2008; Lucassen & Schraagen, 2011; Wathen & Burkell, 2002). People associate information credibility with well-composed text (Oppenheimer, 2008). High-quality prose, including correct grammar, syntax, and spelling, communicates that a source is credible. Direct and simple prose also evokes perceptions of intelligence (Oppenheimer, 2006, 2008). Physical and aesthetic features of information's presentation have a similar effect. Sharp fonts, attractive colors, compelling images, intelligible graphics, visually appealing layouts, and usable navigational guides are among the surface features that can indicate professionalism and that people equate with a credible source. A source's personal appearance can also inform surface credibility.

Choice of dress in a photograph or at a meeting may suggest credibility by providing visual evidence of professionalism.

Experienced credibility refers to firsthand or vicarious experience of a source's impartiality, fairness, competence, and honesty, such as through having read an individual's prior published work (firsthand) or observing that an evaluation's findings were simultaneously published as a report and as a peer-reviewed journal article (vicarious). In the latter instance, peer-reviewed publication serves as an endorsement and provides vicarious evidence that expert peers found the work credible. When an evaluator has direct interaction with individuals who are recipients of evaluative information, the evaluator's level of diplomacy, charm, goodwill, and likeability may decrease or increase experienced credibility of him or her (Wathen & Burkell, 2002). People are biased toward extending credibility to those whom they find likable (Chaiken, 1980).

INFORMATION RECIPIENT

People employ personal algorithms for determining on which criteria a piece of information must be judged satisfactory to be considered credible (Hilligoss & Rieh, 2008; Kahneman, 2011). Information recipients are unlikely to prioritize and synthesize criteria identically. Which criteria matter depends upon many factors, including the level of domain expertise and analytic skills individuals possess. Domain expertise provides people with the depth of information to recognize what is and is not credible in a substantive area whereas analytic skills provide people with the capacity to assess information critically. Confidence in our beliefs and our worldview also affect our judgments.

Domain Expertise

Credibility assessment processes vary as a function of individual differences in domain expertise (Lucassen & Schraagen, 2011). Whereas novices can assess surface characteristics without domain knowledge and may therefore depend upon these characteristics to indicate information quality, experts have the ability to assess information content directly. For example, accuracy, or the absence of factual errors, can only be correctly assessed when an information recipient has sufficient expertise in a given domain to detect errors of fact or when he or she possesses and applies information skills so as to provide him or her with a reasonable basis for making such a judgment in the absence of domain expertise. Information recipients' level of expertise in evaluative thinking and in the substantive issue being evaluated will affect their abilities to make judgments of credibility. Evaluators' level of expertise in evaluative thinking and evaluation methods will similarly impact their judgments of what constitutes credible and actionable evidence. However, the presence of factual errors does not preclude an expert from forming an overall judgment that information is credible (Lucassen & Schraagen, 2011).

Part of what makes an expert an expert and distinguishes him or her from a novice is his or her ability to identify relevant from irrelevant information. However, experts do not rely on content alone to form their judgments. Experts, like novices, use very few cues to make their judgments and, like anyone else, rely on heuristic and intuitive devices to arrive at judgments (Tversky & Kahneman, 1974). *Heuristics* are unconscious working rules of thumb we use to make decisions quickly and easily. Heuristics are similar to substituting simpler questions or problems that can be easily answered or solved for ones that we experience as more difficult (Kahneman, 2011), which means that experts are prone to use irrelevant information to arrive at conclusions. Expert judgment is most likely to be superior to that of novices when experts work in domains in which there are a limited number of patterns to learn to recognize and there is high degree of regularity in the context (e.g., automotive mechanics; Shanteau, 1992). In domains characterized by high pattern complexity and contextual irregularity (e.g., psychiatry), experts are more prone to errors in judgment because it is more difficult to determine what information is relevant and what information is not. Evaluation is more like psychiatry than auto mechanics.

Although experts and novices are each prone to errors in judgment about information, the types of errors in judging the credibility of information to which experts and novices are most vulnerable are dissimilar. Tseng and Fong (1999) observed that novices to a topic are more vulnerable to *gullibility errors*. Gullibility errors occur when an individual accepts false information as true. Novices are at heightened risk of believing untrue information when their need for information on a topic is pressing. Experts are more prone to *incredulity errors*. Incredulity errors occur when people reject true information as false.

CONFIDENCE

Being certain of what you know is based on your sense of how quickly you came to a conclusion and how difficult that process was. You are more confident when coming to a conclusion is quick and easy than when you are challenged by the task. Koriat (2008, 2011) has shown that the process that makes us confident in our judgments is very similar to the process we use to make the judgments themselves (see also Pleskac & Busemeyer, 2010). We believe easily arrived-at judgments are probably correct; the judgments in which we are confident come to us quickly. That means that people can be simultaneously confident, wrong, and difficult to convince this is the case because they equate the ease of arriving at an answer with the accuracy of that answer. Paradoxically, engaging in difficult and careful mental work to arrive at a correct answer may make us less confident simply because the process was arduous. Kahneman

(2011) notes several conditions under which people are more vulnerable to making judgments based on the ease of arriving at a conclusion rather than on more effortful critical analysis of content. These include being in a good mood (e.g., the evaluation shows we are doing terrific work), performing another effortful activity at the same time we are completing a target task (e.g., answering e-mail while listening to the evaluation results being presented via conference call), and being a knowledgeable novice but not a true expert.

ANALYTIC SKILLS

In a classic paper on evidence and confidence, Griffin and Tversky (1992) demonstrate that confidence in inaccurate judgments about things such as facts probably occurs because people give insufficient attention to the weight of evidence as compared to its strength. *Weight of evidence* refers to the reliability and consistency of evidence, whereas *strength* refers to the size of an effect or its position along a dimension, such as a positive–negative continuum. Kahneman (2011) explains that strength of evidence is akin to the main storyline. In the program evaluation context, the storyline might be that a program was well liked by clients, that it improved client well-being on particular indicators, or that is was more cost-efficient than an alternative. The weight of the evidence is akin to the source of the evidence. In program evaluation, the quality of the sampling design and its execution are components of the weight of evidence. Obtaining client feedback only from those clients who attend a program regularly, only through convenience sampling, or only on a single occasion might indicate the evidence has limited weight to address whether the intended client population is satisfied and has benefited from a program.

Cognitive psychology shows us that whereas strength of evidence is intuitively easy to understand and readily captures our attention, weight of evidence is not intuitive and may often be ignored. Think back to the first peer-reviewed research paper that you ever read. Perhaps it was assigned to you in your first semester of graduate training as a budding evaluator or you encountered it in your first evaluation job. Recall your experience of reading the introduction and discussion sections. Now recall reading the methods and results sections. The former was probably easier to grasp than the latter. You could get the gist of the study from the introduction and the discussion. You easily understood the story of the findings as the authors chose to convey and interpret it. You probably struggled more with the methods and results and, given where you were in the process of learning about methods, could not and did not give as careful consideration to the study's technical details as you did to the study's overall message. In other words, you attended to the strength of the evidence to a greater degree than you did its weight. Classic experiments have shown us that even experts may take inadequate account of the weight of evidence (Tversky & Kahneman, 1971).

WORLDVIEW

Although the perceived lack of bias and the impartiality of content produced by a source may factor heavily into credibility judgments, so does the perceived similarity of a source's beliefs to those of the information recipient (Birnbaum & Stegner, 1979). Sources with worldviews similar to those of information recipients may be perceived as more credible providers of information than sources with dissimilar views, independent of any close assessment of the information each offers. Evaluators and their clients are prone to believe information produced by sources who are trusted and who possess compatible worldviews. However, being viewed as an expert can also hinder information recipients' perception that information is credible.

In a set of classic experiments, Birnbaum and Stegner (1979) and Birnbaum and Meller (1983) tested a scale-adjustment model in which expertise was expected to magnify the effect of bias either positively or negatively. Across the various experiments, unbiased sources of greater expertise were judged as more credible than were sources with equivalent expertise but who were perceived as biased. As the model predicted, bias did not always suggest that expert information was perceived as less credible. An expert source had greater weight when his or her judgment was the opposite of what one might expect, based on the expert's known bias. For example, findings supporting the benefits of contraceptive education on delayed sexual initiation would be viewed as more credible when these were produced by an expert evaluator who was known to support abstinence-only education than they would by an expert evaluator known to support contraceptive education. Expert sources also had greater weight when their bias was similar to that of the people judging their expert opinions. Birnbaum and colleagues' findings underscore the idea that when people reach a conclusion about credibility, they have typically combined an assessment of the information's source and message and considered each in light of their preexisting point of view.

Putting It Together:
The Process of Making a Credibility Judgment

Although people should analyze information carefully, judging credibility through systematic information analysis is time and labor intensive (Hilligoss & Rieh, 2008). *Systematic information analysis* refers to thoughtful critical analysis of informational content (Fleming, 2011; Hilligoss & Rieh, 2008; Kahneman, 2011). Systematic information analysis is controlled and taxing rather than autonomic and effortless (Kahneman, 2011; Weber & Johnson, 2009). Perhaps because systematic information analysis rapidly saps mental energy, people will only apply that level of cognitive effort under select circumstances and will limit the frequency and time devoted to it. That means it is not always the case that people will evaluate the credibility of evidence or information through rigorous analytical means. Indeed, the default appears to be *not* to analyze information rigorously and to rely instead on an initial intuitive judgment that is based largely on peripheral informational cues.

Given the effort required to process information in a systematic and rigorous manner, people default to heuristic information processing under ordinary circumstances. As previously noted, *heuristic* information processing refers to the use of simple rules of thumb that allow us to make assessments in an automated manner and with little effort and minimal conscious awareness. Heuristics are substitutes for rigorous analysis and make cognitive assessment processes feel manageable (Kahneman, 2011). Reviewing all of the heuristics that people use and may pertain to evaluating evidence is beyond the scope of the current chapter (for a review of temporal heuristic biases in evaluation, see Sanna, Panter, Cohen, & Kennedy, 2011; for an overview of common heuristics impacting decision making, see Kahneman, 2011, and Tversky & Kahneman, 1974). However, I will highlight select heuristics that are associated with judging the quality of information to illustrate how heuristics work to insinuate peripheral characteristics into the process of making judgments about the credibility of information content.

Empirically derived stage models of the judgments people make to decide on the credibility of information online illustrate the integration of heuristic processes in decision making. When people encounter a webpage entry, people focus first on how the information is presented, noting features such as its organization and ease of use (Wathen & Burkell, 2002). The types of heuristics that people initially use to judge whether information has the appearance of credibility are therefore related to surface characteristics of the source, such as appearance and semantics. People will draw preliminary conclusions about how likely it is they can learn what they want to know easily and with minimal effort. In research on credibility judgments, people equate poorly organized and composed information with low credibility (Hilligoss & Rieh, 2008; Oppenheimer, 2006). If a piece of information does not appear credible, most will discount it prior to any more rigorous examination.

If surface characteristics suggest credibility, the second stage of credibility assessment involves evaluating characteristics of the message's source using heuristics related to other source characteristics (Wathen & Burkell, 2002). Information recipients consider whether the source appears to have the expertise, trustworthiness, credentials, and appeal to be taken seriously. People will take stock of the source's reputation for providing credible information and whether others have endorsed it as a credible source (Chaiken, 1980; Hilligoss & Rieh, 2008; Metzger, Flanagin, & Medders, 2010). People who enjoy a credible reputation are said to have *cognitive authority* (Wilson, 1983). Individuals with cognitive authority are influential because they are considered worthy of belief. Savolainen (2011) observed that a source's reputation was weighted far more heavily than its expertise in judging source credibility.

A superficial assessment of content and message will also occur at this second stage (Wathen & Burkell, 2002). Consistency with previously available information or with widely held opinions are commonly used heuristic short-cuts for determining credibility at this point in the decision-making process. People look to determine if the main messages are consistent with their expec-tations and with what others perceive to be true (Koriat, 2011). Evidence or information that fails to conform to our expectations might be dismissed as false, despite cues that the information ought to be given credence. This phe-nomenon is called an *expectancy violation* heuristic (Metzger, Flanagin, & Medders, 2010). We are biased to dismiss key indicators that information is credible—such as that information is comprehensive, warranted, and well-argued—if the information violates our expectations. In other words, the familiar is perceived to be true and the unfamiliar is viewed skeptically (Wathen & Burkell, 2002). People tend to believe information that is consistent with what they already think they know (Fisher, Jonas, Frey, & Schulz-Hardt, 2005; Koriat, 2008, 2011; Wathen & Burkell, 2002). People also tend to believe statements that are frequently repeated, otherwise known as the *validity effect* (Boehm, 1994). Other heuristic indicators that might be used at this stage could include scanning citations (Hilligoss & Rieh, 2008). Information may be discounted at this stage or be judged worthy of closer examination. If people are motivated to do so, close examination of the content may next occur.

FACTORS PROMOTING HEURISTIC INFORMATION PROCESSING

Why do peripheral cues reduce our impetus to analyze information rigor-ously? Peripheral cues promote a state of cognitive ease (Kahneman, 2011). While some of the lessons from cognitive psychology and information sciences suggest we should be very thoughtful in how we compose information to suggest a professional appearance, these very same features may reduce the inclination to analyze information systematically (Alter, Oppenheimer, Epley, & Eyre, 2007; Oppenheimer, 2008). The problem occurs because when information is pre-sented to us in ways that invoke cognitive ease, we will not necessarily recognize that we are attributing credibility to information because we were put at ease by its surface cues and our heuristic appraisal processes. In discussing the relation-ship between cognitive ease and illusions of truth, Kahneman (2011) explains,

> How do you know that a statement is true? If it is strongly linked by logic or association to other beliefs or preferences you hold, or comes from a

source you trust and like, you will feel a sense of cognitive ease. The trouble is that there may be other causes for your feeling of ease—including the quality of the font and the appealing rhythm of the prose—and you have no simple way of tracing your feelings to their source. (p. 64)

As Kahneman suggests, information recipients' affective or emotional states influence the process of evaluating information (see also Oppenheimer, 2008). In a comprehensive annual review of research on judgment and decision making, Weber and Johnson (2009) describe evidence that people's emotional states at the moment they encounter information becomes an aspect of the information itself within their memory. Affective states can become entangled with information, regardless of whether those states are invoked by the information (e.g., the characterization of program performance in the report provokes staff anger, report readers find the comics used to illustrate key points delightful) or are entirely incidental (e.g., a manager was upset by the fender-bender he had on the way into the office that morning, a staff member received a bouquet of roses just before sitting down to peruse the latest evaluation report). People who are in a positive mood state avoid difficult analytic work in order to preserve their mood. In such an instance, heuristics will be invoked in place of critical analysis. In addition to affecting the extent to which people will critically analyze information and what conclusions they may draw about that information, people can misattribute emotions to information (Weber & Johnson, 2009). Bold print, sharp font, and appealing aesthetics can evoke a positive mood state and a sense of cognitive ease, which may reduce desire to engage in critical analysis (Alter et al., 2007) and create the illusion that information is credible because it feels true.

TEAM A AND TEAM F REVISITED

As noted by Schwandt (2008), credibility judgments are embedded within the specific social context of an individual's attempt to seek, integrate, and use information. Hilligoss and Rieh (2008) also observed that the complex nature of forming credibility judgments leads people to perceive credibility as a relative attribute rather than as an absolute characteristic of information. Team A and Team F illustrate that judging the credibility of information is a relative and multidimensional act. Both teams used peripheral and informational characteristics to arrive at different conclusions about the same evidence.

Team A

Team A was primarily composed of nonexperts in evaluation, surveillance, and research. Team A also had a pressing need for information and the desire to move quickly to deal with an urgent problem. They were poised and eager to take action. These are information recipient characteristics that, in combination, could predispose Team A's members to judge the credibility of information by relying more heavily on its peripheral features than on the validity of the methods used to produce it. These characteristics often also reduce the likelihood of careful analysis of information.

The characteristics that made the information helpful and actionable to Team A are all associated with perceived credibility. Team A said that the data made a *novel* contribution to their immediate and pressing informational needs. No prior first-person accounts related to HIV-risk behavior and accompanying field-based HIV tests had been obtained from this population. The information derived from the data was perceived by Team A as *current, relevant,* and *useful.* These data were viewed as *accurate* enough because they corresponded with what was already known through sentinel surveillance—people in this group are disproportionately HIV-impacted, reflecting the tendency to believe what is consistent with what one already knows to be true. The data also corresponded closely with studies done elsewhere on the same population, increasing Team A's confidence in the findings. The data enriched the emerging picture of risk in the population by contributing strength to the evidence of a coherent storyline.

Particular source characteristics mattered to Team A. The sample was of reasonable size and geographically diverse, which the members of Team A saw as adding weight to the evidence and contributing source credibility. Additionally, indigenous people, including members of the population, had contributed to the production of the data. Indigenous participation enhanced source credibility by giving cognitive authority to the information's producers. Team A's members believed that indigenous people were more authoritative and less biased sources of information on indigenous experiences than cultural outsiders. Team A also included many indigenous people as members, so Team A shared a worldview with the people who were studied and also with many of those involved in producing the evidence (source credibility). Taken together, these characteristics of the decision-making context and the information itself facilitated Team A's conclusion that these data were credible enough to act upon.

Team F

Team F was primarily composed of experts in epidemiology and kindred specialties in public health. These characteristics provided Team F with domain expertise in particular quantitative methods for collecting information and a unique professional rubric for arriving at credibility judgments. Team F preferred approaches to data collection grounded in conventional epidemiologic traditions (validity). Team F was also composed almost exclusively of nonindigenous people. Many of Team F's members believed that professionally trained and seasoned data collectors produced the best quality information (source credibility). Past experience had hardened their skepticism that local people who were not specialists could produce quality information on a reliable basis. Team F also thought that the etic perspective brought by outsiders often enhanced the impartiality of evidence. Team F believed that Team A's data collectors lacked source credibility in multiple respects (limited expertise, low reputed and experienced credibility) and this may have primed Team F to focus on features of the evidence that could undermine its truth value.

Team F was deeply concerned about the information's *accuracy* and, in particular, the *weight of the evidence.* Though they acknowledged the general consistency of the emerging storyline, from their point of view, the data could not be considered credible or actionable because the sampling design provided an unsound basis for determining the period prevalence of HIV (lack of validity). They also seemed doubtful the prevalence could be as high as these data suggested (expectancy violation), which heightened their validity concerns. Because there was no basis for knowing whether the data provided an over- or underestimate of prevalence, there was also no way to confirm or refute the data's accuracy. It was better, in their view, to assume the data provided an inaccurate picture than an accurate one, given no basis for confirmation. Team F concluded that the data on the population members' needs and experiences would also probably be distorted because the representativeness of the sample was unknown. Other features of the information—such as its novelty, relevance, currency, and utility—were of secondary importance to Team F. Moreover, although Team A used instruments and procedures that Team F had sanctioned, these features of the validity of the information were not weighted heavily enough by the members of Team F for them to identify ways in which the data might provide credible evidence on anything that had been assessed.

Human Judgment and Credible Evidence in Evaluation

It seems obvious that the process by which evaluators arrive at credibility judgments will differ within the larger population of evaluators and in comparison to those who are recipients of evaluative information as a function of each individual's domain and information skills expertise. It also seems apparent that though evaluators are likely to be highly motivated to process information systematically as part of their professional obligations to generate and evaluate evidence, we are also prone to use heuristics (rules of thumb) as well because we have to rely on them, given the limits on human information processing. Reliance on heuristics may increase our vulnerability to errors and bias in judging the credibility of evidence. Moreover, despite our domain expertise and motivation to engage in critical analysis of evidence, we may be unconsciously affected by surface and source characteristics to look for and find features of information that confirm what we have been primed to expect. If the notion of credibility is activated by our observing who conducted an evaluation, by the professional look of the report's cover, or by snippets about method gleaned from the executive summary, we may overlook features of information that might give us pause or condition our positive evaluation. If disbelief is activated by these same features, we will be primed to find the flaws and overlook the virtues, and we risk making incredulity errors. Our biases and expectations regarding the programs and policies we evaluate and the methods we favor have the potential to impact us in a similar manner unless we make diligent effort to interrogate and counteract them.

Evaluation users, especially those who lack depth of expertise in evaluation or the time and motivation to assess evaluation information systematically, may be overly dependent on judging surface and source-based indicators of trustworthiness. Users may make intuitive judgments of information plausibility in lieu of careful evaluation of evidence. Users without evaluation expertise may be the most vulnerable to believing information they ought not to trust (Rieh & Danielson, 2007). On the other hand, evaluation users may be quick to dismiss information they should not (incredulity errors) when their motivation and involvement on an issue are low or peripheral features put them off.

Implications

I have purposefully focused on how people make decisions about the credibility of information to help evaluators understand that *all* of us—evaluators and our clients—are prone to make judgments about the quality of evidence that may be imperfect or that differ from the judgments made by others around us. The differences in our credibility judgments are not solely reflections of professional disagreements about issues of method, just as the differences in evaluation users' credibility judgments are not driven solely by methods. Our debates center on issues of method because these are central to the process by which we produce evidence, but methods are only a part of how we and others judge whether findings have credence. As Weiss noted long ago, methods do matter, but how much they matter in leveraging people's attention and influencing their credibility judgments depends on the context (Weiss & Bucuvalas, 1980). We will all systematically assess evidence on some occasions and rely on heuristic appraisals in others; much of the time, evaluators will do both simultaneously. We will all use different algorithms to arrive at decisions about the credibility of information. We will all be wrong about our judgments on some occasions and correct on others and to varying degrees. We will all be influenced by features of information that may not have direct relevance to the problem at hand at one time or another.

PRACTICE DIRECTIONS

To the cynical evaluator, I may have just argued that their copy editor and graphic designer deserve merit raises. However, given the larger mission of the profession to raise the capacity of others to think in an evaluative manner (e.g., critically!) about information and to feed democratic deliberation, cognitive and information sciences suggest we ought to be thinking very seriously about how to encourage systematic critical attention to evaluative information itself. Meta-evaluation offers one promising strategy. To the extent that summative meta-evaluations provide a credibility rating and can delineate the features of information that effect its truthfulness, meta-evaluation can indicate to evaluation audiences that on the whole, particular evaluations offer well-warranted findings and, more importantly, why. Meta-evaluations can illustrate how, given real-world circumstances, a wide variety of approaches and methods can be employed to produce sound evidence. They can also help individual evaluators become more attuned to and transparent regarding their own bases for making credibility determinations.

Innovative approaches to evaluation capacity building offer another promising method for promoting systematic assessment of evidence. Rather than instruct users in how to design a focus group or develop a logic model, capacity building could be designed to help evaluation users to understand the important balance between strength and weight of evidence and to identify how particular methodological elements may contribute to each, generally speaking. Evaluation capacity building could also be developed to help consumers to consider multiple features of information content, such as fairness, impartiality, validity, and accuracy. Developing the cognitive skills associated with evaluative thinking may go farther than developing a limited set of methodological skills among evaluation-capacity–building consumers because users are unlikely to become true experts in designing and conducting evaluations.* Moreover, meta-evaluation and conventional capacity-building activities are probably not enough, particularly if these efforts are not well informed by an understanding of how people evaluate information and form a judgment that evidence ought to be believed.

Although reliance on heuristics is not always a bad thing and may often lead people to the correct answer with little expenditure of cognitive effort, psychologists have identified effective procedures to reduce the impact of common biases and to counteract reliance on heuristics when these might lead to errors in judgment in situations where there is a correct answer (see, for

---

* Schwandt (2013a) suggests that training for evaluators should include greater emphasis on the development of the critical-thinking skills that are necessary for evaluative thinking.

example, Sanna et al., 2011). Some of these procedures, once adapted, could prove useful during evaluations, especially at the dissemination phase. For example, asking people to deliberately think the opposite can work against gullibility errors that are caused by a common priming effect called *anchoring* (Tversky & Kahneman, 1974). Anchoring occurs when irrelevant information that is present in the problem-solving context constrains our thinking, typically without our awareness. Evaluators might also benefit by developing novel approaches to address unresolved credibility claims. For instance, Johnson and Stefurak (2013) suggest combining elements from conflict-management, team-building, and procedural justice strategies to encourage dialogue about differing perceptions of the credibility of evidence.

RESEARCH DIRECTIONS

Although evaluators have a growing body of informative studies on evaluation influence, we have little in the way of empirical studies on credibility judgments about evidence within the domain of evaluation. And, in contrast to writing on influence, evaluation users' perspectives are not well represented in current writing on credibility of evidence. To the extent that theoretical work on persuasion suggests strongly that judgments regarding the credibility of information precondition trust of that information and its active use (Fleming, 2011; Kelton et al., 2008; Mark & Henry, 2004), evaluators would be well served by generating evidence about how audiences for evaluation make credibility decisions. Because many evaluation users are not evaluation experts, differences in expert and nonexpert judgments are especially germane. What kinds of information skills do evaluation users employ? Do users take into account how evaluative information was produced and, if so, what facets of the information influence their judgments? What role does credibility of evidence play in users' assessments that an evaluation's findings can be acted upon? How are users' credibility judgments being impacted by the evolution in innovative formats for presenting evaluation information? Or by our professional debates on issues such as the superiority of one method or approach as compared with another? How can we best use recent developments in guidance on reporting and dissemination to promote systematic information assessment?

A second area for research investigation concerns the impact of evaluation capacity building and similar interventions on judgments regarding the credibility of evaluative evidence and on the critical thinking and information skills necessary to reach those judgments. In particular, research might address how best to reduce gullibility errors in assessing evaluative evidence without increasing incredulity errors. Capacity building and other innovative interventions can promote healthy critical analysis of evidence. Research might help determine the best balance of strategies for reducing the tendency to believe evaluative information when its credibility ought to be questioned without at the same time developing an overly dismissive stance toward evidence that is plausible. Research might also help detect what kind of interventions are most likely to prevent evaluation consumers from developing false expectations about the validity of applying particular approaches in one evaluation context versus another.

A third area would focus on how evaluation expertise and human judgment processes combine to effect evaluators' assessments of the credibility of evidence in their own work and the work of others. Although nearly every chapter on the history of evaluation notes that evaluation is an ancient worldwide practice and part of everyday sensemaking about the world, the logic, knowledge, and skills associated with formal evaluation are learned. To become an expert evaluator requires advanced training in the logic associated with specifying criteria of merit and arriving at judgments regarding value and worth; knowledge of a wide range of methods and the quality standards that underlie evaluation's methodological pluralism; and skills that span critical thinking, interpersonal interaction, communication, and reflexivity. Complex concepts such as triangulation, statistical conclusion validity, authenticity, and coherence may become part of how evaluators think as a consequence of years of training and applied experience. These ultimately may become part of the schema we use to appraise the quality of evidence. We may integrate additional criteria, such as those suggested by leading evaluation standards, to judge the extent to which evaluations are meritorious. Possessing evaluation expertise and defined professional standards provides evaluators with a unique framework for arriving at judgments about the credibility of evidence and the worth of evaluations that distinguishes us from those applied scientists who do not use evaluative logic or favor methodological pluralism and from those who are not expert evaluators. An important question for research on evaluation concerns when and how we use the breadth and depth of our evaluation knowledge and skills in our own practice and how our expertise interacts with biases in human judgment and decision making (see also Schwandt, 2013b).

Conclusion

The research on judgment and decision making makes it plain that understanding the pros and cons of particular evaluation models and methods alone is insufficient to grasp why, in some instances, people will dismiss solid evaluative evidence and, in other instances, will accept weak evidence. If we truly aspire to encourage intelligent belief in evaluation (Schwandt, 2008), we would be wise to consider the simplifying rules of thumb (heuristics) that people—ourselves and those on whose behalf we conduct our work—may use when they make judgments about the credibility of evaluation evidence. We would also do well to learn about the circumstances under which systematic and heuristic assessments of evidence occur. Building into all evaluation capacity endeavors and all evaluations mechanisms to promote reasoned review of evidence to guard against heuristic appraisals when these are not useful may be especially productive. Active and disciplined processes of double-checking, reassessing, following checklists, and searching for the opposite of what we are inclined to believe at first pass may be necessary to guard against false judgments about information credibility. If a skilled evaluator had led Team A and Team F through a checklist of evidence credibility indicators, for example, their respective weighting of particular features of evidence may have been more obvious, providing them with the basis for a collegial discussion.

References

Alter, A. L., Oppenheimer, D. M., Epley, N., & Eyre, R. N. (2007). Overcoming intuition: Metacognitive difficulty activates analytic reasoning. *Journal of Experimental Psychology: General, 136,* 569–576.

American Evaluation Association (AEA). (2004). *Guiding principles for evaluators.* Retrieved April 16, 2014, from http://www.eval.org/p/cm/ld/fid=51

Birnbaum, M. H., & Meller, B. A. (1983). Bayesian inference: Combining base rates with opinions of sources who vary in their credibility. *Journal of Personality and Social Psychology, 45,* 792–804.

Birnbaum, M. H., & Stegner, S. E. (1979). Source credibility in social judgment: Bias, expertise and the judge's point of view. *Journal of Personality and Social Psychology, 37,* 48–74.

Boehm, L. E. (1994). The validity effect: A search for mediating variables. *Personality and Social Psychology Bulletin, 20,* 285–293.

Brandgruwel, S., Wopereis, I., & Vermetten, Y. (2005). Information problem solving by experts and novices: Analysis of a complex cognitive skill. *Computers in Human Behavior, 21,* 487–508.

Chaiken, S. (1980). Heuristic versus systematic information processing and the use of source versus message cues in persuasion. *Journal of Personality and Social Psychology, 39,* 752–766.

Chelimsky, E. (1998). The role of experience in formulating theories of evaluation practice. *American Journal of Evaluation, 19,* 35–55.

Fisher, P., Jonas, E., Frey, D., & Schulz-Hardt, S. (2005). Selective exposure to information: The impact of information limits. *European Journal of Social Psychology, 35,* 469–492. DOI: 10.1002/ejsp.264

Fleming, M. A. (2011). Attitudes, persuasion, and social influence: Applying social psychology to increase evaluation use. In M. M. Mark, S. I. Donaldson, & B. Campbell (Eds.), *Social psychology and evaluation* (pp. 212–241). New York, NY: Guilford Press.

Griffin, D., & Tversky, A. (1992). The weighing of evidence and the determinants of confidence. *Cognitive Psychology, 24,* 411–435.

Henry, G. T., & Mark, M. M. (2003). Beyond use: Understanding evaluation's influence on attitudes and actions. *American Journal of Evaluation, 24,* 293–314. DOI: 10.1177/109821400302400302

Hilligoss, B., & Rieh, S. Y. (2008). Developing a unifying framework of credibility assessment: Construct, heuristics, and interaction in context. *Information Processing and Management, 44,* 1467–1484. DOI: 10.1016/j.ipm.2007.10.001

House, E. R., & Howe, K. R. (1999). *Values in evaluation and social research.* Thousand Oaks, CA: SAGE.

Johnson, R. B., & Stefurak, T. (2013). Considering the evidence-and-credibility discussion in evaluation through the lens of dialectical pluralism. In D. M. Mertens & S. Hesse-Biber (Eds.), Mixed methods and credibility of evidence in evaluation. *New Directions for Evaluation, 138,* 37–48.

Joint Committee on Standards for Educational Evaluation. (2011). *The program evaluation standards: A guide for evaluators and evaluation users* (3rd edition). Newbury Park, CA: SAGE.

Julien, H., & Barker, S. (2009). How high-school students find and evaluate scientific information: A basis for information skills literacy development. *Library and Information Science Research, 31,* 12–17.

Kahneman, D. (2011). *Thinking, fast and slow.* New York, NY: Farrar, Straus, and Girroux.

Kelton, K., Fleischmann, K. R., & Wallace, W. A. (2008). Trust in digital information. *Journal of the American Society for Information Science and Technology, 59,* 363–374. DOI: 10.1002/asi.20722

Koriat, A. (2008). Subjective confidence in one's answers: The consensuality principle. *Journal of Experimental Psychology: Learning, Memory, and Cognition, 34,* 945–959.

Koriat, A. (2011). The self-consistency model of subjective confidence. *Psychological Review, 140,* 117–139. DOI: 10.1037/a0025648

Liu, Z. (2004). Perceptions of credibility of scholarly information on the web. *Information Processing and Management, 40,* 1027–1038. DOI: 10.1016/S0306-4573(03)00064-5

Lucassen, T., & Schraagen, J. M. (2011). Factual accuracy and trust in information. *Journal of the American Society for Information Science and Technology, 62,* 1232–1242. DOI: 10.1002/asi.21545

Mark, M. M., & Henry, G. T. (2004). The mechanisms and outcomes of evaluation influence. *Evaluation, 10,* 35–57.

McKnight, D. H., Choudhury, V., & Kacmar, C. (2002). The impact of initial consumer trust on intentions to transact with a website: A trust building model. *Journal of Strategic Information Systems, 11,* 297–323.

Metzger, M. J., Flanagin, A. J., & Medders. R. B. (2010). Social and heuristic approaches to credibility evaluation online. *Journal of Communication, 60,* 113–439. DOI: 10.1111/j.1460-2466.2010.01488.x

Organisation for Economic Co-Operation and Development, Development Assistance Committee Network on Evaluation. (2010). *Quality standards for development evaluation.* Retrieved March 27, 2014, from http://www.oecd.org/dac/evaluation/qualitystandards.pdf

Oppenheimer, D. M. (2006). Consequences of erudite vernacular utilized irrespective of necessity: Problems with using long words needlessly. *Applied Cognitive Psychology, 20,* 139–156.

Oppenheimer, D. M. (2008). The secret life of fluency. *Trends in Cognitive Sciences, 12,* 237–241.

Petty, R. E., & Cacioppo, J. T. (1986). Elaboration likelihood model. In L. Berkowitz (Ed.), *Advances in experimental social psychology* (vol. 19, pp. 123–205). San Diego, CA: Academic Press.

Pleskac, T. J., & Busemeyer, J. R. (2010). A theory of choice, decision time, and confidence. *Psychological Review, 117,* 864–901.

Rieh, S. Y. (2002). Judgment of information quality and cognitive authority in the web. *Journal of the American Society for Information Science and Technology, 53,* 145–161.

Rieh, S. Y., & Danielson, D. R. (2007). Credibility: A multidisciplinary framework. In B. Cronin (Ed.), *Annual Review of Information Science and Technology* (vol. 41, pp. 307–364). Medford, NJ: Information Today.

Rieh, S. Y., & Hilligoss, B. (2008). College students' credibility judgments in the information-seeking process. In M. J. Metzger & A. J. Flanagin (Eds.), *Digital media, youth, and credibility* (pp. 49–72). Cambridge, MA: The MIT Press. DOI: 10.1162/dmal.9780262562324.049

Sanna, L. J., Panter, A. T., Cohen, T. R., & Kennedy, L. A. (2011). Planning the future and assessing the past: Temporal biases and debiasing in program evaluation. In M. M. Mark, S. I. Donaldson, & B. Campbell (Eds.), *Social psychology and evaluation* (pp. 166–186). New York, NY: Guilford Press.

Savolainen, R. (2011). Judging the quality and credibility of information in Internet discussion forums. *Journal of the American Society for Information Science and Technology, 62,* 1243–1256. DOI: 10.1002/asi.21546

Schwandt, T. A. (2008). Educating for intelligent belief in evaluation. *American Journal of Evaluation, 29,* 139–150. DOI: 10.1177/1098214008316889

Schwandt, T. A. (2013a, October). *Evaluative thinking is critical thinking.* Paper presented at the meeting of the American Evaluation Association, Washington, DC.

Schwandt, T. A. (2013b, October). *Research relevant to improving evaluation use: Studying decision making.* Paper presented at the meeting of the American Evaluation Association in Washington, DC.

Scriven, M. (1980). *The logic of evaluation.* Inverness, CA: Edgepress.

Shanteau, J. (1992). The psychology of experts: An alternative view. In G. Wright & F. Bolger (Eds.), *Expertise and decision support* (pp. 11–23). New York, NY: Plenum Press.

Slater, M. D., & Rouner, D. (1996). How message evaluation and source attributes may influence credibility assessments and belief change. *Journalism and Mass Communication Quarterly, 73,* 974–991.

Tseng, S., & Fogg, B. J. (1999). Credibility and computing technology. *Communication of the ACM, 42,* 39–44.

Tversky, A., & Kahneman, D. (1971). Belief in the law of small numbers. *Psychological Bulletin, 76,* 105–110.

Tversky, A., & Kahneman, D. (1974). Judgment under uncertainty: Heuristics and biases. *Science, 185,* 1124–1131.

Walraven, A., Brandgruwel, S., & Boshuizen, H. (2009). How students evaluate information and sources when searching the world wide web for information. *Computers & Education, 52,* 234–246.

Wathen, C. N., & Burkell, J. (2002). Believe it or not: Factors influencing credibility on the web. *Journal of the American Society for Information Science and Technology, 53,* 134–144. DOI: 10.1002/asi.10016

Weber, E. U., & Johnson, E. J. (2009). Mindful judgment and decision making. *Annual Review of Psychology, 60,* 53–85. DOI: 10.1146/annurev.psych.60.110707.163633

Weiss, C. H. (1988). Evaluation for decisions: Is anybody there? Does anybody care? *Evaluation Practice,* 5–19.

Weiss, C. H. (1998). *Evaluation research: Methods for studying programs and policies* (2nd ed.). Upper Saddle River, NJ: Prentice Hall.

Weiss, C. H., & Bucuvalas, M. J. (1980). *Social science research and decision making.* New York, NY: Columbia University Press.

Wilson, P. (1983). *Second-hand knowledge: An inquiry into cognitive authority.* Westport, CT: Greenwood Press.

Part II

Credible and Actionable Evidence: The Role of Randomized Experiments

- Chapter 4—When Getting It Right Matters: The Struggle for Rigorous Evidence of Impact and to Increase Its Influence Continues

- Chapter 5—Randomized Controlled Trials: A Gold Standard or Gold Plated?

- Chapter 6—Demythologizing Causation and Evidence

The strengths and limitations of scientific experimentation in the form of randomized controlled trials (RCTs) and quasi-experimental designs for producing credible and actionable evidence are explored in Part II. In Chapter 4, Gary Henry sketches out an underlying justification for the U.S. Department of Education's priority for randomized experiments and high-quality quasi-experiments over nonexperimental designs when getting it right matters. His argument has deep roots in democratic theory and stresses the importance of scientifically based evaluations for influencing the adoption of government policies and programs. He argues that high-quality experimental evaluations are the only way to eliminate selection bias when assessing policy and program impact and that malfeasance may occur when random assignment evaluations are not conducted. Henry urges his readers to consider his arguments in favor of the proposed priority in an open-minded, reflective, and deliberative way to do the greatest good in society. He claims that the RCTs conducted since the first edition of this book in response to the U.S. Department of Education's priority for RCTs have produced volumes of credible evidence. Henry concluded this evidence demonstrates the fact that random assignment studies are the most credible way to estimate causal effects and that RCTs are, in fact, more feasible than could have been imagined.

In Chapter 5, Leonard Bickman and Stephanie Reich explore in great detail why RCTs are commonly considered the gold standard for producing credible evidence in applied research and evaluation. They clearly articulate why RCTs are superior to other evaluation designs for determining causation and impact and alert us to the high cost of making a wrong decision about causality. They specify numerous threats to validity that must be considered in applied research and evaluation and provide a thorough analysis of both the strengths and limitations of RCTs. In the end, they conclude, "For determining causality, in many but not all circumstances, the randomized design is the worst form of design except all the others that have been tried" (p. 104-105).

Michael Scriven (Chapter 6) offers strong critiques of the RCT as the gold standard for generating credible and actionable evidence in evaluation practice. He first takes a stand against the "current mythology . . . that scientific claims of causation or good evidence . . . require evidence from . . . RCTs" (p. 115). He asserts,

> [T]o insist that we use an experimental approach is simply bigotry—not pragmatic and not logical. In short, it is a dogmatic approach that is . . . an affront to scientific method. . . . Moreover, to wave banners proclaiming that anything less will mean unreliable results or unscientific practice is simply absurd. (p. 117)

Next, he provides a detailed analysis of alternative ways to determine causation in applied research and evaluation and discusses several alternative methods for determining policy and program impact, including the general elimination methodology or algorithm (GEM). He ends with a proposal for marriage of warring parties—complete with a prenuptial agreement—that he believes would provide a win-win solution to the "causal wars," with major positive side effects for those in need around the world.

The final chapter of the book by Melvin Mark (Chapter 13) precedes Appendix I, which contains a critique of Scriven's perspectives and comments about using randomized experiments to generate credible and actionable evidence. We believe Scriven's critiques and ideas about RCTs are important enough to warrant expanded consideration.

4

When Getting It Right Matters

The Struggle for Rigorous Evidence of Impact and to Increase Its Influence Continues

Gary T. Henry

In 2003, on a slightly warmer-than-usual November 3rd in Washington, D.C., Rod Paige, the Secretary of Education, requested comments on a departmental policy that would give randomized controlled trials (RCTs) and high-quality quasi-experiments extra points in the scoring of reviews for proposals to evaluate the effectiveness of educational programs (U.S. Department of Education, 2003). This turned out to be the spark for a confrontation—the credibility war—that immediately boiled over and has subsequently simmered for the past decade.

The credibility war erupted in 2004, when a group of American Evaluation Association (AEA) members prepared an official response for the organization that ended with the following statement: "We believe that the constraints in the proposed priority would deny use of other needed, proven, and scientifically credible evaluation methods, resulting in fruitless expenditures on some large contracts while leaving other public programs unevaluated entirely" (AEA, 2004). The official response was countered by another group of eight evaluators (including former AEA presidents, AEA board members, and AEA journal editors) who stated, "We believe that the proposed priority will dramatically increase the amount of valid information for guiding the improvement of education throughout the nation" (Bickman et al., 2003).[1] The credibility war had been joined, and nearly ten years later, the tension has receded but not entirely dissipated.

The Institute of Education Sciences (IES), the newly established research arm of the U.S. Department of Education, was formed with a mandate to increase the amount of credible, scientific evidence that was available to serve as a basis for educational decision making. IES was authorized in the No Child Left Behind Act of 2001 (NCLB; Elementary and Secondary Education Act), which mentioned "scientifically based research" 111 times (Neuman et al., 2002). In the days immediately following the adoption of the Act, the conversations about the future of educational research took two very important turns that are relevant to discussions about credible evidence.

First, those engaged in the development of the IES research agenda declared that evaluation—and more specifically, impact evaluation—was the type of research that should be conducted through IES. The rationale for this focus, later implemented by requirements to assess "malleable factors" and evaluate interventions with respect to their effects on student outcomes, was that impact evaluation would be the type of research most useful in improving students' educational outcomes. This focus was consistent with the standards-based accountability system put into place by NCLB. That is, the impact evaluations would provide educational administrators with the evidence that they would need to select the interventions or programs that would enable them to reach the educational performance objectives that were established in federal law and set on a state-by-state basis.

Second, they quickly established a clear hierarchy of research designs or approaches to answering causal questions, which were the type of questions explicitly called for by the focus on impact evaluation. RCT and field experiments (FEs) topped the hierarchy, followed by high-quality quasi-experiments (such as regression discontinuity [RD] and interrupted times series [ITS] designs) and everything else formed the base of the hierarchy. Findings from correlational studies as well as qualitative research were largely deemed too ambiguous to guide education decision making. These studies at the base of the hierarchy, when funded, were to focus on empirical hypothesis generation that should then lead to testing these hypotheses using the designs at the top of the hierarchy that are referred to as high-quality, scientifically sound, or rigorous—mainly RCT, FE, and RD designs.

To an extent that most would have considered impossible for a federal agency in 2002, IES has maintained an unwavering commitment to funding evaluations of the malleable factors and interventions in education that nearly exclusively use the high-quality designs at the top of the hierarchy. In 2001, Cook reported that of the studies planned by the Department of Education in 2000, the year before NCLB was passed, only one of 84 studies was an RCT. In 2011, Murnane and Willett reported that "[o]ne indication of the energy with which IES has pursued [the scientifically-based research] agenda is that, in its first six years of operation, it funded over 100 randomized field trials of the effectiveness of educational interventions" (p. 9). The number and quality of the RCTs and FEs continue to climb. As of September 2013, the What Works Clearinghouse has reviewed the literature for 15 types of educational interventions—for example, teacher incentives and dropout prevention—and has 554 reports on interventions published on the website, all of which are rated by the same type of hierarchy for evidence: The rating "meets What Works Clearinghouse evidence standards without reservation" is bestowed only on "well-implemented randomized controlled trials and regression discontinuity designs that do not have problems with attrition" (downloaded from http://ies.ed.gov/ncee/wwc/glossary.aspx#letterM on September 13, 2013).

In the past decade, IES (along with other organizations such as the Spencer Foundation and the W. T. Grant Foundation) have placed a premium on RCTs, FEs, and other high-quality designs for evaluating educational interventions and provided funding for these types of evaluations. The field has responded—and perhaps been transformed—by producing these types of evaluations and by training many doctoral level researchers, who will in turn become the next generation of educational researchers, to design and implement high-quality evaluation designs. But the presence of research findings from evaluations that implemented these designs have not influenced education policy makers and administrators to the extent that was expected. This is underscored most clearly in the request for applications to operate a center on knowledge utilization in 2013 by IES:

> Education researchers have made enormous strides in studying the impacts of education policies and interventions designed to improve outcomes for students. Despite this accumulation of knowledge, there is pervasive concern that this work has not resulted in widespread adoption of practices shown to have positive effects or improvements in educational outcomes for large numbers of students. (U.S. Department of Education, 2013, p. 11)

In this chapter, I begin by sketching out how the findings produced by high-quality designs implemented in education and a wide variety of other policy areas (including criminology, substance abuse prevention, economic development, mental health, and public health) align with a normative theory of democracy. The case presented here has deep roots in normative democratic theory and acknowledges the vast developments in social sciences in the last quarter-century. I will make four main points and support them in this chapter:

1. Assessing the effectiveness of public policies and programs is a significant presenting problem for modern democracies, and addressing this problem requires accurate and highly credible evidence about the consequences of public policies and programs.

2. The underlying values of the methods-based approach to evaluation are deeply rooted in beliefs about the value that evaluation can bring to society.

3. Incredible developments in social science research methods since most of the original (and still echoed) criticisms of experimental methods were first levied and are now routinely implemented in evaluations provide substantial support for the widespread use of rigorous and well-conducted RCT, FE, RD, and ITS studies and even observational studies conducted under conditions that support causal inference.

4. Transparency of evaluation methods and findings is essential to producing influential information in democracies and guidelines have been developed that can help to make evaluation practices and findings transparent.

In the next four sections, each of these points will be described more fully to create a deeper understanding of the specific approaches for conducting evaluations that are most likely to influence policy and program decisions in a way that improves social conditions in modern democracies. The arguments also provide a coherent justification for the Secretary's priority (U.S. Department of Education, 2003) for evaluation using random assignment to be conducted to aid decision making concerning policies and programs.

The Presenting Problem in Modern Democracies

Modern democracies are representative governments that function in this age of unprecedented flow of information. Perhaps the most surprising turn of the late 20th century was the apparent acceptance by many throughout the world that representative democracy was the most desired form of government and, by virtue of it being desired by the governed, superior to other forms of government, although we need look no further than the Arab Spring to understand the difficulties of forming and sustaining representative democracies.

One quest of philosophers and political scientists is to understand why representative democracies are assumed to be superior to all others or, at least, preferred at this historical moment to all others (Henry, 2001). Hurley (1989) has reasoned that modern representative democracies allow for a cognitive function to be performed that sets them apart from the other forms of governance. Hurley's shorthand for describing this function is that democracies "debunk bad ideas." Certainly, there is no shortage of bad ideas in democracies or any other form of government. Moreover, democracies have no way to prevent these ideas from becoming bad, ineffective, or even harmful policies. Although we hope that the deliberative and relatively open processes in modern democracies filter out the worst of the bad ideas, a quick scan of recent legislative history in modern democracies would indicate that there are no guarantees when it comes to preventing the adoption of ineffective or even harmful policies.

The cognitive justification for democracy lies not in prevention of bad policies but in the fact that the bad ideas promulgated in the form of policies and programs can be detected. Moreover, evidence persuading the public and policy makers that the ideas were in fact bad can be collected; the aspects of the policies that are flawed and ineffective can be brought to light; the need for reform can be accepted by citizens and their elected representatives; and the policies can be reformed, dismantled, or replaced. One could argue that a system guaranteeing welfare payments for people as long as they remained poor was a flawed idea. This idea was debunked over a number of years through a number of studies including randomized FEs, and the policies were reformed in the United States. The fact that the consequences of this aspect of the welfare system were exposed and that the idea was debunked does not mean that it was replaced by a perfect policy but rather that any bad ideas embodied in the last round of welfare reforms will have their chance to be debunked as the process continues to unfold.

Clearly to debunk bad ideas, democracies need accurate and credible evidence about the consequences of public policies. Negative consequences can be used to identify policies that embody bad ideas, while evidence of positive consequences may forestall misguided attacks on policies that are effective in the respects that have been assessed. Negative consequences of policies occur in two ways: (1) failure to meet the original goals or expectations of the policy or (2) negative side effects that have arisen. Positive consequences also occur in two ways: (1) when the expected benefits of the policy have been realized or (2) when negative consequences that were predicted by opponents to its adoption failed to occur. Another possibility, according to Rossi's Iron Law, is that "the expected value for any measured effect of any social program is zero" (Rossi, 1978, quoted in Rossi, Lipsey, & Freeman, 2004, p. 5).

In order for the cognitive function of democracy to be fulfilled, we need accurate evidence that is both truthful and equally capable of finding positive, negative, or null consequences of public policies. In other words, modern democracies need credible assessments of the causal impacts of public policies and the programs developed to carry out the policies to inform voters and policy makers.

Furthermore, the evidence needs to be broadly considered as true and accurate. These are the criteria suggested by credibility. Credibility mandates that the methods be sufficiently sound and sufficiently fair to convincingly indicate that the program consequences are positive, negative, or null. Again, using the welfare reform example, randomized experiments persuaded stakeholders that the welfare system that existed prior to 1996 was less likely to lead to work and independence from welfare than policies based on a work-first strategy and that implementation of work-first reforms was feasible (Greenberg, Mandell, & Onstott, 2000). The accurate assessment of consequences of policies and programs establishes a priority for methodologically sound cause-and-effect studies of public policies and programs.

Certainly, no reasonable person would argue that the only important research questions for evaluation are causal questions, but I maintain that to fulfill their promise, modern democracies must provide significant resources for evaluations of the effectiveness of public policies. Public policies and programs are intentional acts undertaken with the coercive force of government behind them. Authoritative bodies, such as legislatures and administrators, make public policy and program choices in most cases. The choices of these bodies are binding on the governed and therefore, to inform citizens' beliefs about public programs' positive, negative, or null results and potentially to influence voting decisions, democracies require that both the intended and unintended consequences of programs and policies be evaluated and the findings be made widely known in order to encourage reform of negative or ineffective policies and improve the chances that interventions that produce positive effects will be adopted.

The stated purpose of public policies and programs is to produce a different pattern of social outcomes than currently exist. Since Pressman and Wildavsky (1973) pointed out the parallel between cause-and-effect relationships in social science and the cause-and-effect theories embedded in social policies, we have understood that causal methods are fundamental to evaluation and that certain approaches to estimating the effects of policies and programs are better than others. The causal methods required to assess the impacts of intentional interventions must be able to detect the differences in the social outcomes that result from intentional actions that represent a change to the social environment. The policy, program, or intervention in this case represents an intention to change or reform the current state of affairs for the better. The findings must be as conclusive as possible and rule out alternative explanations for the differences detected in the pattern of social outcomes when differences are detected. The most salient of the alternative explanations in this context is that individual characteristics and administrative decisions that affect who receive access to public programs can also affect the outcomes of the individuals after receiving services. The most conclusive and widely regarded as compelling means for producing findings that eliminate these alternative explanations are RCTs and FEs. While other types of designs can be shown under certain conditions to produce effect estimates that are ignorably different that those from random assignment studies, such as regression discontinuity and matching comparison group designs (Cook, Shadish, & Wong, 2008; Shadish, Clark, & Steiner, 2008), it is difficult to ensure the required conditions are met and all require assumptions that are not needed to consider RCT and FE findings as unbiased by selection of a policy or into a social program and, therefore, credible.

Fortunately, the fact that public policies and programs are undertaken with the intent to improve social conditions but are of uncertain benefit effectively rules out many of the ethical arguments against random assignment. Other socially important types of research, such as research to assess the effects of individual behaviors that have been previously shown to be likely to have negative consequences (for example, smoking) cannot ethically assign individuals at random to engage in that behavior. In cases in which the action being investigated has been strongly associated with harmful outcomes and not intended to improve health or well-being, ethical considerations may remove the option of random assignment, and other methods are required.

Thus RCTs and FEs, while limiting in certain respects, can virtually eliminate the most powerful point of contention that arises in disputes about causal estimates—that is, that those who are provided access and chose to participate in public programs were different from those who did not in ways from those that did not that lead to differences in outcomes. All other means to estimating causal effects are second best to a random assignment study in eliminating the differences in the participants and nonparticipants that may cause any observed differences. Specifically, for the study of the effectiveness of public programs, RCTs and FEs produce the most credible and compelling evidence about the consequences of public policies and programs, *and* they are available for almost all situations, since policies and programs are intended to be beneficial but the magnitude of any benefits are uncertain. This leads to the conclusion that random assignment studies are the most accurate, credible, economical, and straightforward means of establishing causal connections between public actions and social consequences that democracies can bring to bear. While this connection is not often made, the methods-oriented approaches to evaluation have values aligned with these theories of democracy deeply embedded within them.

The Value of Evaluation Findings in Representative Democracies

In the classic work on evaluation theories, Christie and Alkin (2013) analyze and describe theories that prescribe how evaluation should be conducted. They metaphorically place prescriptive, normative theories of evaluation on three branches of an evaluation tree—the methods branch, the use branch, and the values branch. The center branch grows out of the interest in social inquiry; they label it the *methods branch* and describe it thusly: "Theorists on this branch are typically concerned with obtaining the most rigorous knowledge possible given the contextual constraints" (p. 12). The evaluators on this branch are those most likely to endorse the hierarchy for evaluation designs described above and appear to be united in terms of the idea that the value of evaluation to society is directly related to the accuracy and credibility of the information produced. This value statement aligns with the need for information described in some theories of democracy.

By 1956, Dahl had laid out a theory of democracy that connected the information on the consequences of public policies to voters' choices for candidates. In his *A Preface to Democratic Theory,* he spelled out the importance of information on the benefits of public policies and the widespread availability of that information, as well as information on the positions of candidates and political parties, for voters to make informed choices in representative democracies. In essence, this theory of representative democracy, which includes a central role for information concerning the consequences of public policies, aligns with the prescriptive theorists from Christie and Alkin's methods branch of the evaluation tree. A theory of evaluation grounded in democratic theory would include the requirement that evaluations be carried out in order to provide information that is accurate and widely accepted as credible about the consequences of public policies and programs. Credibility is likely to hinge on the methods of the evaluation adhering to the standards that are generally accepted by professionals in the particular field of inquiry, if individuals choose to defer to experts (as many will do in order to take cognitive shortcuts), or it may hinge on an individual's own assessment of the accuracy of the evaluation.

But by no means have the potential ramifications for evaluation that this theory of modern democracies has articulated been fully worked out. For example, it is unclear how to set up institutional arrangements for funding evaluations that ensure that evaluation sponsors do not have undue effects on the evaluation questions, designs, methods, findings, and the distribution of the findings, thereby reducing the available and credible evidence about the consequences of public programs. In fact, recent work by evaluation scholars as diverse as Chelimsky (2006) and House (2006) have pointed to the struggle to achieve independence and thereby produce credible evaluation findings.

Another way in which the ramifications of methods-oriented evaluation have yet to be fully worked out is related to another branch of the evaluation theory tree—*use.* Theorists on this branch express "an explicit concern for the ways in which evaluation information will be used and [focus] specifically on those who will use the information" (Christie & Alkin, 2013, p. 13). While some of the evaluation theorists on the methods branch have focused attention on the question of the influence of evaluation findings on policy adoption and termination among other actions (Henry & Mark, 2003; Mark & Henry, 2004), the clear priority of evaluators working in the methods-oriented tradition is producing accurate and credible information. An underlying assumption appears to be that if the information produced by an evaluation is not accurate, acting upon it seems unlikely to produce improvements in social outcomes. Another underlying assumption is that if the findings from an evaluation are not credible, then they will not be influential or persuasive and will not stand up to the withering attacks from those ideologically opposed to the policy direction implied by the findings, especially in the current polarized political climate. However, as noted above in reference to the need for a center to study knowledge utilization, another underlying assumption—that the findings from the evaluations that have been carried out with rigorous designs will be used— has not yet been realized.

In addition, some of the methods-oriented evaluators have recognized the contingent nature of following one prescriptive theory of evaluation or another. For instance, Rossi (1994) made the case that methods-oriented approaches that use designs at the top of the aforementioned hierarchy tend to be more common and more appropriate when evaluating large-scale programs, while qualitative methods that are more likely to be used by use-oriented evaluators may be more appropriate with small-scale, local evaluations. In addition, Mark, Henry, and Julnes (2000) describe the decision to follow one type of evaluation theory as contingent upon the circumstances and purpose of the evaluation. Of course, other evaluation theories may prove more appropriate and valuable when other evaluation questions rise to the fore within democracies. For example, when assessing a local program, organization, or institution *in situ,* democratic, deliberative evaluation as described by House and Howe (1999) may be the best alternative. Their approach is supportive of democratic values such as self-determination and local control, and the criteria they develop for inclusiveness of the participants, dialogue among them, and deliberation over the possible actions and their consequences offer clear guidance for conducting an evaluation as well as providing a basis for judging the quality of the evaluation.

Still, evaluations using designs at the top of the hierarchy are often criticized based on problems experienced in carrying out these evaluations. When social scientists moved from the laboratories into the field during the initial stage of the modern period of evaluation, the logic of their designs transferred, but when the laboratory procedures were applied in the field, many problems arose and the findings were not sufficiently robust to produce conclusive results in all cases. However, the evaluators, social scientists, and statisticians who clung to the need for accurate, credible estimates of the effects of public programs have made substantial improvements in the last quarter-century that have addressed many of the problems with evaluation implementation that undermined the credibility of evaluations undertaken in the 1960s and 1970s.

Methodological Developments Aiding Impact Evaluation

Initially, evaluators who sought to take experiments and surveys using probability sampling into the field to assess the consequences of public programs ran
into significant problems implementing their elegant study designs. The biases
of studies such as the Westinghouse Evaluation of Head Start, which relied on
a flawed matched-sampling procedure, became the subject of much intense
criticism and reanalysis as well as the source of great frustration (Datta, 1982).
Moreover, the information from large-scale evaluations took time to generate
and was costly. Other evaluation approaches were developed that took less time,
cost less, and provided as much (if not more) information about the programs.
But many of these evaluations focused on program processes or stakeholders
opinions and did not provide credible estimates of program effects.

Many evaluators refused to give up on social experiments, painstakingly
identified flaws, and developed and tested remedies to reduce or eliminate the
sources of error. In part, these efforts were motivated by studies that showed
that methods other than well-implemented random assignment studies routinely produced effect estimates that were different and that would support
different policy actions (Glazerman, Levy, & Myers, 2003; LaLonde, 1986).
Therefore, it was apparent that eliminating or at least minimizing error was
most possible by implementing random assignment studies, but doing so
would require systematic efforts to improve them.

Indeed, great progress has been made in the estimation of the effects of
policies and programs by thoroughly and systematically breaking down error
into its sources. In a seminal paper, Imai, King, and Stuart (2008) extend
Rubin's Causal Model (RCM) and break down the types of error in a causal
study into two parts: (1) study sample selection and (2) treatment assignment.
When the study sample is actually the population or a probability sample, error
from study sample selection is reduced to zero or is expected to be reduced to
zero, respectively. When the assignment to treatment is random, the treatment
and untreated groups can be expected to be balanced on the factors that may
affect their outcomes at the time of randomization. By laying out this idealized
model, which Murnane and Willett (2011, p. 46) refer to as the *two-group randomized experiment,* both types of error can be described and specific sources
of those errors exposed and, perhaps, reduced or eliminated. The ideal two-
group experiment has redefined the top of the design hierarchy in a way that
maximizes the ability to produce an unbiased causal effect estimate that can be
generalized (inferred) to the defined target population.

However, the ability to conduct such studies is very limited in practice. A
common source of error in RCTs is attributable to the necessity that members
of the study population must volunteer for the evaluation study or, in the case
of FEs that employ lotteries to select program participants, eligible participants

must volunteer for the program. In these cases, the generalizability of the findings are limited to volunteers, as Murnane and Willett (2011) note with respect to a lottery-based FE study conducted in New York City on a school voucher program for children from low-income families: "Consequently, the external validity of the research findings is limited to generalizations to the [volunteer low-income families] defined population and not to the broader population of children from low-income families in the New York City public schools" (p. 47). As issues—such as the differences between the study population and the target population for a program—are identified, the search for possible remedies begins. For example, Imai and colleagues (2008) show that blocking, or placing the study sample into categories based on variables that have previously been shown to relate to the outcome of interest for the evaluation, and assigning individuals to treatment and control in equal quantities from within each block or category may reduce the error that is commonly associated with having to recruit volunteers to participate in a RCT.

Many types of error that formerly plagued researchers who attempted to accurately and credibly estimate the effects of policies and programs have been taken as a challenge, and innovative methods have been developed to reduce the bias and produce more accurate estimates of a program's effectiveness. For example, the error caused by differential attrition from a study that leads to missing data has been reduced through procedures that have increased researchers' ability to locate and obtain data from participants in the evaluation (Greenberg & Shroder, 2004) and statistical techniques that impute data to avoid losing the participant from the study and reduce the bias and increase the efficiency of the estimates of program effectiveness (Graham 2009; Schafer & Graham, 2002).

Another error that occurs in many evaluation studies results from the fact that the participants whose outcomes are being measured in an evaluation receive the treatment and other services in naturally occurring groups or clusters, such as schools or clinics. Since the individual observations within a specific school or clinic are not all independent, the typical standard errors, which assume the independence of members of the study sample and are used to test statistical significance, are too small, making it more likely to find an effect when the null effect is actually true (Hox, 2002). Methods such as hierarchical linear models (Raudenbush & Bryk, 2001), also known as *multilevel models* (Hox, 2002), and cluster-adjusted standard errors are implemented as a matter of standard practice now to correct for this problem and to accurately test the hypotheses.

As previously mentioned, the most pernicious form of error in estimating the effects of public policies and programs is sometimes labeled *selection bias* or, in the terms of Imai and colleagues (2008), *error arising from treatment assignment*. This error occurs when individuals volunteer or are assigned by the staff to participate in a program and the factors leading to participation in the program are associated with the outcome variable of interest. The most definitive way to eliminate this source of error bias is by random assignment of individuals to treatment. However, some recent studies have begun to show that under certain conditions, other ways to address treatment assignment error may produce estimates of effects that are similar to random assignment studies. For example, Shadish, Clark, and Steiner (2008) show that with numerous measures that are associated with selection into treatment and the outcome of interest used as covariates, both propensity-score–matching methods and covariate-adjusted regression produce effect estimates that are similar to those produced by a RCT. Another recent study reviewed numerous studies that made comparisons between the effect estimates from random assignment studies and studies using other designs such as RD and propensity score matching. In this study, Cook, Shadish, and Wong (2008) show that well-designed and well-implemented studies using RD or propensity score matching produce effect estimates similar to those from FEs.

These are only some of the developments that have occurred in the past few years that both improve the credibility of RCTs and FEs as well as other study designs that are at or near the top of the hierarchy of designs mentioned in the opening section of this chapter. However, few of these developments would have been possible without making evaluation methods and findings transparent and available for all to inspect. The need to ensure that not only the sponsors and those stakeholders directly involved with the evaluation have access to the methods and findings but also those who may be affected by the decisions made by stakeholders, the public, and other researchers have access to methods and findings places another imperative on transparency. This is the topic for the fourth section of this chapter.

Need for Complete Transparency of Method and Sponsorship in Evaluations

Much like the realization that we can't prevent some ideas from becoming bad or harmful policies, we cannot prevent misdirected or careless evaluations from being conducted. In addition, even high-quality evaluations that show that policies that have produced negative consequences may never see the light of day. Professional standards are the first line of defense against evaluations of poor quality and allowing evaluation findings to be dropped into a file drawer, never to be seen. The AEA's Guiding Principles for Evaluators has several principles that have direct implications for transparency and making publicly funded evaluations available to the public (AEA, 2004). One such principle recognizes that "freedom of information is essential in a democracy" (AEA, 2004).

This is fundamentally important. The guidelines go on to indicate that evaluators have the responsibility to actively disseminate the evaluation results to all who have a stake in the policies or programs being evaluated but that these activities may be reasonably constrained by resources. In addition, the Guiding Principles indicate that evaluators should decline to conduct an evaluation that they determine is likely to produce misleading results and that they should not mislead anyone about their procedures or methods.

While the Guiding Principles set the stage for appropriate practice in terms of recognizing an evaluator's responsibility to society, the evaluation community needs to go further. Three areas may need to be considered for evaluation to progress in terms of adding value to society. First, the guidance to clearly communicate the methods and to avoid misleading others about them doesn't establish firm standards about what procedures and methods should be reported nor the level of detail. For example, in terms of potential error from the necessity of finding volunteers to participate in a study, one must know how potential participants were identified, how eligibility was determined, how many volunteered, how many dropped out or were not included in final outcome measures, and how the characteristics of the analytical sample for the study compare to those of the target population for the policy or program. Reporting the sample size and characteristics of the original and analytical sample is not enough.

Second, the principles are silent with respect to intellectual property rights for the data collected as a part of the evaluation. If the evaluator does not explicitly have the right to use the data from an evaluation, then sponsors can prohibit distribution of findings that the sponsor finds detrimental to their interests. In these cases, information needed by the public to support reform of bad or ineffective policies can be censored and the value of evaluation to society undermined. The Guiding Principles do acknowledge the special responsibility of evaluators who conduct publicly funded evaluations but stop short of developing directions that would ensure public access to publicly funded evaluation reports. However, the Guiding Principles do specify that society's interests are rarely the same as specific stakeholder groups, such as the sponsor, and that evaluators have an obligation to society as a whole. This can be used as a basis for the argument that findings should be released, but consideration should be given to requiring that evaluators have intellectual property rights subject only to reasonable review provisions and the requirement to protect human subjects.

Finally, through dialogue, careful reasoning, and (eventually) empirical evidence, we need to begin to consider whether there is a point at which a careful, rigorous assessment of the consequences of public policies and programs should be mandated. It is possible for program administrators who also control evaluation funds to focus evaluations on questions of program coverage, studies of variations in implementation, single-case studies of a program or organization, descriptive studies of program participants, or subjective assessments of satisfaction. At a given time and in a specific situation, any of these could be the best choice for evaluation funding. But continually and indefinitely postponing addressing the public program effectiveness question cannot be in the interest of society.

There is no compelling answer to overcoming situations created by avoiding impact evaluations of public policies and programs. Regulations requiring that efficacy tests of policies and programs be conducted prior to full implementation of a policy are not feasible. Implementation problems may indeed hinder program effectiveness and need to be assessed prior to testing the effectiveness of the program. This situation is likely to be best addressed by establishing and funding alternative institutions to provide priorities for evaluations of program effectiveness. It appears that independent or quasi-independent federal organizations such as IES, the National Institute of Justice, and the National Institutes of Health have rebalanced institutional priorities by providing resources for independent evaluations. While evaluations sponsored and conducted by the agencies administering the programs are likely to be biased toward questions that do not include an assessment of the program's consequences, these quasi-independent institutes can help to ensure that the resources needed to implement designs at the top of the hierarchy to evaluate the consequences of public policies and programs are available.

Conclusion: So What Counts as Credible Evidence?

The IES proposal, which sparked the credibility war (and, to some extent, this volume) presented an opportunity for more evaluations to be conducted using high-quality designs, and the evidence shows that the promise has been realized. Clearly, there are many approaches to evaluation. And under certain conditions, a variety of evaluation approaches that include but are not limited to outcome monitoring, process evaluation, implementation evaluation, and deliberative democratic evaluation may be the best choice for an evaluation and have been used to help make judgments about social policies, programs, and institutions.

However, I believe that Angrist and Pischke (2009) speak for the majority when they say, "The most credible and influential research designs use random assignment" and point to the Perry Preschool Project as a case in point (p. 11). In summary, I draw these conclusions:

1. Accurate and highly credible information on the consequences of policies and programs that can be used to motivate reform of public policies and programs that have negative or no effects and support selection and maintenance of those that have positive effects is essential in order for modern democracies to produce greater social benefits.

2. The prescriptive theory of evaluation that is most closely aligned with the value to society of producing accurate and highly credible information about the effects of social programs is that followed by methods-oriented evaluators.

3. Many of the problems that plagued initial efforts to conduct rigorous evaluations using designs at the top of the design hierarchy have been acknowledged, their sources identified, methods for reducing or eliminating them developed, and the solutions are being implemented routinely in current evaluations. The development of RCM, its subsequent codification (Holland, 1986), and its further development (Imai et al., 2008; Rubin, 2005) have improved our understanding of making causal inferences and opened up the possibility that we can sufficiently specify the conditions that would make designs lower on the hierarchy as credible as random assignment studies.

4. The institutional arrangements for ensuring that rigorous and fair impact evaluations receive adequate resources, given the benefits they produce for society, and making important findings widely available is an ongoing developmental process to which the IES and the other research arms of federal agencies have made significant contributions.

In the original version of this chapter, I argued that Secretary Paige's priority statement could redress an existing imbalance in the allocation of evaluation funds within the Department of Education. I also noted, "Only time, and a high-quality, rigorous evaluation of the impacts of the evaluations funded since 2003, will tell." As I reported earlier in the ensuing years, IES has funded many RCTs and FEs, along with some RD and other high-quality quasi-experimental studies, which make it clear that IES has redressed the imbalance of funds available for educational research and evaluation. These studies have produced volumes of credible evidence. In addition, along with theoretical and methodological developments, they seemed to have convinced many of the fact that random assignment studies are the most credible way to estimate causal effects and that they are, in fact, more feasible than could have been imagined before IES began. But is does seem that the influence of these types of studies is more limited than expected in terms of policy and program reform. The impact evaluation of the studies by IES has not yet been done. Perhaps, in the apparently soon-to-be-funded center for knowledge utilization, such studies using designs high on the hierarchy of designs can produce credible and influential information on the influence of the evaluation findings before this chapter is revised again.

Note

1. For the sake of full disclosure, it is important for you to know that I helped draft this statement and signed it.

Acknowledgments

I wish to acknowledge that I have received funding to conduct research from the Institute of Education Sciences, U.S. Department of Education and have participated in peer reviews and peer review panels conducted by the Institute of Education Sciences, U.S. Department of Education.

References

American Evaluation Association (AEA). (2004). *American Evaluation Association guiding principles for evaluators.* Retrieved March 28, 2014, from http://www.eval .org/p/cm/ld/fid=51

Angrist, J. D., & Pischke, J-S. (2009). *Mostly harmless econometrics: An empiricist's companion.* Princeton, NJ: Princeton University Press.

Bickman, L., Boruch, R. B., Cook, T. D., Cordray, D. S., Henry, G. T., Lipsey, M. W., et al. (2003). *Response to the Secretary's request for comment on the proposed priority on scientifically based evaluation methods.* For a summary of the comments, see Department of Education (200 Scientifically Based Evaluation Methods. *The Federal Register, 70,* 3586–3589).

Chelimsky, E. (2006, November). *Consequences of evaluation: A federal perspective.* Presentation at the Annual Meeting of the American Evaluation Association, Portland, OR.

Christie, C. A., & Alkin, M. C. (2013). An evaluation theory tree. In M. C. Alkin (Ed.), *Evaluation roots: A wider perspective on theorists' views and influences* (2nd ed.). Thousand Oaks, CA: SAGE.

Cook, T. D. (2001). Sciencephobia: Why education researchers reject randomized experiments. *Education Next, 1,* 62–68.

Cook, T. D., Shadish, W. R., & Wong, V. C. (2008). Three conditions under which experiments and observational studies produce comparable causal estimates: New findings from within-study comparisons. *Journal of Policy Analysis and Management, 27*(4), 724–750.

Dahl, R. (1956). *A preface to democratic theory: How does popular sovereignty function in America?* Chicago, IL: University of Chicago Press.

Datta, L-E. (1982). A tale of two studies: The Westinghouse-Ohio evaluation of Project Head Start and the Consortium for Longitudinal Studies report. *Studies in Educational Evaluation, 8*(3), 271–280.

Glazerman, S., Levy, D. M., & Myers, D. (2003). Nonexperimental versus experimental estimates of earnings impacts. *The Annals of the American Academy of Political and Social Science, 589*(1), 63–93.

Graham, J. W. (2009). Missing data analysis: Making it work in the real world. *Annual Review of Psychology, 60,* 549–576.

Greenberg, D. H., Mandell, M. B., & Onstott, M. (2000). Evaluation research and its role in state welfare policy reform. *Journal of Policy Analysis and Management, 19,* 367–382.

Greenberg, D. H., & Shroder, M. (2004). *The digest of social experiments.* Washington, DC: Urban Institute Press.

Henry, G. T. (2001). How modern democracies are shaping evaluation and the emerging challenges. *American Journal of Evaluation, 22*(3), 419–429.

Henry, G. T., & Mark, M. M. (2003). Beyond use: Understanding evaluation's influence on attitudes and actions. *American Journal of Evaluation, 24*(3), 293–314.

Holland, P. W. (1986). Statistics and causal inference. *Journal of the American Statistics Association, 81,* 945–960.

House, E. R. (2006, November). *Blowback.* Presentation at the Annual Meeting of the American Evaluation Association, Portland, OR.

House, E. R., & Howe, K. R. (1999). *Values in evaluation and social research.* Thousand Oaks, CA: SAGE.

Hox, J. J. (2002). *Multilevel analysis: Techniques and applications.* Mahwah, NJ: Lawrence Erlbaum.

Hurley, S. L. (1989). *Natural reasons: Personality and polity.* New York, NY: Oxford University Press.

Imai, K., King, G., & Stuart, E. A. (2008). Misunderstandings between experimentalists and observationalists about causal inference. *Journal of the Royal Statistical Society, 171,* 481–502.

LaLonde, R. J. (1986, September). Evaluating the econometric evaluations of training programs with experimental data. *The American Economic Review, 76*(4), 604–620.

Mark, M. M., & Henry, G. T. (2004). The mechanisms and outcomes of evaluation influence. *Evaluation, 10*(1), 35–57.

Mark, M. M., Henry, G. T., & Julnes, G. (2000). *Evaluation: An integrated framework for understanding, guiding, and improving policies and programs.* San Francisco, CA: Jossey-Bass.

Murnane, R. J., & Willett, J. B. (2011). *Methods matter: Improving causal inference in educational and social science research.* New York, NY: Oxford University Press.

Neuman, S. B., Rich, L., Reyna, V., Towne, L., Feuer, M., Raudenbush, S., . . . Wilson, L. (2002). *The use of scientifically based research in education.* Washington, DC: U.S. Department of Education.

Pressman, J. L., & Wildavsky, A. (1973). *Implementation: How great expectations in Washington are dashed in Oakland; or, why it's amazing that federal programs work at all.* Berkeley: University of California Press.

Raudenbush, S. W., & Bryk, A. S. (2001). *Hierarchical linear models: Applications and data analysis methods* (2nd ed.). Thousand Oaks, CA: SAGE.

Rossi, P. (1994). The war between the quals and the quants: Is a lasting peace possible? In C. S. Reichardt & S. F. Rallis (Eds.), The qualitative-quantitative debate: New perspectives. *New Directions for Evaluation, 61,* 23–36.

Rossi, P., Lipsey, M., & Freeman, H. (2004). *Evaluation: A systematic approach* (7th ed.). Thousand Oaks: SAGE.

Rubin, D. B. (2005). Causal inference using potential outcomes: design, modeling, decisions. *Journal of the American Statistical Association, 100,* 322–331.

Schafer. J. L., & Graham, J. W. (2002). Missing data: Our view of the state of the art. *Psychological Methods, 7*(2), 147–177.

Shadish, W. R., Clark, M. H., & Steiner, P. M. (2008). Can nonrandomized experiments yield accurate answers? A randomized experiment comparing random and nonrandom assignments. *Journal of the American Statistics Association, 103*(484), 1334–1356.

U.S. Department of Education. (2003, November 4). *Scientifically based evaluation methods.* Federal Register, 68, 213. RIN 1890-ZA00. Retrieved March 28, 2014, from http://www2.ed.gov/legislation/FedRegister/proprule/2003-4/110403b.pdf

U.S. Department of Education. (2013, May 2). *Request for Applications: Education Research and Development Center Program.* CFDA Number: 84.305. Retrieved April 11, 2014, from http://ies.ed.gov/funding/ncer_rfas/randd.asp

5

Randomized Controlled Trials

A Gold Standard or Gold Plated?

Leonard Bickman

Stephanie M. Reich

R andomized controlled or clinical trials (RCTs) have been taking on increasing importance, especially outside of the medical field.[1] The number of RCTs is increasing as well as the number of areas in which they are conducted (Bloom, 2008; Boruch, Weisburd, Turner, Karpyn, & Littell, 2009). Moreover, these designs are being recommended and privileged over other designs by prestigious research organizations (e.g., Shavelson & Towne, 2002). In addition, several U.S. federal agencies deemed the RCT as the gold standard that should be used not only in considering the funding of research and evaluation but also in initiating and terminating programs (Brass, Nunez-Neto, & Williams, 2006). However, over the last several years, there has been considerable debate about whether RCTs should be considered the ultimate standard design (Cook & Payne, 2002; Maxwell, 2004).

While most would argue that the RCT is a powerful research design, many debate whether it should be labeled as the *gold standard* for research trying to determine causality. Dissenters of this design as the model for research cite issues of appropriateness, ethics, feasibility, and cost, arguing that other methods can answer causal questions equally well. Most claim that RCTs are more appropriate for medical and basic science investigations,

---

AUTHORS' NOTE: We are not the first to use metals to describe standards. Both Rossi (1987) and Berk (2005) have used similar terms.

where such procedures as blinding or masking of experimental conditions are possible, and not for the bulk of behavioral science research. For instance, Scriven (2005) argues that numerous other designs can infer causation for far less money and with less time than the RCT. He lists cross-sectional designs with triangulation of information, regression discontinuity designs, and interrupted time series designs as just a few equally, if not more, credible designs. Others note that some research areas are not amenable to RCTs, such as safe-sex interventions for HIV/AIDS prevention (e.g., Van de Ven & Aggleton, 1999); broad-spectrum programs (e.g., Cook & Campbell, 1979); and, comically, the efficacy of parachutes (Smith & Pell, 2003).

The debate over RCTs as the gold standard for research is highly relevant to the evaluation of social and educational programs that are designed to improve the quality of lives of others. At the heart of this dispute is whether RCT is the only credible design for testing causal relationship. That is, are the findings believable, trustworthy, convincing, and reliable, and do specific designs, such as the RCT, truly yield more credible findings? To address these issues, this chapter will first briefly focus on the issue of credibility and its subjective nature. Then we will consider how credible RCTs are for the study of cause-and-effect relationships. We will describe some of the important limitations of RCTs and briefly consider alternative designs.

Credibility

Credibility is a highly subjective term. The quality of evidence cannot be determined without knowing which questions were asked and why, what evidence was gathered to answer these questions, who asked the questions and gathered the evidence, how the evidence was gathered and analyzed, and under which conditions the evaluation was undertaken. In addition to these foundational issues, credibility is also influenced by the depth and breadth of the study as well as whether the findings are based on a single study or conclusions drawn about the effectiveness of sets or types of interventions. In other words, much more goes into the judgment of the credibility of research than just the design. While we will discuss some of the broader issues related to credibility, we will concentrate mostly on how the design of the study affects its credibility, since this is the focus of the current debate over whether RCT should be the standard for research and evaluation.

One aim of this chapter is to discuss elements of RCTs that increase or threaten credibility. This is a daunting task, since we believe that credibility is highly subjective. Credibility is a perceived quality and does not reside in an object, person, or piece of information. Thus, what is called credible will be different for different people and under different situations. For assessing credibility in evaluation, we argue that there needs to be a consensus among persons recognized as experts in what they label *credible*. In this chapter, we will describe the elements of an RCT that make it more or less credible to determine causal relations.

It is important to note that the RCT's designation as the gold standard is based on theoretical or potential characteristics of RCTs. It is also the case that many of the limitations attributed to RCTs are more potential problems than proven actual limitations. The chapter will describe some of the issues that arise when implementing an RCT that affect its credibility.

Causation, Epistemology, and Credibility

An important component of credibility is what is defined as knowledge and which methods are used to obtain, discover, or create this knowledge. For instance, in comparing qualitative and quantitative methods, the ontological, epistemological, and theoretical issues of what are "data," how they are analyzed, and what interpretations are drawn from them are viewed quite differently (Brannan, 2005). Although there have been some efforts to critique the quality, trustworthiness, and transferability of qualitative research (e.g., Rolfe, 2006)—and, similarly, the quality and internal, external, statistical conclusion—and construct validity of quantitative research (Shadish, Cook, & Campbell, 2002), epistemological disagreements exist on both sides. Even those who utilize mixed methods acknowledge that the epistemological arguments remain (Howe, 2004; Mertens & Hesse-Biber, 2013; Onwuegbuzie & Leech, 2005).

Although epistemology is an important component of credibility, defining it is beyond the scope of this chapter. Discussing what qualifies as evidence or "truth" would take far more space than this book allows. Therefore, for the purpose of this chapter, we will focus solely on the credibility of studies utilizing quantitative methods. In particular, our discussion will examine claims that the *cause* resulted in the *effect* and whether RCTs should be the standard in quantitative program evaluation and other applied research approaches. While we limit this discussion to post-positivistic quantitative methods, we recognize that no single method can be used to address every question and that different methodologies may yield different answers.

The Cost of Making a Wrong Decision About Causality

We know that there are costs in making a wrong decision. To call a program effective when it is not means that valuable resources may be wasted and the search for other means to solve the problem will be hindered. Some programs may not only be ineffective but also harmful. In such cases, the costs of a wrong decision would be higher. On the other hand, falsely labeling a program as ineffective would mean that clients who would have benefited from the intervention would not have that benefit. Some examples illustrate the point. Imagine the identification of a drug as effective when it is not. Patients taking this drug would not have their condition improve and, in some cases, would continue to deteriorate. Further, if producing the drug takes hundreds of millions of dollars, the financial cost of this mistake is high. Conversely, if the drug were ineffective but costs only pennies to manufacture, there would be little waste of financial resources. While those taking the medication would not benefit from the treatment, the low cost would not inhibit the development of other medications. Thus it is more likely that patients would receive effective medication in the future (assuming pharmaceutical research continues), although not as likely as if the drug was accurately labeled as ineffective. While mislabeling a drug as effective is problematic, this problem is exacerbated when the cost is high. The ramifications of the drug example above are somewhat straightforward, yet for most interventions, the situation is not as clear. Most studies do not compute the costs of the intervention, let alone the cost of a wrong conclusion. Thus credible research is needed to minimize wrong decisions and the subsequent human and financial costs. Later, we will describe some actual medical decisions that were based on the use of a weak design.

The RCT as the Gold Standard of Evidence

RCTs are often thought of as providing more credible evidence than other research designs. This sentiment was demonstrated by the U.S. Secretary of Education's change in funding priorities in 2003 to give highest priority to RCTs.[2] While we agree that an RCT is a powerful research design, it is not immune to threats to validity. In fact, RCTs are just as vulnerable to threats to construct and statistical conclusion validity as other designs. Below, we critique the validity and subsequent credibility of RCTs, with special attention to internal validity—that is, the cause–effect relationship.

Why RCTs Are High in Internal Validity

RCTs have high internal validity because each participant has an equal chance of being assigned to each group, which reduces the likelihood of a systematic bias in the selection and assignment of participants, the main threat to internal validity. Thus random assignment rules out numerous rival hypotheses for the effects found that are based on initial participant differences. We will not describe all the threats to internal validity, as practically any book on program evaluation or research methods will list them. Instead, we will focus on the more visible threats and those that have not been widely discussed in relation to experimental designs.

More Visible Threats to Internal Validity That RCTs Share

While RCTs minimize some of the threats to internal validity, they are not immune from them all. In fact, the majority of threats to drawing valid causal inferences remain. Some of these threats are well known (such as experimenter effects, allegiance, history, and attrition) and others are less often acknowledged. First we will address the more often-cited threats.

EXPERIMENTER EFFECTS

RCTs can be influenced by the behavior of the experimenter/evaluator. The most commonly acknowledged behaviors are experimenter expectancies in which the experimenter knows who is getting the intended treatment or *cause*, and this either influences how the *effect* is recorded or how the participant is treated, thus influencing the observed effect. Using blinding or masking most often controls for this threat. The most common example of this is double-blinded drug studies in which both the participants and researcher do not know who is receiving the experimental drug or placebo. It is rare to have single-blinded let alone double-blinded RCTs in the social sciences (Kumar & Oakley-Browne, 2001). Moreover, although hundreds of studies have been conducted on experimenter expectancy effects (Rosenthal, 1976) and the broader term, *demand characteristics* (Rosnow, 2002), it is not known how strong these effects are in the real world and under which conditions they will produce a significant bias in the results. A similar caution is expressed about the so-called *Hawthorne effect*, for which we believe there is scant supporting evidence (Adair, Sharpe, & Huynh, 1989).

ALLEGIANCE EFFECTS

Similar to experimenter expectancies is the bias caused by allegiance. Allegiance bias occurs when the experimenter develops or supports the treatment (intended cause), and this influences the observed or reported effect. For instance, in the area of clinical psychology, Luborsky and colleagues (1999) compared 29 different individual therapies and found a correlation of 0.85 between differential investigator allegiances and differential treatment outcomes. Even if participants are randomly assigned to conditions, the experimenters' expectations and behaviors can systematically bias results. Making sure that persons other than the originator of the program conduct the evaluation can control for the allegiance effect.

LOCAL HISTORY

The validity of RCTs can be threatened when one group is exposed to external events that can affect the outcome, but not the other group. In these situations, it does not matter how people were assigned, since a systematic bias is introduced to one group of participants and not the other. While it may be impossible for a researcher to prevent such an occurrence, the possibility of such an event requires the monitoring of both experimental and control conditions.

ATTRITION

One of the strengths of random assignment is its ability to minimize the effects of systematic initial differences among participants. However, this equivalence may be threatened when attrition occurs, especially if the attrition differentially affects one group and not the other. When attrition happens more in one condition than another, or if different types of attrition occur, then the experimental design is transformed into a nonequivalent comparison group design and the benefits of random assignment may be lost (Lipsey & Cordray, 2000). Systematic attrition—that is, attrition that is not at random—can have grave effects on the accuracy of causal inferences (Shadish, Hu, Glaser, Kownacki, & Wong, 1998), especially if the reasons for dropping out are inaccessible and how participants vary is unknown (Graham & Donaldson, 1993).

There are several approaches to diagnosing attrition (Foster & Bickman, 2000), but one of the more popular approaches to correcting attrition problems is propensity scoring (e.g., Leon et al., 2006; Shadish, Luellen, & Clark, 2006; VanderWeele, 2006). Propensity scoring may also be useful even if differential attrition did not appear to occur. In these situations, propensity scores help account for differences that are not obvious (Rosenbaum & Rubin, 1983). However, the use of statistical equating techniques is not without controversy (Steiner & Cook, 2013). Some question whether it accomplishes its goal while others argue about how it should be done (Baser, 2006; West & Thoemmes, 2008). Moreover, there are important innovative approaches to strengthening the validity of quasi-experiments that do not use statistical adjustment but focus on designing more internally valid research approaches (Cook & Wong, 2008).

Less Well-Recognized Threats to Internal Validity

When random assignment is feasible and well implemented, it can be an effective method for untangling the effects of systematic participant differences from program effects (Boruch, 1998; Keppel, 1991). However, random assignment alone is not sufficient to ensure high-quality evaluations with credible findings. As noted above, numerous other design, measurement, and implementation issues must be considered in order to make causal inferences. Some of these, which are described above, are commonly noted in the literature. Other threats to internal validity are not often acknowledged. Thus, we would like to draw your attention to a few.

SUBJECT PREFERENCE BEFORE RANDOM ASSIGNMENT

Since properly implemented random assignment ensures an equal chance of assignment to each group, it ignores individual preferences, including individual decision making preferences that might exist (McCall & Green, 2004; McCall, Ryan, & Plemons, 2003). For instance, drawing a sample from only those who are willing to be randomly assigned may not produce equivalent groups if participants have preferences for one condition over another. Suppose 80 people want condition A and 20 prefer condition B. Of the 50 people randomly assigned to condition A, the chances are that 40 (or 80%) will end up in their preferred condition. Of the 50 people assigned to condition B, 10 (or 20%) will be in their preferred condition.

Willingness to be randomly assigned and preferences for a treatment condition are clearly not the same. Faddis, Ahrens-Gray, and Klein (2000) experienced this problem in their effort to compare school-based and home-based Head Start services. In this study, researchers found that many families who were randomly assigned to home-based childcare programs rather than Head Start (school-based) centers never enrolled their children and when they did, they were more likely to attrite. Thus the families that enrolled and remained in the evaluation may have been systematically different by condition from those families that did not complete enrollment. It would also appear from the attrition patterns of this study that some families prefer center-based Head Start to home-based Head Start services. These preferences may have affected how beneficial each type of program was to families and the conclusions drawn from the comparison.

Similar results have been found in mental health services research (Corrigan & Salzer, 2003; Macias et al., 2005). For instance, Chilvers and colleagues (2001) found that patients who chose counseling did better than those who received the services because of randomization. Similarly, in a review of the influence of patient and physician preferences in medical research, King and colleagues (2005) found evidence that preferences can influence outcomes; however, this effect was minimized in larger trials.

In order to address the effect of preference in RCTs, some have advocated for a patient preference RCT/comprehensive cohort design or two-stage randomized design (Brewin & Bradley, 1989; Howard & Thornicroft, 2006). In the first two designs, some of the people with clear treatment preferences are enrolled in their desired treatment while the rest (those with and without strong preferences) are randomly assigned to a treatment condition. In the two-stage randomized design, all participants are randomized into two groups. The first group is able to select their treatment and the second group is randomized to the treatment condition. These variations of the RCT allow evaluators to estimate the degree to which a preference systematically biases results as well as assess how representative the randomized sample is to the general population (those with preferences and without). While this approach may work, it is not feasible in most conditions, since there are rarely the abundant resources (i.e., participants and money) needed to apply these designs.

UNMASKED ASSIGNMENT

Theoretically, RCTs should not have any selection bias because of the random assignment of participants to conditions. Unfortunately, sometimes the random assignment process breaks down. The potential breakdown may be suspected when the person doing the random assignment knows which condition will be used next. This is described as an unmasked trial. Berger and Weinstein (2004) found several instances of this problem in major clinical trials, and Greenhouse (2003) warns that finding significant baseline differences with an unmasked trial is clear evidence of the manipulation of random assignment.

SMALLER SAMPLE SIZE THAN EXPECTED

The reduction of selection bias due to random assignment is based on the notion that with a large enough sample, potentially biasing participant characteristics will be distributed evenly across groups. However, many studies do not include sample sizes large enough to truly protect against systematic bias. As Keppel (1991) warns,

> we never run sufficiently large numbers of subjects in our experiments to qualify for the statistician's definition of the "long run." In practice, we are operating in the "short run," meaning that we have no guarantee that our groups will be equivalent with regards to differences in environmental features or the abilities of subjects. (p. 15)

In small sample studies, the threat of selection bias is much greater, regardless of random assignment of participants to conditions.

ONE-TIME RANDOM ASSIGNMENT

If we took the same people and reassigned them to groups randomly, there would inevitably be differences in group means obtained, as "any observed comparisons between the outcome for the experimental group and the outcome for the control group confounds possible treatment effects with random variation in group composition" (Berk, 2005, p. 422). Thus findings from an RCT only provide information on a specific configuration of people and do not necessarily apply if the people were regrouped. Thus all single studies should be judged with caution. This is a reminder that in science all findings are provisional—regardless of the method used.

INACCURATE UNIT OF ASSIGNMENT

Some evaluation and research questions utilize different units of an organization for random assignment but another level for data analyses. If the data analysis level is used as the level of assignment instead of the organization, then the benefits of the RCT are minimized. For example, a professional training program for teachers that should increase student achievement uses individual student achievement scores for the analysis, which ignores nonindependence of students in the same class. Instead, the proper unit of analyses should be the class average, not the individual student (Boruch, Weisburd, & Berk, 2010). Large threats to validity are introduced when a typical RCT, rather than cluster RCT (described later in the chapter), is used (Raudenbush, 2008). Further, when interventions are at the population level, meta-analyses have found that a bias toward identifying more treatment effects with RCT than observational time series designs exist (Concat, Shah, & Horwitz, 2000; Sanson-Fisher, Bonevski, Green, & D'Este, 2007).

Threats to Between-Group Differences—Even in RCTs

There are other threats to the internal validity of randomized experiments found in almost any textbook on research design that seem plausible but appear to be without any empirical support, at least none we could find.

RESENTFUL DEMORALIZATION

When the control group or a weaker treatment group knows that they are not getting the treatment, they may become demoralized and not perform as well. Thus differences at posttest may be due to decreased performance of the control group and not enhanced performance of the treatment group. Unfortunately, it is difficult to demonstrate that the control group deteriorated while the treatment group held its own rather than a real effect occurring. Blinding or masking helps protect against this. Moreover, we do not know if this artifact is rare or the magnitude of its effect. Thus this may be a potential threat with little practical consequences.

COMPENSATORY RIVALRY—JOHN HENRY EFFECT

Knowledge of whether you are in the treatment or control group can also have the opposite effect of demoralization. Instead of losing motivation, the control group members may become even more motivated to perform, just to "show them." John Henry may have been a real person, but his relevance to research design is based on legend. John Henry was a "steel-driving man" who competed against a steam machine to drive spikes into the railroad crossties. Although he won the race, he died soon after. Because of his knowledge of the machine's advantage, John Henry did not become demoralized but became more motivated to beat the machine. In a similar fashion, a control group's members might compete more strongly against a more heavily resourced experimental condition to demonstrate their prowess.

Lack of External Validity in RCTs

While this chapter focuses on the credibility of RCTs in drawing causal infer-ences, we must note the most often–cited criticism of this design is its reduced external validity. Clearly, if the focus of an evaluation is whether a program is effective, then understanding for whom and under what conditions it is effec-tive is important as well. Unfortunately, the nature of volunteerism and the evaluator's ability only to randomly assign those willing to be in any group can limit the generalizability of findings. This has led many to question whether causal inferences are enough of a benefit when RCTs may create artificial cir-cumstances and findings that may not be generalizable to other settings, peo-ple, or times (Cronbach, 1982; Heckman & Smith, 1995; Raudenbush, 2002). Berk (2005) states this strongly by claiming,

> It cannot be overemphasized that unless an experiment can be general-ized at least a bit, time and resources have been wasted. One does not really care about the results of a study unless its conclusions can be used to guide future decisions. Generalization is a prerequisite for that guid-ance. (p. 428)

The validity of the RCT depends upon the investigators' intention to study the effectiveness of a cause in the real world or its efficacy in more of a labora-tory context. While Cook and Campbell (1979) described internal validity as the *sine qua non* of research, external validity is essential for research in applied contexts. It is clear that the health sector values internal validity over external validity (Glasgow et al., 2006), as the research standards of the medical field (e.g., Consolidated Standards of Reporting Trials [CONSORT]) do not deal with external validity. Currently, it is likely that a tightly designed study that is high in internal validity is more likely to be published and have a grant application approved even if it is low in external validity.

Lack of generalizability is a common concern for medical research, as participants are often selected to be younger, healthier (lacking comorbid diseases than the one being studied), and, for women, not pregnant (Van Spall, Toren, Kiss, & Fowler, 2007). Such selection of participants identifies treatments that may not be effective to the types of people most likely to need treatment (Apisarnthanarax et al., 2013; Bhatt & Cavender, 2013; Rothwell, 2005; Van Spall et al., 2007). For instance, people over the age of 65 account for 53% of new cancer diagnoses but are only 33% of the participants in clinical trials for cancer treatments (Leaf, 2013). Leaf's opinion piece about the generalizability of RCTs in the *New York Times* illustrated concern among the general public about RCTs, given the over 100 commentaries that followed this publication.

Judging external validity is often more difficult than assessing internal validity. How are we to know if the results will apply in the future in some other context? Predicting the future is difficult under any circumstances, but it is especially difficult when we do not know what factors moderate the treatment. We agree that it is too limiting to focus solely on internal validity. The best way to assure external validity is to conduct the study in a setting that is as close as possible to the one that the program would operate in if it were adopted and to include the people that would typically use that setting or be affected by the problem the intervention hopes to ameliorate. We see the recent emphasis on research transportability and bridging science and practice to be a step toward valuing external validity.

APPROPRIATENESS OF THE COMPARISON

Another aspect of external validity beyond volunteerism is the use of the appropriate comparison. Some RCTs are well implemented but conceptually flawed due to the use of an inappropriate comparison group. When this occurs, the internal validity may be high but the utility of the study (i.e., external validity) is low. For instance, in a review of pharmaceutical-funded versus independent investigator-implemented RCTs, Lexchin, Bero, Djulbegovic, and Clark (2003) found that new drugs were typically compared to placebo conditions rather than another medication. As such, large effects were found yet the drugs' performance in comparison to current treatments was unexplored. Here, the RCTs were well executed but were not much of a contribution to science or human well-being. Thus external validity is essential for credibility if the findings are going to be applied.

Other Issues Raised With RCTs

PRIVILEGING CERTAIN TYPES OF RESEARCH

The belief that RCTs are indeed the gold standard of research implies that other studies employing other designs are weaker and thus less credible. The implications of this are that research areas amenable to the conduct of RCTs are by their very nature more credible. This introduces an unintended side effect of championing certain topic areas as having more credible results when randomized designs are easier to conduct in those areas. For example, it is much easier to conduct a randomized double-blind study of a psychotropic drug than to evaluate a type of psychotherapy. This implies that drug studies are more credible, on the average, than psychotherapy studies. In a similar fashion, total coverage or mandated programs cannot be feasibly evaluated using an RCT. In the former, everyone is receiving the treatment and thus none can be randomly assigned because it would be illegal to withhold the benefit. This does not mean that these programs are immune to study, only that they cannot be studied using an RCT. However, their findings can still be credible.

A similar issue of privileging research occurs when the use of RCTs promotes more investigation into a low-priority area, resulting in resources being spent in less beneficial areas. For instance, in the area of HIV interventions, before truly potent antiretroviral therapy was discovered, 25 RCTs found spuriously significant effects for a variety of treatments of approved, controversial, and contraindicated medications. This resulted in what Ioannidis (2006) calls a *domino effect*, when "one research finding being accepted leads to other findings becoming seemingly more credible as well. This creates webs of information and practices to which we assign considerable credibility, while they may all be false and useless" (p. e36).

ETHICAL ISSUES

There are ethical issues in using the RCT because of the possibility that effective treatments may be denied to some. There have been many discussions of the ethics of design (Boruch et al., 2009; Fisher & Anushko, 2008; Sieber, 2009), and we will briefly summarize them here. First, if it is known with some degree of certainty that one treatment is better than another, then one must question why the study is to be conducted. It is only when we do not know the relative effectiveness that an RCT is called for. Second, in almost all cases, a treatment group is compared to another treatment and not to a no-treatment condition. This use of an active control is important for methodological as well as ethical issues. Some conditions are especially appropriate, from an ethical point of view, for using an RCT. When there are more in need than there are treatments, it seems especially fair to distribute the treatment by lot or randomly, thus giving everyone an equal chance of obtaining the experimental treatment.

Other times, an RCT is not appropriate if the outcome of a comparison group is known with certainty. For instance, in designing bulletproof fabrics, researchers draped the cloth over pigs and fired a high-caliber weapon at the fabric. In this study, there was no need to shoot at naked pigs, since the outcome of the control condition was well established (Boruch, 2005a). Further difficulties can arise and bias results when the clinical staff does not believe that the effectiveness of the treatment is unknown. Why select a treatment to test if it is not likely that it is effective? Another bias that may be introduced is when the clinician believes that the treatment will work better with a particular type of client. This is one reason why the investigator should maintain strict control over the random assignment process.

Sometimes the random assignment of participants would be unethical, making an RCT inappropriate. For instance, the attempted Children's Environmental Exposure Research Study of the effects of pesticides on babies in Florida was halted due to national response to the questionable ethics of such a study to be carried out by the Environmental Protection Agency (Johnson, 2005). Just because an RCT is possible does not mean it should be conducted. Smith and Pell (2003) make this point well in their satirical article, "Parachute Use to Prevent Death and Major Trauma Related to Gravitational Challenge: Systematic Review of Randomized Controlled Trials."

MULTILEVEL/CLUSTER DESIGNS

In addition to ethical issues, feasibility factors into whether the RCT is the best design to use. Randomized experiments where the unit of assignment is not an individual but a group (such as a school or classroom) offer a special challenge because of covariation due to nesting of units within other units. This research is most often found in educational research, where the treatment may be introduced at the class, school, or even district level. In such cases, there is a strong consensus that the appropriate analysis is at the unit of random assignment. Thus if schools are randomly assigned, then the school should be the unit of analysis. The major drawback to this position is the drastic reduction of degrees of freedom. In the not-too-distant past, researchers randomly assigning an intervention to, for example, eight schools with 500 students each would analyze the data as if there were 4,000 participants (8 × 500) instead of eight. By not considering nesting, the analyst is not taking into account the intercorrelation coefficient (ICC) between students and classes within a school. This ICC can seriously affect the statistical power of the design.

For instance, Varnell, Murray, Janega, and Blitstein (2004) reviewed 60 group- or cluster-randomized trials (GRTs) published in the *American Journal of Public Health and Preventive Medicine* from 1998 through 2002. The authors found that only 9 (15.0%) GRTs reported evidence of using appropriate methods for sample size estimation. Of 59 articles in the analytic review, 27 (45.8%) reported at least one inappropriate analysis and 12 (20.3%) reported only inappropriate analyses. Nineteen studies (32.2%) reported analyses at an individual or subgroup level, ignoring group or included group as a fixed effect. Thus interclass correlations were largely ignored. In an attempt to deal with this problem, there are now CONSORT standards (described later) that can be used in evaluating the quality of cluster designs (Campbell, Elbourne, & Altman, 2004).

As noted earlier, using the correct level of analysis has important implications for the design of RCTs. Now, instead of counting students, we need to count schools. While there is not a one-to-one loss in statistical power (i.e., one student is equivalent to one school), it will typically take close to 40 schools to detect a small to medium effect size between two conditions. While this is a difficult requirement, it is more feasible in education than in other areas. Fortunately, there are school districts that have many schools within them. However, this is not the case for areas outside of education. In the area of mental health, randomizing at the mental health center level is difficult. We (LB) conducted an RCT using 40 different mental health sites (Bickman, Kelley, Breda, De Andrade, & Riemer, 2011). If we had not been collaborating with the country's largest provider of mental health services for children, we do not believe the study could have been conducted. Moreover, the expense of conducting these multisite studies is very high when compared to single-site research.

Another concern with cluster RCT designs is determining how to measure outcomes (the effect) and who should be viewed as the participant needing consent. Take, for example, the NEXUS study, a cluster RCT of the effectiveness of a physician educational intervention to reduce the use of lumbar radiographs (Eccles et al., 2001). Although the intervention targeted general practitioners and randomization occurred at the clinic level, no doctors were consented. The "effect" was the number of radiographs ordered per 1,000 patients, but no patients were informed that their medical chart was a component of this study (Weijer et al., 2011). Thus additional ethical concerns arise when RCT is used at a group level.

REPORTING OF RCTS

It is beneficial to have standards of quality of RCTs, such as the CONSORT standards (described later) used primarily in the medical field, but it is important to inquire the degree to which these standards are actually followed in journals. This question has been addressed primarily in several medical fields, with uneven reporting of participant characteristics and attrition by group (Lu, Yao, Gu, & Shen, 2013; Post, de Beer, & Guyatt, 2013). Many medical journals now mandate CONSORT reporting, but this is not the standard for many behavioral science publications that disseminate RCT research and evaluation. Such reporting is important in determining the credibility of the findings and determining their generalizability to other people, places, and times.

Do RCTs Have Different Outcomes From Other Designs?

While RCTs are often called the *gold standard* of research, one must question whether these designs yield different results from quasi-experimental designs. A very visible example of an RCT producing findings that were different from those of a nonrandomized design is the research on hormone replacement therapy for women. Previous nonrandom trials indicated positive effects of the therapy, while a randomized trial found negative effects (Shumaker et al., 2003). However, a more detailed examination suggests that differences in outcomes could be explained by differences in the samples studied (Hernan et al., 2008). In a meta-analysis comparison of psychotherapy studies using RCTs and quasi-experiments, Shadish and Ragsdale (1996) concluded that under some circumstances, a well-conducted quasi-experiment could produce adequate estimations of the results obtained from a randomized study; however, they concluded that randomized experiments are still the gold standard.

Since then, other studies have been completed comparing experimental and quasi-experimental designs. These studies have not produced consistent findings. Some research has found different outcomes favoring randomized experiments (e.g., Glazerman, Levy, & Myers, 2003), while others found that quasi-experiments produced outcomes of unknown accuracy (e.g., Rosenbaum, 2002). However, all the previous studies shared a flaw that made the results even less certain. All of them confound assignment method with other study variables. Shadish, Clark, and Steiner (2008) used an innovative doubly randomized preference trial procedure to untangle these confounds by first randomly assigning students to either a random assignment condition or a self-selection procedure. The authors found that both the random assignment condition and self-selection condition produced similar results after adjusting the self-selection procedure with propensity scores. However, the authors caution that these results may not generalize, since they were conducted in a college laboratory using college students as participants, and that the results appear to be sensitive to how missing data in the predictors were handled. The reader is referred to commentaries (Hill, 2008; Little, Long, & Lin, 2008; Rubin, 2008) and a rejoinder by the authors for a more in-depth discussion of comparisons between randomized and nonrandomized designs.

Existing statistical approaches to nonexperimental data appear insufficient to compensate for biases that may arise when the pattern of missing data cannot be properly modeled, such as when there are no standards for treatment, when affected populations have limited access to treatment, or when there are high rates of treatment dropout.

Additionally, due to great heterogeneity among people and their lifestyles, typical RCT may not be able to detect effects for certain people under different conditions. Recent pharmaceutical studies have failed to identify why some people respond well to medications while others do not or how to account for the aggregation of data, which may mask impacts, especially when there is insufficient statistical power to detect effects due to participant heterogeneity (Button et al., 2013). This has led some to argue for the use of "data-intensive mega-trials," with sample sizes of tens of thousands of participants for high-profile (i.e., "blockbuster") medications (Ioannidis, 2013). In considering population variability and sample size needs, there is evidence that registries and administrative data can provide insights into the impact of interventions better than RCTs alone (Joynt, Orav, & Jha, 2013). For instance, in the field of pediatric oncology, the use of a registry has helped identify effective treatment protocols for more and less commonly occurring pediatric cancers (Steele, Wellemeyer, Hansen, Reaman, & Ross, 2006). The registry, in conjunction with smaller RCTs, has greatly increased the survival rates of childhood cancer, even though the incidence of pediatric cancers is increasing (National Cancer Institute, 2008). Cardiology has recently followed suit with the creation of the National Cardiovascular Data Registry (NCDR), which is currently targeting clinical practices and outcomes of cardio catheters nationwide (Dehmer et al., 2012).

Approaches to Judging the Credibility of RCTs

There have been several approaches to evaluating the quality of an RCT. Probably the most widespread is the CONSORT. Around 1995, two efforts to improve the quality of reports of RCTs led to the publication of the CONSORT statement. These standards were developed for medical clinical trials but can be used with some modification in any RCT. The CONSORT statement consists of a checklist and flow diagram for reporting a RCT. It was designed for use in writing, reviewing, or evaluating reports of simple two-group parallel RCTs. The standards apply to the reporting of an RCT but may be considered a proxy of the actual conduct of the study. This assumes that the published article accurately describes the methods. Huwiler-Müntener, Juni, Junker, and Egger

(2002) found that the methodological quality of published articles as rated by reviewers was associated with the reported quality indicated by a subset of the CONSORT standards. Soares and colleagues (2004) compared the published quality of RCTs performed by the Radiation Therapy Oncology Group to the actual protocol used in each study. The authors found that the published version of the article underestimated the quality of the protocol used. Unfortunately, the authors only compared the absolute level of quality and not the correlation between quality of the reports and quality of the protocol. The key aspects of the checklist that relate specifically to RCTs are summarized in Table 5.1.

There have been several studies in quite a few medical specialties that have examined whether research published in their journals has improved since the release of the standards. Kane, Wang, and Garrard (2007) examined RCTs published in two medical journals before and after the CONSORT guidelines were evaluated; one journal used the CONSORT statement (*Journal of the American Medical Association* [*JAMA*]) and one did not (*New England Journal*

Table 5.1   Key Aspects of the Checklist That Relate Specifically to RCTs

Section and Topic	Descriptor
Randomization	
a. Sequence generation	a. Method used to generate the random allocation sequence, including details of any restrictions (e.g., blocking, stratification)
b. Allocation concealment	b. Method used to implement the random allocation sequence (e.g., numbered containers or central telephone), clarifying whether the sequence was concealed until interventions were assigned
c. Implementation	c. Who generated the allocation sequence, who enrolled participants, and who assigned participants to their groups?
Blinding (masking)	Whether or not participants, those administering the interventions, and those assessing the outcomes were blinded to group assignment. If done, how the success of blinding was evaluated.

SOURCE: Based on Moher, Schulz, and Altman (2001).

of Medicine [*NEJM*]). The results indicated that reporting improved in both journals, but *JAMA* showed significantly more improvement in all aspects of RCT reporting. Several other studies found similar results (Moher, Jones, & Lepage, 2001; Plint et al., 2006).

The publication of the CONSORT standards has had a greater effect on research in medicine than on research in the behavioral sciences. For instance, Spring, Pagoto, Knatterud, Kozak, and Hedeker (2007) examined the analytic quality of RCTs published in two leading behavioral journals and two medical journals. One of the criteria used was *intention to treat* (ITT), where the analysis includes all participants kept in the assigned group, regardless of whether they experienced the condition in that group. Not only did more reports in medical journals (48%) state that they were going to use ITT than in behavioral journals (24%) but more also used it correctly in the medical journals (57%) than in behavioral journals (34%). Moreover, the articles in the top psychology journals were less likely than those in medical journals to describe a primary outcome, give a reason for estimating study size, describe the denominators that were used in the analysis of the primary outcomes, and account for missing data in analyses.

In the area of social and behavioral research, the Society for Prevention Research (SPR) has established broader standards that provide criteria with which to judge the credibility of evidence for efficacy, effectiveness, and dissemination (Flay et al., 2005). These broader concerns require criteria dealing with the intervention, measures, analysis, and other aspects of research. We will focus on those standards related to determining the credibility of causal statements. These are

> *Standard 3:* The design must allow for the strongest possible causal statements;
>
> *Standard 3.b:* Assignment to conditions needs to minimize the statistical bias in the estimate of the relative effects of the intervention and allow for a legitimate statistical statement of confidence in the results; and
>
> *Standard 3.b.i:* For generating statistically unbiased estimates of the effects of most kinds of preventive interventions, random assignment is essential. (p. 157)

SPR supports the use of nonrandomized designs when necessary—for example, for total coverage programs or when ethical considerations do not allow such a design. The alternatives suggested are the interrupted time series and regression-discontinuity designs. The requirements of these latter two designs severely limit their use. A third design, matched case-control design, is viewed as acceptable only when there is a pretest demonstration of group equivalence. To be credible, this necessitates demonstrating equivalence by using sufficiently powered tests on several baselines or pretests of multiple outcomes and the inclusion of major covariates. Steiner and colleagues (2010) have shown that it is critical to identify the appropriate covariates if bias is going to be statistically reduced. The key is to provide convincing evidence that the lack of a random assignment process did not result in a correlation between unmeasured variables and condition.

Other Approaches to Establishing Causality

There are other research designs found to be scientifically acceptable in other disciplines that do not involve experiments, let alone RCTs. These disciplines include geology, astronomy, engineering, medical forensics, and medical laboratory testing. In some cases, it is impossible to conduct experiments, such as in astronomy. Like RCTs, approaches in these fields rely on observational methods. These fields have extremely precise predictions, exacting measurement, and exceptionally large numbers of replications in common. While it is important to note that other observational methods are scientifically acceptable ways to establish causality, it is equally important to understand that they are credible only under conditions that rarely, if ever, occur in the social and behavioral sciences.

An approach that is more suitable to the social sciences is known as *program theory, theory-driven method*, or *pattern-matching method* (Bickman & Peterson, 1990; Chen & Rossi, 1983; Donaldson, 2003; Scriven, 2005). These are nonexperimental, observational methods that use complex predictions to support a causal hypothesis. In some ways, they are similar to astronomical research, without the precision. This approach is not in opposition to RCTs and has been used in RCTs and quasi-experiments as a way of understanding what is occurring in the black box of the program. We fully realize that RCTs can directly answer only a very limited number of questions, and we must depend on other approaches to fill the gaps. Further, the use of RCTs can be strengthened by the inclusion of qualitative methods, which may help with the interpretation and credibility of research and evaluations findings. For instance, the New Hope anti-poverty intervention used of post-hoc qualitative case studies to disentangle observed quantitative impacts of the RCT and to create a follow-up survey (Gibson & Duncan, 2005).

While both experimental and quasi-experimental designs have numerous threats to the validity of conclusions drawn, the RCT, when implemented well, controls for more threats than nonexperimental designs (in the social sciences). As such, well-executed RCTs are more credible in determining causal relationships. However, the argument has been made that they are inherently less feasible, more costly, and more difficult to implement. Having conducted many RCTs and quasi-experimental designs, we do not agree.

Feasibility

RCTs have been criticized as being difficult to conduct and lacking feasibility. We would argue that the existence of so many RCTs belies that criticism. In a report to Congress, the Congressional Research Service cited the number of RCTs as of 2002 as 250,000 in medicine and 11,000 in all the social sciences combined (Brass et al., 2006). While the number is 20 times more in medicine, 11,000 is still a significant number of RCTs. Two other examples are the Cochrane Collaboration (www.cochrane.org), which has over 350,000 RCTs registered, and the Campbell Collaboration (www.campbellcollaboration.org; Petrosino, Boruch, Rounding, McDonald, & Chalmers, 2000), which contains over 13,000 RCTs in the social sciences (Boruch, 2005b). While there are some specific conditions in which RCTs could not or should not be implemented, these appear to be rare rather than the modal situation.

Practical Issues in the Conduct of RCTs

Currently, both authors are conducting RCTs in such areas as mental health, education, and parenting. In addition to these studies, the senior author has conducted over 20 large-scale RCTs in his career in several areas, representing over $20 million in external funding. Having worked with numerous types of designs, we have not found RCTs to be more difficult to implement than quasi-experimental designs. In fact, the design is usually not the most troublesome aspect of field experimentation.

LIMITED TREATMENT RESOURCES

The *Congressional Research Service Report* (Brass et al., 2006) suggests that RCTs take longer to conduct, are more expensive, and, in general, are more difficult to implement than nonrandomized designs. This is clearly true when RCTs are compared to preexperimental designs such as the simple post-test-only or pre-post-test designs. As noted earlier, the fair comparison is with designs that include a control group.

There are some conditions that are optimal for an RCT. If there are more people who want a service than can be provided for, then the fairest way to determine who receives the service is usually by lot or random assignment. Often, the service provider might insist that severity should serve as the criteria for admissions. It is possible to argue that within every measure of severity, there is a band of uncertainty within which random assignment could be done. However, this limits the power of the study as well as the external validity. In such cases, the regression-discontinuity design may be more appropriate.

NONEQUIVALENT CONTROL GROUP

Finding a comparison group can often be more difficult than randomly assigning participants to conditions. Assuming that such a group could be found, there is still the difficulty of convincing the control group organization to collect data when there is no benefit to the organization or clients for participating in the study. In addition, more assumptions must be made and more analyses must be conducted to assess pretest group differences and, when possible, propensity for group assignment.

COST IS COST

As mentioned earlier, cost is often raised as a consideration in implementing an RCT. The cost of including a comparison group should be the same whether random assignment is used or not. However, in many quasi-experiments, the control group is not in the same location as the treatment group, often necessitating increased expenses either due to travel or the staffing of a remote site. If the experimenter is very confident of the randomization process (e.g., the sample is very large), then it is possible to do a posttest-only design with the assumption that the treatment and control groups were equivalent before the study started. This would cut data collection costs in half. Hak, Wei, Grobbee, and Nichol (2004) found only one empirical study that looked at the cost effectiveness of different study designs testing the same hypothesis. However, it was not applicable to this discussion of RCTs because it compared a case-control design to a cohort design. We do not have empirical evidence that RCTs are more expensive.

RANDOM ASSIGNMENT

Negotiating for the use of an RCT, where it is ethical and legal, is not as difficult as some may make it appear. For instance, we have implemented random assignment in a study in which parents called to obtain mental health services for their children. While there was initially some resistance by one staff person, the random assignment apparently posed no problem to parents, since 84% agreed to participate in the study (Bickman, Summerfelt, & Noser, 1997).

One of the issues in implementing an RCT is the danger of *crossover* in which those assigned to the treatment group end up in the control group (usually because the organization did not provide the promised services) or when control group participants are exposed to the treatment (also known as *contamination* and *diffusion*). In some situations, physical separation of the participants reduces the probability of this problem, but in the above example, the parents were all in the same community. Moreover, the service organization could not legally or ethically refuse to treat children. The latter issue was dealt with by asking parents, before they became clients, if they were willing to participate in the random assignment, with the incentive that their child would not be put on the waiting list if he or she was selected for treatment. All of the system-of-care clients received care in that system. In the control group, 6% of the cases received services from the system of care at some point in the study. Thus crossover was not a problem in this particular study (Bickman, Summerfelt, & Noser, 1997).

Crossover problems may occur in educational experiments that are implemented at the school level and take more than a school year to conduct. In these cases, it is not unusual for some students to transfer between schools. In one of our studies, 1.4% of the over 1,000 students changed to schools that had a different experimental condition in the first year, and less than 1% changed schools in the second year.

The issue of crossover analysis can be dealt with in a conservative fashion by using an ITT approach in the analysis. In this case, the analysis is conducted using the original assignment, regardless of the condition the participant experienced. It is conservative because it will water down any potential treatment effects but it maintains the advantages of the random assignment. A discussion of the ITT analysis may be found in Nich and Carroll (2002). Subsequent analyses of the sample can be conducted to look at how those who actually received treatment responded. This type of Treatment on the Treated (TOT) analysis can compare outcomes that are based on receiving treatment versus other artifacts (Dobie & Fryer, 2011; Morris & Gennetian, 2003).

Resistance to random assignment may be a problem, but in our experience, we have not found it to be a significant issue. However, in an experiment we conducted on pediatrician diagnosis and treatment of attention-deficit/hyperactivity disorder (ADHD), we found that the pediatricians took an extraordinarily long time to commit to participate. We think there was a conflict between their values as scientists and not wanting to be subjects in a study. Still, this would have probably occurred whether participants were randomly assigned or not.

Conclusion: So What Counts as Credible Evidence?

While RCTs may be prone to numerous threats to validity, they are nonetheless one of the most credible designs available to researchers. We have described many of the problems of RCTs, both in implementation and in concept. However, we still view them to be a credible choice for quantitative research. They are not really a "gold standard" in the sense of being perfect, but to paraphrase what Winston Churchill said about democracy, we conclude, "For determining causality, in many but not all circumstances, the randomized design is the worst form of design except all the others that have been tried."

This chapter has explored the RCT as the gold standard for credible research. As noted, credibility of research is determined by assessing whether the findings are believable, trustworthy, convincing, and reliable. Specifically, judging credibility necessitates information about the research questions asked: What evidence was gathered to answer these questions, who asked the questions and gathered the evidence, how the evidence was gathered and analyzed, and under which conditions the evaluation was undertaken? In addition to these foundational issues, credibility is also influenced by the depth and breadth of the study as well as whether the findings are based on a single study or multiple studies. For assessing credibility in evaluation, we argue that there also needs to be a consensus among persons recognized as experts on what they label credible. While credibility is affected by what is viewed as knowledge or truth, this chapter is limited to discussing only post-positivistic quantitative methods. As such, issues of credibility are influenced by statistical conclusion, internal, construct, and external validity.

The RCT is as vulnerable to threats to statistical conclusion validity and construct validity as other methods. However, it is protected against one of the main threats to internal validity: selection bias. Even with this protection, there are several other well-recognized threats as well as less commonly acknowledged threats to internal validity. As described in the chapter, some of the well-recognized threats include experimenter effects; allegiance effects; local history; and attrition, especially differential attrition. Less-familiar threats include participant preferences prior to randomization, unmasked assignment, small sample size, and one-time random assignment.

When considering issues of external validity, RCTs may create an artificial situation in which the findings are not very generalizable. In such cases, credibility of the application of the evaluation is reduced. When conducting any RCT, it is important to use an appropriate comparison and to be sure that group random trials are used when making comparisons across settings or in situations where interclass covariation will influence results. While RCTs may still be prone to numerous threats to validity, this chapter has argued that they are still one of the most credible designs available to researchers and evaluators.

Notes

1. We will use the term *RCT*, known as a randomized clinical or control trial, to represent all randomized experiments, not just clinical trials.
2. While certain quasi-experimental designs were included in this priority, randomized designs were preferred when possible.

References

Adair, J. G., Sharpe, D., & Huynh, C. (1989). Hawthorne control procedures in educational experiments: A reconsideration of their use and effectiveness. *Review of Educational Research, 59*(2), 215–228.

Apisarnthanarax. S., Swisher-McClure, S., Chiu, W., Kimple R. J., Harris, S. L., Morris, D. E., & Tepper, J. E. (2013). Applicability of randomized trials in radiation oncology to standard clinical practice. *Cancer, 119*(16), 3092–3099. DOI:10.1002/cncr.28149

Baser, O. (2006). Too much ado about propensity score models? Comparing methods of propensity score matching. *Value in Health, 9*(6), 377–385. DOI: 10.1111/j.1524-4733.2006.00130.x

Berger, V. W., & Weinstein, S. (2004). Ensuring the comparability of comparison groups: Is randomization enough? *Controlled Clinical Trials, 25*(5), 515–524. DOI: 10.1016/j.cct.2004.04.001

Berk, R. A. (2005). Randomized experiments as the bronze standard. *Journal of Experimental Criminology, 1,* 417–433. DOI: 10.1007/s11292-005-3538-2

Bhatt, D. L., & Cavender, M. A. (2013). Are all clinical trial sites created equal? *Journal of the American College of Cardiology, 61*(5), 580–581. DOI: 10.1016/j.jacc.2012.10.024

Bickman, L., Kelley, S., Breda, C., De Andrade, A., & Riemer, M. (2011). Effects of routine feedback to clinicians on youth mental health outcomes: A randomized cluster design. *Psychiatric Services, 62*(12), 1423–1429. DOI: 10.1176/appi.ps.002052011.

Bickman, L., & Peterson, K. (1990). Using program theory to describe and measure program quality. In L. Bickman (Ed.), Advances in program theory. *New Directions for Evaluation, 47,* 61–72.

Bickman, L., Summerfelt, W. T., & Noser, K. (1997). Comparative outcomes of emotionally disturbed children and adolescents in a system of services and usual care. *Psychiatric Services, 48,* 1543–1548.

Bloom, H. S. (2008). The core analytics of randomized experiments for social research. In P. Alasuutari, J. Brannen, & L. Bickman (Eds.), *Handbook of social research methods* (pp. 115–133). London, England: SAGE.

Boruch, R. F. (1998). Randomized controlled experiments for evaluation and planning. In L. Bickman & D. Rog (Eds.), *Handbook of applied social research methods* (pp. 161–191). Thousand Oaks, CA: SAGE.

Boruch, R. F. (2005a). Comments on the papers by Rawlings and Duflo-Kremer. In G. K. Pitman, O. N. Feinstein, & G. K. Ingram (Eds.), *Evaluating development effectiveness* (pp. 232–239). New Brunswick, Canada: Transaction Publishers.

Boruch, R. F. (Ed.). (2005b, May). Place randomized trials: Experimental tests of public policy [Special issue]. *Annals of the American Academy of Political and Social Sciences, 599.*

Boruch, R. F., Weisburd, D., & Berk, R. (2010). Place randomized trials. In A. R. Piquero & D. Weisburd (Eds.), *Handbook of quantitative criminology* (pp. 481–502). New York, NY: Springer.

Boruch, R. F., Weisburd, D., Turner, H., Karpyn, A., & Littell, J. (2009). Randomized controlled trials for evaluation and planning. In L. Bickman & D. Rog (Eds.),

Handbook of applied social research methods (2nd ed., pp. 147–181). Thousand Oaks, CA: SAGE.

Brannan, J. (2005). Mixing methods: The entry of qualitative and quantitative approaches into the research process. *International Journal of Social Research Methodology, 8*(3), 173–184. DOI:10.1080/13645570500154642

Brass, C. T., Nunez-Neto, B., & Williams, E. D. (2006, March 6). *Congress and program evaluation: An overview of randomized controlled trials (RCTs) and related issues.* Washington, DC: Congressional Research Service, Library of Congress. Retrieved May 18, 2007, from http://assets.opencrs.com/rpts/RL33301_20060307.pdf

Brewin, C. R., & Bradley, C. (1989). Patient preferences and randomised clinical trials. *British Medical Journal, 299,* 313–315.

Button, K. S., Ioannidis, J. P., Mokrysz, C., Nosek, B. A., Flint, J., Robinson, E. S., & Munafo, M. R. (2013). Power failure: Why small sample size undermines the reliability of neuroscience. *National Review of Neuroscience, 14*(5), 365–376. DOI: 10.1038/nrn3475. DOI:10.1038/nrn3475

Campbell, M. K., Elbourne, D. R., & Altman, D. G. (2004). CONSORT statement: Extension to cluster randomised trials. *British Medical Journal, 328,* 702–708.

Chen, H. T., & Rossi, P. H. (1983). Evaluating with sense: The theory-driven approach. *Evaluation Review, 7,* 283–302. DOI: 10.1177/0193841X8300700301

Chilvers, C., Dewey, M., Fielding, K., Gretton, V., Miller, P., Palmer, B., . . . Harrison, G. (2001). Antidepressant drugs and generic counselling for treatment of major depression in primary care: Randomised trial with patient preference arms. *British Medical Journal, 322,* 772–775. DOI: 10.1136/bmj.322.7289.772

Concat, J., Shah, N., & Horwitz, R. I. (2000). Randomized controlled trials, observational studies and the hierarchy of research design. *New England Journal of Medicine, 342,* 1887–1892. DOI: 10.1056/NEJM200006223422507

Cook, T. D., & Campbell, D. T. (1979). *Quasi-experimentation: Design and analysis issues for field settings.* Boston, MA: Houghton Mifflin.

Cook, T. D., & Payne, M. R. (2002). Objecting to the objections to using random assignment in educational studies. In F. Mosteller & R. Boruch (Eds.), *Evidence matters: Randomized trials in education research* (pp. 150–178). Washington, DC: Brookings Institution.

Cook, T. D., & Wong, V. C. (2008). Better quasi-experimental practice. In P. Alasuutari, J. Brannen, & L. Bickman (Eds.), *Handbook of social research methods.* London, England: SAGE.

Corrigan, P., & Salzer, M. (2003). The conflict between random assignment and treatment preference: Implications for internal validity. *Evaluation and Program Planning, 26,* 109–121. DOI: 10.1016/S0149-7189(03)00014-4.

Cronbach, L. J. (1982). *Designing evaluation and social programs.* San Francisco, CA: Jossey-Bass.

Dehmer, G. J., Weaver, D., Roe, M. T., Milford-Beland, S., Fitzgerald, S., Hermann, A., . . . Brindis, R. G. (2012). A contemporary view of diagnostic cardiac catheterization and percutaneous coronary intervention in the United States: A report from the CathPCI Registry of the National Cardiovascular Data Registry,

2010 through June 2011. *Journal of the American College of Cardiology, 60*(20), 2017–2031. DOI: 10.1016/j.jacc.2012.08.966 DOI:10.1080/13645570500154642

Dobie, W., & Fryer, R. G. (2011). Are high-quality schools enough to increase achievement among the poor? Evidence from the Harlem Children's Zone. *American Economic Journal: Applied Economics, 30,* 158–187. DOI: 10.1257/app.3.3.158

Donaldson, S. I. (2003). Theory-driven program evaluation. In S. I. Donaldson & M. Scriven (Eds.), *Evaluating social programs and problems: Visions for the new millennium.* (pp. 109–141). Mahwah, NJ: Erlbaum.

Eccles, M., Steen, N., Grimshaw, J., Thomas, L., McNamee, P., Soutter, J., . . . Bond, S. (2001). Effect of audit and feedback, and reminder messages on primary-care radiology referrals: A randomised trial. *Lancet, 357*(9266), 1406–1409.

Faddis, B., Ahrens-Gray, P., & Klein, E. (2000). *Evaluation of Head Start family child care demonstration* (Final Report). Washington, DC: Commissioner's Office of Research and Evaluation.

Fisher, C. B., & Anushko, A. E. (2008). Research ethics in social science. In P. Alasuutari, J. Brannen, & L. Bickman (Eds.), *Handbook of social research methods* (pp. 95–110). London, England: SAGE.

Flay, B. R., Biglan, A., Boruch, R. F., Castro, F. G., Gottfredson, D., Kellam, S., . . . Ji, P. (2005). Standards of evidence: Criteria for efficacy, effectiveness, and dissemination. *Prevention Science, 6*(3), 151–175. DOI: 10.1007/s11121-005-5553-y

Foster, E. M., & Bickman, L. (2000). Refining the costs analyses of the Fort Bragg evaluation: The impact of cost offset and cost shifting. *Mental Health Services Research, 2*(1), 13–25. DOI: 10.1023/A:1010139823791

Gibson, C., & Duncan, G. (2005). Qualitative/quantitative synergies in a random-assignment program evaluation. In T. Weisner (Ed.), *Mixed methods in the study of child and family life* (pp. 283–303). Chicago, IL: University of Chicago Press.

Glasgow, R. E., Green, L. W., Klesges, L. M., Abrams, D. B., Fisher, E. B., Goldstein, M. G., . . . Orleans, T. (2006). External validity: We need to do more. *Annals of Behavioral Medicine, 31*(2), 105–108. DOI: 10.1207/s15324796abm3102_1

Glazerman, S., Levy, D. M., & Myers, D. (2003). Nonexperimental versus experimental estimates of earnings impacts. *The Annals of the American Academy of Political and Social Science, 589,* 63–93. DOI: 10.1177/0002716203254879

Graham, J., & Donaldson, S. (1993). Evaluating interventions with differential attrition: The importance of nonresponse mechanisms and use of follow-up data. *Journal of Applied Psychology, 78*(1), 119–128. DOI: 10.1037/0021-9010.78.1.119

Greenhouse, S. W. (2003). The growth and future of biostatistics: A view from the 1980s. *Statistics in Medicine, 22,* 3323–3335. DOI: 10.1002/sim.1634

Hak, E., Wei, F., Grobbee, D. E., & Nichol, K. L. (2004). A nested case-control study of influenza vaccination was a cost-effective alternative to a full cohort analysis. *Journal of Clinical Epidemiology, 57,* 875–880. DOI: 10.1016/j.jclinepi.2004.01.019

Heckman, J. J., & Smith, J. A. (1995). Assessing the case for social experiments. *Journal of Economic Perspective, 9*(2), 85–110. DOI: 10.1257/jep.9.2.85

Hernan, M., Alonso, A., Logan, R. Grodstein, F., Michels, K., Stamfer, M., . . . Robins, J. M. (2008). Observational studies analyzed like randomized experiments: An application to postmenopausal hormone therapy and coronary heart disease. *Epidemiology, 19*(6), 766–779. DOI: 10.1097/EDE.0b013e3181875e61

Hill, J. (2008). Comment. *Journal of the American Statistical Association, 103*(484), 1346–1350.

Howard, L., & Thornicroft, G. (2006). Patient preference randomised controlled trials in mental health research. *British Journal of Psychiatry, 188,* 303–304. DOI: 10.1192/bjp.188.4.303

Howe, K. (2004). A critique of experimentalism. *Qualitative Inquiry, 10*(1), 42–61. DOI 10.1177/1077800403259491

Huwiler-Müntener, K., Juni, P., Junker, C., & Egger, M. (2002). Quality of reporting of randomized trials as a measure of methodologic quality. *JAMA, 287,* 2801–2804.

Ioannidis, J. (2006). Evolution and translation of research findings: From bench to where? *PLoS Clinical Trials, 1*(7), e36. DOI:10.1371/journal.pctr.0010036

Ioannidis, J. (2013). Mega-trials for blockbusters. *JAMA, 309*(3), 239–240. DOI:10.1001/jama.2012.168095.

Johnson, S. L. (2005). *Children's environmental exposure research study.* Washington, DC: U.S. Environmental Protection Agency. Retrieved May 30, 2007, from http://www.epa.gov/cheers.

Joynt, K. E., Orav, E. J., & Jha, A. K. (2013). Mortality rates for Medicare beneficiaries admitted to critical access and non-critical access hospitals, 2002–2010. *JAMA, 309*(13), 1379–1387. DOI:10.1001/jama.2013.2366

Kane, R., Wang, J., & Garrard, J. (2007). Reporting in randomized clinical trials improved after adoption of the CONSORT statement. *Journal of Clinical Epidemiology, 60*(3), 241–249. DOI: 10.1016/j.jclinepi.2006.06.016

Keppel, G. (1991). *Design and analysis: A researcher's handbook.* Upper Saddle River, NJ: Prentice Hall.

King, M., Nazareth, I., Lampe, F., Bower, P., Chandler, M., Morou, M., . . . Lai, R. (2005). Impact of participant and physician intervention preferences on randomized trials: A systematic review. *JAMA, 293*(9), 1089–1099. DOI:10.1001/jama.293.9.1089.

Kumar, S., & Oakley-Browne, M. (2001). Problems with ensuring a double blind. *Journal of Clinical Psychiatry, 62*(4), 295–296.

Leaf, C. (2013, June 13). Do clinical trials work? *New York Times,* p. SR1.

Leon, A. C., Mallinckrodt, C. H., Chuang-Stein, C., Archibald, D. G., Archer, G. E., & Chartier, K. (2006). Attrition in randomized controlled clinical trials: Methodological issues in psychopharmacology. *Biological Psychiatry, 59*(11), 1001–1005. DOI: 10.1016/j.biopsych.2005.10.020

Lexchin, J., Bero, L., Djulbegovic, B., & Clark, O. (2003). Pharmaceutical industry sponsorship and research outcome and quality: Systematic review. *British Medical Journal, 326,* 1167–1170. DOI: 10.1136/bmj.326.7400.1167

Lipsey, M., & Cordray, D. (2000). Evaluation methods for social intervention. *Annual Review of Psychology, 51,* 345–375. DOI: 10.1146/annurev.psych.51.1.345

Little, R. J., Long, Q., & Lin, X. (2008). Comment. *Journal of the American Statistical Association, 103*(484), 1344–1346.

Lu, Y., Yao, Q., Gu, J., & Shen, C. (2013). Methodological reporting of randomized clinical trials in respiratory research in 2010. *Respiratory Care,* published ahead of print, January 9, 2013. DOI:10.4187/respcare.01877

Luborsky, L., Diguer, L., Seligman, D. A., Rosenthal, R., Krause, E. D., Johnson, S., . . . Schweizer, E. (1999). The researcher's own therapy allegiances: A "wild card" in comparison treatment efficacy. *Clinical Psychology: Science and Practice, 6,* 95–106. DOI: 10.1093/clipsy.6.1.95

Macias, C., Barreira, P., Hargreaves, W., Bickman, L., Fisher, W., & Aronson, E. (2005). Impact of referral source and study applicants' preference for randomly assigned service on research enrollment, service engagement, and evaluative outcomes. *American Journal of Psychiatry, 162*(4), 781–787.

Maxwell, J. (2004). Causal explanation, qualitative research, and scientific inquiry in education. *Educational Researcher, 33*(2), 3–11. DOI: 10.3102/0013189X033002003

McCall, R., & Green, B. (2004). Beyond methodological gold standards of behavioral research: Considerations for practice and policy. *Social Policy Report, 18*(2), 3–12.

McCall, R., Ryan, C., & Plemons, B. (2003). Some lessons learned on evaluating community-based, two-generation service programs: The case of the Comprehensive Child Development Program. *Journal of Applied Developmental Psychology, 24*(2), 125–141. DOI: 10.1016/S0193-3973(03)00042-X

Mertens, D., & Hesse-Biber, S. (2013). Mixed methods and credibility of evidence in evaluation. *New Directions for Evaluation, 138,* 5–13. DOI: 10.1002/ev.20053

Moher, D., Jones, A., & Lepage, L. (2001). Use of the CONSORT statement and quality of reports of randomized trials: A comparative before-and-after evaluation. *JAMA, 285,* 1992–1995. DOI: 10.1001/jama.285.15.1992.

Moher, D., Schulz, K. F., & Altman, D. G. (2001). The CONSORT statement: Revised recommendations for improving the quality of reports of parallel-group randomized trials. The CONSORT Group. *JAMA, 285,* 1987–1991. DOI: 10.1186/1471-2288-1-2

Morris, P., & Gennetian, L. (2003). Identifying the effects of income on children's development using experimental data. *Journal of Marriage and Family, 65*(3), 716–729. DOI: 10.1111/j.1741-3737.2003.00716.x

National Cancer Institute. (2008). *Childhood Cancers.* Retrieved on March 30, 2014, from http://www.cancer.gov/cancertopics/factsheet/Sites-Types/childhood

Nich, C., & Carroll, K. M. (2002). Intention to treat meets missing data: Implications of alternate strategies for analyzing clinical trials data. *Drug and Alcohol Dependence, 68*(2), 121–130. DOI: 10.1016/S0376-8716(02)00111-4

Onwuegbuzie, A., & Leech, N. (2005). On becoming a pragmatic researcher: The importance of combining quantitative and qualitative research methodologies. *International Journal of Social Research Methodology, 8*(5), 375–387. DOI: 10.1080/13645570500402447

Petrosino, A., Boruch, R. F., Rounding, C., McDonald, S., & Chalmers, I. (2000). The Campbell Collaboration social, psychological, educational and criminological trials register (C2-SPECTR) to facilitate the preparation and maintenance of systematic reviews of social and educational interventions. *Evaluation and Research in Education, 14*(3), 206–219. DOI: 10.1080/09500790008666973

Plint, A. C., Moher, D., Morrison, A., Schulz, K., Altman, D. G., Hill, C., & Gaboury, I. (2006). Does the CONSORT checklist improve the quality of reports of randomised controlled trials? A systematic review. *Medical Journal of Australia, 185*(5), 263–267.

Post, P. N., de Beer, H., & Guyatt, G. H. (2013). How to generalize efficacy results of randomized trials: Recommendations based on a systematic review of possible approaches. *Journal of Evaluation in Clinical Practice, 19*, 638–643. DOI:10.1111/j.1365–2753.2012.01888.x

Raudenbush, S. W. (2002, February 6). *Identifying scientifically-based research in education.* Paper presented at the Working Group Conference in Washington, DC. Retrieved May 30, 2007, from http://www.ssicentral.com/hlm/techdocs/ScientificallyBasedResearchSeminar.pdf

Raudenbush, S. W. (2008). Many small groups. In J. de Leeuw & E. Meijer (Eds.), *Handbook of multilevel analysis* (pp. 207–236). New York, NY: Springer.

Rolfe, G. (2006). Validity, trustworthiness, and rigour: Quality and the idea of qualitative research. *Journal of Advanced Nursing, 53*(3), 304–310.

Rosenbaum, P. R. (2002). *Observational studies* (2nd ed.). New York, NY: Springer-Verlag.

Rosenbaum, P. R., & Rubin, D. B. (1983). The central role of the propensity score in observational studies for causal effects. *Biometrika, 70*(1), 41–55. DOI: 10.1093/biomet/70.1.41

Rosenthal, R. (1976). *Experimenter effects in behavioral research* (enlarged ed.). New York, NY: Irvington.

Rosnow, R. L. (2002). The nature and role of demand characteristics in scientific inquiry. *Prevention & Treatment, 5*, 37.

Rossi, P. (1987). The iron law of evaluation and other metallic rules. *Research in Social Problems and Public Policy, 4*, 3–20.

Rothwell, P. M. (2005). External validity of randomised controlled trials: 'To whom do the results of this trial apply?' *Lancet, 365*(9453), 82–93.

Rubin, D. B. (2008). Comment: The design and analysis of gold standard randomized experiments. *Journal of the American Statistical Association, 103*(484), 1350–1353.

Sanson-Fisher, R. W., Bonevski, B., Green, L. W., & D'Este, C. (2007). Limitations of the randomized controlled trial in evaluating population-based health interventions. *American Journal of Preventative Medicine, 33*(2), 155–161. DOI: 10.1016/j.amepre.2007.04.007

Scriven, M. (2005, December). *Can we infer causation from cross-sectional data?* Paper presented at the School-Level Data Symposium, Washington, DC. Retrieved May 28, 2007, from http://www7.nationalacademies.org/bota/School-Level%20Data_Michael%20Scriven-Paper.pdf.

Shadish, W. R., Clark, M. H., & Steiner, P. M. (2008). Can nonrandomized experiments yield accurate answers? A randomized experiment comparing random to nonrandom assignment. *Journal of the American Statistical Association, 103*(484), 1334–1356. DOI: 10.1198/016214508000000733

Shadish, W. R., Cook, T., & Campbell, D. (2002). *Experimental and quasi-experimental designs for generalized causal inference.* Boston, MA: Houghton Mifflin.

Shadish, W. R., Hu, X., Glaser, R. R., Kownacki, R. J., & Wong, T. (1998). A method for exploring the effects of attrition in randomized experiments with dichotomous outcomes. *Psychological Methods, 3*, 3–22.

Shadish, W. R., Luellen, J. K., & Clark, M. H. (2006). Propensity scores and quasi-experiments: A testimony to the practical side of Lee Sechrest. In R. R. Bootzin &

P. E. McKnight (Eds.), *Strengthening research methodology: Psychological measurement and evaluation* (pp. 143–157). Washington, DC: American Psychological Association.

Shadish, W. R., & Ragsdale, K. (1996). Random versus nonrandom assignment in controlled experiments: Do you get the same answer? *Journal of Consulting and Clinical Psychology, 64,* 1290–1305.

Shavelson, R. J., & Towne, L. (Eds.). (2002). *Scientific research in education* (National Research Council. Committee on Scientific Principles for Educational Research). Washington, DC: National Academy Press.

Shumaker, S. A., Legault, C., Rapp, S. R., Thal, L., Wallace, R. B., Ockene, J. K., . . . Wactawski-Wende, J. (2003). Estrogen plus progestin and the incidence of dementia and mild cognitive impairment in postmenopausal women: The Women's Health Initiative memory study: A randomized controlled trial. *JAMA, 289,* 2651–2662. DOI:10.1001/jama.289.20.2651

Sieber, J. E. (2009). Planning ethically responsible research. In L. Bickman & D. Rog (Eds.), *Handbook of applied social research methods* (2nd ed., pp. 106–141). Thousand Oaks, CA: SAGE.

Smith, G., & Pell, J. (2003). Parachute use to prevent death and major trauma related to gravitational challenge: Systematic review of randomised controlled trials. *British Medical Journal, 327,* 1459–1461. DOI: 10.1136/bmj.327.7429.1459

Soares, H. P., Daniels, S., Kumar, A., Clarke, M., Scott, C., Swann, S., & Djulbegovi, B. (2004). Bad reporting does not mean bad methods for randomised trials: Observational study of randomised controlled trials performed by the Radiation Therapy Oncology Group. *British Medical Journal, 328,* 22–24. DOI: 10.1136/bmj.328.7430.22

Spring, B., Pagoto, S., Knatterud, G., Kozak, A., & Hedeker, D. (2007). Examination of the analytic quality of behavioral health randomized clinical trials. *Journal of Clinical Psychology, 63*(1), 53–71. DOI: 10.1002/jclp.20334

Steele, J. R., Wellemeyer, A., Hansen, M., Reaman, G. H., & Ross, J. A. (2006). Childhood cancer research network: A North American childhood cancer research network. *Cancer Epidemiology Biomarkers & Prevention, 15,* 1241–1242.

Steiner, P. M., & Cook, D. L. (2013). Matching and propensity scores. In T. D. Little (Ed.), *The Oxford handbook of quantitative methods* (vol. 1, pp. 237–259). New York, NY: Oxford University Press.

Steiner, P. M., Cook, T. D., Shadish, W. R., & Clark, M. H. (2010). The importance of covariate selection in controlling for selection bias in observational studies. *Psychological Methods, 15,* 250–267. DOI: 10.1037/a0018719

Van de Ven, P., & Aggleton, P. (1999). What constitutes evidence in HIV/AIDS education? *Health Education Research, 14*(4), 461–471.

Van Spall, H., Toren, A., Kiss, A., & Fowler, R. (2007). Eligibility criteria of randomized controlled trials published in high-impact general medical journals: A systematic sampling review. *JAMA, 297*(11), 1233–1240. DOI:10.1001/jama.297.11.1233

VanderWeele, T. (2006). The use of propensity score methods in psychiatric research. *International Journal of Methods in Psychiatric Research, 15*(2), 95–103. DOI: 10.1002/mpr.183

Varnell, S. P., Murray, D. M., Janega, J. B., & Blitstein, J. L. (2004). Design and analysis of group-randomized trials: A review of recent practices. *American Journal of Public Health, 94*(3), 393–399.

Weijer, C. Grimshaw, J. M., Taljaard, M., Binik, A., Boruch, R., Brehaut, J. C., . . . Zwarenstein, M. (2011). Ethical issues posed by cluster randomized trials in health research. *Trials, 12*, 100–111. DOI:10.1186/1745–6215–12–100

West, S. G., & Thoemmes, F. (2008). Equating groups. In P. Alasuutari, J. Brannen, & L. Bickman (Eds.), *Handbook of social research methods* (pp. 414–430). London, England: SAGE.

6

Demythologizing Causation and Evidence

Michael Scriven

M yths grow up around all great institutions and grand dreams, from the Greek gods and the master race to democracy and the American West, and science is no exception. The latter are usually based on some oversimplified claim about the nature of science: that it's essentially quantitative or concerned only with general claims or only with claims that are falsifiable or that are intersubjectively testable, and so on. Refuting them is mainly an exercise for the philosophy of science journals. But there are times when we need to separate the myths from reality in a wider forum, and this may be a good time to separate the current myths about causation and evidence from the reality, because the issue is no longer a merely academic dispute. The lives and welfare of huge numbers of human beings now hang in the balance, and we need to bring our best thinking to bear on settling the issues.

Common-Sense Science

The current mythology receiving the most public attention would have it that scientific claims of causation or good evidence, either optimally or universally, require evidence from randomized controlled trials (RCTs).

The truth of the matter—the reality—is very different, as many readers with good general scientific knowledge will realize upon reflection. If you

AUTHOR'S NOTE: My thanks to Ryoh Sasaki and Lynn Gigy for raising some problems with earlier drafts of this overview that I hope to have resolved in this version.

think of the domain of science as represented by a map of the United States, the concepts of causation and evidence are ubiquitous and normally used with great care and precision throughout the whole territory. On this map, let's imagine that the Eastern Seaboard represents the area where RCTs rightly rule, including, for example, pharmacology and some parts of clinical medicine and applied psychology. We'll let the Midwest represent the large area where that approach is often an option, but then, in the rest of the country, RCTs are completely irrelevant to the scientific work of the region, though for slightly different reasons in different areas.

For example, the South on our map can be taken to represent the domain of mathematical physics and astronomy, where laws rule. There have been efforts (for example, by Bertrand Russell) to outlaw the notion of cause from science, based on the observation that mathematical laws, which he thought represented the ideal form to which all science should aspire, do not employ the term *cause*. Common sense prevailed, since those laws (the moment they are applied to any real case) provide an excellent basis for causal claims without invoking experiments. For example, in astrophysics, we have no difficulty in providing causal explanations about the motion of bodies such as comets and meteorites moving under gravitational forces, although we are obviously not able to do any experiments with those bodies.

In the Mountain West, where—let us suppose—geology is king, we don't have any mathematical laws, but we have some good models of causal processes—for example, in explaining the formation of the Rockies or Meteor Crater in Arizona or, for that matter, the craters on the moon. Again, no experiments were or will be called for in support of these claims, although plenty of empirical research in the field provides the evidence to back them up. On the Central Pacific Coast, we might suppose, are located the domains of anthropology and ethnography, where it's considered just plain unacceptable to experiment with one's subjects—but the scientists seem to have no problems about recording their observations of tribal warfare in which one person injures another or forced migration or domestic activities where people make things or do things, all of these being causal claims. In the Pacific Northwest, the home of epidemiology in the analogy, where the cause of epidemics such as lung cancer, obesity, or food poisoning are the hot topics, or in the Southwest, where the forensic sciences reside and where we find plenty of autopsies aimed at determining the cause of death or studies by the National Transportation Safety Board (NTSB) on the cause of airline disasters or the collapse of bridges, there seems to be no mention of control groups. The scientists at work in the West or the South are not dreaming of the day when things will get better so that they can run "true experiments"— they are just getting their jobs done and finding no intrinsic barriers to drawing causal conclusions.

In short, much of the world of science, suffused with causal claims, runs along very well with the usual high standards of evidence, but without RCTs. We all know this very well, once we are reminded of it.

So it's just a myth that science does better if its work in support of causal claims is based on experiments, although the way many of us were taught science, with an emphasis on the great experimental sciences of physics and chemistry and the parts of biology that make good projects at science fairs, tends to foster that illusion. The illusion here is the elevation of a local deity to universal dominance.

So where is the battle being fought, and why is it a battle at all? These questions bring us back to the Midwest, which is another story. This is the land of bipolar allegiance, and there are many localities there where dominance has alternated between the experimental and the nonexperimental forces, with some areas remaining loyal to the midstream party of the quasi-experimentalists. The crusaders from the conservative Northeast are trying to take over the domains of education, psychology, sociology, social work, penology, international affairs, and parts of medicine that occupy this territory, along with other domains, and it's true that in some areas, their takeover has led to improvements—people had indeed been using less-sound approaches when RCTs could have been used. But in many other cases, the attempted takeover is just unnecessarily forcing an issue, and the force used often causes more grief and distortion than benefits. For these are the areas where "it all depends"—that is, the right choice of investigative methodology depends on whether one can get the resources needed, the permissions required, the time-window stretch, and so forth that the demanding RCT model must have.

In such cases, to insist that we use an experimental approach is simply bigotry—not pragmatic and not logical. In short, it is a dogmatic approach that is itself an affront to scientific method, not an improvement in it. Moreover, to wave banners proclaiming that anything less will mean unreliable results or unscientific practice is simply absurd. Look west, young man, or look south, and you'll see there are other ways to go that are just as scientific, just as capable of coming to causal conclusions that are beyond reasonable doubt. Those methods can be used in the Midwest, and often are, and are frequently the best choice.

Before we leave our map, let's add something about what Canada might be thought to represent. That vast stretch of territory represents the proper use of causal language outside science. The two eastern provinces might be taken to represent its use in history by professional historians, who would have some difficulty arranging control groups with long-dead figures but have no difficulty—other than those involved in due diligence—in supporting causal explanations of many historical events. The two western provinces represent its proper use in the law, where it often meets the required standard

for conviction of felonious acts—that is, establishing the facts "beyond reasonable doubt." And the central provinces of Saskatchewan and Manitoba
represent its proper use in ordinary language and technology, where we can
say with complete confidence that we *know* that the reason our car just slowed
down was because we pushed on the brake pedal or that we lost the draft
manuscript *because* we hit Delete at the wrong moment.

The overall picture the map represents is one that shows how RCTs stand
in the grand sweep of causal usage. They own a small slice of it, and there is
sometimes a case for them to be granted a lease on another significant slice,
although they have to earn their place there, and overall, they are often not the
best choice—including some cases where they have talked themselves into a
crucial role they do not deserve.

Logical Building Blocks for an Understanding of Causation

Let's see if we can get the elements of this issue set out plainly, to see how a safe
path can be laid between the patches of quicksand that abound. There are really
just five matters we need to be clear about.

First, it is crucial to understand the difference between (i) the case for
using RCT designs in a wider range of studies in the Midwest, which was
underestimated for a while and is indeed well worth considering, and (ii) the
case for insisting that RCT designs are the only legitimate causal design in that
entire area; that is, the area where it is theoretically feasible. The first is good
practice; the second is methodological imperialism, a kind of program that
could only be justified if the RCT myth about causation were true instead of
being a fantasy. In this situation, the RCT myth, like the Aryan myth, has costly
consequences in human terms: For example, where it has been believed (the
World Bank appears to be the latest proselyte), it has jeopardized the funding
of many large humanitarian projects that think they should not be evaluated
using an RCT design—usually for ethical reasons (i.e., unwillingness to have
some applicants prevented from receiving aid)—by supporting the view that
this means they cannot be shown to be worth funding.

Second, we need to be clear about how we acquire causal language, for that
is where it gets and retains its essential meaning. It will be argued here that this
investigation shows that our original understanding supports bulletproof demonstrations of causal connections based purely on direct observation.

Third, we need to understand the standards of confidence that apply to
causal claims and how they can be met. It will be shown that the highest relevant
standards for scientific purposes are readily attainable by many alternative
designs in many cases, including cases where RCTs cannot meet those standards.

Fourth, we need to be clear about what RCTs do that other designs do not and how this bears on meeting high standards of scientific confidence. In particular, we need to look at half a dozen of the alternative approaches rather carefully to see whether they are in fact inferior in terms of their ability to substantiate causal claims *and* the respects in which they will sometimes have significant advantages over RCTs (e.g., completion speed, resulting confidence level, cost, burden on subjects, generalizability, ethicality, level of expertise required for implementation, and side effects, if any). It will be shown (i) that the usual claimed intrinsic advantage of the RCT design is only a theoretical advantage, and its actual achievements are frequently matched in practice by many other designs; (ii) that even such a theoretical advantage is not present in the RCT designs currently being advocated because they are not in fact true RCT designs; and (iii) that, nevertheless, there are real advantages for a near-RCT approach in some circumstances, although they can only be determined by weighing its comparative merits on the (at least) eight listed considerations (see Sundry Notes section later in this chapter) that bear on the merit of a research design.

Fifth, we need to be clear that there *is* a gold standard of experimental design for causal investigation, although it is not the RCT; it is the logical underpinning of the RCT *and* the many competing designs. This is the *general elimination methodology or algorithm* (GEM), quite easily understood and more easily taught than the RCT.

In the following discussion, we do not segregate the above points, since the overlap and interaction among them is extensive, but all will receive solid support.

The Origin of Causal Concepts

The first of the two foundation stones to be laid in constructing the logic of causation is the proposition that causation is directly and reliably—indeed, trivially and universally—observable. It is perhaps best to approach the proof of this by looking at how we acquire the concept of causation. It is developed in the child's brain before language skills are well developed, and it apparently springs from the palmar ("grip") reflex, which soon develops considerably into (i) the child's realization that he or she can manipulate the environment by shaking a rattle to make a noise, (ii) the recognition and manipulation of crayons for producing marks on paper, and (iii) the discovery that squeezing the cat makes her scratch. These are all cases of understood causation and indeed, by the age of 3 years, the average child has discovered some things that are much more sophisticated, beginning with (iv) how to cause others to do things upon request—and, indeed, becomes notably "bossy" about such demands.

Also acquired are (v) the basic notion of responsibility for his or her actions, resulting in blame when the child is bad and praise when he or she is good, and (vi) the denial of responsibility for "bad" actions (e.g., knocking something over) when the wind or a sibling did it. Soon, there is language to express all of this, and the youngster rightly (vii) claims to see others do things and to be able to get others to do things. In other words, their experience now includes the management as well as the observation of causation and the evaluation of consequences. Maturation simply brings greater range and sophistication to these basics, so there's nothing essentially new about such claims as the adult makes (e.g., that the brakes are working well in his or her car), every datum for this generalization being a (tactile) observation of causation.

The Cognitive Process of
Causal Inference Versus Observation

Despite the commonplace use of our language to the contrary, Cook and many well-trained social scientists and educational researchers, following the great British philosopher David Hume, find it hard to accept the notion of observed causation. They appear to favor the idea that we are really inferring it. But that's like saying we really infer that this person we see in the crowd meeting the passengers from our plane into San Francisco is our spouse. Of course, the neural net is, in some sense, putting bits and pieces together, but that's part of what happens in *perception;* the end result of these neural machinations is *pattern recognition,* not *pattern inference.* Hume's pitch was seductive because we don't see causation in the same way that we see color and motion. Causation, as with many other complex predicates, refers to a learned *holistic* feature of a configuration, not just to a learned *element* in it (i.e., it involves heavy sensitivity to contextual [including historical] factors, not just content). That configuration is what enables the billiards player to say, in suitable circumstances, that he did indeed see the cue ball strike the object ball and thus cause the latter to head for and drop into the pocket. Once one learns how to see this kind of example of causation, it becomes part of the *perceptual vocabulary* (similar to the myriad of instances of your friend's face) or even part of *perceptual evaluation* (for example, what makes a "good seat" in an equestrian event or "good style" in a dismount from the parallel bars in gymnastics).

This epistemic status of causal claims as observable is fully recognized in the one place outside science where doubts are best respected—the court of law. Eyewitness testimony, especially but not only if it meets all the well-defined standards (normal vision, good lighting, clear field, propinquity, recency, corroboration, absence of motive to lie, etc.), is treated there as in science: as an appropriate datum in the court of last resort for establishing a case. The examples of it there regularly include testimony that causation was observed in the standard cases such as battery, vandalism, and shooting. Causation is part of the language of observed acts; and as part of the language of observation, in suitable circumstances, it is established as having occurred with all the credibility that observation deserves in science as in law.

So the first key conclusion here is that the simplest and probably the most reliable of all ways to establish causation is by critical observation. (I use the term *critical observation* here as shorthand for observation subject to the usual checks for the usual sources of error, including reflection on the likelihood of those.)

Interestingly enough, close study of the bible on quasi-experimentation, by Cook and Campbell (1979), turns up a passage in which this view is conceded, although its implications for causal methodology were never developed there: "[W]e do not find it useful to assert that causes are 'unreal' and are only inferences drawn by humans from observations that do not themselves directly demonstrate causation" (p. 33).

This position leads us to studying the second foundation stone for the logic of causal inquiry.

Scientific, Legal, and Practical Certainty

One of the main attractions of the RCT approach is that it appears to provide a greater degree of certainty for its conclusions than the alternatives. There are circumstances in which this is true, but it is not true across the board for several reasons, of which the first is that even causal claims based on direct critical observation can attain the benchmark level of certainty, and it's very hard to find an RCT that matches that standard. The *benchmark level* in scientific research, as in criminal law and in common practice where important matters are at stake, is simply "beyond a reasonable doubt." This is the standard required to establish a case in criminal law and is traditionally and extensively distinguished from *the balance of evidence*, which is the criterion for establishing the occurrence of misdemeanors. This concept of certainty is part of the common language of science so that in the lab or field, the observer or reasoner knows when to make and how to understand a claim that someone is certain that he or she did, saw, or calculated that something occurred or was the case.

This is not careless use or abuse of the term; it is the proper use of the term. It illustrates what the term does in fact mean. Some strands of perfectionist argument in epistemology here, as with perception and causation, have sought to persuade us otherwise, pushing us in this case toward the idea that the proper use of *certain* refers to the complete impossibility of error as in definitional claims and mathematical theorems. But *certain* is a contextually defined term, and the proper standards for its use in the context of empirical discussions is "empirical support beyond reasonable doubt"—not the same standard as applies in talking about the realm of deductive proof. One might as well argue that the term *large* is improperly used to describe an emu's egg or an elephant or anything smaller than the universe. The perfectionist move is just an example of bad linguistic analysis. The law courts remind us that there is a well-established body of rules for the proper use of terms such as *observe* and *certain* that take us well beyond what is sometimes scoffed at as the imprecision of ordinary usage. The courts define the hard core of ordinary use, since that is what the juries understand and that is what good scientific use employs. Even Cook (2001) concedes, in his magisterial review of the arguments for and against the RCT design, that when talking about case studies (where we often rely on reported observations of causation), "I do not doubt that these procedures sometimes reduce all reasonable uncertainty" (p. 38). And that is just the conclusion we need to establish, for that is all that can be reasonably required of any scientific method for establishing causation.

The Alleged RCT Advantage

RCT designs do have an edge, although not the edge that is often claimed for them. As Cook (2001) goes on to say in the quote begun above,

> I do not doubt that these procedures sometimes reduce all reasonable uncertainty, though it will be difficult to know when this has been achieved. However, I do doubt whether intensive, qualitative case studies can reduce as much uncertainty about cause as a true experiment. That is because such intensive case studies rarely involve a totally credible causal counterfactual. Since they typically do not involve use of comparison groups, it is difficult to know [whether] the group under study would have changed over time without the reform under analysis. (pp. 38–39)

The first problem with this passage—and with this position, which is the basic argument for the superiority of the RCT (a.k.a. "true experiment") design—is that the RCT design, as used in the cases under discussion here, does *not* support a counterfactual. The RCT design as used in good agricultural research does have this property. But in educational and community interventions, the design is crucially weakened and is typically no longer double blind as it is in the drug studies. It is not even single blind. That is, both the subjects and the researchers typically can work out (i.e., come to know) who is in the experimental group and, usually, both know which subjects are in the control group since—unlike pills or fertilizers they can reason from their history, the presence or absence of changes in staff interactions with them, the results of communications with other subjects and treatment providers, and so on. This leaves open a gap through which the Hawthorne effect (and its converse) can slip in. (I refer to this situation as a *quasi-blind* condition.) As Cook and the texts define the RCT design, the key point about it is that after randomization (and assuming adequate group size), the only relevant difference between the two groups is the treatment; but in the context we are discussing, there is another difference, namely the difference in the beliefs—indeed the knowledge—of the subjects and experimenters, which we know can cause effects of the type and size we commonly find from treatments, and so we cannot conclude that differences in outcomes must be due to the treatment. (Incidentally, a fully blind design has to be triple blind, not just double blind as in the best agricultural studies.)

So the intensive case study (and the same applies to good quasi-experimental designs [QEDs] and critical observations) is *not* essentially disadvantaged against the RCT; both leave open, in principle, other explanations of whatever effects are claimed.

Might it not still be argued that the RCT has an edge in only having this one loophole, whereas in the other designs, there are (at least typically) more possible counterexplanations? This is not as telling a point as it might appear, since the total probability of the alternative explanations is not additive based on the number of their descriptions; it is entirely situation dependent. There will be situations where the Hawthorne loophole is more threatening to the (so-called) RCT than the totality of the alternatives is to a case study or QED; this will be quite common in the case of the regression-discontinuity design, for example, but also will occur in many other cases. So the RCT edge, significant though it is when the design is truly double blind (although even then not a unique edge on validity), is entirely situation dependent in the normal context of social and educational inquiry. It will still be significant in special cases but nonexistent or negative in others.

The second problem with the quoted argument for the RCT's superiority is that causation can occur in the absence of support for a counterfactual, as it does in the quite-common cases of overdetermination. I have discussed these cases at some length elsewhere and will only remark that it is a significant, although not crucial, weakness of RCTs for the purposes of the present discussion that they will not have any advantage at all in such cases, whereas case studies (and some other approaches, e.g., those based on well-established theory) will have that advantage.

The bottom line here is that the advantage of RCTs is by no means general and must be established in the particular case, a nontrivial task. It remains true that there are cases, including important ones, where the RCT design will settle the issue of causation and no alternative approach will do so equally well.

However, the same is true for many other designs. The conclusion for researchers is simple: Each case needs to be highly specified, including not just the exact question we need answered and the degree to which we want to be able to generalize the answer but also the exact constraints on time, resources, social context, and background before one can decide on the optimal design for an investigation. That analysis is obviously not best done by those who specialize in RCTs alone; it must involve serious discussion by a panel including experts in alternative approaches of several if not all of the kinds listed earlier. As Cook (2001) stresses, relying on a single approach is a methodological error and a serious one, and relying on the wrong one simply compounds the felony. Using a panel that *favors* just one approach is a further felony in itself.

The Other Contenders

Every child acquires a repertoire of possible causes for a large number of effects before reaching school age; for example, children know that the vase on the table by the window can be knocked over by the wind, the shades, the cat, a sibling, a playmate, or a grown-up as well as themselves. When they encounter the effect, they begin to sift through that list and check for indicators, either immediately observable or quickly accessible, that will eliminate or support one or more candidates and eventually may identify the responsible cause. This is the basic case of hypothesis creation and verification, and it is the essential element, even if subliminally and non-inferentially, in all careful causal explanations.

There is a background assumption for this enterprise—the assumption that everything has a cause. The truth of that assumption in the macro domains of everyday experience and scientific investigations is unaffected by the discovery of micro uncertainty, not because the latter phenomenon cannot manifest itself at the macro level—indeed, it can—but because it has a sufficiently small incidence at that level to leave the deterministic principle unaffected as a methodological guide.

The two key components in the basic procedure outlined are the list of possible causes (LOPC), based (of course) on memories or other records of prior observations, and the GEM. Both become increasingly complex as the individual's experience and learning expand—for example, by the addition of theories about possible causes that are *extrapolations*, or extensions by analogy or speculation, from a human's direct experiences. Take, for example, the theory of tectonic plates that added to the list of possible causes for mountain ranges. No one saw those plates collide and raise the Rockies or the Urals, but we all can see what happens on a smaller scale, and once conceived, we add it to the LOPC and can readily project the kind of clues in the geologic record that would confirm this etiology, thus kicking in the GEM process that confirms the hypothesis.

When the hypothesis is about the formation of star clusters, we begin to move beyond models that are based on analogies with ordinary experience and instead create formal models that extrapolate from those based on analogies or even from models that seem to have worked in other areas beyond direct experience. So the piggybacking continues, stretched to its limits with string theory at the macro limit and boson-hadron models at the micro limit. In all of these realms, however, the concept of causation continues, usually unchanged by the changes in the forms to which it applies—except for quantum uncertainty, where it, too, must be modified significantly. And in all these areas, for all these kinds of causal claims, the same procedures of investigation apply—that is, the process of LOPC identification and then the application of GEM to whittle the list down in particular cases by looking for the presence or absence of distinguishing footprints of each possible cause. (I use the term *GEM* rather than *inference to the best explanation* because GEM is not limited to explanation hunting; it applies equally well to inference to the best classification in taxonomy or differential noncausal medical diagnosis; to inference to the best identification in pattern recognition and criminalistics; or, crucially, to inference to the best evaluation category via rubrics, etc.)

This vast web of theory-driven causation is essentially independent of any direct experimental confirmation, since it deals with entities that are largely beyond the range of manipulation. The large hadron collider at Geneva (a giant particle accelerator used by physicists to study the smallest known atomic particles), which was first fired up in 2008, is the culmination of the main exception to this segregation, the zone of experiments with fundamental particles. But even there, where the term *experiments* is always used, it does not refer to experiments with randomized controls but to those ruled by simple pre–post designs, entirely adequate in those circumstances to establish the conclusions to the satisfaction of the Nobel Prize committees. It is simply absurd to suggest that the conclusions arrived at in these circumstances do not deserve to be called *evidence-based* because there is no RCT in sight. To avoid tilting at windmills, it seems that we should modify the overgeneralized claims of the more enthusiastic supporters of RCT and allied terminology so as to retain a reasonable position to consider.

Instead of saying, as the head of the Institute for Educational Science once absurdly pronounced, that there is no scientific basis for any causal claim that is not based on RCT studies, we'll take that as meant to refer to the kind of quasi-blind RCTs used to investigate current issues about the effect of typical large-scale interventions in areas such as education, health, and social services. Correspondingly, we'll take the phrase *evidence-based conclusions*, which is often said to be justified only for the results of RCT studies, to be intended to apply to the kind of quasi-blind RCT studies that pass for the real thing in most experimental contexts.

The thrust of the arguments so far is, then, that these more-limited claims are nevertheless wrong, even if not absurd. That is, even the view that only quasi-RCTs can establish limited causal claims is wrong, since they can be perfectly well established beyond a reasonable doubt in other ways—and the limited RCTs aren't bulletproof themselves. Similarly, the view that the only legitimate evidence-based claims are those supported by quasi-RCT studies is wrong, since even limited evidence-based claims (that is, claims about typical current types of intervention in health, education, and social services) can be established by the even "weaker" quasi-experimental, observational, and theoretical studies. Finally, the claim that *experiment* means a design with random allocation to the two groups should also be modified to the formulation, "quasi-experiments are those in which subjects are carefully matched between the two groups."

This triple modification prevents what many have seen as an extremely tendentious, if unconscious, attempt to hijack an important slice of the scientific vocabulary.

Quasi-Experimental Designs (QEDs)

Let's walk through the consequences of the preceding arguments, using a common "lower-class" QED, the pre–post design with comparison groups. The argument given here would be much stronger with what is commonly thought of as a fancier or more robust design—for example, the interrupted time series design with bounded randomization of the intervals between applications. The example we'll use is of the highly interactive paradigm (HIP) for large introductory lectures at the college level, with enrollments in the low three-digit category. We divide the entering class in about half in some convenient but not random way, such as by taking the morning class as the treatment group in the first semester of the experiment and using the afternoon class for the second semester of the experiment (this is a one-semester class), with the aim of later repeating the experiment with the reverse arrangement. The experimental group receives the new treatment, and the others get the same approach that has been used for several years; the same instructor teaches both classes and teaches the control group just as he has for some years. That claim of approximate constancy in treatment is supported by an experienced colleague who visits a few times unannounced and by a TA who now works for both classes. Let's add that we have an experienced pair of instructional researchers independently look for other differences and find none to remark on. Each class gets the same pretest and posttest; they match closely on the pretest but on the posttest, where the control group shows about one sigma of improvement, the HIP group scores about two sigmas better than that. This effect recurs on the reiteration with reversal of the time slot for giving the experimental treatment.

Now, did HIP have any effect? Given that you know the important "local knowledge" fact that it's extremely hard to kick a one-sigma difference out of any variation in instructional method and that two sigmas is considerably more than twice as hard to get as one, the answer has to be yes, HIP made a big difference. Clearly the size of the difference is crucial here, as is often the case. Conclusion: There are situations where non-RCT designs will provide support for causal claims beyond a reasonable doubt. If you now reflect on exactly what it would take to convert this study into even a limited true RCT study and on the fact that you are not very interested in small differences because they have a track record of not showing up on the replications at distant sites, you should be willing to buy the conclusion that the pre–post comparison study design is better than the RCT here. (That is, you use it knowing that it's a net that will catch only big fish, but you don't want little fish.)

There are a dozen variations on this kind of case, ringing the changes on such matters as dealing with cases where you are only interested in generalizing to the native population in Uganda, but the native population won't give permission for putting their children into the control group; you can't afford the cost of measurement and monitoring for a control group of ex-addicted homeless people; or the memory effects of vitamin shots are small, so interrupted time series will work well.

The bottom line is that there are many cases where non-RCT designs will be better than RCT ones for the cases of interest, cases where the alternative designs will indeed achieve results beyond a reasonable doubt, and even more cases where they will be better than the quasi-RCT designs, the only ones we're really talking about. The limited strategy, which protects the RCT position from absurd overstatement, still cannot save it from being beaten on its own ground—that is, on ground where it can be used. Like a good two-wheel drive car, it can be driven in snow, but it's easily overmatched by the four-wheel drives in those conditions.

The fundamental logic of causal investigation—that is, the rules of inference required for establishing any causal conclusion—is not the use of experiments in the limited sense; it is the use of a critically developed list of possible causes and their *modus operandi* together with critically applied GEM, which is required even for the justification (although not the occurrence) of critical observation.

Funding Strategies

It is now time to turn from the logic of grading and ranking experimental designs to the distribution of resources among them. The first lesson to be learned about the logic of portfolio construction is that the best single investment—better than every alternative—is not the best bet for the whole portfolio budget. Investment managers know very well that the rule about not putting all one's eggs in one basket is not just valid for the medieval housewives who inspired the adage and their successors. Provided only that one's second and third choices still meet the minimum acceptable standards for good eggs, they are better choices than further investment in the top pick for at least half the portfolio.

In research funding, a much-better-than-minimum-acceptable standard is the ability to produce conclusions that are beyond a reasonable doubt, so even if RCTs were generally superior in their ability to yield such results across the board (which is itself a true counterfactual), it would be highly unscientific to back them across the board since they, like all other designs, can go wrong—badly and completely wrong—in a way that is usually not reversible even if detected and is not always detectable at midstream.

But in scientific research, there are two distinct further reasons for the heterogeneous strategy besides protection against failure. It may be helpful to think of the analogy with an investor who decides to put some money into the stock of companies who are working on a new oil field. She could put all her money into one company that has an excellent production hole that is currently the best on the field and is planning to drill more wells on that site. But she knows that a single site can peter out, hit an artesian aquifer that drowns the wells, or run into labor trouble; so for simple *safety* reasons—our first consideration—she will buy into at least one other outfit. She's covering herself against the possibility of failure. But there's another reason to do so: Wells that begin with a less-than-stellar rate of production sometimes hit another pocket below the first and do much better later. So there's a chance of doing better by approaching the formation from two directions, even if the second one is less productive at first. That's the possibility of *superiority* via backing an independent approach. And there's a third reason, too, probably enough reason to justify investment in a third wildcatter. This is the chance to get a better overall picture of the layout of the field, which will be invaluable in guiding further action or withdrawal. This third consideration, of course, corresponds to getting some information about *generalizability* (external validity). Safety, possible superiority, and generalizability—three reasons for avoiding the monolithic strategy. The analogy carries over completely to the issue of funding research, a point that Cook (2001) stresses.

This argument does not dismiss the possibility of doubling the investment in the best option; it just recommends not restricting all investment to it. Doubling in the research case would make especially good sense if combined with slight variations in the research personnel and population used. But it still comes further down the list than variations in the primary strategy. Somewhere in between these two major paths to enrichment of a single design approach, there is the use of the superbly ingenious list of ways to match the comparison group without using random allocation, a list developed and provided by Cook (2001).

The argument given makes an invincible case for the indefensibility of the present situation in which, according to the extensive testimony from members of the review panels that have talked about it, there is no serious consideration of using non-RCT designs instead of RCTs. That strategy is largely based on bad reasoning about the superiority of what are in fact flawed RCT designs, which even if peerless would be no better than many others and clearly worse in many cases. This bad reasoning is combined with the fallacy of assuming that such superiority, if it did exist, would justify a monolithic strategy.

The present ill-based practice is also too often combined with denial of the existence of the monolithic strategy, sometimes accompanied by a gesture in the direction of regression discontinuity funding. If there is any doubt that an essentially monolithic strategy is *de facto* in place, it would be easy enough to establish the facts by doing a survey of funding over the past two years, using a contractor with a team from both sides. It is certainly long past time for a meta-evaluation of the success of the new emphasis on RCT funding, and the absence of any movement toward doing that surely shows either incompetence or a serious lack of interest in finding out the truth about the claims for improvement before proceeding still further with the takeover, especially in the latest area where it has established a beachhead: the evaluation of international aid.

It is important that the reasons against the monolithic strategy apply even if, *per impossible*, the RCTs were superior across the board in the certainty with which they can determine causation. It is an argument designed to be acceptable to both camps.

Cooperation Combined With Competition

It would be unrealistic to suppose that the causal wars will cease in the light of the above treatment of the underlying differences between the competing positions. But it would be good to see some recognition of the very considerable range of cases where both parties can benefit from using the skills of the other. Cook (2001) lists many such cases, although not with quite the spin I'm putting on them, and I'll sum it up in my way by saying that it seems clear that the effective execution of RCT studies depends very heavily indeed on skills that are highly developed in qualitative researchers and extremely rare in the training of quantitative researchers. The converse position is also clear: There is still a considerable area in qualitative research where the skeptical reflexes of the trained quantitative researcher need to be heeded very carefully, not because their usual dismissive judgment is justified, but because by heeding their concerns, the design can be greatly improved, including its credibility to a wider audience—a worthwhile consideration in itself—and also (often enough) its validity. But let's take a final moment to look at the need for qualitative research skills in managing RCTs. We can begin with the two great threats to the validity of the (already limited) RCT design: differential attrition and cross-contamination. No one denies that some very expensive RCT efforts in the past have been completely destroyed by these weaknesses. If these flaws are detected very early, it is sometimes possible to stop them in their tracks, before validity is hopelessly compromised. How can an early warning system for them be set up?

The answer is almost always through a continual process of interviews (with groups and face-to-face) with students and staff and parents and administrators—a program that not only seeks by intelligent and systematic questioning to pick up the warning signs but also builds trust and cooperation in what is, after all, a project with potential benefits for all.

Interestingly, there is a double reward from this activity. It provides not only good insurance for the validity of the study but also vital evidence about the process whereby the causal agent—and any inhibitors of it—operate, which provides key clues to the possibility of generalizations in some dimensions and the improbability of generalizations in other directions and often strong supportive evidence for the causal connection under investigation. Cook (2001) gives a long list of the valuable information that can be picked up by these observers.

And who has the training for this kind of observation and interaction? Of course, it is a job description for a qualitative researcher. These are high-grade skills, not often taught as having top importance in quantitative training programs. Cook (2001) actually gives as his reason for abjuring the term *gold standard* for RCT designs the fact that these skills are of great importance, are hard to acquire, and are rarely available. The bottom line is that all RCTs are really hybrid designs—*mixed method* in the sense of having essential quantitative and qualitative components.

So I end on this note: A marriage of the warring parties is not only possible but would provide a win-win solution, with major winning side effects for those in need around the world. The prenuptial agreement should include (i) recognition of the place of duties for both parties along with (ii) funding for non-RCT studies where they are better fitted to task and context than RCTs and with skilled quantitative researchers collaborating to cover sharpening the design of and analyzing the numerical data, plus (iii) at least one collaborative meta-evaluation panel funding proposals from both parties and (iv) another one evaluating the success of contracts of both kinds. Serious concern with research standards (and human welfare) suggests that we should shortly see some proposals similar to this and/or signs that such proposals would be funded.

Conclusion: So What Counts as Credible Evidence?

Myths are grand stories, fictions that achieve cult status, and they spring up around all powerful structures, whether structures of knowledge or imagination or political or market entities. Some of the myths about science occasionally acquire enough of a cult following to materially alter policy, as, for example, the myth about the inheritance of acquired characteristics altered agricultural policy in the Soviet Union at one stage. The currently popular myths about causation and evidence have now achieved this kind of potentially dangerous cult status. Those who stand to suffer include those who have been served by giant philanthropic programs that are now being attacked as based on inadequate evidence of efficacy. This chapter attacks these myths, mainly by reminding readers of the implications of their general commonsense and general scientific knowledge.

People are usually led to believe myths by charismatic evangelists who have been misled by and promulgate some set of near-truths. In the present case, the evangelists are a group of distinguished scientists, many on the faculty of great universities, and they remind us that scientific excellence is highly compartmentalized. Not only do leading scientists often promulgate highly implausible political or religious doctrines but—as in this case—they can make mistakes of overgeneralization about science itself, thinking that excellent designs for demonstrating causation or providing evidence in their own sphere are definitive for the whole of science. We have often seen this when good physicists, for example, proclaim that the search for general laws expressed in exact quantitative terms is the key task of science and that the behavioral or educational sciences need to be reformed by rigorous efforts to find and report these. Similarly, good mathematicians reacted negatively to the suggestion that statistics should be admitted to the Parthenon of respectable mathematics. In the present case, good scientists have been entranced by the paragon of experimental design, the RCT, and illicitly generalized this into a required standard for all good causal investigation. It is suggested here that this view is completely refuted by a careful look at the way that astronomy, epidemiology, engineering, geology, field biology, and many other sciences establish causal conclusions to the highest standards of scientific (and legal) credibility.

The situation in this myth-busting episode is in fact worse, since the grounds for refutation are as follows: Causation is a key component of much of science (pure and applied) as well as other disciplines outside science (especially history and law). In everyday life, history, and law, causal claims on which lives depend are frequently established conclusively without any need for RCTs, sometimes (*contra* Hume) by direct observation.

So this chapter tracks the way in which we acquire causal concepts in infancy, in the law courts, in scientific field studies, and in the engineering lab, in order to support the counterclaim about the epistemological and common-sensical status of RCTs (i.e., the claim that they are usually not as defined, and even if they were—and certainly as they are—they are not uniquely superior).

The general position here is extended to suggest that (i) the attempted takeover of the terms *evidence* and *cause* is partly inspired by the false dichotomy between *experiment* and *quasi-experiment* and (ii) the whole effort is closely analogous to the attempted annexation of the concept of *significance* by *statistically significant*. While the motivation for both assaults was the highly commendable one of improving rigor in the applied social sciences, which was certainly needed, the way to do that is by increased care in picking the right tool for each job and using it properly, not by an oversimplification of the task. It is to be hoped that repelling this invasion, as well as the recovery from the attempt, takes less time and costs less in human terms as well as scientific terms than the earlier debacle.

Miscellaneous Notes

- For an example of observations that, mediated by a theory, demonstrated causation, think of the observations of the solar eclipse of 1919 that are generally thought to have shown that sunlight is refracted by gravity as predicted by the general theory of relativity.
- The eight methods for detecting causation are those based on (i) direct observation (e.g., visual, affective, tactile), (ii) reported observation (e.g., case studies), (iii) eliminative inference (e.g., autopsy, engineering breakdown), (iv) theoretical inference based on use of an analogy/theory (e.g., physics, geology, astronomy), (v) direct manipulation (e.g., in the kitchen and lab), (vi) "natural experiments" (e.g., meteorology, epidemiology), (vii) quasi-experimentation (e.g., medicine, pedagogy), and (viii) RCTs (e.g., pharmacology).

References

Cook, T. D. (2001). *A critical appraisal of the case against using experiments to assess school (or community) effects.* Retrieved March 31, 2014, from http://media.hoover .org/sites/default/files/documents/ednext20013unabridged_cook.pdf

Cook, T. D., & Campbell, D. T. (1979). *Quasi-experimentation.* Boston, MA: Houghton Mifflin.

Part III

Credible and Actionable Evidence: Perspectives From a Range of Evaluation Designs and Methods

Scientific experimentation in the form of the randomized controlled trial (RCT) is the focus of discussion in the chapters included in Part II. Henry and Bickman both implement RCTs and each discusses issues related to the why, how, when, and under what conditions RCTs are best used for producing objective, credible evidence for decision making. Scriven critiques the RCT as the gold standard for generating credible evidence in applied social research and evaluation and offers what he understands to be a viable alternative to the RCT for yielding objective evidence about the value of a program or policy.

In Part III of the book, the authors address methods other than RCTs and discuss their capacity for producing credible and actionable evidence. Each chapter author describes a particular method or general approach for studying applied problems. Each author considers the questions to be addressed by the study and then offers arguments for why and how the approach described generates systematic and credible information for use in applied settings.

In Chapter 7, Sharon Rallis notes the importance of matching methods to study questions and then argues that qualitative inquiry is ideal for addressing the *how* and *why* questions in evaluation and applied research. Qualitative inquiry involves the use of methods that capture language and behavior as they occur in naturalistic settings. Rallis maintains, "In short, while still adhering to technical rigor, probity, and transparency, my method allows the program participants to tell their own story" (p. 140). For Rallis, a value of the qualitative approach is that it allows the investigation of a social phenomenon to focus on understanding a problem in relation to its context, thereby being interpretative in nature. Unlike the chapters in Part II, which emphasize the relationship between objectivity and credibility, Rallis argues that credibility is dependent upon how evaluators interpret, analyze, and synthesize data into a rich and detailed story. She further contends that the use of this information is dependent upon how it is interpreted by and presented to audiences. She offers a case example of a two-part evaluation she conducted to illustrate how "as evaluators using qualitative tools, we pay special attention to clearly articulating and revealing the criteria we use to organize and analyze our data and to make judgments (interpretations) about the meaning and value of actions and perceptions" (p. 143).

In Chapter 8, Sandra Mathison uses Feyerabend's anarchist epistemology, which accepts all ideas as worthy of consideration as the underlying argument for discussing the use of images as a form of evidence in evaluation and applied research. Mathison defines image-based evidence as "any intrinsically visual data—such as photographs, video/film, drawings, cartoons, graphs and charts, typography, graphic art, graffiti, computer graphics, television, architecture, signs, clothing as well as what is seen in the mind's eye" (p. 162). She explains three ways in which images are used in evaluation: "(1) as data or evidence, (2) as an elicitation device to collect other data, and (3) as a representation of knowledge" (p. 162). Similar to Rallis, Mathison maintains, "The credibility of evidence and the knowledge it generates is contingent on experience, perception, and social conventions" (p. 157). She points to the significance of context and the ways in which context influences credibility. Specifically, she notes the importance of understanding the context in which evidence is produced and for "providing specific criteria for judging the credibility of evidence" (p. 158). Context is particularly salient in participatory evaluation approaches in which, Mathison notes, images are most likely to be used as evidence. This is because participatory approaches are concerned with ensuring that evidence is relevant to a variety of stakeholders, including program recipients. Consequently, notions of what constitutes evidence reflect the values of a wider group. With expanded ideas of what constitutes evidence, images are likely to be a valued form of evidence. Mathison offers illustrative examples of images as data and describes specific evaluation studies in which images have been used and, in particular, how they have been used as evidence.

Eleanor Chelimsky discusses evaluation synthesis as an approach for providing credible and actionable evidence in Chapter 9. In the first part of the chapter, Chelimsky explains how she came to develop the evaluation synthesis method while serving as director of an evaluation-focused unit at the Government Accountability Office (previously the General Accounting Office). She describes the political conditions and information needs of the U.S. Congress and the range of evaluation questions posed to the GAO, all in relationship to when, how, and why evidence is perceived as credible in policy decision making. Reflecting on her work, Chelimsky says, "In short, I had come to see credibility as threefold—involving the quality of the methodological evidence, the quality of the evaluative substance, and the quality of its presentation—and highly influential in the use of our work" (p. 184). This perspective led Chelimsky to develop a credible method that uses retrospective information to address a range of questions, including prospective questions. Synthesizing existing evaluation findings was intended to "dramatize, for legislative users, not only what was known but also what was *not* known in a particular problem area" (italics in original, p. 186). Chelimsky then goes on to describe how the method was experimentally developed in response to a request by the Chairman of the Subcommittee on Select Education, which was preparing for hearings on the Handicapped Act. The information produced in response to this request had great policy use, and so a formal process for developing the evaluation synthesis method was undertaken. Chelimsky explains the six-step process of evaluation synthesis in detail and offers three additional case examples of its use. She concludes by describing the challenges of implementing the method and thus the ways in which its credibility might be questioned as well as the ways information generated from synthesis studies were used in actionable ways.

7

When and How Qualitative Methods Provide Credible and Actionable Evidence

Reasoning With Rigor, Probity, and Transparency

Sharon F. Rallis

E valuation is applied research, so as evaluators, we want our evaluations to make a difference in policy or practice. To produce evidence that stakeholders trust enough to use, we reason through the many choices we make in designing and conducting studies. Our first decisions focus on which evaluation questions and which methods effectively yield data to inform those questions. Then, implementing the method requires numerous selections and ongoing decision making as we collect, analyze, and interpret data to turn them into findings. Finally, we choose how and to whom we report findings. Throughout the entire process, we attend to *rigor* (adherence to established standards for process), *probity* (wholeness, integrity, and moral soundness), and *transparency* (open and detailed documentation or display of all decisions and actions). If the methods we use match the purpose of the evaluation, if we

AUTHOR'S NOTE: I want to acknowledge and thank several people: Rachael Lawrence, my trusty graduate assistant, who was my right arm in conducting the PLBSS study and who provided valuable feedback on drafts of this chapter; Bethany Rallis, a clinical psychologist-in-training who expands my perspectives and forces me to clarify my arguments; and Gretchen Rossman, my colleague and friend, with whom I have explored and written about many of these ideas over the years.

employ these methods ethically with technical competence, and if our decisions and the underlying reasoning are apparent, the evaluation will meet our ultimate goal—to produce credible and actionable evidence. Therefore, we must choose our methods wisely.

Qualitative evaluation is a prudent choice when research questions aim to illuminate the program practices: the *how* and *why* of program implementation on intended effects. When the appropriate method is qualitative, the evaluator's decisions and corollary actions become especially important because the evaluator *is* the "instrument" (Guba & Lincoln, 1989, p. 175; Lincoln & Guba, 1985, p. 236; Patton, 2002, p. 14) or "means through which the study is conducted" (Rossman & Rallis, 2012, p. 5), and the participants are individual (or groups of individual) human beings, each with unique values, perceptions, and experiences. With qualitative methods, we collect data in natural settings, often through face-to-face encounters; thus the moral principles of *respect, beneficence,* and *justice** shape how we treat participants. Our procedures are emergent rather than prefigured. Our analyses and interpretations, while grounded in theories of action or conceptual frameworks, are openly subjective—that is, meanings are generated within perspectives and experiences of the context (see, for example, Blumer, 1969, pp. 78–89; Rallis & Rossman, 2012). Thus articulating our standards and revealing and explaining what we do and why is imperative. If we employ qualitative methods with rigor, ethical practices, and transparency, the evaluation illuminates program practices and effects, and stakeholders are highly likely to use the findings for program improvement, decision making, and informing policy.

In this chapter, I describe the reasoning behind the use of qualitative methods, demonstrating why and how these methods in an evaluation can produce credible and actionable evidence. When are qualitative tools appropriate for meeting the purpose of the evaluation and exploring the evaluation questions? How do qualitative data become information—and what technical rigor is involved? What composes ethical practice in data collection, analysis, and interpretation? I suggest that by addressing the *how* and *why* questions, qualitative methods have the potential to bridge the research-to-practice gap. I ground the reasoning in principles articulated in the National Research Council's *Scientific Research in Education* (Shavelson & Towne, 2002) and in moral principles underlying ethical practice.

---

*These are three basic principles, generally accepted in in Western traditional culture, that guide the ethics of research involving human subjects (National Commission for the Protection of Human Subjects of Biomedical and Behavioral Research, 1979).

Matching Method to Program Theory and Questions

Producing credible and actionable evidence begins with choosing the appropriate method—and this choice does not depend on a preference for a particular method (quantitative or qualitative) or on a belief that one method is considered more rigorous than another. Rather, the decision depends, either implicitly or explicitly, on purposes of the evaluation. We ask the following questions: What do stakeholders want to know about the program? What are the evaluation questions? The program's logic or theory of change generates a series of questions, and stakeholders—whether policy makers, program leaders, practitioners, or users—direct the evaluation toward the particular focus of interest. We choose methods with the tools to collect and analyze the data that will best inform those questions. Making explicit the program's theory of change is therefore critical to designing and conducting the evaluation.

Decision makers choose programs based on theories or arguments that suggest that the programmatic intervention will make a positive difference in the context. "Social programs are based on explicit or implicit theories about how and why the program will work" (Weiss, 1995, pp. 66–67): *If we implement X intervention, then Y outcomes will result.* The following figure illustrates the links between intention, action, and result in a theory of action.

Articulating the theory brings to the surface assumptions and causal inferences and allows evaluators to locate where the research questions fall. Are we interested in the connection between goals and outcomes (Boxes #1 and #3)—What happens as a result of the intervention? If so, we probably choose a method (such as an experiment) that allows causal inference. Do we want to know whether the program was implemented with fidelity? Or do we

Figure 7.1 Theory of Action

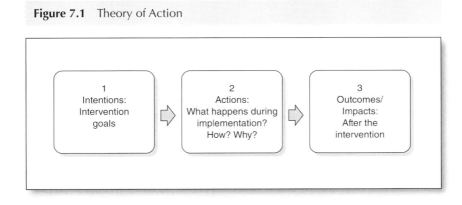

want to explore the complex interactions that take place within what is referred to as the *black box* (Box 2) as the goals become program activities? These latter questions, which fall into explanatory or exploratory contexts, demand descriptive answers that require descriptive statistics or qualitative methods. Given stakeholders and resources, we may choose to look at several questions.

Most evaluations I conduct focus on Box 2, exploring what happens during program implementation:

- What actions take place in the setting? How do people perform these actions? Why?
- What do these actions mean to the participants—both during and afterward?
- What are perceived effects of these actions?
- In what ways do the actions relate to each other and to external forces?
- Are these actions and meanings organized into any patterns that indicate norms for this setting?*

These questions demand descriptive data—data that tell a story—so I use qualitative tools with participants in the setting. I observe the program in operation; I listen to and read the words of program participants; I examine artifacts related to the program operation. Capturing these images, words, voices, objects, and ideas requires intensive interaction with the people and the program activities and materials in order to tell a story that participants can recognize and that sheds light on the program operation and connections. Such descriptions honor the idiosyncratic and contextual nature of participants' experiences in the program and allow complex and dynamic interpretations of those experiences. I borrow tools from ethnography to understand interactions and relationships, from phenomenology to understand perspectives and perceptions about the lived experience, and from sociolinguistics/semiotics to understand how people communicate their meanings for activities, events, objects, and people (see Rallis & Rossman, 2012, for discussion of these genres). I also draw on the program's theory or logic to make sense of what people say and do, I document and display my decisions, and (to the best of my ability) I treat participants with respect and fairness while addressing their needs and concerns. I aim to achieve wholeness, integrity, and moral soundness. In short, while still adhering to technical rigor, probity, and transparency, my method allows the program participants to tell their own story.

For example, in a two-part evaluation we conducted (in 2011 and 2013) of the Professional Learning-Based Salary System (PLBSS), a professional

---

*These questions are loosely adapted from the work of Erickson (1986).

development initiative implemented in the Portland (Maine) Public Schools, the theory of action read as follows:

> If teachers are compensated on the basis of their professional learning, their salaries will increase and they will become agents of their own learning. They will build skills and knowledge, both individually and collaboratively, to improve their instructional practices and a broader culture of learning in the schools. These improvements will result in increased student learning. (Rallis, Churchill, & Lawrence, 2011)

Each conditional action represents a cause and intended effect, so to design the evaluation, we worked with two primary stakeholder groups (the district leadership and the teachers' union) to specify the focus and generate evaluation questions.

The first questions fell into Boxes 1 and 4: Did teachers participate and did their salaries rise? Did student scores increase? An initial study answered these questions with surveys and analyses of district records. Since the program was operationalized during the 2007–2008 school year, participation (and satisfaction) levels in PLBSS were high, salaries rose, and student scores improved. However, since district and union leaders agreed that conducting controlled experiments were impractical, they acknowledged that the achievement increases might not be directly attributed to the professional development intervention—but they still wanted to know how the intervention might be related to the student outcomes. Essentially, they wanted the evaluation to look into Boxes 2 and 3 to explore any causal relationships among teacher learning, classroom instruction, student learning, and school change.

Figure 7.2   PLBSS Theory of Change

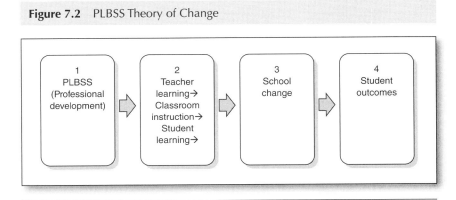

SOURCE: Rallis, Keller, Lawrence, & Soto, 2013

District and union leaders therefore directed their questions toward teacher and student actions related to the professional development activities. Did participation in these activities build skills and knowledge, both individually and collaboratively? Did teachers use their learned skills in their instructional practices? Did student work change relative to instruction? In what ways did teachers work together in the schools? Did the school culture change—and if so, in what ways? We needed evidence of teacher learning, use of that learning, and its affect on student work. Quantifying or measuring teacher learning or use of learning was not possible, given the varying purposes and formats, number, and potential uses of professional development opportunities, so at this point, we chose qualitative tools: observations in schools and classrooms, interviews, reviews of professional development curriculum and teacher lesson plans, and analyses of student work. Put simply, what did both teachers and students *experience* and then *do* with their experience in their instruction and classroom work? In this case, our evaluation design sought to illuminate the black boxes between the intervention and the impact on student scores, thus directing us to qualitative methods.

While this example comes from the education field, my assertions can be generalized to other practical fields that serve social needs, because evaluation is an applied science. For example, current discussion among clinical psychologists considers the need to recognize individual differences in both patients and clinicians in the development of best practices and that naturalistic methods help bridge the chasm between research and practice, as these methods answer questions that quantitative methods cannot (Beutler, 2009; Reed, Kihlstrom, & Messer, 2006).

From Data to Use: Clear Criteria and Thick Description

When using designs that match method with program logic and evaluation questions, evaluators collect and combine *data* (images, words, numbers, impressions) into *information*; if policy makers or program participants use that information, it becomes *knowledge*. Since use may take several and varied forms and since evaluators seldom have full control over how the evaluation information will be used, we seek to provide evidence that can inform the evaluation questions and possible decisions or actions. The relationships among data, information, and knowledge, while not completely linear, might best be illustrated as follows (Rallis & Rossman, 2012, p. 10):

Data (analyzed and synthesized) become → *Information* (interpreted and used) becomes → *Knowledge*

When using qualitative methods, evaluators collect data as words and images and artifacts to capture participants' actions or reports of actions and their perspectives of the experienced actions. Through analysis, we combine these data to build *thick descriptions* that make interpretation possible, suggesting intentions, causal connections, and patterns of behavior (see Geertz, 1973). The descriptions are so detailed that readers (potential users of the evaluation) can see what the evaluator sees. Often best portrayed in narrative form, the combined images and words tell a story that constructs understandings of and generates insights into program operations and effects. The narratives are not intended to be generalizable; they are detailed descriptions of one program or setting. However, they allow potential users to judge the value of the findings and decide which aspects might apply to similar settings and in what ways—and thus potentially suggest future actions.

Credibility depends on how we as evaluators combine those data, how we analyze and synthesize pieces of data into information. *Actionability*—that is, *use*—lies in how the information is interpreted and then presented to audiences. Stakeholders use findings, depending on whether they understand and accept how we have created and told the story, that is, how we made meaning of the words and images. If they can see how and where the data were collected and how conclusions grew out of these data, they become interested in and engage with the findings. As evaluators using qualitative tools, we pay special attention to clearly articulating and revealing the criteria we use to organize and analyze our data and to make judgments (interpretations) about the meaning and value of actions and perceptions.

Whatever the method, technically rigorous analysis and interpretation of these actions—or perceptions of these actions—rely on identified criteria, the underpinnings of an analytic framework. Evaluation is the "systematic assessment of the operation and/or outcomes of a program, compared to a **set of explicit or implicit standards** [bold added for emphasis], as a means of contributing to the improvement of that program or service" (Weiss, 1998, p. 4). Because not all stakeholders are likely to share the same set of beliefs, values, goals, and definitions, we use the program logic to reach agreement on criteria for assigning meaning to data. The standards or criteria emerge from the program logic and serve to bound the selection, analyses, and interpretation of data: What exactly is the intervention intended to do to yield which specific results? How will we know if the intervention happens as intended? How do we judge effects?

In choosing the focus of the evaluation questions and articulating criteria, stakeholders and evaluators emphasize what they consider important, thus making explicit their subjectivity. The criteria serve to guide analysis: What categories of action can we expect? How will we know if or what actions occur? What characteristics describe or define expected quality/success? We specify indicators and details that enable us to recognize these indicators in the images, words, or pictures we collect. Deductively using the program logic, we provide detailed descriptions and identify patterns. We compare what we see, hear, and read to the defined criteria. Identifying expected operations and outcomes also facilitates inductive analysis; the unexpected is highlighted, and we consider how these unexpected actions relate to the program goals and implementation. Throughout the process, we reason through choices and make decisions, embedding our evaluative thinking in program theory and criteria.

To illustrate how criteria are developed and used to support analysis and interpretation, we refer to our evaluation of the PLBSS, in which several levels of criteria emerged. The levels and criteria were articulated together with program and district personnel, beginning with descriptions of the categories of offerings (traditional university courses; district-created, including teacher-led, courses; and individual projects): What counts as an activity in each category to receive salary credit? Criteria included required structure (e.g., length, meeting time, materials) and content. Content had to address either district priorities (technology, English language learners [ELLs], early childhood needs, adolescent literacy, poverty) or instructional needs (literacy and language acquisition, math, cultural competency). Finally, to connect local criteria to national criteria, we cross-referenced content, structure, and process to the *Standards for Professional Learning,* a set of standards and indicators developed collaboratively and adopted by various professional educational associations (Learning Forward, 2011). These criteria provided categories for organizing and coding our data. The images, words, actions, or artifacts did not need to fit the categories; rather, the criteria allowed us to agree on meanings and to build a convincing narrative about what was happening in professional development activities, among teachers, and in classrooms and schools.

We analyzed the data collected in response to the following questions:

- What choices did teachers make among professional development offerings?
- What did the teachers learn in their professional development choices?
- How do teachers use these learnings in their classroom instruction?
- What student performance examples in classrooms illustrate use of or response to instruction related to specific professional development of the teacher (e.g., how student writers develop their characters)?

We asked how teachers' choices met instructional needs or district needs. We sought descriptions of the activity, its format, and its content. We captured stories in which teachers described what they learned and how they used these strategies in their classroom instruction. We spent time in their classes observing instruction and students working. We looked at lesson plans. The stories were enhanced by collecting evidence that illustrated students' performance in response to specific instruction related to their teacher's professional development.

In one school, for example, the data told the story of a turnaround that was shaped largely by teachers' participation in professional development that changed the way they worked with each other and with children in their classrooms. With a majority population of ELLs, the school was identified as failing; the district chose to use a school improvement grant to develop teachers' skills for teaching reading and writing to ELLs through job-embedded language and literacy acquisition workshops that met during the school day with push-in literacy coaching. We heard, "We did not choose [to participate]—at first, we hated it. You cannot teach these kids." Soon, teachers began to say, "I need to learn how to teach these children" and "I'm learning strategies I can use in my classroom." Their words described how planning and instruction of reading and writing concepts and skills became coherent across years and grades by using common calendars and consistent writing prompts and sentence frames, which changed developmentally from grade to grade. Teachers showed us student work (displayed throughout the school) that represented evidence of activities related to the workshop curriculum; for example, at every grade level, we saw student essays on how writers develop characters. We documented, often with pictures, teachers working together, moving between classrooms with ease and relating to students in any classroom. Their words added credibility to our findings:

- I find that when taking a class or course together with other teachers from the same school or district, discussions often develop about what we learned. It's constructive adult talk with peers.
- It's not just that we like each other; it is about the work. The learning and sharing continues.
- We use more common language, more common strategies . . . [and understand] what other teachers at different levels need you to do at your level. And I know what to expect from the children before they come to my class.
- Again, all of this, I never could have done any of this if I hadn't spent those lousy credit hours, and the payback is really good . . . for the kids. I have been teaching for quite a few years, but I needed to enhance my ability to teach ELLs. . . . [I]t's been a wonderful experience for me because our school has grown in diversity immensely over the last few years and will continue to do so, and I feel it's important for me. . . . You really learn how to teach—much more so than the college courses that certify you as [an] ELL [teacher].
- The [workshops] changed the content and focus of independent reading. I built an extensive classroom library, created a blog for students to discuss their independent reading, [and] revised the focus of the writing prompts related to reading, and as a result, increased my students' interest in and practices around independent reading. These practices, I believe, transfer to more in-depth and comprehensible reading in all content areas.
- Triangulating the assessment data on my ELL . . . offers evidence of success that I can credit to some degree to the specific emphasis I have placed on the workshops—differentiation, tiered instruction, and language frames. Building

background knowledge has enhanced my work around curriculum mapping, which in turn has generated clearer learning targets for students who, for their part, have demonstrated stronger work products [writing pieces] over time.

- When you walk around our school, you see the evidence and volume of student writing, and you see students in primary grades writing nonfiction reports, which is such a keystone of the common core [standards]. It's amazing, when you walk the school [to see all of their work].

- Really, what is it students need to do to comprehend the text at a higher level of thinking, critical thinking[?] . . . I actually learned what moves a kid from a level . . . to the next band of reading that you come to, what kinds of things do I need to teach them—to move a student to the next level. . . . An example is being able to have them give evidence, like a character trait, that they know who a character is. Humor, as well, what is the evidence that shows it . . . or what is the author [saying]. . . . [I]f he isn't coming right out and saying it, can the student infer what the author was implying?

Analyzed and synthesized using the criteria, these images and words become the rich and detailed story we offered as evidence of what happened with the PLBSS. When we presented the findings, leaders and practitioners recognized the story and engaged with questions, additions, critiques, and comments such as: "That's a lot to think about."

From Data to Use: Trust, Transparency, and Everyday Ethical Practices

The relationship we built with the district and program leadership as well as with the teachers and other participants contributes to the credibility and usability of the stories offered as evidence. Turning qualitative data into findings that illuminate practices and linkages between intents and outcomes requires evaluators to interact with other human beings—namely, the participants (policy makers, funders, planners, and practitioners at various levels). As evaluators using qualitative methods, we enter the program world; we both shape and are shaped by the actions and interactions. We are satisfied that program logic, criteria, and thick description have kept our interpretations bounded and relevant. Still, why should the stakeholders and potential users trust that interpretations and findings bear any relationship to reality and have any potential for use? The answer is this: Transparency and ethical practices are imperative. Can our audiences see and understand how we reached these conclusions? Is the chain of reasoning evident and coherent and grounded in moral principles? Are the relationships continually assessed as respectful, beneficial, and just?

Transparency and ethical practices are important at all stages of the evaluation. As the evaluation begins, participants must know what evaluators will be doing and why; they must trust that the evaluator's actions will be respectful and not bring harm and that the motivation to evaluate this program is fair. At the end, whether they are practitioners or policy makers, potential users want to trust the integrity and social value of the evaluation; as Phillips (2007) argued,

> [a] policymaker no doubt will consult the empirical data, but rightly will be swayed by ethical premises and by notions of what constitutes a good and caring society, and by his or her conceptions of the rights that all individuals possess. (p. 383)

Ultimately, according to Weiss (1998), the purpose of evaluation *is* ethical. Evaluators are not judges; rather, "with the information and insight that evaluation brings, organizations and societies will be better able to improve policy and programming for the **well-being of all** [bold added for emphasis]" (p. ix).

Grounding evaluation in ethical purposes and relationships adds a moral dimension to the evaluator's reasoning: What moral principles guide my decisions and interactions with stakeholders? "The point of moral principles is to regulate interactions among human beings" (Strike, Haller, & Soltis, 1998, p. 41). Again, the relational aspect is especially present when using qualitative methods, which rely on human interactions. While human subject reviews have emphasized procedure over relationships in real settings, the principles can provide guidance for ongoing moral reasoning. The *principle of respect for human persons* implies a moral obligation to honor participants' rights and to treat them as an end in themselves, not as mere means to an end. The *principle of beneficence* is a moral obligation to act to benefit others and protect them from risk, recognizing that an evaluator cannot know what is best for participants; it does not imply a balance of benefits and risks. Finally, the *principle of justice* ensures that both selection and receipt of benefit should be equitable and that procedures are nonexploitative. Only through a morally reasoned relationship between the evaluator and the participants can the dimensions, parameters, and expectations of these principles be ethically defined, negotiated, and shared (see, for example, Hemmings, 2006; Rallis, 2010; Rallis, Rossman, & Gajda, (2007; and Rossman & Rallis, 2010, for further discussion of ethical practice and moral principles).

Ongoing ethical dialogue about standards for conduct necessarily occurs because not everyone agrees upon or acts on a common ethic. In fact, ethical theories can be grouped into two broad categories that may conflict. One set of moral principles form consequentialist theories that focus on results of actions: Any particular action is neither intrinsically good nor bad; rather, it is good or bad because of its results in a particular context—its consequences. If the end has value, the means are less important. Such a view argues for programs that result in the greatest good for the greatest number. Nonconsequentialist ethical theories, on the other hand, advocate ethics of individual rights and responsibilities and of justice. These ethics recognize universal standards or rights to guide all behavior, regardless of the consequences in a specific context. The protection of these rights may not be denied, even for the greatest good for the greatest number. Principles of fairness and equity are used to judge whether program purposes and actions are right and wrong, seeking to ensure the well-being of all, even though the allocation of benefit may differ (Rawls, 1971).

Evaluators' reasoning moves from abstract principles to concrete circumstances of the evaluation, asking where the evaluation questions and criteria actually focus: on the consequences, on the outcomes, or on the rights and treatment of participants as the intervention is implemented? *Communitarianism* ethics (MacIntyre, 1981) acknowledge that communities differ on what is morally good or right, and evaluators know that stakeholders often hold different fundamental values. Those values may even conflict with the evaluator's own values. Which values define the evaluation questions, guide the decisions, and shape interpretations? Nonconsequentialist theories of justice and individual rights raise questions of power and representation: Who defines what is right in this program? Whose values are used in rating or in choosing criteria? Are all voices given opportunity to be heard? Different stakeholders in a given situation might call for an evaluator to draw on more than one moral principle or from various ethical perspectives. For example, influential stakeholders or clients might demand consideration of outcomes over process in the program while program recipients would be concerned with potential benefits, costs, or harm.

Addressing ethical issues is not a single event nor is it facilitated by any codified procedure. Rather, ethical reasoning consists of ongoing decisions made throughout the evaluation in *caring* interactions with those affected by the decisions at the moment. Instead of turning to a principle for guidance, the caring evaluator returns to the participants: What do they need in this place at this time? Will filling this need harm others in the network of care? Am I, as evaluator, competent to fill this need? Is the expressed need really in the best interest of the participant? (Noddings, 1995, p. 187). *Care theory* emphasizes the moral interdependence of people: "As [evaluators], we are as dependent on our [participants] as they are on us" (Noddings 1995, p. 196). Reciprocity in mutual care and respect bridges the gap between purposes and needs of the evaluator and the evaluated.

As caring evaluators, we respect the connections among the participants, the program, and ourselves. We want to understand the interactions and the relationships themselves, the interdependencies: How does one person's meaning making interact with and influence another's? A *caring ethic* expects the relationship to be dynamic, symmetrical, and connective; we give respect, and we are respected (Lawrence-Lightfoot, 2000). At the same time, as we honor the participants, we work to create conditions that allow them to respect our efforts to discover and understand their experience.

In the end, the task of reasoning out the ethic to apply in each case falls to the evaluator. Again, I illustrate our ethical reasoning as we conducted the PLBSS evaluation, framing our decisions with the three principles commonly used to guide human subjects research. First, we discussed with everyone we encountered, whatever the relationship to the program or evaluation, the purposes and expected procedures of the study—and to the best of our ability, we made sure these were understood; thus we gained informed consent.

RESPECT

To honor participants' individuality and rights, each interview was a unique conversation. We considered our participants to be capable professionals and treated them as such, engaging in dialogue about their motivations and experiences. Because the policy to change salary allocation to teachers had several motivations—including the need to increase salaries in order to retain quality teachers, the desire to give more autonomy to teachers by allowing them to choose their own professional development, and the belief that increased teacher learning would increase student learning—we explored the reasons behind each personal or group decision and ensured that each was included in the program logic and in the criteria for analysis and interpretation. We were open to concerns about process and content and considered collaboratively which interview and observation strategies would be least intrusive and would respect each participant's right to privacy. We aimed to build mutual relationships that facilitated authentic dialogue about their choices and their use—or nonuse—of professional development. In fact, because we were genuinely interested in what they were doing, teachers and school leaders readily shared their experiences, ideas, and critiques. The conversations (interviews) often lasted longer than scheduled and led to participants' willingness to let us use direct and identifiable quotes.

BENEFICENCE

Given that we could not intuit what different stakeholders would consider benefits or burdens of the evaluation, we sought collaboration in the design: What theory of change guided the program and participation? What might they want to learn from the study? How might they use the information? Then, together, we explored data sources: Which schools would offer the most informative data—and would not suffer from the intrusion of the evaluators for interviews and observations? When might be best times to collect data? What might be best ways to deliver the findings—and to whom? Similarly, to articulate criteria, we discussed their expectations and how they might define quality or success. Regarding interviews and observations, we noted that any promises for complete confidentiality and anonymity would be false and promised that were we to use a direct quote, we would check with the speaker first. We tried to consider each case individually to meet the needs of each person in that instance. For example, when a person who held a singular role such as coach or principal did not want their words identified, we discussed and reached agreement in how to meet mutual needs, such as disguising the role. These agreements were open to ongoing negotiations and revisions when needed. For example, as the study progressed, more people wanted to own their words and waived anonymity. In short, we were guided by the question, What is right for her, him, or them?

JUSTICE

Our efforts to ensure fairness focused on site selection, data collection strategies, and the analysis-interpretation stage. We reasoned through site selection and strategies to be sure that no group was either exploited or received special reward. Satisfied that no special interests or private agenda was in play, we agreed to select schools that were facing specific and publically acknowledged challenges: one that had been labeled by the U.S. Department of Education as a school requiring corrective action and one whose student population demographic had drastically changed in the past two years. While analyzing and interpreting data, we explicitly considered the following questions: Whose data are these? What voices may be missing? What alternative interpretations are likely? What influence might power relationships play in meaning making? For example, we encouraged meetings that brought together potentially conflicting stakeholders (e.g., administration and union leaders). Also, we were vigilant about speaking to a range of teachers with varying needs, noting (for example) a comment questioning the system's equity of opportunity: "For teachers who coach, have young families, or actually correct student papers, there is not enough time in life to complete the hours of [professional development] and the paperwork to advance [salary]" (personal communication [interview], April 9, 2013).

The PLBSS evaluation met our standards for rigor, probity, and transparency as well as the standards of the district leaders, union personnel, and teachers. But would it pass muster with a larger and external audience?

Applying Standards for Scientific Inquiry

Ultimately, the users—both intended and accidental—of the evaluation hold the key to its credibility and actionability. Those who believe the evaluation has value will use it in some way commensurate to the perceived value. Still, what is considered science and the scientific community influence credibility and actionability by legitimizing particular forms or methods of research with its promulgated definition of standards for scientific inquiry. Even groups within the scientific community disagree. In 2004, the U.S. Department of Education in the No Child Left Behind Act labeled randomized controlled trials (RCT) as the gold standard for evaluation, but other groups argue for broader under-standings of science. As a science educator who reviewed the Rossman and Rallis (2003) qualitative methods manuscript wrote, "There is more art in sci-ence than you recognize." Watson (1968) describes in *The Double Helix* how the discovery of the structure of DNA required rigorous reasoning, but it also involved creativity, politics, mystery, and love. "Science seldom proceeds in the straightforward logical manner imagined by outsiders. Instead, its steps for-ward (and sometimes backwards) are very often very human events in which personalities and cultural traditions play major roles" (p. ix). Kuhn (1970) reminds us that we accept something as truth until the scientific community accumulates enough evidence that another truth exists and iteratively until more evidence is uncovered to alter this truth.

The point is that scientific knowledge is a social construct, so credible and actionable evidence becomes what the relevant communities of discourse and practice accept as valid, reliable, or trustworthy. Judgments about the quality of inquiry represent "the social construction of knowledge. . . . [T]he key issue becomes whether the relevant community of scientists evaluates reported findings as sufficiently trustworthy to rely on them for their own work" (Mishler, 2000, p. 120). A relevant community to inform evaluators' understandings of legitimate scientific inquiry might be the National Research Council, whose Committee on Scientific Principles for Education Research defined *scientific inquiry* as

> [a] continual process of rigorous reasoning supported by a dynamic interplay among methods, theories, and findings. . . . Advances in scien-tific knowledge are achieved by the self-regulating norms of the scientific community over time, not, as sometimes believed, by the mechanistic application of a particular method to a static set of questions. (Shavelson & Towne, 2002, p. 2)

The committee members declare what scientific inquiry is *not* (static or mechanistic) while recognizing the role of discourse. Science requires the dis-play of findings, along with the reasoning that led to those findings, for others in the community to contest, modify, accept, or reject. Their discourse con-cludes that scientific research studies do the following:

- pose *significant questions* that can be investigated empirically
- link research to *relevant theory*
- use methods that permit *direct investigation* of the questions

- provide a coherent and explicit *chain of reasoning*
- replicate and *generalize* across studies
- disclose research to encourage *professional scrutiny and critique*

In short, the National Research Council implies that scientific research involves human judgment—reasoning—so applying these principles to the use of qualitative methods for evaluation seems appropriate for judging the legitimacy of the method. The PLBSS evaluation offers a tangible case from practice to apply the following principles:

1. Collaboratively chosen, the evaluation posed observable, practical, realistic (all terms used to define *empirical*) questions deemed significant among district leaders, union personnel, teachers, and ourselves (the evaluators).

2. We articulated a strong program theory from which evaluation questions, design, and criteria emerged. As well, we reviewed literature on professional development as grounding for developing the program theory of change with participants.

3. To investigate the questions directly, we conducted real-time on-site observations and interviews and personally reviewed program materials.

4. To ensure that our chain of reasoning was both coherent and explicit, we included program stakeholders in decision making, transparently discussed our methods, revealed data and analyses behind interpretations, and sought feedback and alternative perspectives.

5. While findings apply directly only to the sites studied, we have shared the story of PLBSS with national audiences (with express permission from the program participants); feedback indicates that the insights offer deep understanding of activities that can apply to other turnaround schools in districts elsewhere.

6. Finally, we presented the findings in various forums in the district, the community, and the nation. In these discussions, the study and findings were scrutinized and critiqued. And, as academics, we are writing about the process and findings for publication, thus further disclosing our information to encourage professional scrutiny and critique.

Applying the National Research Council principles is itself an exercise of reasoning with rigor, probity, and transparency. However, missing from the list of principles is a criterion I view as critical to determining the value of evaluation as an applied science: *use.* Therefore, final essential questions I ask of my evaluations include the following: Does the evidence inform the program operation to improve the well-being of participants? In what ways do the findings bridge the gap between theory and practice? We believe that the PLBSS study used question-driven methods that produced a credible story to which audiences responded and that illuminated the initiative, informing both policy and practice improvements for sustainability and even transferability—that is, action.

Question-Driven Inquiry: Matching Method to Purpose

In designing a study, evaluators first determine the program theory of action (*program/intervention X will produce Y results*) and locate the focus of the evaluation within that logic. When the evaluation questions seek to measure results, quantitative methods are employed. When the evaluation questions what happens between the X and Y of the program theory—that is, the activities, events, experiences, and perceptions related to program implementation and operation—qualitative methods can access the data that build exploratory or explanatory descriptions that tell the story of the program. Both methods require reasoning with rigor, probity, and transparency to produce credible and actionable evidence. Methods are chosen to match evaluation purposes, not for the method's status in the research world or on evaluators' preferences or expertise. The method appropriate to the evaluation question can yield data to build information that decision makers may use for program improvement. In summary, evaluation is a question-driven inquiry process.

References

Beutler, L. E. (2009, September). Making science matter in clinical practice: Redefining psychotherapy. *Clinical Psychology: Science and Practice, 16*(3), 301–317.

Blumer, H. (1969). *Symbolic interaction*. Englewood Cliffs, NJ: Houghton Mifflin.

Erickson, F. (1986). Qualitative methods in research on teaching. In M. C. Witrock (Ed.), *Handbook of research on teaching* (3rd ed.). New York, NY: MacMillan.

Geertz, C. (1973). *The interpretation of cultures*. New York, NY: Basic Books.

Guba, E. G., & Lincoln, Y. S. (1989). *Fourth generation evaluation*. Newbury Park, CA: SAGE.

Hemmings, A. (2006). Great ethical divides: Bridging the gap between institutional review boards and researchers. *Educational Researcher, 35*(4), 12–18.

Kuhn, T. (1970). *The structure of scientific revolutions* (2nd ed.). Chicago, IL: University of Chicago Press.

Lawrence-Lightfoot, S. (2000). *Respect*. Cambridge, MA: Perseus Books.

Learning Forward. (2011). *Standards for professional learning*. Retrieved July 7, 2013, from http://learningforward.org/standards

Lincoln, Y. S., & Guba, E. G. (1985). *Naturalistic inquiry*. Newbury Park, CA: SAGE.

MacIntyre, A. (1981). *After virtue*. Notre Dame, IN: University of Notre Dame Press.

Mishler, E. G. (2000). Validation in inquiry-guided research: The role of exemplars in narrative studies. In B. M. Brizuela, J. P. Stewart, R. G. Carillo, & J. G. Berger (Eds.), *Acts of inquiry in qualitative research* (pp. 119–145). Cambridge, MA: Harvard Educational Review.

National Commission for the Protection of Human Subjects of Biomedical and Behavioral Research. (1979, April 18). *The Belmont Report. Ethical Principles and Guidelines for the Protection of Human Subjects of Research.* Washington, DC: Office of the Secretary Ethical Principles and Guidelines for the Protection of Human Subjects of Research.

Noddings, N. (1995). *Philosophy of education.* Boulder, CO: Westview.

Patton, M. Q. (2002). *Qualitative research & evaluation method* (3rd ed.). Thousand Oaks, CA: SAGE.

Phillips, D. C. (2007). Adding complexity: Philosophical perspectives on the relationship between evidence and policy. In P. A. Moss (Ed.), *Evidence and decision making: The 106th Yearbook for the National Society for the Study of Education* (pp. 376–402). Malden, MA: Blackwell.

Rallis, S. F. (2010, July–August). "That is NOT what's happening at Horizon!": Ethics and misrepresenting knowledge in text. *International Journal of Qualitative Studies in Education, 23*(4), 435–448.

Rallis, S. F., Churchill, A., & Lawrence, R. B. (2011). *Supporting professional learning: Impacts of the PLBSS in Portland Public Schools.* Amherst, MA: Center for Education Policy.

Rallis, S. F., Keller, L., Lawrence, R., & Soto, A. (2013). *Revisiting PLBSS.* Amherst, MA: Unpublished report.

Rallis, S. F., & Rossman, G. B. (2012). *The research journey: Introduction to inquiry.* New York, NY: Guilford Press.

Rallis, S. F., Rossman, G. B., & Gajda, R. (2007). Trustworthiness in evaluation practice: An emphasis on the relational. *Evaluation and Program Planning, 30,* 404–409.

Rawls, J. (1971). *A theory of justice.* Cambridge, MA: Harvard University Press.

Reed, G. M., Kihlstrom, J. F., & Messer, S. B. (2006). What qualifies as evidence of effective practice? In J. C Norcross, L. E. Beutler, & R. F. Levant (Eds.), *Evidence-based practices in mental health: Debate and dialogue on the fundamental questions* (pp. 13–55). Washington, DC: American Psychological Association.

Rossman, G. B., & Rallis, S. F. (2003). *Learning in the field: An introduction to qualitative research* (2nd ed.). Thousand Oaks, CA: SAGE.

Rossman, G. B., & Rallis, S. F. (2010). Everyday ethics: Reflections on practice. *International Journal of Qualitative Studies in Education, 23*(4), 379–391.

Rossman, G. B., & Rallis, S. F. (2012). *Learning in the field: An introduction to qualitative research* (3rd ed.). Thousand Oaks, CA: SAGE.

Shavelson, R., & Towne, L. (Eds.). (2002). *Scientific research in education.* Washington, DC: Committee on Scientific Principles for Education Research, National Research Council.

Strike, K., Haller, E., & Soltis, J. (1998). *The ethics of school administration.* New York, NY: Teachers College Press.

Watson, J. D. (1968). *The double helix: A personal account of the discovery of the structure of DNA*. New York, NY: New American Library.

Weiss, C. H. (1995). Nothing as practical as good theory: Exploring theory-based evaluation for comprehensive community initiatives for children and families. In J. P. Connell, A. C. Kublsh, L. B. Schorr, & C. H. Weiss (Eds.), *Approaches to evaluating community initiatives* (pp. 65–92). New York, NY: Aspen Institute for Humanistic Studies.

Weiss, C. H. (1998). *Evaluation: Methods for studying programs and policies* (2nd ed.). Upper Saddle River, NJ: Prentice Hall.

8

Seeing Is Believing

Using Images as Evidence in Evaluation

Sandra Mathison

As for a picture, if it isn't worth a thousand words, to hell with it.

Ad Rheinhardt, minimalist American painter

I mages are evidence; this chapter explores the credibility and usefulness of images as evidence in evaluation. While there are unique features of images, their credibility exists within a larger framework for establishing facts and values. The credibility of evidence and the knowledge it generates is contingent on experience, perception, and social conventions. As such, knowledge changes over time (consider that Pluto once existed as a planet, and now it doesn't) and can and should be arrived at through many means, eschewing the dominance of any one method or data type. Embracing Feyerabend's (1975) anarchist epistemology, the notion that every idea or strategy however new or old or absurd is worthy of consideration, we can expand the possibilities for knowing the social world. Credible evidence is not the province of certain methods (such as observations or experiments) and cannot be expressed only one way (such as statistical averages or vignettes). To extend Feyerabend's notion, credible evidence should be humanitarian, including embracing political ideology as a source of credibility since such ideologies may be important in overcoming the chauvinism of particular perspectives, especially ones that maintain the status quo.

At any given time, our knowledge is the best it can be and a commonsense realism prevails—we are reasonably certain at a given time of what is true, and we act on that knowledge with relatively high degrees of confidence. In some senses, certainty is based on cultural norms or intersubjective meanings, those things we collectively know even if that knowledge is tacit. But because knowledge is contingent, there are limits to its certainty, and what we know will inevitably change. The issue of certainty often turns on sustaining a Cartesian dualism of a mind and a separate real world—rejecting this dualism refocuses the issue of certainty away from mapping mind onto a physical reality and toward usable and sensible knowledge.

Information becomes evidence within a context at both pragmatic and philosophical levels. Sometimes information becomes evidence because it is acquired in certain ways, such as through the use of randomized clinical trials (RCTs) within a post-positivist framework or through the telling of stories within a narrative framework. These are contexts of formal research and evaluation. But information becomes evidence through lived experiences, including professional practice. These are contexts of everyday life. Contextuality is important in two respects. First is the contextuality of the evidence itself, and the charge that something is taken out of context is always a serious challenge to the credibility of evidence. Knowing the point of view (for example, economic, aesthetic, or political), who generates evidence, and how are critical aspects of credibility. The more context provided for evidence, the better able we are to judge its credibility. Context is important in a second sense of providing specific criteria for judging the credibility of evidence. The most obvious example of this is culturally different criteria for establishing credibility—one might contrast Western scientific notions of credibility with aboriginal notions of what makes evidence credible. Adopting the anarchist position offered by Feyerabend allows for open-ended possibilities for what can count as credible evidence and therefore knowledge of the social world.

Seeing Is Believing, or Is It?

Images are all around us. We are all image makers and image readers. Images are rich data for understanding the social world and for forming and representing our judgments of that social world. Image-based research has a long history in cultural anthropology and sociology as well as the natural sciences (Collier & Collier, 1986), but it is still relatively uncommon in program evaluation (Hurworth, 2004). Nonetheless, in this discussion, I want to explore both the uses of images and the possibilities for their use in evaluation.

I do not assert that images are better evidence than any other. Images should not be romanticized but neither should their value as data and knowledge be denigrated. Especially in Western industrialized cultures, images are associated with artistic expression, entertainment, and persuasion. Images are seen as intuitive, representing implicit and subjective knowledge, while numeric, text, and verbal data are more associated with fact, reason, and objective knowledge. Images are no more suspect than any other sort of data, such as numbers or text. Images, as any data, can be used to lie, to question, to imagine, to critique, to theorize, to mislead, to flatter, to hurt, to unite, to narrate, to explain, to teach, to represent.

We do not necessarily need to see to believe, and indeed, we believe many things we cannot or do not see directly. The Humean skepticism about the knowability of causation is a key example of knowing something without seeing it. The billiard ball example illustrates this skepticism—in the Humean perspective we cannot see causation, but we infer it from seeing one billiard ball moving across the table, hitting another, and causing that second ball to move. Understanding DNA is another example. Most of us cannot see the genetic code, but we understand genetics when we look at siblings or parents and their children and note their similar appearance and behavior. Even when we do not directly see what we know, knowing is based on seeing and we typically call this *observation*. Seeing, even if in the form of indirect observation, is intricately connected with believing and thus knowing at the individual, cultural, or global levels of knowledge. Indeed, there is biological evidence that seeing, at least in the context of space, is more reliable than other sources of data, and the central nervous system summarizes visual information in statistically optimal ways (Witten & Knudsen, 2005).

SITUATING IMAGES AS EVIDENCE IN CURRENT EVALUATION APPROACHES

Images are most likely to be used as evidence within participatory, empowerment, and responsive evaluation approaches. These are evaluation approaches that actively involve stakeholders in planning and implementing evaluation studies as well as using evaluation results. Stakeholder involvement takes a particular form in this genre of evaluation—it must be broad and fundamental to decisions made in the evaluation process, often including defining evaluation questions, deciding what methods best answer those questions, deciding from whom to collect data, analyzing data, and disseminating and using evaluation results.

Participatory approaches to evaluation can be collaboration between an evaluator and program stakeholders, or program stakeholders might assume responsibility for the evaluation. In the collaborative scenario, evaluators and stakeholders work together to identify the evaluation focus, questions, and data collection, but the evaluator has responsibility for the execution and quality control of the evaluation process. When program stakeholders assume responsibility, they call on evaluators to lend technical expertise if and as needed. The goal is increased stakeholder participation but also increased self-determination at individual, organizational, and/or community levels. Additionally, these approaches can be characterized by the following underlying motivations: (1) a pragmatic interest in making evaluation meaningful and useful, (2) a social constructivist epistemology, and/or (3) a political interest in social justice and fairness.

When evaluation perspectives, such as those described above, emphasize evidence meaningful to all stakeholders, and particularly service providers and recipients, there will likely be wide variation in evidence used in program evaluations. Careful attention is given to what is meaningful and sensible to not only evaluators but also to those who deliver and receive programmatic services. Encouraging program participants to use their own means to understand, analyze, and communicate the value of programs and services may include traditional social science research techniques but will likely extend to more commonsense, pragmatic forms of evidence including, although not limited to, images. Potential benefits of images as evidence in evaluation are highlighting personal experiences, engaging emotions, surfacing assumptions, understanding complex and multidimensional experiences, and respecting cultural differences.

For example, photography is used for exploring and analyzing personal, cultural, and social experiences and the photographs, individually and collectively, can be evidence for judging the efficacy of interventions at each level (Wang, 1999). Sands, Reed, Harper, and Shar (2009) used Wang's PhotoVoice to evaluate a school gardening program for fifth graders. Asking students, "If you were going to teach young children about growing food, what would you show them?" (p. 18) generated photographs used by the students for an analysis of core ideas about growing food, understandings that resulted from their participation in the program. The California Endowment (2007) describes grassroots program evaluations that "give program participants a chance to tell their own stories in their own ways," which can take "many forms, from oral and written narratives to gesture, movement, art, music, movies and more" (p. 2).

The Center for Digital Storytelling has embarked on a project called Capturing Value directed at philanthropic grant makers wishing to expand the tools to convey the value of their work. Using a participatory evaluation framework, the Center invites work with funders wishing to use digital storytelling to explore what can be learned from funders' "investment in work for the public good" and that "can help others know how to move forward, sparking new ideas, inspiring new investments, guiding future choices" (Center for Digital Storytelling, n.d.). This initiative seeks to generate evidence that complements more traditional evaluation data by combining images and storytelling to engage audiences (other funders and policy makers, for example) through thought and feeling in ways that capture imagination, hold attention, and still communicate with nuance. Similarly, the Digital Clubhouse, with centers on both the U.S. east and west coasts, uses the technology of digital storytelling to support people of all ages in considering how to improve the quality of their lives and communities. Both the Center for Digital Storytelling and the Digital Clubhouse provide instruction and support for using media technology, but the end goal is to use new media in service of giving authentic voice to individuals as they explore and try to enhance the social fabric of their lives, whether through a personal healing experience or a community development project.

Perhaps one of the most frequent contexts within which images are used in evaluation is when youth are primary stakeholders and a transformative partici-patory and empowerment evaluation approach is adopted. The school gardening project is an example of this, and the Digital Clubhouse emphasizes intergenera-tional involvement and several initiatives specifically involve school-age children. Art Reach Toronto, a program that supports arts initiatives for engaging normally excluded youth, outlines a wide range of arts-based evidence and data-collection strategies to facilitate youth-focused program evaluations. In their Arts-Based Evaluation toolkit, creative strategies for expressing value are advocated to express complex ideas, to use multiple modes of expression, to build on creativity inherent in projects, and to generate data appropriate for communicating about value in reports (Art Reach Toronto, n.d.). PhotoVoice was the platform for youth involve-ment in the evaluation of Minnesota's Statewide Health Improvement Program. Youth from thirteen communities created a snapshot of Minnesota's health by focusing on how healthy eating affects them and their communities and what limits and supports physical activity and healthy eating in their community (Minnesota Department of Health, n.d.). These evaluation examples illustrate empowering youth to explore value with an eye to social improvement by using familiar and compelling technology tools, ways of exploring the world that may resonate more with their experience and skill than traditional social science tools.

WHAT IS IMAGE-BASED EVIDENCE IN EVALUATION?

Images in evaluation include found and evaluator- or participant-produced videos, photographs, drawings, collages, cartoons, and other visual forms of expression and representation. In anthropology, sociology, and psychology, images have been used for some time as data and as a compelling representation of knowledge because they are fundamentally human ways of expressing experi-ences, values, and knowledge.

Images are essential to human sense-making. We see and think and communicate using images. Like words, images can be used, construed, and read in different ways and can serve multiple functions.... Like words, images are part of who we are, who we think we are, and who we become—they are integral to questions of identity and purpose. Like other aspects of sense-making, how images create meaning is a dynamic process involving dialectical negotiation or interaction between the social and the personal aspects in any give culture. (Weber, n.d.)

Image-based evidence is any intrinsically visual data—such as photographs, video/film, drawings, cartoons, graphs and charts, typography, graphic art, graffiti, computer graphics, television, architecture, signs, clothing, as well as what is seen in the mind's eye. This last sort of image may not be recognized as truly visual, but indeed, we give meaning to and judge the adequacy of people, events, and products by the images we hold only in our mind. Images of failing schools, successful classrooms, urban blight, and healthy communities reside in our mind, even if we have never seen those places.

Images are used in three ways: (1) as data or evidence, (2) as an elicitation device to collect other data, and (3) as a representation of knowledge.

IMAGES AS DATA

In the first case, the images are themselves the data or evidence in an evaluation. The classic example of images as data comes from Mead and Bateson's (1942) photographic study of Balinese life. This book includes 759 still photographs with captions including the context of the photos, complemented by theoretical discussion. Mead and Bateson were motivated to move beyond what Mead described as "ordinary English words" because of their inadequacy for capturing and communicating the emotions of the South Sea Islanders; photography and film became their alternate grammar.

Children's drawings are an example of images as data. In my investigations of high-stakes testing in schools, children's experiences of testing have been captured in drawings of themselves, the testing context, and their relationships with their teacher and classmates. Figure 8.1 shows a cartoon and Figure 8.2 a self-portrait by a fourth grader taking the state-mandated English Language Arts Test. The Performing Arts Workshop's quasi-experimental design evaluation of a school-based artist in residence program asked students in grades three to five to complete pre- and post-program surveys that included drawings as a response (Performing Arts Workshop, n.d.). These drawings, along with more traditional survey item data, allowed for an investigation of changes over time in student perspectives in and of art.

Figure 8.1   Cartoon Drawing as Data

SOURCE: Freeman and Mathison (2005).

IMAGES TO ELICIT OTHER DATA

Using images to elicit other data, such as cultural or personal meaning, is perhaps the most common form of image-based research (Harper, 2002); auto-driven photography is a good example (see, for example, Clark, 1999). In general, evaluation participants are given the opportunity to take photographs related to the evaluation questions at hand. The specific subject matter is left to participants and the photographs become the physical manifestation of what

Figure 8.2 Joseph's Self-Portrait as Data

Joseph (Hispanic urban fourth grader): "[I was] worried 'cause if I don't, if I fail again 'cause I did third grade, 'cause in third grade . . . my teacher said 'some of you going to pass into fourth grade,' and I didn't . . . 'cause if I fail then I have to go to summer school. And I don't want to go to summer school again."

SOURCE: Freeman and Mathison (2005).

participants pay attention to and, by inference, what they value. The photographs are not the end goal, however. The meaning the photographer-participants make of the photographs, expressed in interviews, is the key data. In assessing customer satisfaction with a hotel, Pullman and Robson (2007) asked guests to photograph things that influenced their opinions of the hotel. The photographs became the basis for discussions with guests about what they did and did not like.

This same strategy is used with photographs or video not generated by participants. Evaluators who bring a theoretical framework to their work may take photographs or videos that focus the elicitation on specific evaluation issues. White, Sasser, Bogran, and Morgan's (2009) use of Photolanguage in evaluation illustrates this strategy. Photolanguage uses black-and-white photographic images specifically chosen for their aesthetic qualities; their ability to stimulate emotions, memory, and imagination; and their capacity to stimulate reflection in the viewer. Evaluators may find [that] Photolanguage provides a valuable tool for use with evaluation participants who experience barriers to involvement, actual or perceived.

Similarly, in a study of a therapeutic camp for children with cancer, investigators hypothesized that the nature of physical space was a critical dimension of the camp's therapeutic quality. Researchers took photos of camp spaces and used them as elicitation devices in interviews with campgoers to explore this idea (Epstein, Stevens, McKeever, & Baruchel, 2006). Regardless of who makes the images, photographs, or video recordings, they are used to elicit participants' thoughts, decisions, reasoning, and reactions *in situ* (see, for example, Meijer, Zanting, & Verloop, 2002).

IMAGES AS REPRESENTATION

The third use of images is to represent knowledge generated within an evaluation. Visual images can illustrate the interpretive text—a legitimate and particular use of images. This use of images in evaluation challenges a taken-for-granted assumption that legitimate knowledge of what is or is not valued is best expressed in words, whether spoken or written. And the dominance of print media in academia reinforces this assumption. The idea of using a broad range of communicative devices is not new in evaluation (Torres, Preskill, & Piontek, 2005), and images can augment or be the primary communicative device for reporting findings.

Media, other than text, have become increasingly accessible and communicable with the Internet, such as Kaplan and Howes's (2004) web-based compilation of photographs taken by secondary school students and staff. The Kellogg Foundation summarized the issues from evaluations of rural community leadership programs (what the Foundation calls *cluster evaluation*) by developing a short video combining video images of rural communities, interview clips with program participants, and voice-over narration (Kellogg Foundation, 2013).

While not specific to evaluation, the Kids With Cameras projects illustrate the use of photographs as representation, made popular by the movie *Born Into Brothels*. While this project uses photography as an empowering skill for these children, their photographs also stand as representations of their life, a representation that needs no further interpretation or embellishment. The idea is that participant photography permits participants to speak directly and empowers them to influence their community as well as decision and policy makers. The generic strategy is called PhotoVoice (Wang, 1999; Wang & Burris, 1997). Photo essays are another example of images as representation, such as Lauren Greenfield's (n.d.) representation of growing up in Los Angeles in *Fast Forward*, a series of photographs with contextualizing text. Peter Menzel's (1995) *Material World: A Global Family Portrait* (photographs taken by the photographer) and Jim Hubbard's (n.d.) *Shooting Back* (photographs taken by homeless children) illustrate images as knowledge. While examples of photo essays in evaluation reporting are scarce, the Asian Development Bank (ABD) uses this strategy extensively, including for reporting evaluation findings. The evaluation of ABD social protection programs includes a more traditional written report augmented by a photo essay (Asian Development Bank, 2012).

While it is easy to focus on the numbers represented in graphs, tables, and charts, these are also images, ones used by all evaluators, and there are many resources providing guidance for and examples of their effective use in evaluation reporting. Innovative ways of summarizing data and information into images are emerging with the increased use of infographics and digital dashboards in evaluation as well as attention to presentation aesthetics. Big Brothers Big Sisters used infographics to summarize Youth Outcomes Survey findings, an image that illustrates program goals, criteria for success, and outcomes (see Figure 8.3). Infographics go beyond summarizing data in a table or chart and employ graphic design to facilitate visualization of data, often communicating large data sets in simple, intuitive ways—Tufte's work is significant and instructive in this area. Combining an aesthetic sensibility with a goal to communicate information, Tufte illustrates how descriptive information can be visualized to tell stories of multidimensional relationships. He describes this as envisioning information, which is at "the intersection of image, word, number, art" (Tufte, 1990, p. 9). The potential of dynamic infographics for evaluation reporting are illustrated in the amazing video of Hans Rosling's *200 Countries, 200 years, 4 Minutes,* an animation of huge amounts of global health data in real space (https://www.youtube.com/watch?v=jbkSRLYSojo). (See Evergreen Data for a wide range of data representation ideas in evaluation; http://stephanieeve rgreen.com/.)

Credibility of Images in Evaluation

All data are susceptible to manipulation, distortion, or misuse, but images no more so than any other data. Just as statistics can distort meaning, so too can images distort meaning. *Photoshopped* has become a verb indicating an image has been digitally changed to deliberately distort meaning, but its meaning extends to other uses, such as when the media focuses on celebrity breakups rather than Hurricane Katrina victims or when history textbooks exclude embarrassing moments of racism or sexism. The technical term for photographic manipulation is *scitexing* (named for the company that developed the technology) and can include overlaying multiple

Figure 8.3   Infographic of Evolution Criteria and Program Outcomes for Big Brothers Big Sisters Student Outcome Survey

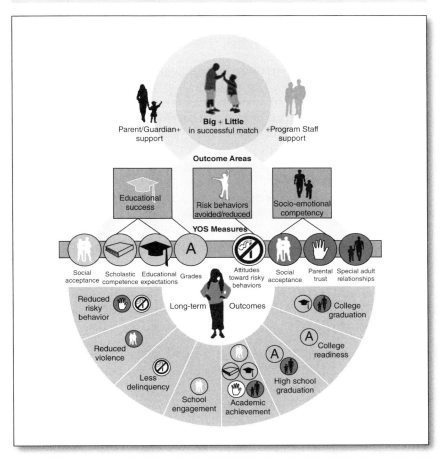

SOURCE: Wheeler and Valentino (2013).

negatives, airbrushing, image quilting, and so on. There is a long history of image manipulation for whimsical, commercial, and political purposes, and the credibility of images as evidence must necessarily consider such possibilities (see Loizos, 2000, and the website *Is Seeing Believing?* at www.frankw baker.com/isb.htm for more on the manipulation of images). But evaluators are no more likely to manipulate image data than they are to manipulate statistical data.

Four considerations for establishing the credibility of images are discussed below: (1) quality of the evaluation design, (2) attention to context,

(3) adequacy of the image from multiple perspectives, and (4) the contribution images make to new and useful knowledge.

EVALUATION DESIGN PROVIDES
THE FRAMEWORK FOR CREDIBILITY

In part, the credibility of any data can be judged by reference to the evaluation design (Wagner, 2004). There is a debate about what constitutes the best evaluation design, marked by a recent advocacy for RCTs. There is not, however, unanimity about what is best, in part because best for what and in what context is an important part of the equation. Without indulging in a discussion of the very different perspectives about what constitutes an adequate design, the credibility of images can be established within the context of whatever evaluation design is used.

Image-based evaluation can operate within a post-positivist framework where image data are treated as any other kind of data. The credibility of the evidence, and the threats to credibility, are established procedurally. Evaluation studies intend to answer questions or test hypotheses. Whether the evidence collected provides credible answers depends on such strategies as establishing the validity of the measures (i.e., are the images actually what is of interest), the reliability of images (i.e., do individuals or researchers agree on images and what they represent), the sampling of images from a knowable population in an explicit and defensible way, and whether the analysis follows understood conventions.

A participatory- or empowerment-oriented evaluation study that employs images as evidence will also make reference to procedures to establish credibility. For example, it is likely that participant-generated images would be favored over researcher-generated images, to be coherent with the intention to understand the meaningfulness of a construct, experience, or program from the participants' point of view. Another example would be a clear and transparent justification for the selection of images to use in elicitation strategies. Yet another example would be a description of how analytic categories are generated and used in the analysis and conclusions. In addition, other conventions such as prolonged engagement (images collected over time in multiple contexts) and responsiveness (the use of images reflects a respectful interaction between evaluator and participants) might be the focus.

Regardless of the underlying epistemologies, the credibility of images in evaluation can be judged by the defensibility of the evaluation design. Truth or credibility is, at least in part, established through conventions. While different camps of inquiry accept different conventions for establishing credibility, there is a set of conventions to which a particular image-based evaluation study can be compared. Image-based evaluation, as with any evaluation, can therefore be established by reference to procedures that, by agreement of a community of inquirers, have come to be acceptable.

CREDIBILITY OF IMAGES AS EVIDENCE REQUIRES ATTENTION TO CONTEXT

When they photographed social life in Bali, Bateson took pictures while Mead noted when, where, and under what circumstances the photograph was taken (Mead & Bateson, 1942). In presenting the images in their book, careful attention was paid to sequencing the photographs in the order they were taken. This was done because the photographs sometimes illustrate an event that has a temporal quality (a dance, a ceremony, preparation of a meal), but in a larger sense Mead and Bateson were providing a context for understanding Balinese social life.

Visual sociology and other image-based research often use and make images that resemble other uses of images, such as photojournalism or art.

> Visual sociology, documentary photography, and photojournalism, then, are whatever they have come to mean, or been made to mean, in their daily use in worlds of photographic work. They are social constructions, pure and simple. In this they resemble all the other ways of reporting what we know, or think we have found out, about the societies we live in, such ways as ethnographic reports, statistical summaries, maps, and so on. (Becker, 1998, p. 74)

In his analysis, Becker (1998) illustrates that knowing who is creating and using images is a critical aspect of establishing their credibility. He asserts that images, as do all cultural objects, get meaning from their context. A common means for providing context is the combination of images with text. Using Mead and Bateson's (1942) book on Balinese life as an example, when opened, the pages facing each other provide a complement of image and accompanying contextualizing text: Photographs appear on one page and two kinds of text on the other—a few paragraphs of interpretation and captions indicating when, where, and by whom the photograph was taken and what was going on at the time as well as interpretive text suggesting the theoretical meaning of the photographic evidence. Detail, then, is one way to provide context:

> [I]n visual reasoning, art, typography, cartography, even sculpture, the quantity of detail is an issue completely separate from the difficulty of reading. Indeed, at times, the more intense the detail, the greater the clarity and understanding—because meaning and reasoning are contextual. (Tufte, 2003, p. 12)

While talking about data displays in general, Tufte's (2006) emphasis on detailed documentation as the key to credibility applies to images of all types (p. 132).

Mead and Bateson's (1942) work exemplifies explicit, detailed contextualizing of images, but credible images may also imply context.

> Because the images themselves, sequenced, repetitive, variations on a set of themes, provide their own context, they teach viewers what they need to know in order to arrive, by their own reasoning, at some conclusions about what they are looking at. (Becker, 1998, p. 14)

The credibility of images is enhanced by providing or implying context (whether through text, narration, or other images) and by using complex, detailed images.

ADEQUACY OF THE INTERPRETATION OF THE IMAGE

The adequacy of the interpretation of images is the third aspect of credibility and can be understood in terms of the focus on the subject matter, the creation, or the viewers of the images (Werner, 2006). One or the other of these three foci may be more relevant in establishing the credibility in any particular evaluation study, but at the heart of the adequacy of the interpretation is a sense of authenticity. Table 8.1 summarizes each foci, including key questions one might ask to establish the credibility of an image or an image-based study.

In assessing the adequacy of the interpretations of images, one can look first at the content of the image. In other words, what sense is made of the image? The content can be read in ways that range from relatively low inference (such as describing what is in the image) or much higher inference (such as imputing particular states of mind to people in images). The key concern is the degree to which the interpretation is supported by the images themselves. Table 8.1 lists the kinds of readings that may be part of the interpretation and accompanying questions to test the credibility of those interpretations. Take, for example, the common image of a map. The map's content can be interpreted in a relatively straightforward, literal way—What place is portrayed and what features of the place are included? But the map also lends itself to higher inference interpretations—such as what kinds of places or things are valued—perhaps by being given prominence (museums, personal events) and what is devalued by its absence. If one looks at the common iconic map of the London Underground, the image portrays a sense of places in relation to one another, communicates distances between places, and evokes a sense of neatness and symmetry to the city. If one then compares this iconic map to the less common but geographically correct map of the London Underground, a different sense of place is communicated.

Table 8.1   Features of the Interpretation of Images

	Readings of Images		Questions to Establish Credibility of Images
Focus on subject matter	• Literal reading • Biographical reading • Empathetic reading • Iconic reading • Psychological reading	Low Inference ↓ High Inference	• What are the physical features of the image? Who or what is portrayed? What is the setting? • What is the relationship of the image to current practices? To identities? How is the image socially situated? • What common experiences are invoked? • How does the image relate to bigger ideas, values, events, or cultural constructions? • What are the intended states of mind and being?
Focus on image creation	• Technical reading • Editorial reading • Indexical reading • Spectatorship reading		• What are the design features? Are images scaled or mapped? • What value or knowledge is communicated by the author or creator? • How does the image relate to values of the time and place? • Where is the viewer situated in relation to the image?
Focus on audience/ viewers	• Reading of effects • Reflexive reading		• What impact does the image have on viewers? • How do viewers see themselves within the interpretation? How does the image interact with biography?

But images are not just of something, someone, or someplace. They are created by the evaluator, by other stakeholders, or are a collaborative endeavor. Judging the image's credibility may also require attention to the creator. At one level, the credibility of the image can be judged by its technical qualities. If appropriate, does the image include elements of scale that provide adequate context for its interpretation? How is the image set up with regard to perspective? No image is a transparent window, and the creator's choices in its creation provide a point of view for understanding the context. This point of view includes not only the technical decisions (black and white or color, line drawing or oil painting, distant or close up, front or back images) but also reflects the creator's cultural context and values in a particular time and place. In Table 8.1, these are referred to as *editorial* and *indexical* readings. The last sort of reading is one that considers the interpretation of the image in relation to the viewer: Where does the image situate the viewer, the reader of the image?

Look again at Figure 8.2, Joseph's self-portrait while taking the English Language Arts Test. In this case, the image creator is known, which is not always the case, especially if images are found rather than created. Joseph can tell us things about what the image means, and he does so in the interview excerpt. There are things about the drawing that Joseph may not be able to tell us but that may be meaningful, such as the significance of the colors he chose and the fact that Joseph looks directly at us out of his portrait.

Images imply a viewer, thus the interpretations of images require attention to audience. What impact do the images have on viewers? Are the evaluator and stakeholders' interpretations coherent with the viewer's interpretations? How do the images and the interpretations of them interact with the biographies of viewers? Take Joseph's self-portrait again as an example. We might ask, how do we see Joseph in the testing situation and how do others understand Joseph's experience? I have a large matted version of this drawing, along with several others, in my office. These pictures draw people in, and inevitably visitors talk about them. Seeing these pictures, people ask me questions—about the kids, about the research, about why I used drawing. But they are also speculate about what they mean, show empathy by feeling sad for kids like Joseph, share in the satire inherent in some drawings, share the happiness in doing well on the test, and tell stories of their own experiences with assessment in schools.

CREDIBILITY IS DEPENDENT ON THE EXTENT TO WHICH IMAGE CONTRIBUTES TO USEFUL KNOWLEDGE

It is a truism that evaluation should result in new knowledge, new understandings about the evaluand. In a traditional social science framework, a relatively small, particular, and focused audience is often implied. Study results are reported in peer-reviewed journals and books read by others with similar interests. New knowledge in this context is new to a group of colleagues working hard on inquiry about the same phenomena, and the study is indexed to an existing body of literature. This test of credibility may apply to image-based studies. Attention is paid to whether the claims follow from the evidence and whether the arguments are well-founded, defensible, and coherent.

Evaluation assumes a broader audience though, including policy makers, funders, communities, practitioners, and service recipients. Evaluation is complex, and the field has moved well beyond the simplistic instrumental-use notion to more nuanced and varied uses of evaluation and evaluation findings (Kirkhart, 2000; Preskill & Caracelli, 1997; Weiss, 1979). In some arenas, policy makers have regrettably and effectively redefined credible and useful evidence by specifying which evaluation designs are best, resulting in what Weiss, Murphy-Graham, Petrosino, and Gandhi (2008) call *imposed use*. Results of evaluations that use experimental designs are categorically defined as more useful, but at the end of the day, imposed use still begs questions about the credibility of evidence, discounts local knowledge of program effects, and privileges bureaucratic procedures over arguments to demonstrate usefulness (Weiss et al., 2008).

The ubiquity and accessibility of images may suggest alternatives for judging the credibility and usefulness of evaluations that rely on images as evidence. Because images have a populist character, image-based evaluations and evaluation findings may be more accessible to study participants (and people similar to them), the public, and even policy makers, and therefore, potentially broader contexts for knowledge generation may be important in considering a study's credibility. Credibility in this more populist context might also involve questions about verisimilitude, authenticity, and usefulness as a catalyst for change. Instead of a scientific proceduralism rhetoric, the rhetoric is one of believability, often a call to join the evaluator and other stakeholders on a journey to understanding and knowing (Wagner, 2004, p. 1500). In this context, the balance of interpretation to evidence will tip toward evidence, in contrast with the social science reports where interpretation is illustrated by evidence.

This populist context of credibility does not seek legitimation within a body of literature created by a relatively small community of scholars and does not fit with the imposed use now common in the federal government arena but rather seeks legitimation in its ability to communicate with diverse consumers. Evaluation studies are first and foremost about understanding value and merit within a particular context, often with an eye to making things better. While images are not a singular answer to how to do this well, they may have certain advantages given this intent. Wagner (2004) suggests that inquiry should be multifaceted:

> Being smart about that requires that we learn what we can from not only social scientists but also documentary photographers and filmmakers, at least some of whom celebrate both art and empiricism and aim for both telling images and telling truths. (p. 1505)

Conclusion: Do Images Count as Credible and Useful Evidence?

It is simplistic to assert seeing is believing, but because our eyes sometimes deceive us does not obviate the credible knowing from using and viewing images in evaluation. This chapter focused on how we use and establish the credibility of images in program evaluation not because images are better or more compelling evidence but because any evidence may be credible, truthful, and useful. As suggested in the introduction, the credibility of evidence ought not to be established solely or even primarily by the methods by which it is generated. Whether one is doing ethnography or randomized experiments or survey research is not the only feature in establishing the credibility of the evidence generated. What counts as credible evidence is defined within inquiry traditions, within epistemological traditions. In evaluation theory and practice, fundamental epistemological differences exist, so the credibility of evidence within any particular tradition is first established within a particular tradition.

As we investigate and evaluate social phenomena, we should eschew the hegemony of any particular tradition and assume all kinds of evidence might increase our knowledge of and methods of valuing social phenomena. Images, correlations, effects sizes, vignettes—indeed, any and all evidence—must be taken seriously and examined in ways that reject the search for a single conclusion about what is good and right. Considering any and all evidence fosters thinking about the usability and sensibility of evidence within the larger social context.

References

Art Reach Toronto. (n.d.). *Arts-based evaluation 101.* Retrieved April 16, 2014, from http://www.artreachtoronto.ca/toolkits/the-goal-toolkits/art-based-evaluation/

Asian Development Bank. (2012). *Special evaluation study on ABD's social protection strategy.* Retrieved April 9, 2014, from http://www.adb.org/sites/default/files/ses-socialprotection.pdf

Becker, H. S. (1998). Visual sociology, documentary photography, and photojournalism: It's (almost) all a matter of context. In J. Prosser (Ed.), *Image-based research: A sourcebook for qualitative researchers* (pp. 84–96). London, England: Falmer.

California Endowment. (2007). *Storytelling approaches to program evaluation: An introduction.* Los Angeles, CA: Author.

Center for Digital Storytelling. (n.d.). *Capturing value.* Retrieved on April 16, 2014, from http://www.storycenter.org/capturing-value/

Clark, C. D. (1999). The auto-driven interview: A photographic viewfinder into children's experiences. *Visual Sociology, 14,* 39–50.

Collier, J., Jr., & Collier, M. (1986). *Visual anthropology: Photography as a research method.* Albuquerque: University of New Mexico Press.

Epstein, I., Stevens, B., McKeever, P., & Baruchel, S. (2006). Photo elicitation interview (PEI): Using photos to elicit children's perspectives. *International Journal of Qualitative Methods, 5*(3), Article 1. Retrieved April 9, 2014, from http://www.ual berta.ca/~iiqm/backissues/5_3/PDF/epstein.pdf

Feyerabend, P. (1975). *Against method.* New York, NY: Humanities Press.

Freeman, M., & Mathison, S. (2005). *Urban and suburban students' reported experiences with high-stakes testing in New York State.* Paper presented at the Annual Meeting of the American Educational Research Association in Montreal, Quebec, Canada.

Greenfield, L. (n.d.). *Fast forward.* Retrieved April 16, 2014, from http://zonezero.com/exposiciones/fotografos/lauren2/portada.html

Harper, D. (2002). Talking about pictures: A case for photo elicitation. *Visual Studies, 17,* 13–26.

Hubbard, J. (n.d.). *Shooting back.* Retrieved April 16, 2014, from http://www.shooting back.net

Hurworth, R. (2004). The use of the visual medium for program evaluation. In C. Pole (Ed.), *Seeing is believing? Approaches to visual research* (pp. 163–180). Oxford, England: Elsevier Ltd.

Kaplan, I., & Howes, A. (2004). Seeing through different eyes: Exploring the value of participative research using images in schools. *Cambridge Journal of Education, 34*(2), 143–155.

Kellogg Foundation. (2013, February 5). *God made a rural* [video]. Retrieved April 16, 2014, from http://www.youtube.com/watch?v=0LusMW84c5Y

Kirkhart, K. E. (2000). Reconceptualizing evaluation use: An integrated theory of influence. *New Directions for Evaluation, 88,* 5–23.

Loizos, P. (2000). Video, film, and photographs as research documents. In M. W. Bauer & G. Gaskell (Eds.), *Qualitative researching with text, image, and sound.* Thousand Oaks, CA: SAGE.

Mead, M., & Bateson, G. (1942). *Balinese character: A photographic analysis.* New York, NY: New York Academy of Sciences.

Meijer, P. C., Zanting, A., & Verloop, N. (2002). How can student teachers elicit experienced teachers' practical knowledge? Tools, suggestions, and significance. *Journal of Teacher Education, 53*(5), 406–419.

Menzel, P. (1995). *Material world: A global family portrait.* San Francisco, CA: Sierra Club Books.

Minnesota Department of Health. (n.d.). *A snapshot of health in Minnesota: Youth PhotoVoice project.* Retrieved on April 15, 2014, from http://www.health.state .mn.us/healthreform/ship/events/policyconference/photovoice.pdf

Performing Arts Workshop. (n.d.). *ARISE student survey.* Retrieved on July 9, 2013, from http://www.performingartsworkshop.org/pages/resources_administrators .html

Preskill, H., & Caracelli, V. (1997). Current and developing conceptions of use: Evaluation use TIG survey results. *Evaluation Practice, 18,* 209–225.

Pullman, M., & Robson, S. (2007). A picture is worth a thousand words: Using photo-elicitation to solicit hotel guest feedback. *Cornell Hotel and Restaurant Administration Quarterly, 48*(2), 121–144.

Sands, C., Reed, L., Harper, K., & Shar, M. (2009). A PhotoVoice participatory evaluation of a school gardening program through the eyes of fifth graders. *Practicing Anthropology, 31*(4), 15–20.

Torres, R. T., Preskill, H., & Piontek, M. E. (2005). *Evaluation strategies for communicating and reporting: Enhancing learning in organizations.* Thousand Oaks, CA: SAGE.

Tufte, E. R. (1990). *Envisioning information.* Cheshire, CT: Graphics Press.

Tufte, E. R. (2003). *The cognitive style of PowerPoint.* Cheshire, CT: Graphics Press.

Tufte, E. R. (2006). *Beautiful evidence.* Cheshire, CT: Graphics Press.

Wagner, J. (2004). Constructing credible images: Documentary studies, social research, and visual studies. *American Behavioral Scientist, 47*(12), 1477–1506.

Wang, C. (1999). Photovoice: A participatory action research strategy applied to women's health. *Journal of Women's Health, 8*(2), 85–192.

Wang, C., & Burris, M. (1997). Photovoice: Concept, methodology, and use for participatory needs assessment. *Health Education and Behavior, 24*(3), 369–387.

Weber, S. (n.d.). *Concerning images.* Retrieved April 16, 2014, from http://iirc.mcgill.ca/

Weiss, C. H. (1979). The many meanings of research utilization. *Public Administration Review, 39,* 426–431.

Weiss, C. H., Murphy-Graham, E., Petrosino, A., & Gandhi, A. G. (2008). The fairy godmother—and her warts: Making the dream of evidence-based policy come true. *American Journal of Evaluation, 29*(1), 29–47.

Werner, W. (2006). Reading pictures of people. In E. W. Ross (Ed.), *The social studies curriculum: Purposes, problems, and possibilities* (pp. 217–240). Albany, NY: SUNY Press.

Wheeler, M., & Valentino, S. (2013, April 23). *Using infographics to translate evaluation evidence: The 2013 BBBS youth outcomes report.* Retrieved on August 1, 2013, from http://chronicle.umbmentoring.org/research-corner-using-infographics-to-translate-evaluation-evidence-the-2013-big-brothers-big-sisters-youth-outcomes-report/

White, R., Sasser, D., Bogran, R., & Morgan, J. (2009). Photos can inspire a thousand words: Photolanguage as a qualitative evaluation method. *Journal of Extension, 47*(3). Retrieved April 15, 2014, from http://www.joe.org/joe/2009june/iw1.php

Witten, I. B., & Knudsen, E. I. (2005). Why seeing is believing: Merging auditory and visual worlds. *Neuron, 48*(3), 489–496.

9

Credibility, Policy Use, and the Evaluation Synthesis

Eleanor Chelimsky

This chapter is about the analytical method known as evaluation synthesis, viewed from a combined theory/practice perspective. It explains how the need arose to develop this method at the Government Accountability Office in 1980, recounts the uncertainties involved in implementing it, and details its policy use in all three branches of government over the next decade. Synthesis credibility is considered not only from the viewpoint of methodological validity but also from the various viewpoints of policy actors, sponsors, and other potential users of evaluation findings in a political environment. Four examples of policy use (by the Congress, various federal agencies, and the Supreme Court) are outlined, along with some general reflections on lessons learned in the process of moving the method from development to use.

When I went to the Government Accountability Office (GAO) in 1980 to build an evaluation unit there, I had the usual set of expectations about the kinds of evaluation questions we would be likely to get from the U.S. Congress, based on prior experience with executive-branch agencies. For example, I expected the questions to be retrospective; to be focused largely on program improvement; to be dominated by the subject areas of defense, health, education, and welfare; and to reflect a single political outlook, mostly determined by the latest election returns. Instead, I found that prospective questions came regularly from congressional policy makers and staff (either because they needed predictive information to support upcoming legislation or because they already had such information and wanted an analysis of its accuracy). I discovered that the legislative purpose of an evaluation question was as often to establish accountability as it was to improve programs (because accountability to the public is a crucial part of the congressional oversight function). As for subject-area diversity, it turned out to be almost infinite (because of the specific coverage assigned to each congressional committee, combined with the nation-monitoring character of the committee structure as a whole), but, unfortunately, without the strong subject-area staff support to be found in executive-branch agencies. And I learned that every legislative request for evaluative information, regardless of which party was in power, needed to be considered from the standpoint of politics *in general* (because of the majority/minority structure of every congressional committee, because of the constituency issues that would face Members of Congress at the next election, and because of the importance of past history and politics in legislative policy making).

Evaluation Settings and Evaluation Questions

What I grasped, then, was that differences in evaluation settings bring differences in the kinds of questions evaluators must be prepared to answer, although evaluators working in academic settings always have at least some freedom to independently determine the study question they want to examine. But in a government or foundation or consultant setting, this is not usually the case: Evaluators working in such settings must answer the questions posed to them (albeit with the possibility of negotiation regarding feasibility, cost, and other issues). Still, even though these evaluative questions may emerge from different purposes and may address widely divergent information needs, they do tend to fit within four general types or categories:

- *Management* questions (e.g., What do performance data tell us about what is happening in a program over time? What changes does this imply for the program going forward?)
- *Knowledge* questions (e.g., How can we learn whether the measured outcomes of a program are, in fact, attributable to the program or whether there are other causal factors involved in those outcomes? What does the answer to that question say about the validity of the theory and objectives on which the intervention was based?)
- *Accountability* questions (e.g., Does the intervention's implementation meet established criteria for quality? Does the program reflect all the relevant knowledge about the public problem targeted?)
- *Development* questions (e.g., How familiar with evaluative thinking are the expected users of the findings? Are efforts required to build understanding on

the part of these users, including the acquisition of experience with administrative data systems and other evaluative tools?)

Of course, the likelihood that evaluators will be asked a particular kind of question also varies somewhat by setting. For example, knowledge and development questions tend to occur in any setting. But accountability questions originate most often in the legislative branch, spurred by the oversight function, whereas management questions, which emerge naturally from within the programming agency, are just as likely to be asked as part of accountability evaluations requested by legislative policy makers. As for the prospective questions that surprised me so much when I first went to the GAO, these used to be a hallmark of legislative evaluation, but today, they are often posed by executive-branch policy makers as well.

Evaluation Methods (Both Retrospective and Prospective) and Their Credibility

With respect to the evaluation methods used for answering these diverse questions—questions that are different both with regard to purpose and to the kinds of information sought—these also are typically different. For example, data from a performance measurement methodology can satisfactorily answer certain questions posed by executive-branch program managers who want a continuing check on the changes occurring in their initiatives, but those data won't tell us *why* such changes may be occurring. That is, performance measurement alone cannot typically answer knowledge questions, accountability questions, or development questions. With respect to the experimental method (or the randomized controlled design), it is splendid for answering knowledge or accountability questions about program effectiveness (especially the degree to which the program may be the cause of the observed outcomes), but it is not so good at answering, say, management questions about scale-up (that is, whether a finding of program effectiveness in one place is generalizable to other places). Similarly, the case study method can bring—as performance measurement data and the experimental design cannot—an in-depth understanding of the other factors which may contribute to program effectiveness, including the particular local environment, the institutional context, the organizational constraints, and the specific program experience of individual practitioners and participants. On the other hand, case studies have trouble attributing outcomes to interventions because their study design does not rule out plausible competing causes for those outcomes (as the experimental design does).

Therefore, to produce evidence useful for answering the different kinds of questions posed in different settings, evaluators must rely on a host of different methods, sometimes employed alone, sometimes in combination. Since no one method is uniquely suited to answering all questions, and since evaluators have a great deal of experience with the warts and flaws of each of these methods, different approaches that are appropriate to both the specific question and its purpose can be (and are) used together—one method's strength bolstering another one's weakness—to produce answers to the evaluative questions and to ensure the quality of the evaluative evidence.

Where prospective questions were concerned, however, evaluators in 1980 had few methods to draw upon and little experience in applying them. Indeed, these questions were not typically even considered to be part of the evaluation repertoire, in which the quintessential question is "What happened?" (and not "What's likely to happen?"). Prospective questions were usually referred instead to policy or economic analysts and forecasters (Chelimsky, 1987). Nonetheless, given the volume of prospective questions coming to us from the Congress, I realized that a unit whose mission was to show that evaluation could be routinely useful to policy makers in any of the three branches of government could not long resist dealing with these questions and still survive. So I started looking at what was known about the track record of some of these methods, based on a concern for their credibility. For example, the fact that the accuracy of a forecast can be determined only in retrospect, perhaps years later (by comparing the predicted outcomes to what actually occurred), means that in the immediate, its accuracy could be very hard to defend. In addition, I noticed that in many cases, those crucial after-the-fact determinations of accuracy were never undertaken (United States General Accounting Office [USGAO]/PEMD-88-8). So, given this uncertain state-of-the-art in prospective methodologies, the serious data problems I had already experienced with econometric models (missing data, old data, unvalidated data, etc.), and also that there was as yet little evaluative experience with time-series models, I was worried about our ability to answer prospective questions—using any of these methods and having to assure their credibility—in a turbulent political environment. But how then does one *normally* establish credibility in a political environment, even with methods that have long been used in evaluation?

Establishing the Credibility of Evaluative Evidence

Clearly, determining whether the quality of the evidence produced by an evaluation is methodologically sound constitutes a hugely important question for evaluators. However, it isn't necessarily, or always, a difficult one. To answer it, most evaluators typically rely on existing theory, experience, and expert research review. At the GAO, for example, I immediately established various panels of reviewers with wide theoretical and practical knowledge of different methods and subject matters to judge the quality of our evaluative evidence to make sure, say, of the appropriateness of the study design and methods to the question posed, of the care taken in the implementation of that design and its methodology (especially issues involving sampling, data collection, and statistical analysis), and of the logic and validity of the study's findings and conclusions (e.g., the strength of the conclusions allowed by the methods employed). The evaluators I had brought in to the GAO were themselves experts in various methodologies to begin with, and we paid serious attention to the issues raised by our reviewers, some of whom were illustrious in their fields.

As such, I thought the credibility of our methods and evidence would be well defended, at least with respect to retrospective questions. And indeed, if evaluations were produced only for the research or evaluation community, such review would probably have been enough to assure the general credibility of our work. But the fact is that evaluations are conducted for use in a world of politics, where ideologies differ and special interests abound. This means that methodological credibility, while crucial for the thoughtful defense of a study, is only a first step for evaluators working in a political environment who want to see their findings used in policy making. Other aspects of credibility, in addition to the quality of the evaluative evidence, may be just as important to the political actors (nonresearchers) who will use, or not use, the evaluation's findings. What then are these aspects?

The Credibility of Evidence and the Evidence of Credibility

A first problem here in thinking about what credibility may mean to our users and what information we need to give them in support of that credibility is that in the world of politics, it can be rare to find a level playing field for evaluation. Biases against a study can exist even before the evaluation begins so that its general credibility will be hard to achieve, no matter what efforts the evaluators may undertake. And if the findings, once reported, run counter to the predetermined agendas of corporate, bureaucratic, or ideological interests, credibility will need to be established in the face of sometimes severe opposition by these interests. This opposition typically begins with an effort to destroy the *overall* credibility of the evaluation. For example, doubt will usually be cast on the study's methodological quality, but even more attention will be paid to attacking the competence, independence, objectivity, social or political agenda, and "over-intellectuality" of the evaluators. So ensuring general evaluative credibility in the face of special-interest attacks is both important and difficult.

But such credibility is important as well for others in a political world. For example, even the evaluation's sponsors, no matter how well they understand its findings and how much they want to act on them, may need to defend it to other actors who are not researchers: to local groups, state administrators, or program practitioners who may be charged with implementing the evaluation's findings or to political appointees in their agency. So when evaluation findings are controversial—politically, bureaucratically, or in terms of practitioner traditions—it often turns out that even when their methods are acclaimed by the research community, evaluators may still face an uphill fight and some entrenched obstacles to use that they must struggle to overcome.

Obviously, this is no simple matter. And there is worse. Above and beyond the difficulty that our various audiences may be biased or use multiple criteria in deciding on the credibility of a study, there is a second problem for us that goes back to the initial level of credibility. That is, methodological validity, no matter how strong, is never absolute: Our evidence can never be entirely complete, correct, or permanent. Of course, we share this problem with scientific efforts generally, even those that—unlike evaluations—have the added security of being performed in the laboratory. For example, Dyson (2012) writes that in scientific endeavor, there is never a "sharp boundary, with truth on one side and fantasy on the other. All of science is uncertain and subject to revision" (p. 39). Or as Campbell (1984) puts it, "All scientific knowing is indirect, presumptive, obliquely and incompletely corroborated at best. The language of science is subjective, provincial, approximate, and metaphoric, never the language of reality itself. The best we can hope for are well-edited approximations" (p. 105). And Shadish (2005) reminds us of Einstein's comment that "[a]n experiment is something everybody believes, except the person who made it" (p. 129). In short, we can no more expect to produce *perfect* evidence (since knowledge is always imperfect) than we can expect to be credible to all audiences (since some may always be biased). What we should be aiming for, then, as evaluators is the greatest *possible* validity in our methods, combined with the greatest *possible* persuasiveness in our explanations and accounts.

On the other hand, even though our credibility is affected by limitations on our knowledge and the good faith of our audiences, it's also the case, with respect to the latter issue, that there exist many people—in Congress, within agencies, and in the courts—who are imbued with a sincere desire for accurate information about the successes and failures of government interventions. I had this experience almost continually over the years, and it is still true as I write this today. Even in climates of extraordinary political partisanship, public servants who recognize the importance of evaluation for good government can still be found. However, whether the political climate is stable or unstable, the overall credibility of an evaluation still counts as a major factor in their decision to use its findings.

With respect to the eternal imperfections of evaluative and scientific knowledge, it should also be noted that evaluation, in its short life, has already done a good deal to answer *factual* questions in government or society about such things as what the relevant choices may be for addressing a public problem, whether an intervention proposed and implemented was the right one, whether it had the expected results or not, why it had those results, and whether and how it should be modified in consequence. Evaluations have produced strong answers with solid and sustained evidentiary support to policy and program questions concerning, say, infant mortality and how it can be reduced; the effects of adolescent drinking on highway fatalities; the size and ingredients of contamination in our water supply; the effects of various prison policies (and social theories) on crowding, costs, racial disparities, and recidivism; the relationship of car size to highway safety; and many other public problems.

In sum, then, there do exist audiences who will, in fact, look for evidence of evaluative credibility, and although the "truth" produced by even the strongest evaluations may always be partial, uncertain, and mobile, evaluation today has generated more than enough valuable information for policy making and program management to make clear that evidence of its credibility is worth building. But how should that be done? For which policy actors do we need to offer a credibility defense? And what kind of credibility are we talking about?

The Substantive and Presentational Credibility of an Evaluation

If we listen carefully to our users and to the policy makers who ask us evaluative questions, they tell us that there are two important sources (other than methodological validity) that evaluators can draw upon for credibility in a political arena. These are the actual *substance* of an evaluation (from which its audiences will—or will not—take away a perception of its authenticity and integrity) and its *presentation* (i.e., the clarity, precision, balance, candor, vivacity, and absence of grandiloquence or exaggeration in the report language).

At the GAO, having convinced myself of the need to *always* build a credibility defense at the beginning of any evaluation, I ended up developing a two-part checklist for my own use (Chelimsky, 1996). This checklist was fairly mobile, depending on the context and subject matter of the evaluation, but the first part always included evaluation-wide, *substantive* issues such as:

- the quality of the literature review; the evaluators' understanding of program context, theory, history and politics; and the conclusions drawn in consequence to support the logic of the evaluation design;
- the completeness of the evaluators' description of the relevant program theory, the program treatment, and the areas of match and discrepancy between the two;

- transparency in discussing the evaluation questions, including their origin, how and why they were chosen, and their ramifications for study methodology;
- careful and complete explanation of the methods selected to answer the questions, their appropriateness, the alternatives excluded, and the methods' costs and benefits;
- attention to the conclusiveness of statements relative to the methods employed;
- candor in the evaluators' assessments of the major strengths and weaknesses of their evaluation, with discussion of the efforts made to compensate for weaknesses; and
- overall persuasiveness of the findings and recommendations (relative to the methodology used), their relationship to those of prior evaluations, how and why these evaluations differ, their practical applicability, and the degree of their likely usefulness (immediately and/or over time) to the evaluation's sponsor.

The second part of the checklist addressed issues of *presentational* credibility such as:

- the balance achieved between the evaluator's desire to present every detail of the work and the reader's willingness to absorb only quite small quantities of technical information;
- the presence of unintentional expressions of subjectivity or advocacy in the writing that could undermine the perceived honesty or objectivity of the report;
- the degree of transparency in communicating the report's essential messages, such as the short- and long-term lessons of the work, the areas of continuing ignorance, problems encountered, and relevant arguments brought to bear against the study and/or its conclusions;
- the existence of a complete, nonrepetitious, well-written executive summary that acquaints readers with the main points of the evaluation (stating clearly whether and how the findings are important, how they confirm or depart from prior findings, and what is significant about the evaluation's methods or experience that might benefit future evaluators) and lures them into exploring the detailed report; and
- the quality of the language and its avoidance of the kind of "mumbo-jumbo, pretentiousness, jargon and over-theologizing" that had caused past evaluation report audiences to find them "spooky, unfathomable, tedious to read and complicated to understand" (Chelimsky, 1977, p. 49).

In short, I had come to see credibility as threefold—involving the quality of the methodological evidence, the quality of the evaluative substance, and the quality of its presentation—and highly influential in the use of our work. Therefore, when I realized that we would surely need to address prospective as well as retrospective questions, my first concern went to the question of how I would defend the viability and credibility of forecasting methods (such as economic models, Delphi panels, etc.). Based then on the set of considerations I've just outlined—involving the close connections between evaluative settings, questions, methods, and credibility on the one hand to the policy use of findings on the other—it seemed sensible to look at the potential benefits of developing and using a method for synthesizing the findings of existing evaluations.

The Evaluation Synthesis: Beliefs and Expectations

To me, a first reason for believing in the importance of synthesizing already-completed evaluation findings was that it would allow us to use *retrospective* information to answer a wide variety of questions (including prospective ones). And this could bring us greater methodological credibility than would normally be the case, because the evidence would emerge not from a single study but from a group of carefully selected, well-designed evaluations. As such, I thought we could bring to a congressional committee a solid foundation of knowledge about past findings; past successes and failures; and past suggestions by practitioners, participants, and evaluators for improvement to a particular intervention and thereby help point the way toward the development of more promising future policies or programs.

Second, since a part of the mission of my new unit was to familiarize legislative committees with evaluation (as well as increase their use of its findings), I saw our role as being that of presenting the widest possible variety of evaluative information to the Congress: information that would stand up under hostile scrutiny. After talking to people on the Hill and reading a fair number of legislative records, it was clear that many sound and relevant evaluations were virtually unknown to the Congress and thus had never had an opportunity to influence legislative policy making. Based on the writings of Gene Glass about meta-analysis in 1976, I thought synthesis could help us in that role. However, synthesis was then in its infancy as an evaluative method, and there were only a few dissimilar, tentative approaches to look at. For example, one immediate difficulty I had with Glass's approach was his stipulation that syntheses needed to include *all* relevant studies. He wrote that "eliminating the 'poorly done' studies is to discard a vast amount of important data" (Glass, 1976, p. 4). Perfectly true, of course, yet for us, to include the less-good studies would have meant losing the crucial advantage of starting an analysis based on studies whose methodological credibility had already been established. On the other hand, Glass's faith in the potential of synthesis both as a way of answering evaluative questions and as a way of making better use of the information we already have was inspiring. In his words:

> Before what has been found can be used, before it can persuade skeptics, influence policy, affect practice, it must be known. Someone must organize it, integrate it, extract the message. A hundred dissertations are mute. Someone must read them and discover what they say. (Glass, 1976, p. 4)

A third reason for finding synthesis attractive was that, judging from some rather acerbic criticisms about timeliness and the "ivory tower" leveled at social scientists by Members of Congress whom I interviewed, I knew that our legislative users would inevitably ask us to answer policy questions under time frames too tight for us even to think about original data collection. So my calculation was that the use of existing studies could allow us to produce findings more quickly and without increasing credibility risks.

Fourth, I'd seen that major congressional policy debates often hinged on differences in findings from only two or three studies, differences that could presumably have been better illuminated as real or spurious by engaging in a broader synthesis of the available research. (I also found comfort and reassurance in the idea of pooling the results of many studies after long experience with the hazards of single, often "exemplary" evaluations whose vulnerabilities only became obvious when their findings were compared to those of other studies, done in different ways and, of course, later.)

Fifth, I worried—correctly, as it turned out—about our being perceived on the Hill as unresponsive if we gave our sponsors a steady diet of studies requiring three-year timeframes. So a balanced methods portfolio that included the use of evaluation syntheses seemed like a prudent notion.

Finally, and perhaps most importantly from a knowledge or theoretical point of view, I hoped that synthesis could dramatize, for legislative users, not only what was known but also what was *not* known in a particular problem area. In that way, I thought we could then focus attention on what needed to be learned (and how to learn it) in time to answer that same policy maker's questions before, say, the next program reauthorization. Based on the legislative record for some programs, it seemed obvious that, on the one hand, the distinction between well-established knowledge and opinion often went unrecognized, and on the other, that what needed to be researched, *as a very next step,* was sometimes not even glimpsed.

So for all these reasons, evaluation synthesis seemed like a good idea. However, in 1980, nobody had had much experience with it, there was as yet no defined methodology, and I realized that moving ahead undoubtedly involved some fairly shaky assumptions about how, in fact, knowledge contributes to policy within a political environment. On the other hand, methodology development—and sharing it within the GAO—was also one of the new evaluation unit's functions, and so, with the agreement of Elmer Staats (then Comptroller General of the United States and Head of the GAO) and the encouragement of Richard Light and Fred Mosteller, both of whom sat on my Advisory Board and knew a good deal about synthesis, I decided to go ahead with the project.

Developing the Evaluation Synthesis

The very first request our evaluation unit received from the Congress (dated March 25, 1981) was almost unbelievably serendipitous. The Chairman of the Subcommittee on Select Education, which was preparing for hearings on the Handicapped Act, wanted us to obtain, in his words,

> an assessment of existing evaluation information on: (1) the numbers and characteristics (such as age, race, handicapping condition, and severity of handicap) of children receiving special education, (2) the characteristics of children less often included in the special education program, (3) the characteristics of children over-represented in the program, and (4) factors related to who gets special education. (USGAO/IPE-81-1, 1981, p. 123)

The Chairman wrote,

> It would be beneficial if this work could be based on a technical review of existing evaluation studies so that it presents and integrates the soundest findings. And it would be most helpful if a written report could be available to me sometime in June. (USGAO/IPE-81-1, 1981, p. 123)

Thus the initial effort of the GAO's new evaluation unit would not focus on a type of evaluation any of us had previously conducted or even heard of but instead would require us to develop and use a methodology that existed only in our heads, with a generous time frame of two months in which to do it.

In a day or so, three members of our evaluation unit—Garry MacDaniels, Linda Morra, and I—came up with a very rough working procedure for doing a synthesis that we saw, of course, as iterative: to be corrected and amended as the study progressed. We enlisted other staff and outside evaluators to help us review 15 evaluation studies and two databases (the sum total of what was published and available). Then, with much burning of the midnight oil, we delivered a draft copy of the report, entitled *Disparities Still Exist in Who Gets Special Education*, on time (June 15, 1981) to the Chairman.

From the viewpoint of our ongoing methods development (which was, of course, as interesting to us as the substantive findings), we learned from this first synthesis—with respect to my hopes of using only high-quality evaluations to ensure credibility—that, in the words of our report,

> Many studies did not adequately describe the methodology they employed. This scarcity of information prevented determining the technical adequacy of these studies and thus limited placing confidence in the

findings. While a study may have been well designed and conducted, a reviewer forced to judge from the report could not have made such an inference. (USGAO/IPE-81-1, 1981, p. 82)

(Of course, we didn't actually "judge from the reports": Our only recourse was to interview the authors.) Even though in this first synthesis, we were deprived of the ability to use studies of already-recognized methodological quality, the studies and databases did still allow us (1) to answer all four of the Chairman's questions with varying degrees of confidence, (2) to indicate important issues that had been left unaddressed, (3) to push hard for more attention to methodological quality in the evaluations commissioned by the Department of Education, and (4) to conclude that "the overall findings indicate the value of using a variety of studies to evaluate a program, rather than relying on a single 'definitive' study" (USGAO/IPE-81-1, 1981, pp. 80–82).

The success of this first modest effort went far beyond anything we had expected. Chairman Murphy responded (July 1) with thanks and a host of new questions, and the Committee then went on to hold hearings and to use our work in reauthorizing the Handicapped Act. On the executive-branch side, the Department of Education not only decided to implement our recommendations but actually applauded the synthesis effort. Among other things, the Assistant Secretary for Special Education and Rehabilitative Services wrote us (1) that "a requirement for a complete description of the methodology used by contractors would be written into future Requests for Proposals" and (2) that

reviewers throughout the Department found the GAO Report to be objective, clearly presented, and useful.... The Department also found the methodology to be appealing. The use of existing studies as a data base, coupled with a clear conceptual model and a standardized procedural framework to analyze and systematize these data, is an extremely useful process for the purpose of isolating gaps in knowledge as well as describing what is currently known about various topics. (USGAO/IPE-81-1, 1981, p. 130)

This remarkable degree of policy use convinced us to move ahead with developing a formal methodology, and Richard Light came in to consult. We also received reviewing help from Fred Mosteller, Carol Weiss, Peter Rossi, John Evans, and Ernie Stromsdorfer. As we worked, we continued to perform syntheses for the Congress (as requested) in various subject areas, which contributed usefully to our thinking in developing the new methodology.

The Evaluation Synthesis Methodology

The method we eventually proposed (USGAO/IPE, 1983) was, of course, intended for use in a policy making context, where evaluators do not develop their own questions. From a methods viewpoint, then, this meant that in an evaluation synthesis (as opposed to a meta-analysis in which a question is derived from the available studies), there could be special difficulties in matching the available studies to policy questions, since the latter did not emerge from a knowledge of the database. We dealt with this either by developing subquestions that could better relate the policy questions to the available evaluations or by simply renegotiating the policy questions themselves.

The approach that we adopted contained six steps with subtasks as follows:

1. *Negotiate the Specific Policy Question and the Evaluation Subquestions With the Sponsor.* Subtasks here included the following:

   (a) Identify the sponsor's information need and underlying issues.

   (b) Review the literature and legislative history.

   (c) Conduct interviews with researchers and other stakeholders, and do snowball sampling when necessary to learn about all relevant work.

   (d) Estimate the feasibility and appropriateness of answering the policy question via the synthesis method, especially the likelihood of answering it in the specified timeframe.

   (e) Refine the policy question as well as the evaluation subquestions and, if necessary, renegotiate them with the sponsor.

2. *Identify and Collect the Relevant Studies.* This consisted in making an exhaustive search to locate all available evaluations, both published and unpublished, through

   (a) bibliographic searches and

   (b) interviews with researchers, subject-matter professionals, public interest groups and other stakeholders, and "snowball" samples.

3. *Assess the Quality of Each Evaluation and Decide Which Ones to Synthesize.* Subtasks here included the following:

   (a) Classify the evaluations in terms of the policy question.

   (b) Appraise each one against the appropriate methodological criteria and research standards.

   (c) Interview as many study authors as possible.

   (d) Summarize the review findings for each evaluation.

4. *Synthesize the Information Distilled From Step 3.* Subtasks here included the following:

   (a) Assess the evaluations and their findings in terms of their strengths and weaknesses, their similarities and trends, and their generalizability.

(b) Combine the data: That is, use quantitative methods (such as computing an average effect size or conducting a combined significance test) when possible or nonquantitative methods when quantitative approaches were infeasible because, say, the basic assumptions required by the quantitative approach could not be met; the character of the question posed presented problems vis-à-vis its relation to the database; or the disparate, fragmented nature of the existing evaluations didn't lend themselves to quantitative techniques. (For an extended discussion of the quantitative and nonquantitative approaches we used, often in combination, see USGAO/IPE, 1983, pp. 23-38.)

(c) Relate the findings to the policy question.

5. *Summarize the Status of Knowledge With Respect to the Policy Question.*

(a) Explain what can be stated with confidence, what can be stated with less confidence, and so on.

(b) Discuss and explain any research disagreements.

(c) Note gaps in the knowledge that need to be addressed.

6. *Provide for a Review of the Synthesis and Its Findings by Methodological and Subject Matter Experts.*

With a draft of this paper in hand, I felt considerably more confident in accepting a new, major, and obviously risky synthesis request, this time from the Chairman of the House Foreign Affairs Committee (dated March 18, 1982) to "assess and synthesize the nature, extent, and quality of the documented information relating to deterrence against the use of chemical weapons; Soviet and U.S. chemical warfare capabilities; binary chemical weapons; and the implications of binary weapons production for disarmament" (personal communication).

Evaluation Synthesis and Chemical Warfare

This effort on chemical warfare, which would clearly be highly visible because it involved a project important to the Department of Defense (DOD), was developed by Richard Barnes, Linda Morra, and Kwai Chan, among others, and it brought to us a new and different example of how the synthesis could be used in legislative policy making over time. Our initial work showed that there had been a large number of gaps in the information available to DOD policy makers before they decided to move ahead with a chemical weapons program; that most of the studies alleged to have supported their policy decisions were opinion based, sometimes without data of any kind; and that there was almost no analysis of the advantages and disadvantages of substituting the binary chemical weapons DOD was proposing (in particular, the Bigeye bomb) for the unitary ones they would replace. As a result, in our report's seven observations, we questioned the basis for a number of DOD's policy decisions, especially that of moving ahead with the Bigeye bomb.

Members of Congress actually read the 120-page report carefully, despite its technicality; discussions of it occupied hours and hours of debate on the Hill and hundreds of pages of the Congressional Record. For us, it was the first political test of the synthesis method, and although it required a strong stomach to get through the controversy raised by the findings, our ability to use the synthesis data to successfully rebut the arguments raised gave us a better idea of the strength, resilience, reach, and viability of the method (USGAO/IPE-83-6, 1983).

In terms of policy use, it was altogether remarkable. The first synthesis was followed by requests from the House Foreign Affairs Committee for nine more evaluations on the subject, and the Chairman wrote me a decade later (June 14, 1990) that our evaluative efforts had

> proven to be a crucial factor in the formulation of U.S. policy. Your work made an important contribution to the bilateral chemical weapons agreement between the U.S. and U.S.S.R. and your contributions made the congressional debate over whether or not to fund these weapons well-informed and substantive. (personal communication)

Eventually, in fact, DOD was obliged to decommission all chemical weapons facilities in the United States.

The methodological learning experience here was also considerable in that it gave us our first taste of the "publication bias" problem. As we tried to identify and collect all the relevant studies, we discovered through interviewing researchers that (a) there was a great deal of unpublished work we would need to find and examine and that (b) there was a tricky classification problem we would need to address. Working through the DOD materials, we discovered that though there existed, overall, a mix of studies taking both "dove" and "hawk" positions vis-à-vis chemical warfare capability; the former had been classified (and couldn't be accessed without a security clearance) while the latter had not. This meant that all unclassified documents placed in the public record to support congressional authorization for the new proposal were "hawkish"—that is, automatically biased in its favor. (We resolved this difficulty by including all studies in our analysis but publishing two reports, one classified and the other unclassified.)

A second part of our learning experience was an all-out attack by DOD on the synthesis method, which required a rebuttal. The Deputy Undersecretary of Defense for Research and Engineering (DDR&E) wrote me a letter saying that our study method was weak and amounted to nothing more than a literature review and that we had failed to do a "real study" (personal communication). What did he mean by a real study? Well, it would have involved talking to the program people who "knew what was what." In other words, to answer our synthesis finding that there existed almost no data to support the decisions taken by DOD policy makers on binary weapons, DOD's response was to attack our method and say that had we "talked to people," we would have "understood" the decisions. But of course, as part of the synthesis, we *had* talked to the very people DDR&E suggested (along with many, many others) but neither better data nor better logic had been forthcoming. (I wrote back, explaining how a synthesis was done, what the advantages of such an approach were, and how and why it was much more than a literature review and suggested—offering a draft copy of the new method—that DOD might want to use it for their own research [USGAO/IPE-83-6, 1983].)

In short, based on our two initial experiences with the synthesis method, one could conclude by looking at the immediate legislative user that the method was highly credible both to those who agreed with our findings and those who questioned them. On the other hand, with respect to the secondary executive-branch user, the credibility of the method seemed to depend entirely on the findings: That is, the method was either highly credible (as seen, for example, by the Department of Education, which agreed with our findings) or lacking in all credibility (as seen by the Department of Defense, which disagreed with our findings). Still, both papers were, in the end, important to legislative- and executive-branch policy making and had to be dealt with seriously by both primary and secondary users.

An Evaluation Synthesis of the Women's, Infants', and Children's Program (WIC)

A third example of our synthesis work involves the Women's, Infants', and Children's (WIC) program, a safety-net intervention that, in the early eighties, was funded at about $1.2 billion a year. It provided nutrition supplements to approximately 3 million people, and the population served was comprised of pregnant women and children (from birth to age 5) in low-income families thought to be at high nutritional risk. The Chairman of the Senate Committee on Agriculture, Nutrition, and Forestry asked us, in a letter dated June 30, 1983, to analyze the

> evaluations which have attempted to assess the WIC program and the extent to which the evaluations support the claims being made. . . . I want to emphasize that I am not requesting a new study of the WIC program itself, but rather a careful examination of existing research to determine the technical and methodological soundness of these

evaluations and the credibility of the claims which have been made based on them. (USGAO/PEMD-84-4, 1984, p. 59)

I went immediately to talk to the Chairman and some of his staff to get a clearer understanding of how they wanted to use our study, and I came away with two important pieces of information: The Committee was in a quandary about what to do with conflicting evaluation reports it had received about the quality of the WIC program (one group said it was highly effective in improving a variety of maternal and child health conditions, while another group criticized the first group's studies as being methodologically unsound, ungeneralizable, and unable to sustain assertions about program benefits). I also learned that the Chairman did not support the program and wanted to make heavy cuts in its appropriations.

In sum, our job here was once again to find and use strong existing evaluations to come up with judgments about a program, even though at first, it appeared as if we were only being asked to critique the evaluations. But in point of fact, the evaluations could only be strong or weak in terms of their methodological soundness for making judgments about WIC, so of course, we were also evaluating the program. In any case, it seemed likely from the beginning that this synthesis would be mired in controversy and that, as usual, we would need to prepare a viable credibility defense. So I asked Richard Barnes, Christine Fossett, David Cordray, and others to develop this synthesis, with Richard Light as consulting methodologist.

We identified 61 evaluations of the WIC program and asked both outside experts and our own staff to assess each study independently and rate it for methodological quality. Only six studies qualified as methodologically valid. However, these six did provide some credible evaluative evidence of favorable program effects with respect to infant birth weight: Average birth weights were 30 to 50 grams higher for infants whose mothers had participated in the program, and the proportion of infants who were at risk at birth (because of low weight) decreased by as much as 20% (USGAO/PEMD-84-4, 1984, p. 54).

We got the results in on time, and the Committee then held a hearing on our synthesis. In the Chairman's remarks, he called our work "balanced and objective" and said that "based on the actual evidence, it seems that some past witnesses clearly have exaggerated the effectiveness of the program." He *also* went on to recognize that, based on our work, WIC did appear to have positive effects "in some areas" (U.S. Senate Committee on Agriculture Nutrition and Forestry, January 30, 1984, p. 1). In the end, instead of cutting the program's appropriations as planned, the Committee maintained its existing funding level.

After the hearing but before the Committee's decision, we received some criticism in the press, with one analyst and a number of program advocates saying that we had "overstated the consequences of the methodological flaws" in the WIC studies (Pear, 1984). So we prepared a release showing the criteria we had used and explaining our inter-rater reliability procedures. We also discussed the issues with the 55 evaluators whose studies had been winnowed in the selection process, and the matter appeared to end there, since there were some serious methodological shortcomings in the studies we had eliminated. Nonetheless, it seemed at first as if this synthesis had become more about judging the methodology of program evaluations than about determining the effectiveness of a public program, which had not been our goal in developing the synthesis approach. Still, at the end of the day, from the viewpoints of program effectiveness and good government, the synthesis was used exactly as it should have been in legislative policy making, despite a climate of ideological confrontation, considerable special-interest rhetoric, and some pre-synthesis bias against the program on the part of the user.

Evaluation Synthesis, Drinking and Driving, the Congress, and the Supreme Court

The last example I want to cite here is probably the most interesting of all the syntheses we did at the GAO. There are a number of reasons why this is so: the degree of interest expressed by the requesting Committee in the methodological credibility of evaluations; the life-and-death questions that were directly related to the subject matter; the echoes of constitutional issues aired long ago by Jefferson and Hamilton regarding the proper scope of federal power; and the amazing ability of special interest groups—in this case, the beer lobby—to affect public policy.

On October 21, 1985, the Chairman of the Subcommittee on Investigations and Oversight, of the House Committee on Public Works and Transportation, wrote asking us to look at the evaluations that had been done to assess the effects of minimum drinking age laws on highway safety. He asked us to

> critically examine existing evaluations to determine the technical and methodological soundness of those evaluations, and the credibility of the claims which have been made based on them. For those studies which seem to offer the most credibility, we would expect a GAO assessment as to the observed range of effects of minimum drinking age laws. (USGAO/PEMD-87-10, 1987, p. 66)

The Chairman then posed nine questions about what was known about the effects of instituting minimum drinking age laws and followed them with this paragraph:

> While this request is directed specifically at the issue of minimum drinking age laws, we have a broader concern that your report may be able to

address. This is the question of what constitutes a "good" evaluation. The subcommittee has for years held hearings on transportation safety issues and notes the frequency with which evaluations that are submitted for the record support opposing conclusions, even though they use similar data bases and assumptions. (USGAO/PEMD-87-10, 1987, p. 66)

He asked for a briefing no later than late spring (1986)—eight months away.

As background to this request, it's probably useful to understand that the Congress had enacted legislation in 1984 requiring that a portion of federal highway funds be withheld from states that did *not* raise their minimum drinking age to 21. Many states had complied, but some resisted and based their resistance on evaluations showing that raising the drinking age did not reduce accidents or fatalities on the road. These evaluations, combined with pressure by the beer lobby (whose profits were threatened by these laws), had produced a situation where some of the states that had already passed minimum drinking age laws were debating their repeal. Finally, South Dakota decided to take its case to the Supreme Court, alleging that the legislation enacted by the Congress was unconstitutional in the first place.

For this synthesis (performed by Richard Barnes, Roy Jones, Phil Travers, and Tom Laetz), we identified 400 evaluations, 49 of which looked at laws that raised the drinking age and examined their effects on traffic accidents and 14—using different evaluation approaches—that met our minimum methodological threshold for quality. We found that based on those 14 evaluations, raising the drinking age to 21 had, on average, had a direct and significant effect on reducing alcohol-related traffic accidents among youths affected by the laws across the states. We also found that states could generally expect reductions in their traffic accidents and that raising the drinking age would likely result in a decline in alcohol consumption and in driving after drinking for the age group affected by the law. The Subcommittee Chairman held a hearing on our report on September 18, 1986 (USGAO/PEMD-87-10).

It was a very unusual hearing. Of all the testimonies I gave to Congress, this is the one in which Members of Congress showed the most interest in issues of methodology. After an all-day session focusing on the smallest details of our work, it ended with plaudits from the Subcommittee Chairman. On the executive-branch side, the Department of Transportation had also received the synthesis well. They wrote, "We commend GAO for an excellent report" and went on to say that "the criteria utilized to select documents for consideration are logical and objective" and that the consistency of the studies' results "increases one's confidence in the generalization of the findings" (USGAO/PEMD-87-10, 1987, p. 100). The Solicitor General then decided to submit our synthesis to the Supreme Court for consideration in the Court's deliberations on the drinking-age law's constitutionality. In the end, the Court upheld the law's constitutionality after using our findings to set aside questions about the effectiveness of raising the drinking age.

After the verdict, all 50 states and the District of Columbia increased the drinking age to 21, and none of the existing laws was repealed, despite intense lobbying by the liquor industry and college students. Finally, at a conference on traffic safety, an official from the National Highway Safety Administration credited us with convincing state legislatures to raise the drinking age to 21 and, as a result, saving an estimated 1,000 lives in 1987.

Some Further Synthesis Efforts

Over the 14 years I spent at the GAO, we did some 30 evaluation syntheses for the Congress, along with two other methods papers which were developed based on our ongoing experience. The first, called the Prospective Evaluation Synthesis, which I drafted with Peter Rossi and Lois-Ellin Datta, was "a systematic method for analyzing proposed pieces of legislation to provide the best possible information on their likely outcomes"—that is, to apply the evaluation synthesis approach directly to prospective questions from the Congress (USGAO/PEMD, Transfer Paper 10.1.10, 1989, p. 2). The second methods paper, which was developed by Judith Droitcour and George Silberman, addressed problems and options in combining data and synthesizing results from studies with complementary designs, principally randomized studies and database analyses. We called this work the Cross-Design Synthesis (USGAO/ PEMD-92-18, 1992). The issue addressed here was that

> definitive answers about the effects of various treatments in medical practice can be provided only by a body of research that meets two key criteria: (a) methodological quality in comparing treatment outcomes, and (b) generalizability to the conditions of medical practice. (Droitcour, Silberman, & Chelimsky, 1993, p. 440)

As such, this method was an effort to develop information on both quality *and* generalizability by selecting studies with complementary designs and then following a strategy that included the following:

- A focused assessment of the study biases that may derive from characteristic design weaknesses;
- Individual adjustment of each study's results to "correct for" identified biases; and
- Development of a synthesis framework and an appropriate model for combining results (within and across designs) in light of all assessment information. (Droitcour, Silberman, & Chelimsky, 1993)

A Few Reflections on the Synthesis Experience at the GAO

During the period between 1980 and 1994, we produced syntheses, both retrospective and prospective, in a great many different subject areas. The approach we used, as already noted, differed in a number of ways from the meta-analysis process described by Glass (1976). Four of these differences in particular seem noteworthy: (1) Our questions were derived from our legislative user and did not emerge from the database of available studies (as in meta-analysis) thus making the relation between the database and the question critical to establish in the synthesis process; (2) because of credibility issues in a political environment, such as the ones encountered in the WIC program synthesis, we looked only at high-quality evaluations rather than at all available information, as in meta-analysis; (3) we were more likely to use nonquantitative techniques for combining synthesis data than was typical for meta-analysis; and (4) we made heavy use of outside expert panels "to suggest additions to the list of studies for review, to critique the technical approaches used for combining synthesis data, and to comment on the study findings" (Light & Pillemer, 1984, pp. 39, 164).

Although the policy use of our 30 syntheses was excellent overall, we nonetheless had some general and specific problems in performing them, not all of which we were able to resolve. First, conducting a synthesis for policy use always depends on the availability of a sufficient number of primary studies, but in the 1980s, these studies didn't always exist. This improved, of course, as time went on. Second, locating all the appropriate studies could be arduous. The publication bias problem dogged us from the beginning, and not only at DOD. In some agencies, there was a highly selective process by which studies that came to the "wrong" (i.e., unfavorable) conclusions were hidden away or classified. We talked with authors/ researchers, we brought in panels of experts, and we inquired exhaustively, but we were often uncertain as to whether we had found all the relevant studies.

Third, poor reporting—rather than poor quality—in some studies made it impossible to use them in a synthesis. On occasion, we found that the explanation of research procedures could be so opaque, so sketchy, and so summarily documented that it was hard to make judgments about the evaluation's technical quality. Treatments also were often minimally described, which made it hard to determine similarities and differences across studies. Of course, we tried to make up for these gaps by discussions with the evaluators, but we didn't always succeed. Fourth, the recency of the evaluations turned out to be important. If the studies in a synthesis are antiquated, there is a risk that the problems they identify may already have been addressed and no longer characterize the program. We tried to counter this by checking on the use that had been made of the evaluation findings. Finally, the difficulties of combining data, especially across studies with different designs, were sometimes hard to work through.

We dealt with these by being honest about uncertainties, acknowledging the frailties of our approach, and developing the Cross-Design Synthesis for merging data from different types of studies.

Overall, however, despite these problems, evaluation synthesis proved from the beginning to be a useful method for us, and it was immediately accepted by Congress. Even when subjected to severe and intensive political grilling, the method held its own and may actually have been a more effective shield against partisan slings and arrows than a single study could ever have been, no matter how well done. Politically, I would say we were most often hit with two types of controversy: when our findings suggested shifts in traditional roles, responsibilities, or resources and when the topic being treated was already mired in political mud before we had even started our work.

Of course, the synthesis caused us our worst problems when the findings were not what people wanted to hear; but this would have been true with any other method we might have used. We did learn to be highly explicit—*ad nauseam*, some said at the GAO—about our procedures: for example, documenting our methods to ensure inter-rater reliability saved our lives on more than one occasion. But overall, in fields where there were many good studies to synthesize, I'd say the approach served us well, even under a hail of bullets.

Looking back, it seems that our synthesis findings were used by policy makers in at least seven different ways:

- to implement the oversight function
- to make legislative reauthorizations
- to make changes or modifications in agency studies and programs
- to develop new legislation
- to strengthen methodological requirements in agency procurement requests
- to make budgetary markups
- to formulate new policy in various agencies

Some syntheses were used in more than one way, and the approach was quite versatile in being able to address programs at different points in their evolution: those still at the concept stage, those already in existence for some period of time, and those so venerable that their evaluations might go back forty years and number in the hundreds.

It seems likely that, deprived of the synthesis approach, we would have been unsuccessful in addressing many important congressional requests for information. Instead, the experience was positive; it worked well with both Democrats and Republicans; the use of the findings was appropriate and considerable in all three branches of government; new agency research was commissioned or mandated when information was missing; strong studies were used and reused; and, perhaps most importantly, evaluation became, because of the synthesis operations, a much more routine tool in the legislative consideration of public programs.

References

Campbell, D. (1984). Numbers and narrative. In R. J. Light & D. B. Pillemer (Eds.), *Summing up: The science of reviewing research* (pp. 104–143). Cambridge, MA: Harvard University Press.

Chelimsky, E. (1977). *An analysis of the proceedings of a symposium on the use of evaluation by federal agencies* (vol. II). Mclean, VA: Metrek, MITRE Corporation.

Chelimsky, E. (1987, June). Retrospective and prospective methods. *Evaluation Review, 11*(3), 355–370.

Chelimsky, E. (1996, September). Producing credible evaluations of federal health programs. In L. J. C. Riggin (Ed.), *Evaluation and the health professions, 19*(3), 264–279.

Droitcour, J., Silberman, G., & Chelimsky, E. (1993, Summer). Cross-design synthesis. *The International Journal of Technology Assessment in Health Care, 9*(3), 440–449.

Dyson, F. (2012, April 5). Science on the rampage. *The New York Review of Books.* Retrieved April 11, 2014, from http://www.nybooks.com/articles/archives/2012/apr/05/science-rampage-natural-philosophy/

Glass, G. V. (1976, November). Primary, secondary, and meta-analysis of research. *Educational Researcher, 5*, 3–8.

Light, R., & Pillemer, D. B. (1984). *Summing up: The science of reviewing research.* Cambridge, MA: Harvard University Press.

Pear, R. (1984, January 31). Food program may improve mothers' health, report says. *The New York Times.* Retrieved April 11, 2014, from http://www.nytimes.com/1984/01/31/us/food-program-may-improve-mother-s-health-report-says.html

Shadish, W. R. (2005). Prudent inquiry: Conceptual complexity versus practical simplicity in knowing what works. In J. S. Carlson & J. R. Levin (Eds.), *The No Child Left Behind legislation: Educational research and federal funding* (pp. 129–134). Greenwich, CT: Information Age Publishing.

United States General Accounting Office/IPE. (1983, April). Methods paper I. *The evaluation synthesis.* March 1992 edition retrieved April 11, 2014, from http://www.gao.gov/assets/80/76108.pdf

United States General Accounting Office/IPE-81-1. (1981, September 30). *Disparities still exist in who gets special education.* Retrieved April 11, 2014, from http://www.gao.gov/assets/140/135323.pdf

United States General Accounting Office/IPE-83-6. (1983, April 29). *Chemical warfare: Many unanswered questions.* Retrieved April 11, 2014, from http://www.gao.gov/assets/150/140095.pdf

United States General Accounting Office/PEMD. (1989, July). Methodology transfer paper 10.1.10. *Prospective evaluation methods: The prospective evaluation synthesis.* Revised (1990, November) edition retrieved April 11, 2014, from http://www.gao.gov/special.pubs/10_1_10.PDF

United States General Accounting Office/PEMD-84-4. (1984, January 30). *WIC evaluations provide some favorable but no conclusive evidence on the effects expected for the special supplemental program for women, infants, and children.* Retrieved April 11, 2014, from http://www.gao.gov/assets/150/141083.pdf

United States General Accounting Office/PEMD-87-10. (1987, March). *Drinking-Age laws: An evaluation synthesis of their impact on highway safety.* Retrieved April 11, 2014, from http://www.gao.gov/assets/150/145107.pdf

United States General Accounting Office/PEMD-88-8. (1988, April). *USDA's commodity program: The accuracy of budget forecasts.* Retrieved April 11, 2014, from http://www.gao.gov/assets/150/146335.pdf

United States General Accounting Office/PEMD-92-18. (1992, March). *Cross-design synthesis: A new strategy for medical effectiveness research.* Retrieved April 11, 2014, from http://www.gao.gov/assets/160/151472.pdf

United States Senate Committee on Agriculture, Nutrition, and Forestry. (1984, January 30). *Press release.*

Part IV

Credible and Actionable Evidence: General Perspectives

- Chapter 10—How Evidence Earns Credibility in Evaluation

- Chapter 11—Actionable Evidence in Context: Contextual Influences on Adequacy and Appropriateness of Method Choice in Evaluation

- Chapter 12—Credible Evidence of Effectiveness: Necessary but Not Sufficient

- Chapter 13—Credible and Actionable Evidence: A Framework, Overview, and Suggestions for Future Practice and Research

The distinction between the chapters in this section and the previous one involves a matter of degree. Although the chapters in Part III dealt with general issues of credibility, each focused primarily on a specific method or method family. Rallis addressed qualitative methods, Mathison emphasized image-based evidence, and Chelimsky considered evaluation syntheses. In contrast, the three chapters in Part IV tend not to focus on a single method or method type. Rather, these chapters tend to engage in more general discussion about what leads to credibility, actionability, and related attributes of evidence.

In Chapter 10, Jennifer Greene points out that the credibility of evidence, in evaluation and presumably more generally, is a political and social matter as well as an empirical one. She contends that credibility "is not automatically granted via the use of particular empirical methodologies but rather is *earned* through inclusive, relational, and dialogic processes of interpretation and action that happen on the ground, in context, and in interaction with stakeholders" (italics in original, p. 206). Greene roots her position in a particular view of democracy and of the place that evaluation (and presumably other applied research) should have within a democracy. According to that vision, "Evaluation conducted for the public good aims to enlighten and inform the relevant policy conversation and *especially* to include therein diverse voices, perspectives, and experiences" (italics in original, p. 207). Greene presents what she sees as the conditions that affect the potential credibility of evidence and further describes how one can best achieve that potential credibility. For instance, she emphasizes the importance of cultivating respectful relationships and communication as an underpinning of credibility. To illustrate her position, Greene describes an actual evaluation, which used a randomized experiment. In addition to summarizing the experiment, Greene offers hypothetical additions of the kind she contends will increase credibility.

George Julnes and Debra Rog provide a pragmatic approach to making choices about what methods to use. In Chapter 11, they argue that in evaluation and applied research, "the 'worthiness' of evidence is better framed as whether it is *actionable* rather than *credible*" (p. 252). They emphasize the importance of the context in which findings might be used: "[T]he worthiness of evidence . . . cannot be judged in the abstract but, rather, only in terms of the needs and constraints of specific situations" (p. 252). Expanding on this general idea, Julnes and Rog provide a framework suggesting how method choices can be guided by thinking about (a) alternative evaluation questions and tasks that might be addressed; (b) attributes of the phenomenon being investigated, such as whether change is likely to be easy and quick or difficult and slow; (c) characteristics of the program or policy to be investigated; (d) specific circumstances of the evaluation or study; and (e) more general characteristics of the context in which the program or policy operates. Julnes and Rog discuss specific issues within each of these five categories and show how they can make one method more or less suitable than others for particular situations. Julnes and Rog also describe the circumstances in which randomized trials and strong quasi-experiments are most likely to be valuable in providing credible and actionable evidence. They conclude with the hope that if more consensus can be achieved about the implications of situational factors for methods choices, then "[d]oing so will support method choice better suited to yielding actionable evidence in context" (p. 255).

In Chapter 12, Thomas Schwandt, like Julnes and Rog, notes that the quality of evidence a method provides is not universal but instead depends on the nature of the question under investigation. Unlike Julnes and Rog, however, Schwandt does not focus on categories of situational factors that might guide method choice. Instead, he describes four general contexts in which evidence might be used: persuasion, negotiation, deliberation, and inquiry. He notes that method hierarchies and other rule-based approaches to evidence use presume one of these contexts rather than the others. Schwandt also emphasizes multiple properties of evidence. Credibility is one property of evidence, according to Schwandt, but there are others, specifically probative value and relevance. Schwandt also discusses ethical issues related to the production, interpretation, dissemination, and use of evidence. More generally, given what he sees as the intrinsic limits of evidence, Schwandt warns us about terms such as *evidence-based* programs or decision making: "To claim that evidence may figure importantly in our decisions is one thing; to claim it is foundation for our actions is another. We would be well advised to talk about *evidence-informed* decision making instead" (italics in original, p. 261).

Melvin Mark closes this section, and the book, with Chapter 13. Mark draws in part on other chapters in this section to sketch a broader framework surrounding judgments of credibility and actionability. Expanding on parts of Schwandt's chapter, he refers to multiple judged attributes of evidence: credibility, inferential potency, relevance, and comprehensiveness. In Mark's framework, these four together are thought to influence judgments of actionability. In addition, the threshold that needs to be exceeded in order to think that action is called for is not a constant but instead varies across situations. Also in the framework are the five aspects of context discussed by Julnes and Rog. These are presumed to influence judgments about credibility and the other attributes of evidence. Yet another aspect of Mark's framework is the idea that different "levels" of processes can influence judgments about credibility and the rest. Some processes are at the individual level (as when a person hears a briefing about an evaluation's findings and is dismissive because of spelling errors in the PowerPoint); others are interpersonal (with Greene's suggested interactions between evaluator and stakeholder being a prime example); and yet others are collective (such as when the legislation enabling a pilot program also dictates the kind of evaluation to take place). Mark uses the components of this framework to review selectively and comment on various points made in previous chapters of the book. The primary goal of this review is to better understand *why* people take different stances about method preferences, with the hope that this understanding can lead to more productive debates and discussions in the future. Mark also notes the future research agenda that can be based on the framework. More importantly, he uses the framework as the springboard for a set of recommendations for evaluation and applied social research practice. Mark's chapter precedes Appendix I, wherein he reviews and responds to Scriven's comments about randomized experiments. In the previous edition of this book, an earlier version of this material was integrated into Mark's chapter. The Scriven material does not fit well in Mark's current chapter, given its new focus on a framework, but we believe that Scriven's ideas are important enough to warrant expanded consideration, so we have retained this in the Appendix.

10

How Evidence Earns Credibility in Evaluation

Jennifer C. Greene

E valuation is an *empirical, political,* and *social* practice in which evaluators gather and interpret data and then use these interpretations to render consequential judgments regarding the quality and effectiveness of targeted programs and policies. The *empirical* face of evaluation is grounded in its central task of gathering information—in targeted contexts—about a program's design, implementation, and outcomes. The *political* face of evaluation is engendered by its central role of making judgments of quality, which in turn inform policy decisions and directions, a role inevitably imbued with values and politics. "A theory of evaluation must be as much a theory of political interaction as it is a theory of how to collect data" (Cronbach et al., 1980, p. 3; see also House, 1980; House & Howe, 1999; Weiss, 1991, 1998). And the *social* countenance of evaluation is inherent in its enactment as a relational and negotiated practical process (Schwandt, 2002, 2003; Schwandt & Burgon, 2006). That is, the particular focus and form of an evaluation study take shape through interactions with multiple stakeholders, as does the collection of evaluation data, which happens predominantly in context, on site, and up close. And the rendering of evaluation's consequential judgments is most effectively a dialogic process, inclusive of the stances and perspectives of diverse stakeholders and thereby of meaning and relevance to a plurality of stakeholder standpoints.

There are considerable pressures on evaluation today to generate *credible evidence* upon which to base decisions about policies, practices, and concomitant resource allocations (Coalition for Evidence-Based Policy, http://coalition4evidence.org/wordpress/; Donaldson, Christie, & Mark, 2009). The most prized evidence concerns the attainment of targeted outcomes, including the causal connections between particular interventions and these desired outcomes. The pressures for such evidence are part of the larger "new public management" philosophy's insistence on outcomes and results. That is, the push for credible, also called *scientific*, evidence in government decision making must be seen as part of contemporary accountability politics.* Notably, in focusing evaluation around particular ideas about scientific evidence, evaluation becomes a tool for institutional control and policy argument (House, 1993, 2004; Schwandt, 2007). As a tool, evaluation can be used to advance policy in particular directions, for example, privatizing prisons in the United States.

Further, accompanying the demand for credible/scientific evidence has been a privileging of a particular evaluation methodology viewed as best at generating the scientific outcome evidence desired, and this privileged methodology is the randomized experiment. Yet, in heavily promoting experimentation, proponents of this view reverse the time-honored order of decisions involved in conducting social inquiry. First, the social inquirer identifies the inquiry purposes and questions and only then selects a methodology that fits these purposes and questions (Chelimsky, 2007). Method is always the servant of substance, never the master. Moreover, questions about the causal effects of social interventions are characteristically those of elite policy and decision makers, while the legitimate questions of other stakeholders are ignored or overlooked (Chelimsky, 2007). In these ways, the demands for credible evidence in evaluation obscure the political and social faces of evaluation by almost exclusively emphasizing its empirical face. Yet all of evaluation's countenances must be present and engaged when assessing the credibility of evidence generated in any given evaluation.

This chapter offers an alternative understanding of the nature of credible evidence in program evaluation, particularly democratic evaluation. In this alternative understanding, the credibility of evaluative evidence is not automatically granted via the use of particular empirical methodologies but rather is *earned* through inclusive, relational, and dialogic processes of interpretation and action that happen on the ground, in context, and in interaction with stakeholders. Conceptualizing credibility as *earned* is particularly important within a democratic vision for evaluation. In the next section of the chapter, I offer a brief portrait of democratic evaluation, positioned in service of the public good. Then, I outline the logic of an earned form of credibility for evaluative evidence. This is followed by an extended example and then by some final reflections.

---

*Parts of this and the next paragraph are derived from Greene (2009).

Evaluation in Service of the Public Good[*]

Within the evaluation community, the evaluation of social, educational, and health programs is (nearly) consensually envisioned, at least in North America and parts of Europe, as a practice intended to contribute broadly to societal improvement and progress and to social betterment (Mark, Henry, & Julnes, 2000). Yet we continue to debate the particular form of this evaluative commitment to societal improvement and social betterment. We advance different kinds of commitments to improve the program or the organization being evaluated (Patton, 2008), to contribute to wise policy and decision making (Chelimsky, 1997), to provide enlightenment or illumination of the issues at hand (Cronbach et al., 1980; Stake, 2003; Weiss, 1998), to contribute to meaningful and democratically oriented social change (House & Howe, 1999; Karlsson Vestman & Segerholm, 2009; Whitmore, 1998), and to serve the public good (Greene, 2003).

At root, these differences in evaluative commitments to doing good are about evaluation's political face or the political positioning of evaluation in society—that is, the ways in which evaluators engage with the political disputes and value conflicts that permeate our evaluation contexts. My political vision positions evaluation as intentionally and democratically conducted for the public good. And the *Guiding Principles* of the American Evaluation Association provide some support for this vision. The fifth of the five Guiding Principles refers to evaluators' "responsibilities for general and public welfare" and further specifies as one of these responsibilities:

> Evaluators have obligations that encompass the public interest and good. These obligations are especially important when evaluators are supported by publicly-generated funds; but clear threats to the public good should never be ignored in any evaluation. Because the public interest and good are rarely the same as the interests of any particular group (including those of the client or funder), evaluators will usually have to go beyond analysis of particular stakeholder interests and consider the welfare of society as a whole. (http://www.eval.org/p/cm/ld/fid=51)

So, in this vision, I am not defining the public good as a simple list of policy priorities but rather as an emphasis on the quality of public reason and the inclusiveness of public discourse. Evaluation conducted for the public good aims to enlighten and inform the relevant policy conversation and *especially* to include therein diverse voices, perspectives, and experiences. The public good (the quality and inclusiveness of public debate about important public issues) is precious enough to compel the caretaking of all citizens (Barber, 1984).

---

[*]This section is adapted from Greene (2010).

It is within this vision of democratic evaluation that the meanings of credible evidence take the particular form outlined next.

Earning Credibility

The credibility of evidence in evaluation is of vital importance to the integrity of the evaluation enterprise and to the value of the contributions the evaluation profession can make to society. Our very business is the generation of information about the quality of a given program and the fostering of meaningful use of that information in the service of greater well-being for program beneficiaries. Of course, we need and want the evaluation information generated to be defensible, on target, and actionable—in short, credible. But warranting the credibility of our evidence is more of a dynamic process than a conferred status. It is more contextual than universal. And it is more dialogic than univocal.

CONDITIONS FOR POTENTIAL
CREDIBILITY OF EVALUATIVE EVIDENCE

At the base of credible evidence in democratically oriented evaluation are several requisite conditions that, if fulfilled, signal the *potential credibility* of evidence from a given evaluation. These conditions include the following:

- The *design and methodology* of the evaluation are technically sound, contextually defensible, and implemented with adherence to appropriate methodological guidelines and conventions. Adequacy of the technical components of our evaluation craft is a necessary but not sufficient condition for the generation of credible evidence.
- The evaluation is directed toward issues, concerns, and questions of *contextual meaning and relevance*; the evaluation is designed to generate information of import and consequence to stakeholders *in the contexts* being evaluated. Evidence that is relevant only for remote stakeholders does not have the potential for credibility.
- The evaluation is directed toward issues, concerns, and questions of meaning and relevance to a *diversity of stakeholders* in the contexts being evaluated, with special inclusion of the interests of stakeholders who are least well served in those contexts.

> It would not be right for evaluators to provide evaluations only to the most powerful or to sell them to the highest bidders for their own uses.... The interests of all stakeholder groups are central [to evaluation], and the interests of all relevant parties should be represented, as genuine democracy would require.... Evaluators must design evaluations so that relevant interest are represented and so

that there is some balance of power among them, which often means [specially] representing the interests of those who might be excluded in the discussion, because their interests are likely to be overlooked in their absence. (House & Howe, 1999, p. 98)

Evaluation is a values-engaged process; it addresses questions and renders judgments based on selected criteria and values (Greene, DeStefano, Burgon, & Hall, 2006). Following House and Howe (1999), I believe that evaluation most defensibly advances democratic values of inclusion, justice, and equity, which are values that serve the general public good (Greene, 2003, 2010). And with these values comes the quiet insistence on including the perspectives, experiences, and standpoints of *all* legitimate stakeholders, with special provisions— as necessary—to include those least well served in the contexts at hand.˙

So the *potential* for evaluative evidence to be credible is established when the methodology is defensible and sound; when the key questions and foci of the evaluation are relevant and meaningful to stakeholders whose lives are affected by the program being evaluated; and when these key questions and foci represent the interests of a meaningful diversity of these stakeholders, with special inclusion of those least well served.

REALIZING THE POTENTIAL CREDIBILITY OF EVALUATIVE EVIDENCE

Next, how is such potential for credibility in democratic evaluation realized? The answer comes in two parts.

Cultivating Respectful Relationships and Communications

First, confidence in the merit and value of the evidence generated by the evaluation is cultivated through the trustworthy, respectful character of the relational and communicative dimensions of the evaluation. These relational and communicative dimensions of the evaluator's craft refer to how we as evaluators interact with stakeholders in the contexts in which we work and to the social and moral character of these interactions. For it is in these micro relationships that the macro political and value commitments of our work are importantly enacted and therefore realized or not (Greene, 2003; Greene et al., 2006). In this way of thinking, the character of the actual practice of evaluation— of what we do in the places in which we work—helps to constitute relational

---

˙Clearly, practical constraints limit any given evaluation's ability to serve *all* stakeholder interests and needs. Yet, in this presentation, credible evaluative evidence still requires that the evaluation and its evidence are meaningfully inclusive of and responsive to a plurality of stakeholder interests and needs.

norms, values, and ideals in that place—notably, about status, power, and privilege; trust, reciprocity, and caring; and respect, tolerance, and acceptance. This relational enactment of evaluation refers to the relationships, roles, interactions that take place as the evaluation is conducted—who speaks and who doesn't, how self and other are negotiated and constructed (Fine, 1994; Fine, Weseen, Weseen, & Wong, 2000), where power and privilege are located, and so forth. A kind of hermeneutic dialogue—characterized by mutual respect, acceptance, and affirmation—represents the ideal for these relational dimensions of evaluation.

More profoundly, in this relational view of the practice of evaluation, the very knowledge that is generated in evaluation—our results, our findings, our judgments of program quality—are understood to be generated *by* a particular set of evaluative relationships and interactions and thus, to a significant degree, are actually constituted by these relationships and interactions. What we do and how we interact in a setting matter to what we learn. These relationships become constitutive of our evaluation findings. Specifically, evaluative findings of relevance to the public good are grounded in an inclusive diversity of perspectives and experiences that are, in turn, generated through mutually respectful, accepting, and trusting (that is, dialogic) evaluative relationships.

So evidence that meets the criteria for being potentially credible earns actual credibility through evaluative relationships enacted with norms of trust, acceptance, and respect and through evaluative communications that are inclusive and dialogic.

Rendering Inclusive Judgments of Consequence

Credibility of the evidence or knowledge generated in a democratic evaluation further earns credibility through its transformation to judgments that are (a) anchored in an inclusive (and democratic) set of values for that context and (b) restoratively consequential and action oriented, again for the context being evaluated.

The core work of evaluation is the generation of judgments of value. Findings from evaluation methods must be transformed into such judgments using criteria identified for that context. And different criteria intrinsically represent different values. For example, in educational evaluation settings, student learning can be judged against criteria that represent normative, comparative, criterion-based, collective, processual, or other values regarding important dimensions of learning and development. So evidence in evaluation conducted in service of the public good earns credibility when transformed into judgments that are explicitly based on inclusive and democratic values, for example, values of equity or social justice (Greene et al., 2006; House & Howe, 1999).

Moreover, these evaluative judgments earn credibility when they are contextually and constructively consequential. Evaluation is fundamentally intended to be of use—instrumental, conceptual, or symbolic. Any of these possible uses can be contextually consequential, meaning that the evaluation results and judgments matter in the context being evaluated. To be credible, evaluation results and judgments need to also matter in a constructive, affirming, restorative way, thus engaging affirmative accountability pressures that encourage understanding and development rather than punitive accountability pressures that motivate through directives and punishments (Benjamin, 2008).

So evidence that meets the criteria for being potentially credible earns enacted credibility through transformation to judgments that are anchored in inclusive criteria and values and that are contextually and constructively consequential.

The next section of this discussion presents an example of the argument about how evaluative evidence earns credibility. The example is purposefully selected to represent the current default meaning of credible evidence, which again refers to evaluation data on expected outcomes from high-quality experimental studies and which again is narrowly confined to the methodological countenance of evaluation. The example presented is based on the article cited. The conversations and dialogues presented are all imagined.

A Multisite Cluster Randomized Field Trial of Open Court Reading

This experimental evaluation study assessed the intended achievement outcomes of a commercially published (by SRA/McGraw-Hill) K–6 literacy curriculum called Open Court Reading (OCR; Borman, Dowling, & Schneck, 2008). The evaluators located this evaluation within the context of continuing challenges in American literacy education, especially for children of color and children from poor families. The OCR curriculum, which has been widely used since the 1960s, emphasizes phonics and is grounded in research-based literacy practices (National Reading Panel, 2000). The OCR program includes student materials (grade-appropriate texts and workbooks, anthologies) and teacher materials (lesson plans and exercises for students) as well as teacher professional development opportunities. Despite the popularity of the OCR program and some evidence regarding its efficacy, it has "never been evaluated rigorously through a randomized trial" (Borman et al., 2008, p. 390).

A randomized experiment at the classroom level (not the individual student level) within five schools in six different states comprised the methodology for this evaluation. During the spring of 2005, SRA/McGraw-Hill recruited schools for this study from among those expressing interest in purchasing the OCR program. Selected schools were offered the OCR materials for free in exchange for study participation, with the proviso that the control classrooms in that school maintain the existing literacy curriculum. A final sample (both experimental and control) of five schools, 49 Grade 1–5 classrooms, and close to 1,000 students was secured. Pre- and posttests (October 2005 and May 2006) of reading comprehension and vocabulary (the CTBS/5, Terra Nova) were administered to all students in both groups.

CREDIBLE EVIDENCE?

The evaluators carefully documented the considerable methodological care they took in designing this study. The methodological issues they engaged included the following: diversity in student demographics and equivalence therein between experimental and control groups (or possible selection bias), the nonrandomness of the sample selection, fidelity of program implementation, possible treatment spillover from treatment to control classes within the same school, inevitable sample attrition, and multilevel statistical modeling, among others. In fact, about one-half of the pages in the article published on this study were devoted to discussions of these methodological issues. The empirical face of evaluation was well documented in this account.

According to the evaluators of this study, there were no statistically significant differences on the reading measures between experimental and control groups (on the average) at pretest, and the samples were both internally and externally robust. A carefully designed hierarchical linear model analysis of the OCR treatment effects yielded the following results. "In all cases, the treatment indicator revealed a statistically significant [positive] classroom-level effect of assignment to OCR" (Borman et al., 2008, p. 402). These results are also practically significant, argued the authors. For example, on the vocabulary test, "the average student from an OCR classroom outperformed nearly 58% of his or her control group counterparts" (Borman et al., 2008, pp. 402–403).

According to the default meaning of credible evidence, these findings suggest* that the OCR is an effective literacy curriculum, on the average, for elementary school children, where effectiveness means adequate mastery of comprehension and vocabulary skills (as defined by the CTBS/5).

CREDIBLE EVIDENCE, REVISITED

But, as I argued above, sound methodology alone does not credibility of evidence make. Rather, credibility is an earned phenomenon, involving interactive processes. Using the threefold set of criteria for evidence credibility in

---

*The evidence is not definitive, given the extent of the methodological challenges in this experimental study. Different readers will have different views on degree to which these challenges compromise the integrity of the evidence obtained.

democratic evaluation, let us imagine what these credibility-earning activities and processes might have looked like in this particular evaluation study.

At the outset, it is important to recognize that this evaluation was not conducted with an explicit democratic framework, ambition, or values. Rather this was a policy-oriented evaluation intended to assess attainment of intended outcomes and to establish causal linkages between the OCR program and these outcomes. And although this is a legitimate and important role for evaluation, it can also be critiqued from a democratic standpoint. So one way of framing this exercise is to imagine how a policy-oriented evaluation of this kind could become more democratic in intent and form (given an assumption of sufficient resources) and thereby generate evidence that earns credibility in all of evaluation's countenances (empirical, political, and social). The present tense will be used in these imaginings, as it is more fresh, alive, and active than others.

Conditions for Potential Credibility of Evaluative Evidence

Three conditions to establish the *potential credibility* of evaluative evidence were recommended above. The first concerns the soundness and defensibility of methodology used in the study. In the OCR evaluation, I believe we can safely assume that this condition was met for the experimental methodology used and, for sake of argument, for any other data-gathering and analysis methods that may be added to the study during this exercise.

The second two conditions necessary to establish the potential credibility of evaluative evidence concern the extent to which and ways in which the evaluation is directed toward issues, concerns, and questions of *contextual meaning and relevance* to a *diversity of stakeholders* in the contexts being evaluated, with special inclusion of the interests of stakeholders who are least well served in those contexts. At least as reported in the published article, the OCR did not meet these conditions. The key evaluation questions pursued were those of the evaluation and program funders, and there was no targeted attention to underserved children (or teachers or schools).

How might the evaluators fulfill these other potential credibility conditions? Here are two ideas, again imagined.

The OCR evaluation team decides to go beyond their contractual charge from SRA/McGraw-Hill and assess additional program components of interest to the teachers and principals in the schools selected. From their side, team members believe that teachers and principals could usefully inform

(Continued)

(Continued)

the evaluative assessment of fidelity of treatment implementation. Beyond this, they believe that the longer-term quality and sustainability of the OCR program depends on local stakeholder support and enthusiasm and want to assess the current nature of such support in this evaluation. Further, they understand that the experimental design could create some tensions within participating schools and wish to help ease these tensions by being responsive to local stakeholder concerns and issues about the program.

In order to better understand teacher and principal program concerns, the evaluation team makes a one-day site visit to each of the five participating schools. During each visit, they meet with several small groups of teachers and administrators for open discussions about the OCR program and its promise and challenge for their school and their students. The evaluators endeavor to listen well and respectfully and to understand in some depth these local perspectives on the OCR program.

After the site visits, the team analyzes all of the input they had received and generates two additional questions for their evaluation, which they send back to all participating teachers and principals for review and critique. The final version of these two additional questions is

- How well does the OCR program permit and support differentiated instruction for different kinds of learners? and
- In what ways and to what extent do the OCR teacher materials and professional development support facilitate contextually appropriate and meaningful program implementation, and what improvements to these materials and support are needed?

The evaluation team adds an online teacher questionnaire and a handful of key informant interviews to the evaluation design to gather the data that could help address these questions.

Prompted partly by their conversations with local stakeholders, the evaluation team also decides to go beyond test score averages and investigate possible differential OCR effects for different kinds of learners. They consult with literacy experts and again, with the teachers and principals in the OCR evaluation study, and ask them to identify the kinds of children who are placed most at risk of literacy learning problems in each of the schools in the study. The team then plans to disaggregate the pre–post data by these subgroups of more fragile learners. Recognizing they would not have enough statistical power to conduct multivariate analyses, they opt to portray the data for these subgroups in a variety of spatial arrays and send interesting relevant arrays back to the teachers for their interpretations and sensemakings. Although a modest addition to the study, these specialized analyses and data reports could hopefully contribute to the future teaching and learning—through OCR or other literacy programs—of children least well served in these study contexts.

With these additions, the OCR evaluation could likely meet the conditions for potential credibility of evaluative evidence because the evaluative questions addressed now include issues of direct relevance to key stakeholders in the contexts being evaluated and also attend to the well-being of a diversity of children with particular attention to those least well served. What activities and processes are now needed to begin to realize such potential?

Realizing the Potential Credibility of Evaluative Evidence

With the site visits and inclusive additions to the evaluation plan described above, the OCR evaluation team has already initiated the kinds of respectful, reciprocal, and inclusive relationships needed for their evaluative results to be credible. Again, the argument is that the very knowledge that is generated in evaluation—our results, our findings, our judgments of program quality—are generated *within and by* a particular set of evaluative relationships and interactions, and thus, to a significant degree, are actually constituted by these relationships and interactions. Distant, disengaged relationships risk the generation of findings that are similarly distant and removed from the contexts being studied. Exclusive relationships can too easily privilege some perspectives and experiences and overlook others, thus risking the generation of findings that do not pertain to the full range of schools, teachers, and children involved in the OCR program and, particularly, that overlook the interests of those least well served in the contexts being studied.

Working in part toward the cultivation of respectful, accepting, and trusting evaluative relationships with local stakeholders, the evaluation team has visited each school and spent time on site interacting with and listening to the teachers and principals involved in the study. These visits resulted in additional evaluation questions and data to be gathered and analyzed—signaling the importance of local stakeholder perspectives and experiences in the evaluation study.

To substantiate and further advance relationships with local stakeholders (and have a faint hope of staying within budget), the evaluation team decides to establish an interactive website for the evaluation and to post a series of biweekly memos to this website about the evaluation's progress while inviting comments and critiques from all involved stakeholders. The intent of the website is to foster an inclusive ongoing conversation about the implementation and effects of the OCR program and thereby to establish interactive norms of inclusion, respect, trust, and acceptance.*

What follows are two illustrations of the evaluation team's biweekly website memos, one relatively early in the one-year evaluation study and one a few months later.

Hello OCR evaluation participants!

Thanks to you all for welcoming the evaluation team to your school last month and for hosting such an enjoyable and rewarding set of conversations. We hope the additional evaluation questions that emerged from this effort will capture some of the important and thoughtful perspectives on the OCR program that we heard during our visits. We are also compelled to comment that food served during our visits was uniformly excellent, though varied in cuisine and tradition. Again, please accept our appreciation for your generous and kind hospitality.

We also thank you all for a nearly flawless pretest experience. We fully realize the challenges and disruption that pretesting invokes in your classrooms and schools. So we are especially appreciative of your exceptional cooperation and assistance with this evaluation activity.

We also would welcome any comments and feedback you may have about the pretesting activity. How did your students experience it? Were there particular students who found the pretest easy or boring, and others who struggled to get through it? What insights might you have about these particular students' literacy development?

And here is our question of the biweek: What aspect or strand of the OCR has been particularly successful with your students over the past month? Why do you think it is working so well with your students?

Thanks!
Evaluation Team

---

*The evaluation team recognizes that a number of parents and guardians of children involved in the OCR evaluation will still be excluded from having an active voice in the study and the program's implementation in their child's school. They vow to strive to remedy this exclusion in the next curriculum evaluation study they conduct.

Hello OCR evaluation participants!

In this post, we take up the observation—noted by many of you—that the OCR is particularly effective with some children who have struggled in the past with learning to read. This could be an especially important insight from this evaluation study, and we are eager to learn more about it from all of you.

So we are inviting anyone who has observed a child being successful in her or his literacy learning with the OCR program—despite a more troubled history—to share the story of this child as you have experienced it. What specifically has drawn your attention to this child? Can you give examples of what he or she has learned to do? To what in the OCR program do you attribute these accomplishments? And what else is important to this story?

To encourage your narrative posts, we have attached a brief example of a literacy learning narrative written by an elementary school teacher last year.

We are eager to read *your* stories.

Thanks!

The Evaluation Team

So the potential credibility of evidence generated from our enhanced OCR evaluation has earned (at least some) enacted credibility through the evaluators' cultivation of ongoing conversations with key stakeholders (notably, teachers) and the respectful and affirming relationships supporting such conversations.

Credibility of evaluative evidence from the enhanced OCR evaluation can be further enacted through the inclusive and dialogic (House & Howe, 1999) rendering of evaluative judgments of constructive consequence. Such judgments can be accomplished through an open process of dialogue and deliberation (House & Howe, 1999) in which the criteria for judgment (a) incorporate democratic commitments (for example, equity in program access and outcomes across diverse children) and (b) are made fully explicit. These evaluative judgments earn additional credibility when they are contextually and constructively consequential—that is, they matter to involved stakeholders and offer meaningful routes to continued (educational) excellence and/or improvement.

In the enhanced OCR evaluation, the evaluators could convene an open forum in each participating school for discussion of the evaluation results toward the generation of judgments with constructive implications for each local community. What follows is one possible invitation to such a forum.

Good day, elementary school community members!

The results of the evaluation of your school's literacy program, Open Court Reading, are now available for discussion and deliberation. We welcome all interested teachers, administrators, and parents/guardians to an open forum on April 20th, during which we will collectively discuss the evaluation results and what they mean for the quality of the OCR program at your school. A high-quality literacy program helps *all* children master the critical skills of reading and writing. So we hope you will come and help make sense of the evaluation results with your particular child or classroom in mind.

The discussion will also seek to map the way forward. In what ways is the OCR a good literacy program for your school? What modifications in or enhancements to the program may be needed? How else can children's development of literacy competence and confidence be developed at your school?

Juice and cookies will be provided at the forum. We hope to see you all there!

The Evaluation Team

Reprise

The language of evaluation (and indeed, other forms of social inquiry) is intrinsically value laden precisely because the practice of evaluation is a social, contextual, and relational activity. Value-laden ideas and concepts can—and often are—used for political positioning and advantage. So it is with the concept of credible evidence. A seemingly neutral, even quasi-scientific term, *evidence*, in everyday parlance refers to an outward sign or an indication as to the truth of a matter or something that furnishes proof (http://www.merriam-webster .com/dictionary/). The political discourse about evaluation priorities over the past decade has concentrated on what the most important kinds of evidence to collect in an evaluation study are and, concomitantly, what kinds of evaluation studies can best produce this evidence. In this discourse, credible evaluative evidence has acquired a more particular meaning, referring to causal claims about intended program outcomes, and credible evaluation designs (that can produce this evidence) have been rank ordered in a hierarchy.

The argument in this paper seeks to reclaim the concept of credible evidence from its narrow definition as causal claims regarding intended outcomes and its pristine position as requiring only a methodological warrant. The argument seeks to reassert the key importance of democratic values in assessing the credibility of evidence and thus also to reframe this assessment as an inclusive, dialogic process rather than a matter of methodological purity. Well beyond good method, making meaningful and consequential judgments about the quality and effectiveness of social and educational programs requires engagement, interaction, listening, and caring.

References

Barber, B. (1984). *Strong democracy: Participatory politics for a new age.* Berkeley: University of California Press.

Benjamin, L. M. (2008). Evaluator's role in accountability relationships: Measurement technician, capacity builder or risk manager? *Evaluation, 14*(3), 323–343.

Borman, G. D., Dowling, N. M., & Schneck, C. (2008). A multisite cluster randomized field trial of Open Court Reading. *Educational Evaluation and Policy Analysis, 30*(4), 389–407.

Chelimsky, E. (1997). The coming transformations in evaluation. In E. Chelimsky & W. R. Shadish (Eds.), *Evaluation for the 21st century: A handbook* (pp. 1–25). Thousand Oaks, CA: SAGE.

Chelimsky, E. (2007). Factors influencing the choice of methods in federal evaluation practice. In G. Julnes & D. Rog (Eds.), Informing federal policies on evaluation methodology: Building the evidence base for method choice in government sponsored evaluation. *New Directions for Evaluation, 113,* 13–33.

Cronbach, L. J., Ambron, S. R., Dornbusch, S. M., Hess, R. D., Hornik, R. C., Phillips, D. C., Walker, D. F., & Weiner, S. S. (1980). *Toward reform of program evaluation.* San Francisco, CA: Jossey-Bass.

Donaldson, S. I., Christie, C. A., & Mark M. M. (Eds.). (2009). *What counts as credible evidence in applied research and evaluation practice?* Thousand Oaks, CA: SAGE.

Fine, M. (1994). Working the hyphens: Reinventing self and other in qualitative research. In N. K. Denzin & Y. S. Lincoln (Eds.), *Handbook of qualitative research* (pp. 70–82). Thousand Oaks, CA: SAGE.

Fine, M., Weiss, L., Weseen, S., & Wong, L. (2000). For whom? Qualitative research, representations, and social responsibilities. In N. K. Denzin & Y. S. Lincoln (Eds.), *Handbook of qualitative research* (2nd ed., pp. 107–133). Thousand Oaks, CA: SAGE.

Greene, J. C. (2003). Evaluators as stewards of the public good. In S. Hood, R. K. Hopson, & H. T. Frierson. (Eds.), *The role of culture and cultural context: A mandate for inclusion, the discovery of truth and understanding in evaluative theory and practice* (pp. 7–20). Greenwich, CT: Information Age Publishing.

Greene, J. C. (2009). Evidence as "proof" and evidence as "inkling." In S. I. Donaldson, C. A. Christie, & M. M. Mark (Eds.), *What counts as credible evidence in applied research and evaluation practice?* (pp. 153–167). Thousand Oaks, CA: SAGE.

Greene, J. C. (2010). Evaluation in service of the public good: The views of one US American evaluator. *Zeitschrift fur Evaluation* [the journal of the German Evaluation Society], *9*(2), 199–210.

Greene, J. C., DeStefano, L., Burgon, H., & Hall, J. (2006). An educative, values-engaged approach to evaluating STEM educational programs. In D. Huffman & F. Lawrenz (Eds.), Critical issues in STEM evaluation. *New Directions for Evaluation, 109,* 53–71.

House, E. R. (1980). *Evaluating with validity.* Thousand Oaks, CA: SAGE.

House, E. R. (1993). *Professional evaluation.* Thousand Oaks, CA: SAGE.

House, E. R. (2004, October). *Democracy and evaluation.* Keynote address presented to the European Evaluation Society in Berlin, Germany.

House, E. R., & Howe, K. R. (1999). *Values in evaluation and social research.* Thousand Oaks, CA: SAGE.

Karlsson Vestman, O., & Segerholm, C. (2009). Dialogue, deliberation, and democracy in educational evaluation. In K. E. Ryan & J. B Cousins (Eds.), *The SAGE international handbook of educational evaluation* (pp. 465–482). Thousand Oaks, CA: SAGE.

Mark, M. M, Henry, G. T., & Julnes, G. (2000). *Evaluation: An integrated framework for understanding, guiding and improving policies and programs.* San Francisco, CA: Jossey-Bass.

National Reading Panel. (2000). *Report of the National Reading Panel. Teaching children to read: An evidence-based assessment of the scientific research literature on reading and its implications for reading instruction.* National Institutes of Health Publication No. 00–4769. Washington DC: Government Printing Office.

Patton, M. Q. (2008). *Utilization-focused evaluation* (4th ed.). Thousand Oaks, CA: SAGE.

Schwandt, T. A. (2002). *Evaluation practice reconsidered.* New York, NY: Peter Lang.

Schwandt, T. A. (2003). Back to rough ground! Beyond theory to practice in evaluation. *Evaluation, 9*(3), 353–364.

Schwandt, T. A. (2007). Thoughts on using the notion of evidence in the controversy over methods choice. In G. Julnes & D. Rog (Eds.), Informing federal policies on evaluation methodology: Building the evidence base for method choice in government sponsored evaluation. *New Directions for Evaluation, 113,* 115–119.

Schwandt, T. A., & Burgon, H. (2006). Evaluation and the study of lived experience. In I. Shaw, J. C. Greene, & M. M. Mark (Eds.), *The SAGE handbook of evaluation* (pp. 98–117). London, England: SAGE.

Stake, R. E. (2003). *Standards-based and responsive evaluation.* Thousand Oaks, CA: SAGE.

Weiss, C. H. (1991). Evaluation research in the political context: Sixteen years and four administrations later. In M. W. McLaughlin & D. C. Phillips (Eds.), *Evaluation and education: At quarter century* (pp. 210–231). Chicago, IL: National Society for the Study of Education, University of Chicago Press.

Weiss, C. H. (1998). *Evaluation* (2nd ed.). Upper Saddle River, NJ: Prentice Hall.

Whitmore, E. (Ed.). (1998). Understanding and practicing participatory evaluation [Entire issue]. *New Directions for Evaluation, 90.*

11

Actionable Evidence in Context

Contextual Influences on Adequacy and Appropriateness of Method Choice in Evaluation

George Julnes

Debra Rog

P hilosophers have long struggled with what it means for evidence to be credible (Weinberg, 1973). For much of this volume, the focus is on understanding what constitutes credible evidence for informing policy and program decisions. Our pragmatic approach extends the concept to suggest that for evidence to be useful, it not only needs to be credible but actionable as well, deemed both adequate and appropriate for guiding actions and decisions in targeted real-world contexts (Julnes & Rog, 2007). Certainly, credibility helps evidence to be actionable, but the level of credibility necessary or useful to guide action depends on the situation. Further, evidence can be credible in one context but of questionable relevance for guiding actions in other contexts (Argyris, 1996). As such, credibility alone is typically not sufficient; relevance also plays a role in what is deemed actionable.

Many factors influence the degree to which a given set of evidence is judged as actionable for a particular purpose and in a specific context. Our interest in this chapter is with those factors related to methodology: To what extent are certain research designs and methods better suited for yielding actionable evidence, and more specifically, what role does the particular context play in determining whether the evidence generated by a particular method should be considered actionable? We address this question for one type of evidence of interest in evaluation—evidence about the causal impacts of programs and policies that we can use to improve them and judge their worth. The methods we consider are the design methodologies, either qualitative or quantitative, that support our confidence in these causal conclusions.

As background, there is general agreement that different methods are more suited to different contexts (Datta, 1997). Indeed, the Evaluation Roadmap published by the American Evaluation Association formalizes this consensus in stating, "All evaluation methods should be context-sensitive, have cultural relevance, and be methodologically sound" (2013, p. 7). However, conflict comes when developing specific recommendations about which particular methods fit the needs of particular contexts. This lack of consensus at the level of specifics has a long history in evaluation (see Reichardt & Rallis, 1994), leading to such distrust that even when one group believes it is offering a context-sensitive recommendation, such as the relative value of random assignment experimental methods compared to other techniques for addressing one class of evaluation questions (Lipsey, 2007), others see an attempt to impose a particular methodology on the field.

Part of the problem may be that we have not developed yet a language of context that is adequate to support more meaningful communication among adherents of different methodological traditions (Datta, 1994). Building on our prior contextual frameworks (Julnes & Rog, 2007, 2008), this chapter is organized in sections around Rog's (2012) delineation of five areas of context that affect evaluation practice: (1) decision context, (2) problem/phenomena context, (3) context of the program/policy intervention, (4) evaluation context, and (5) environmental context. In highlighting these five areas, no claim is being made that these represent some definitive statement of all that can be considered part of context or that there are not other frameworks or perspectives of context that can inform evaluation practice; they are used here to stimulate more meaningful dialogue that will support an evolving development of our appreciation of context. Similarly, although we treat each area of context separately, we do not want to overemphasize their fundamental distinctiveness; in practice, these identified areas are overlapping, intertwined, and considered together in making method choices. We do believe, however, that discussing each in turn can elucidate contextual influences that affect our choice of methods and, hence, improve overall practice.

Implications of the Decision Context for Method Choice

Efforts to advance our understanding of what constitutes actionable evidence need to consider multiple perspectives, not simply those of evaluators. It is important to know who the decision makers are who need the evidence and the standards or rigor expected in the area before a method is chosen. Moreover, method choice is influenced by the degree of confidence that policy makers and other stakeholders feel that they need before taking action. Therefore, in this section, we address several dimensions of the decision context that affect method choice: the types of decisions and information needs of stakeholders; the multiple questions and tasks the evaluation is expected to address; the multiple levels of conclusions and decisions that need to be made; and the form in which the decision makers would like to see the conclusions.

DELINEATING TYPES OF DECISIONS AND INFORMATION NEEDS

Primary among those factors influencing method choice are the decisions that evaluation is to support. One way to distinguish decisions is in terms of the stakeholders making them (e.g., individuals deciding on whether to participate in a program, managers deciding how to implement a program, and policy makers deciding on reauthorization of programs). More common, however, is to frame decisions in terms of the types of decisions and the information needs.

Types of Decisions

Scriven (1967) made an early attempt at providing a framework that distinguished formative and summative purposes for evaluation, with *formative* focused on improving programs and *summative* on supporting judgments of value. The implication is that more exploratory methods are appropriate for formative evaluation and more rigorous experimental designs for summative evaluations. Weiss (1998) moved the focus to types of decisions: choosing among alternative programs; making decisions about scale of funding (e.g., increase, decrease, or maintain funding); and making midcourse corrections. Mark, Henry, and Julnes (2000) continued this approach by distinguishing four purposes for most evaluations—oversight and accountability (note: *accountability* in this context refers to following proper procedures rather than to representing a good use of resources), program and organizational improvement, assessment of merit and worth, and knowledge development—and connecting them to the primary decisions that the particular evaluation needs to support. Making explicit connections among these purposes and appropriate methodologies, the conclusions were that rigorous experimental designs would likely not be appropriate for the first two purposes in that list but might be called for in assessment of merit and worth (intended as the purpose of summative evaluation) or for some efforts at knowledge development. (This last purpose is a broad category that includes efforts to learn about the mechanisms responsible for program effectiveness as well as lessons about evaluation capacity building.)

Information Needs

What information is needed to support decision making in a particular context? One issue to consider is the current state of knowledge in a particular area. For example, evidence that might appear weak and unworthy of confidence in one situation can be judged actionable in others. For example, early in a public health emergency, such as the HIV/AIDS crisis of the past quarter century, anecdotal evidence can play a role in guiding action that would not be appropriate in the context of better evidence and greater understanding. Similarly, for emerging problem areas where little is known about a phenomenon, it may be premature to mount an experimental study. There may not be adequate information on the population in need, the nature of the interventions, and so on to warrant a study or risk the chances of it failing.

In addition, for an evaluation to produce knowledge that can have cumulative force, it is necessary to be aware of the understanding already attained in an area. For example, as Boruch (2007) notes, if current knowledge is limited such that the solution to an issue is extremely debatable, a randomized study may be warranted; otherwise, other methods may suffice. There is also often a responsibility to learn as much as possible about the phenomenon as one is evaluating solutions to deal with it. Thus the depth of underlying knowledge in an area may influence the methods that are appropriate to promote knowledge accumulation.

With this focus on accumulation, the question of the relative importance of strong causal conclusions changes in that the pool of relevant stakeholders telescopes to include those who will make use of the evaluation evidence at some point in the future. This increases the incentive to strengthen the technical adequacy of the knowledge produced. Whereas improvements in the technical adequacy of methods are unlikely in themselves to resolve the debate over evaluation methodology, they can reframe the debate by showing us how to retain rigor while also moving beyond some standard design solutions to strengthen causal conclusions. That is, there will always be cogent and passionately held differences in opinion about how evaluators can and should best contribute to the social good in particular contexts. This is good—debates between strong positions in evaluation (e.g., between Campbell and Cronbach) have yielded much that is to be valued. However, it is also the case that failure to understand the technical advances already available can prolong debates unnecessarily (Shadish, 2002). The need for defensible knowledge, especially in charged policy situations, requires us to continue these advances.

Confidence Required

Some decision situations call for greater confidence in the conclusions that result. For example, it is generally accepted (see Mark et al., 2000) that efforts to improve programs through incremental program changes require less confidence in causal conclusions (e.g., that hiring more staff will "cause" a reduction in client dissatisfaction and complaints) than do efforts to help determine which of two alternative programs should be funded (e.g., an assessment of the relative worth of two approaches to teaching English as a second language) or whether to continue or expand a program. Not only are incremental improvement efforts better able to rely on previous evidence of effectiveness, there is also the expectation that incremental changes can be reversed more easily if subsequent evidence supports very different conclusions.

This variation in desired confidence in causal conclusions occurs in the context of other priorities, including understanding the degree to which the program impacts can be expected to generalize to other settings. While the tension between strong causal conclusions (internal validity) and generalizability is not inevitable or absolute, trade-offs between the two are common in practice. Other priorities that often compete with the accuracy and precision of the findings include timeliness, cost of the evidence that is to result, and whether there are opportunity costs for conducting one study as opposed to another.

MULTIPLE EVALUATION QUESTIONS AND TASKS

A standard frame for organizing evaluation questions is in terms of the tasks that need to be accomplished to address them. Because the most controversial differences in perspectives about methods choice among evaluators are primarily about conducting summative evaluations, or evaluations with the purpose of assessing merit and worth, we focus here on the different tasks that are typically required in well-designed summative evaluations.

Evaluation Tasks

To illustrate the relationships between evaluation questions and the tasks that address them, consider the 14 evaluation questions offered by Weiss (1998, p. 273), arranged in Box 11.1 according to the five traditional evaluation tasks—implementation assessment, outcome assessment, impact evaluation, valuation (e.g., assessment of worth), and critical review (compare these with the related evaluation tasks delineated by Rossi, Lipsey, & Freeman, 2004). Building on the framework offered by Mark et al. (2000), evaluations conducted for the purposes of oversight and program improvement, for example, generally depend on one or both of the first two tasks, implementation evaluation and outcome assessment, with valuative judgments sometimes included.

Box 11.1 Weiss's Evaluation Questions, Organized by Evaluation Tasks (With Our Elaborations in Brackets)

A. Implementation Assessment

- Describing. What went on in the program over time? [e.g., What has been the reach of the program?]
- Comparing. How closely did the program follow its original plan? [e.g., Did it reach the expected target population in the numbers expected? Did the population receive the "dose" of the program intended?]

B. Outcome Assessment

- Comparing. Did recipients improve? [e.g., pre–post scores and rate of change]
- Comparing. Did recipients do better than nonrecipients? [e.g., differences in change or rate of change]

C. Impact Evaluation

1. Aggregate Program Impacts

- Ruling out rival explanations. Is the observed change due to the program? [Is attribution possible? Is an assessment of contribution possible?]

2. Disaggregated Impacts

- Disaggregating. What characteristics are associated with success? [interpreted as causal factors moderating impact]
- Profiling. What combinations of actors, services, and conditions are associated with success and failure? [interpreted as combinations moderating impact]

3. Causal Explanation (Assessment of Causal Mechanisms)

- Modeling. Through what processes did change take place over time? [What are the key mediators? Underlying mechanisms?]

D. Valuation

- Costs. What was the worth of the relative improvement of recipients? [Are the costs of the intervention or program, whether quantifiable or not, commensurate with the benefits of outcomes?]

E. Critical Review

- Locating unanticipated effects. What unexpected events and outcomes were observed? What are the limits to the findings? [e.g., limits of generalization]
- Interpreting. What are the implications of these findings? What do they mean in practical terms? [What decisions can they guide?]
- Fashioning recommendations. What recommendations do the findings imply for modifications in [or continuation of] program and policy?
- Policy analysis. What new policies and programmatic efforts to solve social problems do the findings support?

SOURCE: Thirteen questions are quoted from Weiss, 1998, p. 273

A summative evaluation, on the other hand, often requires all five of the tasks listed in Box 11.1. There is generally a need to document and make judgments about the quality of the program's implementation, measure as many of the relevant outcomes as practical, develop conclusions about the contributions of the program in influencing changes in these outcomes, support judgments about the relative or absolute value of these program influences, and foster critical review about both the evaluation and the broader consequences of the program.

Implications of Tasks for Methodology

If summative evaluation is the main battleground in the method conflict, and if summative evaluations often require all five of the tasks delineated in Box 11.1, which tasks are most problematic in debating the value of experimental evaluation designs over other designs? For this, note that the first two tasks—implementation assessment and outcome monitoring—begin with representing what is observed, whether it is the program activities or outputs (e.g., the number of training modules provided to teachers) or the outcomes of interest (e.g., student scores on state exams). Both the qualitative and quantitative approaches have recommended practices and standards for ensuring the reliability and construct validity of these representations.

Impact evaluation begins with this representation of activities and outcomes but also requires making judgments about causal impacts. This requires judgments about the unique impacts of the program as distinguished from all other likely influences. Most in the evaluation community would acknowledge that failure to tease apart the program influences from other influences and confounds generally leads to invalid conclusions about program impacts. A range of methodologies—especially experimental and quasi-experimental designs, but some qualitative approaches as well—attempt to address these other influences, either through control groups or detailed explanation. How well these methodologies succeed in distinguishing the possible influences is a matter of debate. As such, the most visible fundamental difference in viewpoint among methodologists is over the *adequacy* of different designs in addressing questions of causal impacts, such as those listed in Part C of Box 11.1 (an emerging area of fundamental differences concerns assessing the value of programs and policies, addressed briefly in part D of Box 11.1; see Julnes, 2012, for more details). Significantly, adequacy, as described in this section, depends on context.

MULTIPLE LEVELS OF CONCLUSIONS AND THE TYPES OF DECISIONS TO BE MADE

A second way to frame the variation in evaluation questions is in terms of what can be called *the level of conclusion* (Julnes, 2011). In line with our focus on the impact evaluation task, the levels of conclusions can be understood by building on the distinction of three types of questions that Weiss suggests in the area of impact evaluation. The most basic of Weiss's (1998) impact questions in Box 11.1 is the following: "Is the observed change due to the program?" A more general form of this question is, What are the impacts due to the program? This reflects a concern with the magnitude of program impacts, which may differ from the observed change when, for example, selection bias has resulted in program participants who are more disadvantaged or at risk than those in a comparison group. One of the realities acknowledged with broad-based initiatives, such as those that attempt to change systems or environments, is the possibility that clear attribution to a program or policy or initiative may not always be possible, especially when multiple other types of interventions are occurring at the same time and in the same space. In these instances, funders are often realistic about the inability to trace outcomes to their own funding streams with available resources but are interested in understanding whether their funding and interventions at least contribute to the outcomes that emerge.

In addition to estimating whether a program has an overall impact, impact evaluation often addresses, as indicated in Box 11.1, two questions related to influences on that impact. First, evaluators are often concerned with moderated relationships wherein the size of the impact of a program is dependent on other factors (e.g., whether the effects of a training program differ for men and women; whether the effects of a housing program is different for urban versus rural areas). A second ancillary question addresses what are believed to be the underlying mechanisms responsible for the observed outcomes. Gathering evidence about those mechanisms or processes allows one to reassess the theory that guided the program and to suggest modifications to the program theory. This is often addressed through *mediation* (e.g., Petrosino, 2000), in which certain mechanisms mediate between the program and the outcomes. For example, the success of a mental health program may be mediated by the therapeutic alliance achieved between the provider and the client.

As background, it is useful to note that these three groups of questions— the overall aggregate questions, the questions about moderated relationships, and those focused on inferences about some underlying reality—apply to much that we do in evaluation. For example, when assessing outcomes (section B in Box 11.1) such as the prevalence of homelessness in the United States, aggregate statistics are often made more meaningful through disaggregation across time or across geographical regions. Inferences about underlying constructs come to the fore in discussions on different definitions of homelessness, particularly in characterizing different types of homeless individuals (e.g., those without any shelter versus those staying with family). In addition, there is often an important distinction made about differences in context, especially between urban and rural homelessness. Similarly, the results of cost-benefit analysis as an approach to valuation (section D of Box 11.1) are generally presented both in the aggregate (overall net/present value) and disaggregated by major stakeholder groups. For example, homelessness studies are increasingly examining the outcomes of housing interventions compared to shelter and more emergency options in relation to their costs for those served overall and often with a specific focus on those individuals who have been the highest utilizers of services or those who have been chronically homeless. The focus on an underlying reality comes when, often through critical review, we consider whether real human needs are being met by programs and are reflected in the analyses. In this chapter, however, we are especially interested in how these three levels affect the type of causal analysis needed in impact evaluation.

Aggregate Description

The exemplar of aggregate causal analysis in evaluation is the random assignment experiment that finds that the treatment group has higher average scores on some desired outcome than the control group. For example, a random assignment experiment could be conducted to demonstrate an overall impact of calculator use on scores on a standardized mathematics exam (e.g., the National Assessment of Educational Progress [NAEP]). Based on such an experiment, we would feel justified in concluding that using the calculator caused the difference in average scores for the two groups. This is an important piece of knowledge, representing what Shadish, Cook, and Campbell (2002) call a *descriptive causal conclusion*. It is descriptive in the sense of claiming that something about the treatment caused the observed difference but not trying to explain how the impact occurred. This is the classic domain of internal validity, distinguishing the "treatment as a package" from other causal factors, such as history and selection bias.

Sometimes fairly simple methods are sufficient for identifying causal impacts. For example, monitoring outcomes can, under select circumstances, seem sufficient for supporting conclusions on impacts and thus guiding action. However, in many of the contexts faced by evaluators, measured outcomes provide only ambiguous evidence of impacts and more formal approaches to supporting causal analysis are seen as having distinct advantages. Even when the methods used seem adequate, however, there are limits to what aggregate descriptive causal conclusions can tell us, leading scholars such as Cronbach (1982) to claim that internal validity is trivial. In general, such limits are addressed by disaggregated analyses and analyses that seek to identify underlying causal mechanisms and attribution to interventions of interest.

Disaggregation

Disaggregation for causal analysis can result from separate analyses for different groups but also often makes use of moderated relationships yielded by including interaction terms in the analysis. For example, the calculator use described above might have the greatest impact on certain subsets of students taking the mathematics exam, such as helping most those with prior training

Table 11.1 Analysis of Methods Addressing Causal Questions in Evaluation

Method	Impact Evaluation
Aggregate Description	Causal description of impacts (internal validity), e.g., "The supportive housing program improved the housing stability of families compared to the stability of families that did not participate in the program."
Disaggregation	Generalized causal inference (including external validity), e.g., "The program improved the mental health outcomes of women but had its greatest effect for women with higher clinical needs."
Inferences of Underlying Phenomena	Causal explanation based on underlying mechanisms, e.g., "The program was effective because it provided financial housing assistance that made stability possible."

in calculator use. Quantitative analyses of moderated relationships typically make use of interaction terms in multiple regression and analysis of variance (ANOVA), in multilevel models such as hierarchical linear models, or in survival models that can examine outcomes over time. For case study methods, Yin (1994) describes how multiple-case designs in case study research can reveal how outcomes are dependent on moderated relationships.

Inferential Analysis: Underlying Constructs and Causal Mechanisms

The inferential level for causal analysis involves methods that go beyond descriptive conclusions to say something about the underlying causal mechanisms that are responsible for the descriptive causal relationships. In this sense, we are trying to explain the observed causal relationship. For example, we might use research in cognitive science to understand how calculator use helps on exams (e.g., reducing time required for computation, helping students try out different solutions, or helping students focus on the conceptual elements of the question). This understanding can then support the goal of disaggregation described above, such as allowing us to better understand the types of questions or the types of students that should benefit from calculator use.

The point for this inferential analysis is that though we might be grateful to have an accurate understanding of the descriptive causal relationship, we are rarely satisfied for long with this alone. We generally, though not always, would like to understand the mechanisms that are responsible for the observed causal impact. In traditions such as regression analysis and structural equation modeling, the study of mechanisms is the study of mediated relationships, or causal linkages, that relate the program activities to the targeted outcomes. An emphasis on logic models, program theories, and the search for underlying generative mechanisms is consistent with this focus on mediated relationships. The use of mixed methods, with qualitative accounts of the reasons underlying observed outcomes, is of particular use in both validating and deepening the understanding of our findings (Caracelli & Greene, 1997). Increasingly, decision makers are in need of this type of analysis that goes beyond accountability findings to those that can help refine current efforts and guide future ones.

Implications of Levels of Conclusions for Methods

Having agreed that a major current method debate is focused on supporting the causal analysis required for impact evaluation, we now see that there are several levels of causal questions likely to be of interest. This is relevant here, as the value of random assignment experiments in specific settings varies according to which level of conclusion is of greatest concern.

Among those who accord some value to random assignment experimental designs for evaluation, there is broad agreement that such designs are particularly appropriate for aggregate causal questions, such as estimating the overall effect of a program or policy innovation. Indeed, the prototypic justification for randomized controlled trials (RCTs) is in providing somewhat definitive answers to this aggregate-level question.

The assessment is more complicated when considering the value of random assignment experiments in revealing the moderated relationships that underlie efforts to disaggregate results. On the one hand, reasonable sample sizes and the availability of fairly standard demographic data can allow evaluators to identify differential program effects on different groups of program participants. Experimental methods, for example, often make use of random assignment within subgroups (using strata or blocking variables) to support strong conclusions about the strength and importance of these factors in demonstrating moderated relationships.

Other types of disaggregation can be more difficult in experiments. For example, if, after data are collected, it becomes clear that implementation varied across the different settings, it can be misleading to attribute differences in outcomes to differences in implementation. Similarly, conversations with program participants might suggest differing impacts on different outcomes, only some of which were measured. In contrast, qualitative methodologies make it easier to learn about and incorporate attention to emergent outcomes of interest as the program and evaluation progress.

Understanding the underlying causal mechanisms via experimental methods is at least as difficult as supporting disaggregated conclusions. Critics contend that experimental methods are incapable of identifying causal mechanisms (Pawson & Tilley, 1997), yet these criticisms are not entirely fair. Experiments can improve one's understanding of the underlying mechanisms, though in relatively subtle ways. Note first that the experimental method in social sciences such as psychology is employed primarily when there are theories about underlying mechanisms, and the series of studies in an experimental research program are designed with modifications that progressively clarify the nature of those mechanisms. So it is that an experimental evaluation of disability policy, for example, will likely involve policy variations that reflect presumed psychological mechanisms that influence the willingness of people receiving disability-based public benefits to increase their earnings (Silverstein, Julnes, & Nolan, 2005). On the other hand, it is certainly true that experimental methods can only address a small number of presumed mechanisms and can offer limited insight on how multiple mechanisms interact. Adding qualitative methods in a mixed-methods approach can provide the needed insights about complex mechanisms, and at times, the rich understanding that results can make the *a priori* experimental contrasts seem ill-advised at best.

Thus, experimental methods are argued as appropriate for strengthening impact-evaluation conclusions, but the value of these methods is dependent on the level of conclusions needed. While the decisions confronting some stakeholders will involve aggregate conclusions (e.g., those making go/no go decisions about programs and policies or the level of funding it should have), others require the results of disaggregated analyses (e.g., decisions concerned with expanding programs to different contexts and/or populations) or analyses of underlying mechanisms (e.g., program development decisions); being explicit about these multiple levels will help clarify what are claimed as advantages of one method over another in specific settings.

DESIRED FORM OF CAUSAL CONCLUSIONS

Even if it is agreed that an evaluation planned for a specific setting needs to yield valid aggregate causal conclusions, there is another consideration that affects the value of different methodologies. This final frame builds on a distinction made by Dawid (2000) that concerns whether stakeholders are interested primarily in determining the causes of known effects (e.g., what was responsible for improved education test results) or in identifying the effects of a known cause (e.g., what happens to employment and earnings when there is a change in Social Security Disability Insurance policies). The first question is often addressed with case comparison methods (e.g., looking at those who experienced a serious side effect from a drug and trying to understand how they differ from those who did not experience that side effect) and the second with experimental manipulations (Shadish et al., 2002).

The typical debate around this is between those arguing for the adequacy of qualitative methods for the first question (you can spot this when you hear phrases such as *establishing causality* or *modus operandi method*) and those insisting that only rigorous quantitative methods can provide unbiased answers to the second (as in *estimating program impacts*). Without distinguishing the two causal questions, the debate is never really engaged. A reasonable clarification is that both quantitative and qualitative methods can be effective in establishing causality, but quantitative experimental methods have a distinct advantage in estimating the magnitude of program and policy impacts, particularly when it is possible to employ random assignment and make population estimates based on sampled data.

Problem/Phenomena Context

We have connected decisions about evaluation design to the questions of primary interest to identified stakeholders. However, here again, context matters.

The nature of the phenomena under study (e.g., school dropout rates among transitioning at-risk youth or weight change among those with eating disorders) can be critical in determining the type of design to use but is rarely acknowledged explicitly in the evaluation literature. Before even outlining a causal study, it is important to determine the readiness of the area to mount a controlled study (i.e., how much is already known about the problem or phenomena, tools available to provide accurate outcome measurement, etc.). At times, calls for assessments of impact are premature and may need to be preceded by more descriptive assessments of the problem and the interventions designed to address them.

COMPLEXITY OF MECHANISMS STUDIED

One key method-related aspect of the phenomena studied is the degree to which the presumed causal mechanisms can be easily identified. As an example, contrast the differing implications of studying school dropout rates, as noted above, with studying waiting times in airport security lines under different inspection procedures. The relevant mechanisms are likely understood better in this latter category than in the school dropout example, affecting the methods needed to maintain confidence in causal conclusions.

One difference is that the notion of *mechanism* is quite different in physical systems from how it is used in human psychological and social systems (Mohr, 1996). This is the point made by Boruch (2007), citing as an example the testing of bullet-protective material on pigs. The outcome of shooting pigs with the protection does not require establishing the counterfactuals of shooting a pig without such protection—we know that the pigs would be seriously or mortally wounded. However, when we are considering volitional behavior or complex systems with many confounding factors, it is more difficult to think of situations when the counterfactuals are as clear as they are with physical systems.

PATTERNS OF CHANGE

A second aspect related to both the phenomena that is relevant for method choice is the manner in which change in the outcomes of interest can be expected. The greater the latency between the onset of an intervention and changes in measured outcomes, the more difficult it is to rule out alternative causal explanations. On the other hand, if the outcomes most relevant in judging program effectiveness are likely to improve quickly after the onset of the intervention, degrade quickly after the intervention is discontinued, and improve again after reinstatement of the intervention, then independent manipulation of the intervention without a comparison group (as in an ABAB design), and certainly without one based on random assignment, might be adequate for confidence in causal inferences (Shadish & Rindskopf, 2007). Unfortunately, such responsive patterns of change are more likely with less-complex mechanisms in less-complex systems.

Context of the Program/Policy Intervention

Several factors that condition the type of evidence needed for action are inherent in the types of interventions needed to create change, including the complexity of the system-context dynamics involved and the degree of program readiness. Each of these is described more fully below.

COMPLEXITY OF THE SYSTEM-CONTEXT DYNAMICS

The sheer complexity of some interventions, such as comprehensive reforms (Yin & Davis, 2007), questions the applicability of some evaluation designs including random assignment. Conducting a set of mini-studies to try to answer the central questions also is often misplaced, as they often miss the critical questions about the initiatives as a whole. A number of authors (Connell, Kubisch, Schorr, & Weiss, 1997; Fulbright-Anderson, Kubisch, & Connell, 1998; Rog & Knickman, 2004) note the challenges in evaluating comprehensive reforms, such as the role and dynamics of the context; the evolutionary nature of the initiatives and the fact that they are often designed from the bottom up; variations in what they do, whom they serve, and where they take place; the difficulty in quantifying and measuring the goals (e.g., increasing community efficacy, systems change); and the fact that, because they often encompass entire communities or neighborhoods, there are often few places that lend themselves for comparison. In addition, attribution to a specific funding source or initiative is often difficult, if not impossible, in areas where multiple funders are involved and often blend money and efforts to tackle a problem. Finally, the intervention under study and the broader context are typically often hard to distinguish, with boundaries blurred (Yin & Davis, 2007).

DEGREE OF PROGRAM READINESS

Evaluation theories have long addressed the need for the primary evaluation questions and preferred methods to change as the focus moves from initial pilot demonstrations to established programs or policies. Some of the initial attention focuses on whether a program is evaluable at all, and issues affecting method choice include the degree to which there is clear program logic, the extent to which stakeholders agree on that logic, and the extent to which there is consistency between what is designed and what is implemented.

Clear and Appropriate Program Logic

The internal logic of a program or policy is too often assumed and not examined before an evaluation is designed and mounted. The lack of a solid program theory tying the program to the intended outcomes can render an evaluation meaningless and indicate the need for greater attention to informing the redevelopment of a program.

The program logic, however, needs to be in line with resources. For example, a program may be designed to be staffed by 10 professionals, but resource cuts now mean that only four professionals and four paraprofessionals can be hired. How does this change affect the program's ability to achieve the outcomes? Are there different outcomes that should be considered? The program logic needs to be adapted to such changes.

Degree of Program Maturity and Stability

As Weiss (1998) points out, a concern prior to evaluation is whether the program "operates as intended" and is "relatively stable" (p. 73). This is particularly important to discern before mounting an intensive evaluation that seeks to estimate program impacts. Indeed, one of the major criticisms of randomized experiments, accepted fully even by proponents of experiments, is that they are conducted before programs are ready for this type of inquiry (see Datta, 2007; Lipsey, 2007; Tharp, 2007). Related to this readiness, some programs are quite dynamic in their orientation and their stability may be greatly influenced by outside factors (e.g., funding, weather conditions). This fluctuation can necessitate design features that track and measure these changes and incorporate them into both conceptual and analytic models. This need is even more pronounced when conducting multisite evaluations, where each site may have fluctuations that need to be examined, and judgments need to be made about the suitability of including the site in the outcome evaluation and design features to add to understand these contextual dynamics.

Evaluation Context

Each evaluation has its own *context*—the budget, time, data, and other resources available are all factors within that context that influence the type of evidence possible. Each outcome design has its own requirements. Longitudinal designs, for example, require either the ability to collect primary data over the desired time frame (often after an intervention has ended) or the availability of data through secondary sources to assess change in outcomes over time. Development evaluations, in particular, are often constrained by the limitations of data, complicated by limited funding and tight time frames that require innovative strategies for addressing change in outcomes and estimates of impact (Bamberger, Rugh, & Mabry, 2011).

PROGRAM CONSTRAINTS

Even if there is consensus that a more controlled, randomized study is the best technical choice to address the questions of interest, there are often practical, political, and conceptual constraints that function as hurdles that must be surmounted before an experimental design is accepted as appropriate. One way to understand these constraints and to determine if they can be surmounted is through the conduct of an *evaluability assessment* (see, for example, Wholey, 2004)—an evaluation planning tool designed to judge the readiness of a program for rigorous evaluation. Among its features are an assessment of program readiness (examination of the logic of the program as designed and as implemented, the stakeholder agreement with the logic and especially the outcomes of interest, and the program stability and potential for impact) and evaluation feasibility (requisite capacity for measurement and other conditions, such as appropriate control groups) to conduct a study that is appropriate and has the requisite rigor to guide discussion. In particular, by determining the extent to which decision makers agree upon the desired outcomes of a program and can articulate how they would use the potential evaluation results, evaluability assessment directly unearths and confronts any political tensions and constraints that need to be eliminated before an evaluation can produce actionable evidence.

EVALUATION CAPACITY

As noted above, there may be additional issues with the evaluation and measurement capacity of a program and the overall environment that make certain designs less possible. There may not be the conditions in place for a randomized study or the data system in place to examine "dosage" of services provided. In addition, as Datta (2007) notes, in program areas such as Head Start, it may not be feasible to construct a no-treatment comparison group due to the spread of early intervention. Being able to obtain enough participants to yield a sufficient sample size is a related problem. Some programs may lack a sufficient pool of possible program participants in the community that meet the study eligibility criteria; some may lack the staffing capacity to serve clients in the study period given the number of clients that can be served by each staff member, the amount of time they are expected to receive program services, and so on. For other programs, there may not be the systems in place to monitor programs over time, and thus circumstances would not be conducive for ongoing performance monitoring. Time is also a critical capacity issue often not taken into consideration (or ignored because the funding time frame is set) when examining the plausibility of achieving stated outcomes; often those outcomes agreed upon by stakeholders are well outside what is plausible to achieve within the evaluation time frame, and the more proximal and intermediate outcomes that the program could achieve have not been considered or delineated.

Environmental Context

As Greene (2005) states, there are often layers of settings in which a program or intervention is placed. An educational intervention designed to reduce school dropout rates, for example, may be affected not only by the environment of a classroom but by the environments of the school, the district, the community, and the state. Complex interventions, such as those focused on impacting communities, are often intertwined with their environments, as noted above. The extent to which the context is likely to affect the implementation and outcomes of an intervention has a bearing on the types of methods that are appropriate, depending on the questions of interest. Although RCTs are often designed to control the effects of these external factors, this control can limit the generalizability of the findings. Stratifying interventions across settings where possible (i.e., different classrooms, schools, districts, etc.) can provide for greater generalizability but may increase costs greatly, especially if there is interest in understanding effects of the different types of contexts. A more cost-effective method may be to consider a mixed-methods approach that provides for more qualitative understanding of the role in which context affects the outcomes.

POLITICAL CONSTRAINTS

As noted above, political constraints, especially those unattended to, can undermine the potential value of an evaluation. In particular, understanding how the stakeholders of a program view its purposes and intended outcomes can be important in developing an evaluation that is accepted and produces findings that have influence. Where evaluators differ is on which stakeholders should be included and the priority their views should be given. Evaluators with a focus on social justice believe that too much attention has historically been given to decision-making stakeholders and too little attention has been given to the beneficiaries of programs and others affected by their consequences. The implication of this belief for method choice is that resource-intensive methods are less defensible when there is insufficient consensus on a program's purposes and intended outcomes on the part of those it affects or when there is only a limited chance of the results being used to inform future practice that could benefit those a program serves.

ETHICAL CONSIDERATIONS

The final domain addressed here, though it might be the first constraint to consider in practice, concerns the range of ethical considerations that can lead us to choose one design over another, even if they are in conflict with some of the other considerations. For randomized studies in particular, Boruch (2007) has suggested a list of questions at one level of ethical thinking that guide whether a randomized study is ethically warranted.

Protecting Human Subjects

Whatever design is chosen, there are ethical implications for study participants. For example, the 1978 Belmont Report charged Institutional Review Boards with protecting human subjects of research in terms of three principles: respect for persons (protecting personal dignity and autonomy), beneficence (maximizing anticipated benefits and minimizing possible risks), and justice (making sure the benefits and burdens of research are distributed fairly).

Respect for persons includes the requirement of informed consent and the need to respect the values of participants—without intending harm, being included in a study can hurt participants in many ways, some of which are only poorly understood when informed consent documents are signed. Beneficence requires that the evaluation be expected to yield real benefits (i.e., the problem being studied is serious and the findings are likely to guide future decisions) and entail only the minimal risks necessary to achieve this benefit. If, for example, an experimental evaluation design results in more defensible findings than other approaches and is found to have more influence in guiding policy decisions than other approaches, this would argue for use of that design in similar situations as long as there were only a minimal risk to participants. The concern with justice includes whether it is ethical to withhold treatment from those assigned to the control groups (e.g., those denied treatment perhaps bearing an unacceptable burden for the benefits to others that might result). However, in most current-day evaluations, the control groups are not no-treatment groups but, rather, continue to receive any treatment or services as usual. The case can be made that if a treatment is in fact known to be better than receiving other services, then it is not an obvious candidate for summative evaluation.

Promoting Social Justice

In addition to justice as it relates to protecting participants, there is also a broader concern with social justice. In particular, there may be subtle or not-so-subtle consequences of method choice that work against the interest of some stakeholder groups. As Datta (2007) noted, some federal agencies, such as the Bureau of Indian Affairs, might need to be especially sensitive to cultural issues that might not be addressed well with rigorous designs, such as with randomized field trials. A related point is that different stakeholder groups might want and need different sorts of information from an evaluation, and so prioritizing the needs of one group could be in conflict with the needs of others. Indeed, maximizing the utility of the findings for one stakeholder group may make them relatively useless (or worse, insulting) for other stakeholders. Social justice requires that those least advantaged not be further disenfranchised by focusing only on the information needs of those with the greatest resources. This latter concern may not suggest one method over another but rather the conduct of multiple or mixed methods in instances where the information needs are varied and diverse. It might also mean that in the evaluation planning/evaluability assessment phase, the evaluator has the obligation to share these various stakeholder perspectives, especially with the decision-making stakeholders, in an early effort to bridge some of these differences and help develop a constructive approach to the evaluation.

Attending to Procedural Justice

There are several concerns related to procedural justice in evaluation. One is the concern that many have with the federal government imposing standards on others. While part of this concern is that federal standards tend to be too uniform to meet different needs in different contexts, in this instance, there is also simply the procedural concern with maintaining autonomy in decision making with regard to evaluation methodology (see Chelimsky, 2007). This procedural concern applies also to those who are the intended targets or recipients of the programs to be evaluated. Federal policies may make it more difficult for these program consumers to have input into the evaluation methodologies to be used. For example, persons with disabilities, in line with the phrase *not about me without me*, are asking for and expecting more input into the design and implementation of evaluations of disability policies and programs as well as the interpretation and application of their results (Julnes, McCormick, Nolan, & Sheen, 2006).

How Are We to Judge the Adequacy of Methods for Providing the Needed Evidence?

Even if we can agree on the information (or evidence) needed to address identified stakeholder questions, there is considerable controversy over the degree to which specific evaluation methods are adequate for providing the needed information. Complicating a resolution to this controversy is the lack of consensus on how we determine what is adequate.

VARIETIES OF ACTIONABLE EVIDENCE ABOUT METHODOLOGY

Just as we advocate for evaluations to produce evidence to guide program and policy decisions, we should be guided by evidence or data in our work—specifically, in what methods we choose to use in specific situations. Box 11.2 provides an overview of three general sources of evidence for method choice that we propose to guide method choice based on others' work—outcome based, practice based, and critical review (see Boruch, de Moya, & Snyder, 2002, p. 52). In this section, we discuss criteria for judging each type of evidence for determining methods to use and offer conclusions about the value and shortcomings of each.

Outcome-Based Evidence

Outcome-based evidence implies assessing alternative research designs by the outcomes produced with respect to their accuracy and precision and

---

Box 11.2 Sources of Actionable Evidence for Informing Policies on Method Choice

Outcome-Based Evidence: What is the impact of method choice on evaluation outcomes? Major concerns include

- accuracy and precision of findings,
- reliability and validity of the outcomes/findings, and
- depth of findings and explanatory power.

Practice-Based Evidence: Is there wisdom and evidence of effectiveness in practice? Major concerns include

- agency policies and preferences,
- general quality of implementation, and
- use and persuasiveness of the findings.

Critical Review as Evidence: What are the broader social impacts of methodological choices? Major concerns include

- analysis of ethical implications and
- reflection on broader social consequences.

their persuasiveness and influence. This is the standard approach used in quantitative studies wherein, for example, the outcomes of interest might be the calculated effect sizes that result from a random assignment design as compared to the average effect sizes produced when using nonrandomized comparison groups. Boruch (2007) marshals this type of evidence in describing systematic studies of the effect of method choice on study outcomes.

For qualitative studies, the parallel concern would be whether different approaches yield different conclusions when applied in similar settings. One might be interested, for example, in whether a case study approach using semistructured interviews applied to one facet of school reform yields different outcomes from an ethnographic approach based on ongoing observations and interactions with program participants.

This issue of corroboration highlights the importance of criteria for outcome-based approaches when there are differences in study findings across different designs. Specifically, if different designs tend to yield different assessments of program effectiveness, we need to make sense of these differences. For many quantitative and qualitative designs, there are established criteria determining the reliability and validity of the data collection, with measures of reliability (inter-rater, internal consistency, and test–retest) and validation procedures (criterion-related validity, but also the more general construct validity paradigm). For quantitative designs as well, however, there is also a long tradition of assessing the adequacy of internal validity in terms of ruling out alternative mechanisms that might be responsible for program-related outcomes. Illustrating that these criteria transcend the traditional comparison group paradigm, Shadish and Rindskopf (2007) make the case that single-subject research has developed corresponding ways of strengthening our confidence in conclusions derived without large samples or distinct comparison groups.

There are less-established bases for determining the accuracy and precision of the evidence from qualitative designs or those that lack comparisons. Designs that employ triangulation incorporate the ability to judge the significance of particular outcome data. In addition, designs that build in "contrarian" and alternative views allow one to determine if even divergent perspectives yield convergent findings or results. However, standards differ across various designs and approaches and, in some instances, are absent. It is in this context that the work of Robert Yin (1994; Yin & Davis, 2007) has been particularly helpful in developing criteria for judging the adequacy of case study research and evaluation.

Accuracy and precision are not, however, the only outcome-related criteria generally used in assessing the value of evaluations. The extent to which an evaluation can provide answers to the *why* and *why not* questions that revolve around outcome findings also operates as criteria for determining whether a particular methodological approach will provide actionable evidence. The affinity toward logic models and program theory is in part guided by a need to understand the elements within a program that may be key ingredients causing the outcome as well as generative mechanisms that are linking agents to the ultimate outcomes of interest. Growth in the attention to moderators and mediators in our evaluation designs and analyses is responsive to the need to understand not only if something made a difference but also for whom and under what conditions. Studies that have simplistic designs that can be easily analyzed with ANOVA may not be suited to the complex program and policy situations we are asked to evaluate.

Practice-Based Evidence

Another source of justification for matching a method to a situation is to assess how well they are aligned in terms of the method preferences and practices of various agencies. The rationale for using this type of evidence is that, over time, one expects some form of environmental pressure to lead people to use those practices that meet their needs and provide the best information. To the extent that this dynamic does indeed select for more useful and more context-sensitive methodologies, one can talk of there being "wisdom in practice" that needs to be explicated.

Examples of this source of practical evidence include formal agency policies regarding preferred methodologies for different types of studies, actual historical trends in the use of alternative methodologies, and patterns of current use (Boruch et al., 2002). One might hope that adaptive selection would also be sensitive to the quality with which the various methodologies are often implemented. If a random assignment design is excellent in the abstract but is rarely implemented effectively in certain contexts, this might be taken as evidence of its limited appropriateness in such contexts. Datta (2007) documents potential examples of "wisdom in practice," noting, for example, that agencies that make the most use of qualitative evaluation may have particular needs that are addressed less well by quantitative approaches. Further, she delineates several factors, both institutional and personal, that might account for these patterns of practice. In particular, she notes differences among agencies with varying cultural needs that respect, value, and demand different ways of knowing.

Another practice-based concern is whether the methods did in fact produce actionable evidence that were put to use by policy makers and administrators. It might be, for example, that the questions best addressed by random assignment designs constitute a narrower set than what policy makers want answered for informing policy. On a related note, Gueron (2002) emphasizes the greater persuasiveness of the results of random assignment studies, but the stories of actual people collected through qualitative inquiry are often held up as particularly important to policy makers. Either way, the work by Weiss (1988, 1998; Weiss, Murphy-Graham, & Birkeland, 2005) and many others (e.g., Cousins, 2004; de Lancer Julnes, 2006; Kirkhart, 2000) on the utilization of evaluation highlights the difficulties in using some measure of influence of findings as a yardstick to measure the appropriateness of the approaches used. First, the latent nature of how studies often have an effect, and the less-common instances of immediate instrumental use challenge our ability to measure the true impact findings have. Moreover, the nature and receptivity of the results, the extent to which a "policy window" exists, and competing priorities have as much to do in determining whether an evaluation is successful in affecting public policy as does how the results were derived.

The challenge for accepting actual practice as evidence of best practice alone is that practices can and do persist without necessarily being the best choices. Some of the factors identified by Datta (2007) can lead to suboptimal practices as well as particularly effective ones. Accordingly, practice-based evidence is rarely persuasive by itself for those interested in understanding the desired fit between method and context. Conversely, neglecting patterns of practice puts a greater burden on the other sources of evidence in trying to understand the contextual nuances that should condition use of different methods in different circumstances.

Critical Review as Evidence

A third source of evidence about method choice can be discussed under the general label of *critical review*. The issue for critical review is whether our current policies and practices for method choice are taking us where we want to go as a society (Henry & Julnes, 1998). One focus of critical review for evaluation is to consider the ethics of the evaluation practices. For example, one might make use of ethical analysis to argue that a particular methodology, such as random assignment to experimental or control groups, leads to undesired social consequences for particular groups of those affected by a study. This seems to be Lincoln's (2004) view when, in reviewing the Cook and Payne chapter in Mosteller and Boruch (2002), she points out that random assignment designs might be more acceptable with willing adults than with the small children who are often the focus of educational evaluation.

A related point for this ethical analysis is that experimental methodologies may be used in an elitist mode that neglects the values and voices of those being studied (e.g., Greene, 2007; Schwandt, 2007; Smith, 2007). As mentioned above, for example, the phrase *not about me without me* is often used to express the right of a person with a disability to be involved in research that claims to represent the issues affecting him or her (Julnes et al., 2006). On the other hand, ethical analyses could also lead to the conclusion that random assignment is the most just way of allocating scarce resources in particular settings (Boruch, 2007). In addition, in highly political situations, having more defensible data that fit agreed-upon standards of accuracy and precision may be more defensible and provide stronger evidence to support change in areas that have been heretofore resistant.

Critical review can also involve a consideration of other long-term consequences of using particular designs. For example, while cognizant of the criticisms of experimental methods, the thrust of the critique by Cook and Payne (2002) of the long-term failure to advance our understanding in education is that there has been an overreliance on less-effective (i.e., nonrandom assignment) designs. Tharp (2007) addresses the balance of methods from a developmental perspective, arguing that it is the *process* of development that must be supported and that different methods are valuable at different stages in organizational and social development. This is a reminder that context-appropriate method choice is a means to an end and that the desired "end" is better viewed as an ongoing process than as some fixed and final outcome (Julnes, Pang, Takemoto-Chock, Speidel, & Tharp, 1987). The larger point for critical review is that policy debates on method choice take place within the broader governmental arena of competing interests and competing values (Julnes & Foster, 2001), some consistent with our notions of social betterment, some not.

Discussion

This chapter has presented the value of different methodologies in generating actionable evidence in addressing various evaluation questions. Our goal in this chapter was to approach the topic of method choice from a pragmatic perspective, one that can guide the choice of research designs to produce findings that, in turn, guide action. We begin this concluding discussion, therefore, with a review of the pragmatic elements of our contribution, then summarize the contextual factors that influence method choice, and finally, suggest some steps that can be taken to continue to inform the variety of perspectives on evaluation methodology.

PRAGMATIC FRAMEWORK FOR METHOD CHOICE

One point of agreement among many commentators on the current methodology debate is that it can, at times, be fueled by ideology. Although many qualitative and quantitative methodologists have a deep appreciation of a wide range of methods, too often proponents of one approach construct extreme images of opposing approaches as dogmatic and insensitive to context. Taking the knocking down of such caricatures as support for one's own position, this approach, with its *reductio ad absurdum,* makes it too easy to conclude that one's own approach is (almost) always preferred to other approaches and, hence, too difficult to promote meaningful dialogues on this controversy.

The pragmatic approach is to focus on the contextual contingencies that make our various research designs and methods more or less useful. West (1995) emphasizes this contextual step in clarifying our thinking by noting that "[t]o demythologize is to render contingent and provisional what is widely considered to be necessary and permanent" (p. 314). Our sense is that the dialogue on what methods are appropriate and adequate would be more productive if the claims made in favor of and against specific methods were more contingent and provisional.

Contingent View of Best Evidence

As the chapters in this volume make clear, there will always be different views of what is required for evidence to be judged actionable, but this shift to judging evidence not simply on the methodological rigor with which it is derived but also on what we and others view as persuasive is important and necessary. We need to remind ourselves, however, that evidence is not to be viewed as credible in some universal, abstract sense. In the area of measurement theory, measures (such as an intelligence test) are not judged as valid in general; instead, one speaks of the validity of particular conclusions derived from the measure as employed under specific conditions. So it is with judging credibility: The same evidence might be judged as credible under some conditions but not others. Failure to acknowledge this contextual nature would leave us with a dimension of credibility, ranging from low to high, on which some evidence is better than others and some is even viewed as the "best" as in a gold standard for evidence.

Therefore, our approach has been to emphasize *actionable* rather than *best* evidence to add to the contextual frame for judging the value of evidence. The value of evidence in such settings is dependent not only on whether evaluators judge it as credible but also on the degree to which the evidence is considered relevant to both the major stakeholder questions and to the contexts in which the actions of policy or program change are to take place.

Contingent View of Best Methodology

Just as there is little hope of defining what would be the best evidence independent of specific settings, so there is consensus that we should avoid holding up one methodology, such as the randomized experiment, as the gold standard or best methodology without regard to context. The label of *gold standard* has inflamed the controversy unnecessarily with its implication of a best methodology to be aspired to or approximated by many, if not all. This in turn distracts attention from the important task of matching methods with the needs of particular situations.

But if we know that methods must be selected to meet contextual needs, then perhaps we can organize our understanding of context into a decision-analytic framework, guided by the fives sets of contextual factors offered earlier, that recommends the best methodology for the particular constellation of factors for the specific evaluation situation. For example, given stakeholder concerns, available resources, and a few other considerations, it may be reasonable to conclude that a particular design is to be recommended. We support efforts in this direction but are skeptical that any final product will yield automatic choices of methodology. Not only is it difficult to consider so many factors at once, but there will also be little consensus on how to weight the various factors in selecting the best methodology. Some will likely apply greater weight to stakeholder questions than many other evaluators would; others will view ethical issues as trumping other factors more often than is typical among evaluators. Thus, efforts to consider context in identifying best methodologies represent an improvement over universal claims, but ultimately, the same issues apply and situated judgments will always be of some value.

Context-Based Decision Rules

Although unable to specify best methods in the abstract, we can at least identify and organize the factors that need to be considered in matching methods to specific contexts. In this chapter, we have offered what might be seen as the first steps in such a project by identifying the areas of relevant contextual factors. Specifically, Table 11.2 summarizes the factors addressed. We note that RCTs are particularly valuable when (1) stakeholder questions require population estimates of the magnitude of program or policy impacts, (2) a high degree of confidence is desired in causal conclusions about impacts and the current knowledge is ambiguous and controversial, (3) the phenomena of interest do not allow for alternative approaches of estimating the counterfactual (what would have happened in absence of the intervention) because of the complexity of the presumed mechanisms involved and the time lag of intervention impact complicates using an ABAB design, (4) the program appears to be at near-optimal functioning and there are sufficient resources to implement the necessary components of the RCT methodology, and (5) there are no major ethical concerns with implementing the RCT methodology.

In sum, as our theories and methods are tools, so are the frameworks offered in this chapter and elsewhere in this book to help guide method choice in evaluation and research. Accordingly, we have discussed and organized an array of factors that reasonable people will and should consider in deciding the appropriateness of different methods in specific situations. We have, however, resisted the temptation to offer anything as prescriptive as a decision model that takes our discussed factors as inputs and yields as an output the appropriate methodology for an evaluation in a specific setting. Rather, we seek to be systematic in understanding the factors that should influence method choice but are realistic in expecting that this issue will continue to be debated as government policies are advanced to guide method choices.

Table 11.2   Review of Factors Influencing the Value of RCTs

Contextual Factors	Conditions Favoring RCTs and Strong Causal Conclusions
Decision Context: Stakeholder Questions	When questions about the merit and worth of programs are foremost, particularly if evaluators are interested in estimating the aggregate impacts for populations of interest Information needs: particularly when current knowledge about these impacts is ambiguous or controversial
Problem/ Phenomena Context	When the presumed mechanisms affecting outcomes are complex (e.g., psychological mechanisms, in contrast to some simpler mechanical mechanisms) and it is difficult to estimate the counterfactual outcomes that would have occurred without the program (however, confirming the actual mechanisms at work generally requires supplemental methods)

Contextual Factors	Conditions Favoring RCTs and Strong Causal Conclusions
Program/Policy Intervention Context	When high levels of confidence about causal impacts are desired, when program is embedded in systems of interventions (although understanding the counterfactual is complicated, random assignment can still create an evaluable contrast)
Evaluation Context: Resources and Ethical Considerations	Resources: when resources are sufficient to conduct a rigorous RCT and the program to be evaluated is stable and operating at what is believed to be near its peak level of functioning Ethical: when conducting the RCT would not compromise the rights of participants and would not contribute to social or process injustice
Environmental Context: Political and Cultural Issues	Political: ideological conflicts Cultural: lack of cultural value consensus

PROCESS IMPLICATIONS FOR PROMOTING APPROPRIATE AND ADEQUATE EVALUATION METHODS

Given the arguments developed above about the need to inform a debate that is not likely to end, we suggest several ways to promote an emphasis on conducting quality evaluations.

Embrace the Gray in a Black-and-White Debate

Part of what has led to less-than-productive dialogues over methodology is the tendency to oversimplify opposing positions. This was seen in prior qualitative–quantitative debates, where those criticizing the qualitative position bolstered their own position by ascribing a disbelief in causality to qualitative evaluators. Qualitative evaluators returned the favor by labeling quantitative evaluators as *positivists*, a philosophical position that had been abandoned a half century earlier. This human tendency to overrepresent our own views and oversimplify the opposing view is relevant to current debate over the methods needed to yield actionable evidence. On the one hand, opponents of efforts to promote RCTs see attempts to enshrine experimental methods as a gold standard to be pursued whenever feasible; on the other hand, proponents of RCTs see a resistance to ever funding experimental methods. Our approach has been to find the gray commonality in this black-and-white debate so as to foster dialogue and help determine when certain methods are indeed agreed upon to be the more useful and pragmatic choice.

Pursue Consensus Where It Can Be Found

The points above about a developmental model of inquiry apply as well to other areas with potential consensus. In this chapter, we have developed a set of factors that most would acknowledge as relevant in assessing the adequacy and appropriateness of different methods. This potential for partial consensus highlights the potential of pushing this consensus as far as it can go. In contrast, agreeing on which methods to use in specific settings is likely to be more problematic and likely less satisfying in the short run.

Relatedly, we might have more success reaching consensus on the criteria used to judge the value of different methods than we do in applying those criteria for actual method choice in specific settings. Outcome-based evidence, though most compelling, is generally best suited for quantitative designs, specifically randomized studies. Standards of quality for judging other designs are lacking and need to be developed. In particular, there is a need for standards in assessing the quality of a study's conceptualization and how a study is implemented. The same applies for the analyses used in qualitative studies; in particular, they need a level of transparency that allows for critical review and assessment of accuracy.

Adopt a Process Orientation to Methodology

In affirming evaluators as serving an inquiry process that is itself in service to social betterment, we affirm that our primary loyalty is to the quality of evaluation rather than to any particular methods or ideologies underlying these methods. From this view, it is well accepted that evaluation needs evolve over the life cycle of a program, beginning with exploratory attempts to improve implementation and to understand how the program might address the targeted needs, and much later moving toward a full summative evaluation to assess and document overall effectiveness. Tharp (1981) made this point a quarter century ago, using an ecological metaphor to argue for a natural progression of methods applied during the life of a program: Current texts (e.g., Rossi et al., 2004) offer systematic conceptions of these evolving needs and associated methods and government agencies (e.g., the U.S. Government Accountability Office) offer concrete recommendations that relate appropriate methodology to the program life cycle.

There are, however, other process issues that could improve the methods used in evaluation. One issue is that our views of effective methods in particular settings may change faster than our capacity to execute effectively evaluations based on these methods. Thus, even if there is a need to conduct more RCTs in certain evaluation areas, we might not have enough appropriately trained evaluators to implement the designs successfully. This could affect our judgments about the value of RCTs in general rather than their value given the current lack of capacity. The alternative conclusion would be that RCTs hold promise but require more capacity building in the sense of training in experimental methods, experience in running experimental evaluations, and dialogues on lessons learned among those who have been involved with experimental methods.

A second process-related point is that we do not want to presume enduring answers to questions about methodology. As new techniques are developed, designs and approaches formerly viewed as inadequate can be strengthened to yield evidence accepted as actionable. For example, statistical controls (e.g., adding control variables in multiple regression analysis) have generally been judged as less adequate than design controls (e.g., employing experimental and control groups), but empirical studies that suggest that, with recent advances in statistical control methods (e.g., propensity scores, but also even OLS regression), and under some conditions, "adjusted results from nonrandomized experiments can approximate results from randomized experiments." (Shadish, Clark, & Steiner, 2008, p. 1341)

Strive to Fight Fair

If we accept that our methods are tools and that we will always be revisiting and renegotiating the value of different methods in different situations, it will behoove us to approach this never-ending process in more productive ways. While such advice is obvious in the abstract, there may be much to learn from other traditions for dealing with conflict. For example, there is a tradition of family and marriage counseling that emphasizes learning to "fight fair" when addressing family conflicts. Focusing on the specific application of methods and designs and agreeing ahead of time upon criteria for assessing design fit can, we believe, help develop a fairer playing field than one that is based solely on ideological versus pragmatic grounds.

Conclusion: So What Counts as Actionable Evidence?

Interest on the part of government as well as foundations in using evidence to inform decision making has increased the potential for program and policy evaluation to contribute to improved governance and, more generally, to social betterment. This increased interest, however, has also cast a brighter light on evaluation methods and their adequacy in yielding evidence worthy of guiding decision making. This, of course, requires some consensus on the desired quali-ties of the evidence used to inform program and policy decisions.

This volume seeks to advance our understanding of this issue by addressing, "What constitutes quality evidence?" Our chapter contributes to this discussion in two ways. First, we argued that in evaluation, as opposed to theory-building research, the "worthiness" of evidence is better framed as whether it is *actionable* rather than *credible*. While, in general, more credible evidence is more worthy of guiding action, this reframing makes the quality of evidence less a matter of logic and more one that is concerned with the needs of actual managers, policy makers, and other interested stakeholders.

Second, we developed the notion that the worthiness of evidence, whether the focus is on being credible or actionable, cannot be judged in the abstract but, rather, only in terms of the needs and constraints of specific situations. We make no claim that this is an original insight; indeed, we would argue that everyone understands that different types of evidence are needed for different decisions. We do claim, however, that this general platitude has been underde-veloped and that much of the conflict over methodology in government-sponsored evaluations could have been managed better if we had elaborated in greater detail the factors that condition the adequacy of evidence in different contexts. It is to this second point that we devoted most of our chapter, which can be framed in terms of five aspects of context, while also asking how we are to judge the adequacy of methods for providing the evidence needed in specific contexts.

HOW ARE METHODS TO BE RELATED
TO THE QUESTIONS THAT STAKEHOLDERS WANT ADDRESSED?

We began by affirming the primacy of the evaluation stakeholder ques-tions in influencing the types of evidence needed in guiding decisions. Here, however, we have gone beyond traditional distinctions (e.g., program improve-ment questions vs. program continuation questions) to progressively localize the conflict in terms of:

- the *tasks* required in addressing evaluation questions (representation, causal inference, and valuation), with a focus on the controversy over causal inference;
- the *level of analysis* (aggregate description, disaggregation, and inferences about underlying phenomena) of causal inference desired by stakeholders; and
- the *type* of causal conclusion of most interest (identifying the causes of a known effect or identifying the effects of a known cause).

WHAT CONTEXTUAL FACTORS CONDITION THE EVIDENCE NEEDED TO SUPPORT CAUSAL CONCLUSIONS?

This delineation of evaluation questions and implications for methodology might suggest guidelines for which methods produce credible or actionable evidence for specific questions, but the method implications are more complex and subtle than that. Equally important are a number of contextual factors that further condition the nature of the evidence needed to guide action. Although the least typically considered, the nature of the phenomena being studied is relevant in that some causal relationships are so simple that even casual observational evidence suffices to establish the relationship (e.g., the Boruch example recounted above of pigs not being hurt when covered with protective material before being shot). In addition, the nature of existing knowledge on the topic also conditions what is needed (weaker evidence can be actionable when little else is known; conversely, evidence consistent with a large body of existing evidence is reasonably judged as more credible than evidence without such corroboration).

The context of the intervention influences method choice. The more complex the system relationships in the domain being studied (as in evaluating the impact of a new curriculum in school districts also participating in other school policy experiments and in neighborhoods targeted by various social policy initiatives), the more important it is that multiple sources of evidence support the resulting conclusions. In addition, the ability to establish a pattern of change is critical. If an organizational policy affects employee behavior in a way that corresponds to the implementation, rescinding, and subsequent re-implementation of the policy (as in a classic ABAB experimental design), then the causal contribution can be established through outcome monitoring. When the impacts of a policy change can take years to reveal themselves (e.g., employment outcomes in response to changes in Social Security Administration policies), confident conclusions require evidence that other causal factors were not responsible. Further, within the decision-making context, the desired degree of confidence conditions what is actionable (decisions that can be reversed easily require less evidence than those with more permanent implications). Finally, the context of the evaluation itself (its funding, timeframe, and budget) determines what is possible.

HOW ARE WE TO JUDGE THE ADEQUACY OF METHODS FOR PROVIDING THE NEEDED EVIDENCE?

Having addressed the types of program-related evidence desired in different contexts, how are we to assess evidence on the adequacy of available methods for yielding quality evaluation evidence? The standard approach has been to examine the conclusions that result from different methodologies. For this approach to be definitive, however, there needs to be an accepted yardstick against which to judge the results of other methods. That random assignment experiments were accepted as this yardstick, and hence given the *gold standard* label, has further inflamed the method controversy and increased interest in other standards for judging methods. Accordingly, in addition to the traditional focus on outcome-based standards, we argued for considering practice-based standards that view the patterns of use of different methodologies in different agencies and contexts as evidence of potential effectiveness. In addition, we promote the importance of conducting critical reviews of the adequacy of alternative methodologies. For those interested in measurement, this multifaceted marshalling of evidence is parallel to the emphasis on the "nomological net" of construct validity when there is no singular yardstick to employ for criterion-related validity.

WHEN IS IT APPROPRIATE TO USE PARTICULAR METHODS OF CAUSAL ANALYSIS?

On what basis do we judge it appropriate or not to use particular methods? In some cases, we have experience with the conditions or requirements that must be met for more involved methods to be useful. In other cases, it is an ethical frame that determines our views on appropriateness. Our chapter has addressed the contextual requirements from the perspective of evaluability assessment, discussing the elements needed for a program to be ready to be evaluated (clear program logic and program maturity), the needed evaluation resources (financial, organizational, and timing), and the political constraints (degree of stakeholder engagement and likelihood of evaluation evidence having a meaningful impact). Ethical considerations include the importance of protecting human subjects, the concern with promoting social justice, and the need to consider as well the implications for procedural justice.

PRAGMATIC IMPLICATIONS OF OUR ANALYSIS

Our analysis of the different types of evidence needed in different contexts and of the adequacy and appropriateness of methods for providing this evidence is consistent with Greene's (2007) conclusion that method choice in evaluation should be "contextual, contingent, and political" (p. 111). We have tried to clarify the relevant contextual contingencies but have also cautioned against simple frameworks that drive method choice in a somewhat automatic fashion based on a couple of these factors. This reflects our process orientation toward understanding actionable evidence in context; we need to push toward greater ability to recognize patterns without being seduced into accepting our resulting frameworks as final or even adequate (or, put differently, "seek system-ization but distrust it"; Julnes, 2012, p. 129). Instead, our hope is to promote greater consensus on the implications of the factors we identify. Doing so will support method choice better suited to yielding actionable evidence in context.

References

American Evaluation Association. (2013). *An evaluation roadmap for a more effective government.* Retrieved May 12, 2014, from http://www.eval.org/d/do/472

Argyris, C. (1996). Actionable knowledge: Design causality in the service of consequential theory. *Journal of Applied Behavioral Science, 32*(4), 390–406.

Bamberger, M., Rugh, J., & Mabry, L. (2011). *RealWorld evaluation: Working under budget, time, data, and political constraints.* Thousand Oaks, CA: SAGE.

Boruch, R. (2007). Encouraging the flight of error: Ethical standards, evidence standards, and randomized trials. In G. Julnes & D. J. Rog (Eds.), Informing federal policies on evaluation methodology: Building the evidence base for method choice in government-sponsored evaluation. *New Directions for Evaluation, 113,* 33–73.

Boruch, R., de Moya, D., & Snyder, B. (2002). The importance of randomized field trials in education and related areas. In F. Mosteller & R. F. Boruch (Eds.), *Evidence matters: Randomized trials in education research* (pp. 50–79). Washington, DC: Brookings Institution.

Caracelli, V. J., & Greene, J. C. (1997). Crafting mixed-method evaluation design. In J. C. Greene & V. J. Caracelli (Eds.), Advances in mixed-method evaluation: The challenges and benefits of integrating diverse paradigms. *New Directions for Evaluation, 74,* 19–32.

Chelimsky, E. (2007). Factors influencing the choice of methods in federal evaluation practice. In G. Julnes & D. J. Rog (Eds.), Informing federal policies on evaluation methodology: Building the evidence base for method choice in government sponsored evaluation. *New Directions for Evaluation, 113,* 13–33.

Connell, J. P., Kubisch, A. C., Schorr, L. B., & Weiss, C. H. (Eds.). (1997). *New approaches to evaluating community initiatives: Concepts, methods, and contexts.* Washington, DC: Aspen Institute.

Cook, T. D., & Payne, M. R. (2002). Objecting to the objections to using random assignment in educational research. In F. Mosteller & R. F. Boruch (Eds.), *Evidence matters: Randomized trials in education research* (pp. 150–178). Washington, DC: Brookings Institution.

Cousins, J. B. (2004). Minimizing evaluation misutilization as principled practice. *American Journal of Evaluation, 25,* 391–397.

Cronbach, L. J. (1982). *Designing evaluations of educational and social programs.* San Francisco, CA: Jossey-Bass.

Datta, L-E. (1994). Paradigm wars: A basis for peaceful coexistence and beyond. In C. S. Reichardt & S. F. Rallis (Eds.), The quantitative-qualitative debate: New perspectives. *New Directions for Evaluation, 61,* 53–70.

Datta, L-E. (1997). A pragmatic basis for mixed-method designs. In J. C. Greene & V. J. Caracelli (Eds.), Advances in mixed-method evaluation: The challenges and benefits of integrating diverse paradigms. *New Directions for Evaluation, 74*, 33–45.

Datta, L-E. (2007). Looking at the evidence: What variations in practice might indicate. In G. Julnes & D. J. Rog (Eds.), Informing federal policies on evaluation methodology: Building the evidence base for method choice in government sponsored evaluation. *New Directions for Evaluation, 113*, 35–54.

Dawid, A. P. (2000). Causal inference without counterfactuals. *Journal of the American Statistical Association, 95*, 407–424.

de Lancer Julnes, P. (2006). Performance measurement: An effective tool for government accountability? The debate goes on. *Evaluation, 12*(2), 219–235.

Fulbright-Anderson, K., Kubisch, A. C., & Connell, J. P. (Eds.). (1998). *New approaches to evaluating community initiatives: Theory, measurement, and analysis* (vol. 2). Washington, DC: Aspen Institute.

Greene, J. C. (2005). A value-engaged approach for evaluating the Bunche–Da Vinci Learning Academy. In M. C. Alkin & C. A. Christie (Eds.), Theorists' models in action. *New Directions for Evaluation, 106*, 27–45.

Greene, J. C. (2007). Method choices are contextual, contingent, and political. In G. Julnes & D. J. Rog (Eds.), Informing federal policies on evaluation methodology: Building the evidence base for method choice in government sponsored evaluation. *New Directions for Evaluation, 113*, 111–113.

Gueron, J. (2002). The politics of random assignment. In F. Mosteller & R. Boruch (Eds.), *Evidence matters* (pp. 15–49). Washington, DC: Brookings Institution.

Henry, G. T., & Julnes, G. (1998). Values and realist valuation. In G. T. Henry, G. Julnes, & M. M. Mark (Eds.), Realist evaluation: An emerging theory in support of practice. *New Directions for Evaluation, 78*, 53–72.

Julnes, G. (2011). Reframing validity in evaluation: A multidimensional, systematic model of valid inference. In H. Chen, S. I. Donaldson, & M. M. Mark (Eds.), Beyond the traditional validity model: Alternative views and options for program evaluation. *New Directions for Evaluation, 130*, 55–67.

Julnes, G. (Ed.). (2012). Promoting value in the public interest: Informing policies for judging value in evaluation. *New Directions for Evaluation, 133*.

Julnes, G., & Foster, E. M. (2001). Crafting evaluation in support of welfare reform. In G. Julnes & E. M. Foster (Eds.), Outcomes of welfare reform for families who leave TANF. *New Directions for Evaluation, 91*, 3–8.

Julnes, G., McCormick, S., Nolan, R., & Sheen, J. (2006). *Experiences and outcomes of the Utah Medicaid Work Incentive Program*. Technical report submitted to the Utah Department of Health.

Julnes, G., Pang, D., Takemoto-Chock, N., Speidel, G., & Tharp, R. (1987). The process of training in processes. *Journal of Community Psychology, 15*, 387–396.

Julnes, G., & Rog, D. J. (2007). Pragmatic support for policies on methodology. In G. Julnes & D. J. Rog (Eds.), Informing federal policies on evaluation methodology: Building the evidence base for method choice in government sponsored evaluation. *New Directions for Evaluation, 113*, 129–147.

Julnes, G., & Rog, D. J. (2008). Evaluation methods for producing actionable evidence: Contextual influences on adequacy and appropriateness of method choice. In S. I. Donaldson, C. A. Christie, & M. M. Mark (Eds.), *What counts as credible evidence in applied research and evaluation practice?* (pp. 96–132). Thousand Oaks, CA: SAGE.

Kirkhart, K. E. (2000). Reconceptualizing evaluation use: An integrated theory of influence. In V. J. Caracelli & H. Preskill (Eds.), The expanding scope of evaluation use. *New Directions for Evaluation, 88,* 5–23.

Lincoln, Y. S. (2004). High modernism at the National Research Council: A review of F. Mosteller and R. Boruch's *Evidence Matters. Academe, 90*(6), 110–111, 113–115.

Lipsey, M. W. (2007). Method choice for government evaluation: The beam in our own eye. In G. Julnes & D. J. Rog (Eds.), Informing federal policies on evaluation methodology: Building the evidence base for method choice in government sponsored evaluation. *New Directions for Evaluation, 113,* 113–115.

Mark, M. M., Henry, G. T., & Julnes, G. (2000). *Evaluation: An integrated framework for understanding, guiding, and improving public and nonprofit policies and programs.* San Francisco, CA: Jossey-Bass.

Mohr, L. B. (1996). *The causes of human behavior: Implications for theory and method in the social sciences.* Ann Arbor: University of Michigan Press.

Mosteller, F., & Boruch, R. (2002). *Evidence matters.* Washington, DC: Brookings Institution.

Pawson, R., & Tilley, N. (1997). *Realistic evaluation.* Thousand Oaks, CA: SAGE.

Petrosino, A. (2000). Mediators and moderators in the evaluation of programs for children: Current practice and agenda for improvement. *Evaluation Review, 24,* 47–72.

Reichardt, C. S., & Rallis, S. F. (Eds.). (1994). The qualitative-quantitative debate: New perspective. *New Directions for Evaluation, 61.*

Rog, D. J. (2012). When background becomes foreground: Toward context-sensitive evaluation practice. In D. J. Rog, J. L Fitzpatrick, & R. F. Conner (Eds.), Context: A framework for its influence on evaluation practice. *New Directions for Evaluation, 135,* 25–40.

Rog, D. J., & Knickman, J. (2004). Strategies for comprehensive initiatives. In M. Braverman, N. Constantine, & J. Slater (Eds.), *Foundations and evaluations: Contexts and practices for effective philanthropy* (pp. 223–235). San Francisco, CA: Jossey-Bass.

Rossi, P. H., Lipsey, M. W., & Freeman, H. E. (2004). *Evaluation: A systematic approach* (7th ed.). Thousand Oaks, CA: SAGE.

Schwandt, T. A. (2007). Thoughts on using the notion of evidence in the controversy over method choice. In G. Julnes & D. J. Rog (Eds.), Informing federal policies on evaluation methodology: Building the evidence base for method choice in government sponsored evaluation. *New Directions for Evaluation, 113,* 115–119.

Scriven, M. S. (1967). The methodology of evaluation. In R. W. Tyler, R. M. Gagne, & M. S. Scriven (Eds.), *Perspectives of curriculum evaluation* (vol. 1 of *AERA Monograph Series on Curriculum Evaluation,* pp. 39–83). Skokie, IL: Rand McNally.

Shadish, W. R. (2002). Revisiting field experimentation: Field notes for the future. *Psychological Methods, 7,* 2–18.

Shadish, W. R., Clark, M.H., Steiner, P. M. (2008). Can nonrandomized experiments yield accurate answers? A randomized experiment comparing random and non-random assignments. *Journal of the American Statistical Association, 103* (484), 1334-1343.

Shadish, W. R., Cook, T. D., & Campbell, D. T. (2002). *Experimental and quasi-experimental designs for generalized causal inference.* Boston, MA: Houghton Mifflin.

Shadish, W. R., & Rindskopf, D. M. (2007). Methods for evidence-based practice: Quantitative synthesis of single-subject designs. In G. Julnes & D. J. Rog (Eds.), Informing federal policies on evaluation methodology: Building the evidence base for method choice in government sponsored evaluation. *New Directions for Evaluation, 113,* 95–109.

Silverstein, R., Julnes, G., & Nolan, R. (2005). What policymakers need and must demand from research regarding the employment rate of persons with disabilities. *Behavioral Sciences and the Law, 23,* 1–50.

Smith, N. L. (2007). Judging methods. In G. Julnes & D. J. Rog (Eds.), Informing federal policies on evaluation methodology: Building the evidence base for method choice in government sponsored evaluation. *New Directions for Evaluation, 113,* 119–123.

Tharp, R. G. (1981). The meta-methodology of research and development. *Educational Perspectives, 20,* 42–48.

Tharp, R. G. (2007). A developmental process view of inquiry and how to support it. In G. Julnes & D. J. Rog (Eds.), Informing federal policies on evaluation methodology: Building the evidence base for method choice in government sponsored evaluation. *New Directions for Evaluation, 113,* 123–126.

Weinberg, J. (1973). Causation. In P. P. Weiner (Ed.), *Dictionary of the history of ideas* (pp. 270–278). New York, NY: Scribner.

Weiss, C. H. (1988). Evaluation for decisions: Is anybody there? Does anybody care? *Evaluation Practice, 9*(1), 5–20.

Weiss, C. H. (1998). *Evaluation: Methods for studying programs and policies.* Upper Saddle River, NJ: Prentice Hall.

Weiss, C. H., Murphy-Graham, E., & Birkeland, S. (2005). An alternate route to policy influence: How evaluations affect DARE. *American Journal of Evaluation, 26*(1), 12–30.

West, C. (1995). Theory, pragmatism, and politics. In R. Hollinger & D. Depew (Eds.), *Pragmatism: From progressivism to postmodernism* (pp. 314–325). Westport, CT: Praeger.

Wholey, J. S. (2004). Evaluability assessment. In J. S. Wholey, H. P. Hatry, & K. E. Newcomer (Eds.), *Handbook of practical program evaluation* (2nd ed., pp. 33–61). San Francisco, CA: Jossey-Bass.

Yin, R. K. (1994). *Case study research: Design and methods* (2nd ed.). Thousand Oaks, CA: SAGE.

Yin, R. K., & Davis, D. (2007). Adding new dimensions to case study evaluations: The case of evaluating comprehensive reforms. In G. Julnes & D. J. Rog (Eds.), Informing federal policies on evaluation methodology: Building the evidence base for method choice in government sponsored evaluation. *New Directions for Evaluation, 113,* 75–93.

12

Credible Evidence of Effectiveness: Necessary but Not Sufficient

Thomas A. Schwandt

> *The core standards of good evidence and well-conducted inquiry are not internal to the sciences, but common to empirical inquiry of every kind. . . . Respect for evidence, care in weighing it, and persistence in seeking it out, so far from being scientific desiderata, are the standards by which we judge all inquirers, detectives, historians, investigative journalists, etc., as well as scientists. In short, the sciences are not epistemologically privileged.*
>
> Susan Haack, 2003, p. 23

Every field of disciplined inquiry and every professional practice (such as law, criminal investigation, auditing, and so forth) that draws on means of systematic inquiry is concerned with credible evidence. For example, in the field of policy analysis, evidence drawn from analysis of speeches, internal memoranda, and interviews has been used to argue that the Bush administration expressed strong disdain for international law (Urquhart, 2006); in sociology, evidence drawn from extensive participant observation, interviews, and analysis of government documents has been offered in support of the hypothesis that the Chinese Communist Party's rule has been a disaster for rural people (Mirksy, 2006); and evidence gleaned from historical documents was used to make the case that slavery was central to the history of the New World, and its distinguishing feature was its appeal to racial doctrine to justify the persistence of slavery (Fredrickson, 2006). These examples illustrate that what comprises credible, believable, convincing, and trustworthy evidence spans a range of methods choices experimental science hardly has the only grasp on what constitutes evidence.

When it comes to the matter of what constitutes credible evidence, the field of evaluation seems captivated by discussions of methods needed to produce evidence of impact—witness the several chapters of this book discussing the merits of experimental and nonexperimental approaches to generating evidence of program or policy effectiveness. Of course, there is nothing inherently mistaken about investigating how various methods can be used to warrant claims of effectiveness. However, the preoccupation with the connection between methods and evidence of effectiveness has two unfortunate side effects. One obvious consequence is that it encourages a focus on too narrow a range of claims that need evidencing; the other is that it distracts us from carefully attending to a variety of important issues related to evaluative evidence and its use, including the character of evidence, the ethics of evidence, the contexts of the application of evidence, and the nature of rationality and argumentation (including the notion of an evidence base for decision making). While credibility of evidence is a critical matter, that property cannot be considered in isolation from a number of other issues related to the nature and use of evidence.

Evidence as Foundation?

Evidence generally means information helpful in forming a conclusion or judgment. Framed in a more rigorous epistemological perspective, evidence means factual information bearing on whether a belief or proposition is true or false, valid or invalid, warranted or unsupported. Evidence, however, cannot be the foundation (a source of absolutely secure knowledge) for a hypothesis or conclusion as is implied in the phrases *evidence-based policy* and *evidence-based practice*. This is not possible for two reasons. First, whether evidence is so strong as to rule out *all* possibility for error (i.e., the evidence is conclusive in the sense of being beyond all doubt) is always a matter of interpretation. The long-standing tradition of epistemological skepticism reminds us that we lack conclusive evidence for almost every topic we can think of. Second, evidence over time is obsolete—that is, it is "provisional, and always capable of being overturned, modified, refuted or superseded by better evidence" (Upshur, 2002, p. 114). These characteristics of evidence are consonant with our understanding of the fallibilistic and nonfoundational character of knowledge. Moreover, evidence per se cannot be wrong or right in some absolute sense. Our interpretations of it, however, can be flawed. We may choose to ignore the evidence—recall, for example, the Bush administration's claims that there were weapons of mass destruction in Iraq. We may make an incorrect inference based on the evidence—as that sage columnist, Ann Landers, once said, "Don't accept your dog's admiration as conclusive evidence that you are wonderful." We may leap too quickly to a conclusion absent sufficient corroborating evidence. This is the worry addressed by such methodological moves as data source triangulation and the use of multiple methods, and it is why a good physician always integrates evidence from the clinical examination, the patient's history, pathophysiological rationale (reasoning from principles of physiology to presumed clinical effect), knowledge of previous cases, and results of empirical studies in reaching a diagnosis and recommended treatment. Thus the term *evidence base* must be interpreted with caution: To claim that evidence may figure importantly in our decisions is one thing; to claim it is foundation for our actions is another. We would be well advised to talk about *evidence-informed* decision making instead.

Multiple Properties of Evidence

Credibility, probative force, and relevance are three interrelated properties of evidence. *Credibility* is a matter of whether the evidence is true, and that judgment is subject to interpretation by the relevant reference group charged with making that judgment—a given community of inquirers in the case of disciplined-based scientific inquiry or some other body convened to make the determination (as for example, a jury). In evaluation and applied research, judging whether the evidence gathered is credible will depend, in large part, on whether agreed-upon methodological rules for generating the evidence were followed (and, of course, this is a matter of interpretation). Whether the evidence is credible will be a matter of argument and rational consensus, because it is widely accepted that there is no foundation of unquestionable evidence in terms of which the validity of any knowledge claim can be adjudicated (Hammersley, 2000).

   Probative force of evidence is closely related to the question of credibility. It has to do with how strongly the evidence in question points to the claim or hypothesis under consideration, and it is, in part, a function of the strength of evidence. Probative force can be understood in this way—some evidence literally clinches or all but guarantees a hypothesis; other evidence vouches for a hypothesis; that is, it makes the hypothesis more likely (Cartwright, 2007b). The case for the use of randomized controlled trials (RCTs) is often made on the basis that if a particular set of assumptions is met, then this method clinches the results. But that certainty is bought at a cost, because the situations in which the assumptions are likely to be true are rare (Reiss, 2011).

In the assessment of evidence of impact in the socio-behavioral, psychological, and medical sciences, strength of evidence is often determined by grading schemes, such as a hierarchy of evidence. These schemes are qualitative rankings of different types of support for judgments of the effectiveness of one intervention over another. A simplified hierarchy of strongest to weakest evidence of policy or program effectiveness might look like this:

1. Systematic reviews and meta-analysis of RCTs

2. RCTs with definitive results (large and well-conducted studies)

3. RCTs with nondefinitive results (including smaller RCTs)

4. Cohort studies

5. Case control studies

6. Case studies

7. Expert opinion

The philosopher Nancy Cartwright (2007a, 2011a) has pointed out two major problems with this view of evidential strength. First, grading schemes that rank types of evidence offer no guidance on combining evidence, and decision situations in policy and practice almost always demand multiple kinds of evidence forthcoming from the use of a variety of methods (e.g., evidence of whether a practice or policy is morally, socially, or politically acceptable; evidence of cost; evidence of deleterious side effects; evidence of *Will it work here?*). For example, when writing about the shortcomings of relying on evidence hierarchies in the field of public health, Abeysinghe and Parkhurst (2013) note,

> There are almost no decisions at a political level that simply require an analysis of epidemiological or clinical evidence. Every decision has opportunity costs, and most health issues touch on a range of important concerns beyond morbidity and mortality—such as economic impact (not just cost-effectiveness), fairness and equality, solidarity and justice, or human rights. Many health interventions further involve social norms and behaviours, or government actions over which the population may have moral or ideological concerns (such as views about state control versus individual freedom, or the "right" and "wrong" way to behave). The vast majority of these issues cannot, and should not, be addressed with evidence that easily fits into a single hierarchy. For public health actors to achieve their policy goals—goals such as improvements in population health, reductions in avoidable morbidity and mortality, and decreases in health inequalities—they must ensure not only that they use evidence to guide their decisions, but that they use the right evidence to do so. (p. 13)

Second, grading schemes have led to the unproductive debate about whether a given method, particularly an RCT, is the so-called gold standard for generating evidence. Cartwright (2007a) has argued that gold standard methods are "whatever methods will provide (a) the information you need, (b) reliably, (c) from what you can do and from what you can know on that occasion" (p. 11). RCTs sometimes meet these criteria, but they underperform in other contexts.

Evidential *relevance* has to do with how the evidence bears on the hypothesis or conclusion in question. Relevance is a three-place relation involving an empirical (evidence) claim (E), a hypothesis or conclusion (H), and an argument (A)—E is evidence for H relative to some good argument A (Cartwright & Hardie, 2012, p. 18). This shifts the focus from the matter of the method used to generate evidence to the issue of how evidence plays a part in the argument for a claim that involves many premises. Consider, for example, the multiple premises involved when a detective reaches a conclusion about the commission of a crime. Or imagine the many premises involved in making an argument for the merit or worth of a policy or program when employing Michael Scriven's Key Evaluation Checklist (http://www.wmich.edu/evalctr/archive_checklists/kec_feb07.pdf), which presents an evaluator with the responsibility of conducting an evaluation of process, outcomes, costs, comparisons, and transferability in order to come to a reasonable, evidence-based synthesis. A recent National Research Council (2012) report, *Using Science as Evidence in Public Policy*, makes the argument that understanding how scientific evidence is used in policy making

[r]equires investigating what makes for reliable, valid, and compelling policy arguments *from the perspective of policy makers and those they need to persuade.* For example, arguments that certain consequences will follow from an intervention in a specific circumstance may involve a chain of reasoning with multiple premises. Surfacing and examining those premises and the extent to which they are accepted is critical to understanding whether the argument is perceived as valid (Cartwright, 2011b). For arguments that involve statistical or probabilistic reasoning, it is critical to understand how probabilities are perceived and interpreted (Kahneman, 2011). It is necessary to investigate the ways in which argumentative strategies can mislead by making unwarranted assumptions, relying on unwarranted premises, or relying on fallacies in reasoning (Thouless, 1990; Toulmin, 1979) and, in general, why flawed arguments can nonetheless be persuasive.... We can now more explicitly see that science—data, findings, theories, concepts, and so on—becomes *evidence* when it is used in a policy argument. Although the term "evidence" so used is frequently encountered as claims about predicted or actual consequences—effects, impacts, outcomes or costs—of a specific action, that is but part of the story. (emphasis in original, pp. 55–56)

Obviously, evidence of impact or effectiveness is but one of many considerations that enter into determining a policy or practice decision. Relevant evidence is also needed for understanding political expediency, available resources, values, choice of goals, side effects, and costs and benefits (Davies, 2005). Chelimsky (2007), for example, pointed out that in policy making, evidence is sought for answers to four broad types of questions—descriptive questions that ask *how many*, *how much*, and *in what proportion*; normative questions that invite an assessment of what is actually being done in some program or process versus what is the agreed upon or preferred way of doing things; cause-and-effect questions that inquire whether observed outcomes are attributable to a program or policy; and knowledge-based questions that ask about the current state of knowledge on a given issue. Davies (2005) addresses a similar concern arguing that in policy making, many types of evidence are required: implementation evidence, descriptive and analytical evidence (i.e., administrative data), attitudinal evidence, statistical modeling (multivariate analysis), economic and econometric evidence, ethical evidence, and (the general concern of the authors of this book) evidence of impact.

Evidence Is Linked to the Nature of Questions

It follows in part from what was noted above that what comprises evidence has to do with the kind of question at hand. The basis on which we substantiate the use of any method to generate evidence is not a hierarchy of method—with RCTs at the highest level and expert opinion at the lowest level—but a judgment of the aptness of a given method to generate the kind of information needed to produce evidence needed to answer the question under investigation (Petticrew & Roberts, 2003). There are two ways in which this can be illustrated. First, Table 12.1 shows the kinds of evidence (and methods needed to obtain it) that are required to answer different kinds of questions. In this case, all the questions have to do with the determination of the value of a particular medical treatment.

Second, we can think of the range of evidence necessary to address problem in terms of the model in Figure 12.1 (adapted from Upshur, VanDenKerkhof, & Goel, 2001).

The vertical axis represents the range of methods used to generate evidence. *Meaning* is forthcoming from methods that generate and analyze qualitative data and evidence of frequency, or *measurement*, from quantitative methods. The horizontal axis represents the context of evidence—ranging from individual perspectives to population estimates. In the upper left-hand quadrant (1), evidence takes a narrative form often generated through case profiles, interviews, and focus groups. It consists of data on individual stakeholder and

Table 12.1   Types of Research Questions and Actionable Evidence

Research Question	Research Methodology/ Study Design	Evidence
1. What is the importance of patient preferences in the choice of treatment for benign prostatic hyperplasia?	Open-ended, in-depth interview study	Identification and characterization of reactions of individual patients to their disease and their assessment of risks and benefits of alternative treatment
2. In men with benign prostatic hyperplasia, is laser prostatectomy superior to transurethral resection of the prostate in terms of symptom relief, blood loss, and length of hospital stay?	RCT	Efficacy of the two treatments compared on outcome variables
3. Are we providing effective care to patients with benign prostatic hyperplasia in our region, and are they appearing to benefit from it?	Nonexperimental cohort study	Longitudinal description of interventions patients receive and events and outcomes they experience

SOURCE: Based on Sackett and Wennberg (1997).

participant perceptions, beliefs, experiences, and so on. In the upper right-hand quadrant (2), evidence illustrates social views and preferences as documented in policy studies, case studies, and Delphi group analyses. These studies often rely heavily on qualitative or narrative data. In the lower left-hand quadrant (3), evidence is primarily numerical and personal, focused on the measurement of attitudes, beliefs, and preferences using psychometric and sociometric instruments. In the lower right-hand quadrant (4), evidence is numerical and focused on average effect or efficacy of an intervention. Evidence from the use of RCTs and quasi-experiments is to be found here.

Viewing evidence in this way makes it possible to recognize two important implications: First, evidence is the result of the search for useful knowledge (Banta, 2003). In evaluation, *useful* knowledge is that which bears on the question

Figure 12.1 Conceptual Taxonomy of Evidence

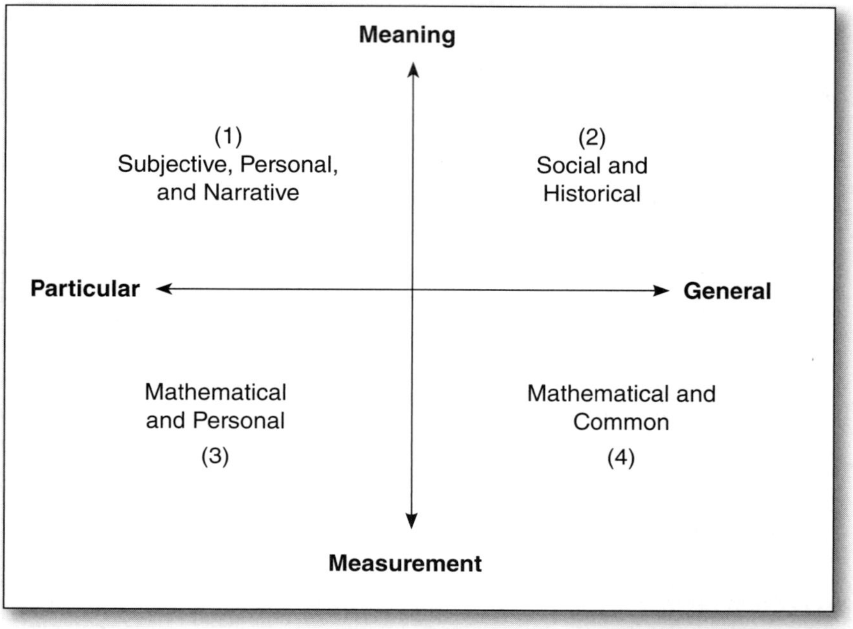

Meaning

(1)
Subjective, Personal,
and Narrative

(2)
Social and
Historical

Particular ← → **General**

Mathematical
and Personal
(3)

Mathematical and
Common
(4)

Measurement

SOURCE: Adapted from Upshur, VanDenKerkhof, and Goel (2001).

of the *value*: (a) Value is not solely determined by causal efficacy; and (b) useful knowledge takes both numerical and nonnumerical forms—experience as well as statistics produces information that can become evidence in decisions about value. In other words, there is a range of evidence that is not simply admissible but required for an evaluation judgment.

Evidence and Ethics

Evaluation is unquestionably an aspect of policy making. Try as we may, it is not possible to eliminate matters of value, ethics, purpose, or politics from policy making, for, by its very nature, policy making "requires making choices that are not value free or reducible to technical issues over which there is little controversy" (Rodwin, 2001, p. 439). Because scientific evidence of various kinds forthcoming from evaluation plays a part in policy decisions, we ought to attend specifically to ethical issues in matters of the production, interpretation, dissemination, and use of evidence. The physician and senior Fellow at the Center for Bioethics and Human Dignity, Edmund Pellegrino (1999), argues, "Because evidence has the power to convince others, it has an inescapable moral dimension. It can lead or mislead, enhance or diminish the lives of individuals and communities" (p. 34). Evaluation clearly seeks to convince in this way—it aims to make a persuasive case for the value (or lack thereof) of a given program or policy.

Drawing on Pellegrino's (1999) work, we identify several ethical considerations. First, the *collection, production,* and *interpretation of evidence* require that the evaluator knows how to competently evaluate evidence so as to avoid using evidence that is fraudulent, meaningless, or misleading. This is no small undertaking, for the question of what constitutes evidence that is sufficient as well as persuasive enough to warrant accepting a hypothesis or strong enough to compel action is not a matter of employing decision rules but of argumentation. This is readily apparent in legal proceedings as well as in the social and behavioral sciences, where it is widely accepted that setting thresholds for statistical significance, effect sizes, confidence levels, or odds ratios is not equivalent to determining the practical significance of an experimental finding.

Second, ethical considerations entailed in the *dissemination of evidence* for any purpose depend on a number of facts, which may be taken singly or in various combinations:

> the audience to which the evidence is being addressed, the particular use to which the evidence is being put, the complexity of the evidence, and the degree of certainty of the evidence presented with respect to the truth, as well as the logic used to arrive at the conclusion. (Pellegrino, 1999, p. 37)

We are, for example, on reasonably solid ground in assuming that peers in the evaluation profession have the technical competence to evaluate evidence within their specific fields of expertise. However, with lay audiences or the general public, Pellegrino argues, there is a much greater obligation to reveal the limitations and weaknesses in data or methodology, the incompleteness or preliminary state of evidence, and so on. He claims that

> [c]ulpability in presenting evidence or understanding its fallibilities varies with the context within which the information is presented. The greater the gap in expertise between the purveyor of the evidence and her or his audiences, the greater the complexity of the evidence itself, and the more general or serious the policy implication, the greater culpability. (p. 39)

Third, the *use of evidence* by those who are not the primary source of the evidence they use—for example, policy makers, physicians, patients, parents, teachers, administrators, and social workers—raises questions about the obligations of evaluators to assist the users of evaluations to reflect on the moral responsibilities for the quality of evidence they invoke for their decisions. In other words, evaluation utilization is not simply a matter of understanding legitimate types of use (e.g., instrumental, conceptual, and symbolic) but also involves questions of the consequences of illegitimate use of evidence by consumers or clients of evaluation, what Cousins (2004) described as *mistaken use* (incompetence, uncritical acceptance), *mischievous use* (manipulation, coercion), or *abuse* (suppression of evidence).

Finally, the credibility and use of evidence (be it quantitative or qualitative) are always implicated in a normative discourse of policy options and individual decision making. Upshur (2001) specifically speaks to this matter in the context of health interventions:

> There is a need to recognize the mutual relationship between health outcomes, outcome measures and normative discourse. There is no denying that medical practitioners and the public respond to media descriptions of health research. Whether to reduce cholesterol intake, increase green tea consumption, have one's PSA [prostate-specific antigen] checked, or get a bone densitometry are all influenced by perceptions of effectiveness. The important point to make is that health outcomes and risk factors are not simply statistical measures or quantitative objective facts. They are manifestations of valued or desired states of being. . . . [T]here are individual and policy implications to how evidence is created and interpreted. This dimension of evidence has hitherto received scant attention in medicine, though it is well recognized in the social sciences and humanities. (p. 572)

In other words, the kinds of discussions we associate with talk of credible evidence, such as the attainment of program and policy objectives or program and policy outcomes and their measures, cannot be neatly separated from discourse about the normative intent of programs and policies. Scientific evidence of effect or outcome is implicated in our understanding of valued states of being, such as *being educated, living a productive life, becoming adjusted to society and community, overcoming addiction,* and so forth.

Using Credible Evidence

Research in informal logic (Upshur & Colak, 2003; Walton, 1998) reveals that credible evidence is used differently in different contexts for dialogue and argumentation. Four of these contexts that have particular relevance for the practice of evaluation are briefly described below. In the first three contexts, the evidential standard—that is, the extent to which credible scientific evidence is *required* as part of the argument—is variable. In the fourth context, evidence is absolutely required for the dialogue to take place.

1. Persuasion—In this context, there is a difference of opinion between the parties, and the goal of the dialogue is to resolve or clarify the issue and persuade the other party. Empirical evidence may be offered in support of a party's view, but values and preferences are equally involved. Evidence, in fact, may be neither necessary nor sufficient to persuade.

2. Negotiation—In this situation, trade-offs and bargaining are rooted in the different interests of the parties dominates. Adjudicating the burden of evidence may be subordinated to other needs, interests, goals, or beliefs of one of the parties involved.

3. Deliberation—The parties in this situation face a dilemma or practical choice of agreeing on the best course of action. Evidence may come (and probably ought) to bear on the deliberation, as, for example, House and Howe (1999) have argued. Other considerations are, however, equally likely to influence the course of the deliberation, such as professional or expert opinion, preferences and values of the parties, and so on.

4. Inquiry—The issue is burden of proof in this context, and the aim is to verify evidence and, consequently, to support or reject a hypothesis. This is the context in which research evidence is absolutely necessary. The evidential standard is fixed, relatively speaking, within the rules of method adopted within a particular methodological or disciplinary practice.

Whether intended or not, many advocates of the idea of evidence-based practices often appear to adopt the point of view that the kinds of evaluative decisions made in practices of clinical medicine, criminal justice, health care, education, social work, and the like are all best characterized as *inquiry dialogues*. What is assumed here—and reflected in hierarchies of evidence that practitioners are instructed to use as guides to decision making—is "a particularly robust kind of rational judgment: judgment that can be codified in rules or guidelines" (Thornton, 2006). It is well-known, however, that most of the decisions faced by practitioners as well as policy makers about whether to adopt, implement, continue, revise, modify, or discontinue a policy or program are matters of practical judgment that involve simultaneous consideration and integration of empirical evidence, expertise or professional opinion, and values and preferences (Chelimsky, 2007; Fischer, 2003). Practitioners and policy makers are embodied agents, and their practices are often best characterized as "dialectical, dynamic, pragmatic and context bound"; what is plausible and reasonable for them to do in a given situation is determined by the context of that situation, not by the existence of a hierarchy of research evidence (Upshur & Colak, 2003, p. 295).

Conclusion: So What Counts?

A moment's reflection on everyday life reveals that navigating our way through—and judging the value, significance, and consequences of—events and relationships demands knowledge of the patterns as well as the peculiarities of human behavior; understandings of the common as well as the idiosyncratic meanings we attach to actions and language; wisdom to respond appropriately and effectively to complex circumstances in situations lacking rules for conduct; and a dependable grasp of the contributory, if not causal, relationship between human actions and their effects. To put it a bit more plainly, to be ordinary, conscious, aware, attentive, and responsive evaluators, citizens, parents, friends, teachers, administrators, health care workers, and the like is to employ a very catholic epistemology that seeks reliable evidence bearing on three broad, important questions—What happened here? What does that mean? Why did that happen? We routinely make use of a variety of empirical means to generate this evidence. As a result, we know different things about ourselves and our actions and we know them in different ways. Taken collectively, these different understandings, and different ways of reaching those understandings, help us form a comprehensive picture of what we are up to, why and how, what it means, and whether we are doing the right thing and doing it well. Thus there is little genuine merit in debating whether any particular method of investigation is superior for producing credible evidence in and for evaluation. Evaluating the merit, worth, or significance of our judgments, actions, policies, programs, and so on requires a variety of evidence generated via both experimental and nonexperimental methods.

Three important considerations ought to guide our discussion of what constitutes credible evidence in evaluation practice: First, deciding the question of what constitutes credible evidence is not the same as deciding the question of what constitutes credible evaluation. In an evaluation, a number of different kinds of claims are put forth in arguing the case for the value (merit, worth, or significance) of a program, project, policy, and so on. Some of these claims are factual; others express value judgments, state definitions or principles, provide causal explanations, and recommend courses of action. Organizing and presenting credible evidence in support of causal claims is, of course, an important part of what an evaluation entails. Yet what constitutes a *credible evaluation* will depend, in part, on how each of the different claims is explained and defended (and how they are collectively assembled into an argument). However necessary, developing credible evidence of effectiveness in evaluation is not sufficient for establishing the credibility of an evaluation.

Second, what constitutes credible, trustworthy, believable, or convincing evidence cannot be decided by method choice alone. This is so for several reasons: (a) Evidence is always put together in defense of some *particular* claim. Thus we cannot discuss the matter of evidence in the abstract—that is, absent a thorough understanding of "Evidence for what?" So, for example, if the claim in question is "X is important in understanding Y," "We are doing the best we can to achieve Y, given the resources at our disposal," or "This community ought to do Y," the kind of evidence we assemble in defense of these claims and the methods by which we assemble it are likely to be different from the kind we would gather if the claim is "Compared to A, B is a superior treatment for reducing the incidence of Y." (b) Appraising the credibility of evidence is never simply a matter of asking about the method used to generate it. Other relevant considerations include the credibility of the source/person (e.g., whether the person employing the method has the relevant expertise, a vested interest or bias, etc.); whether the claim itself is considered plausible and relatively in keeping with what we already know or (very unlikely) is novel and so forth; whether the evidence is derived in a more or less straightforward way from observation or involves a significant amount of inference; how the claim in question fits with other beliefs one holds; and whether there is corroborative evidence from other sources. (c) The circumstances and particular practice in which evidence is being argued influence appraisals of the probative (inferential) force of that evidence. Thus, for example, the same evidence generated with the same method is judged differently in a criminal court than it is judged in a civil court.

Third, there is likely to be considerable payoff for the conduct of evaluation if we frame the account of evidence and its properties (e.g., credibility) in a practical-theoretical way rather an abstract/general-theoretical way. The latter is an attempt to develop a general theoretical account of what evidence is that originates in discussions of what constitutes correct beliefs about knowledge and its justification, the world, and methodology. It seeks to settle things, so to speak, by providing sure guidelines for testing the correctness of our beliefs or principles about evidence. The former, in contrast, is more or less a map of the kinds of practices and decisions within those practices in which we have come to regard evidence as something that matters. A practical theory guides us through those reason-giving practices, drawing our attention to the ways we construct the relationship between knowing and acting in particular situations. Put somewhat differently, concerns about the character of evidence, the ethics of evidence, the contexts in which evidence is used, and the kinds of arguments we make in which evidence plays an import role signify problems of action. Such concerns invite us to answer questions of how we act together meaningfully in making sense of and using evidence in evaluation.

References

Abeysinghe, S., & Parkhurst, J. O. (2013). *"Good" evidence for improved policy making: From hierarchies to appropriateness.* Working Paper #2, London School of Hygiene and Tropical Medicine GRIP-Health Programme. Retrieved August 8, 2013, from http://www.lshtm.ac.uk/groups/griphealth/resources/better_evidence_for_policy:_from_hierarchies_to_appropriateness.pdf

Banta, H. D. (2003). Considerations in defining evidence for public health. *International Journal of Technology Assessment in Health Care, 19*(3), 559–572.

Cartwright, N. (2007a). Are RCTs the gold standard? *Biosocieties, 2*(2), 11–20.

Cartwright, N. (2007b). *Hunting causes and using them.* Cambridge, England: Cambridge University Press.

Cartwright, N. (2011a). A philosopher's view of the long road from RCTs to effectiveness. *The Lancet, 377,* 1400–1401.

Cartwright, N. (2011b). Predicting what will happen when we act: What counts as warrant? *Preventive Medicine, 53*(4), 221–224.

Cartwright, N., & Hardie, J. (2012). *Evidence-based policy: A practical guide to doing it better.* Oxford, England: Oxford University Press.

Chelimsky, E. (2007). Factors influencing the choice of methods in federal evaluation practice. In G. Julnes & D. Rog (Eds.), Informing federal policies on evaluation methodology. *New Directions for Evaluation, 113,* 13–33.

Cousins, B. (2004). Commentary: Minimizing evaluation misuse as principled practice. *American Journal of Evaluation, 25*(3), 391–397.

Davies, P. (2005). *Evidence-based policy at the cabinet office.* Overseas Development Institute, London, Impact and Insight Series. Retrieved August 8, 2013, from http://www.odi.org.uk/sites/odi.org.uk/files/odi-assets/events-documents/2866.pdf

Fischer, F. (2003). *Reframing public policy: Discursive politics and deliberative practices.* Oxford, England: Oxford University Press.

Fredrickson, G. M. (2006, May 25). They'll take their stand. *New York Review of Books, 53*(9), 34–36.

Haack, S. (2003). *Defending science—within reason: Between scientism and cynicism.* Amherst, NY: Prometheus.

Hammersley, M. (2000). *Taking sides in social research: Essays on partisanship and bias.* London, England: Routledge.

House, E. R., & Howe, K. R. (1999). *Values in evaluation and social research.* Thousand Oaks, CA: SAGE.

Kahneman, D. (2011). *Thinking, fast and slow.* New York, NY: Farrar, Straus and Giroux.

Mirksy, J. (2006, May 11). China: The shame of the villagers. *New York Review of Books, 53*(8), 37–39.

National Research Council. (2012). *Using science as evidence in public policy.* Washington, DC: The National Academies Press

Pellegrino, E. D. (1999). The ethical use of evidence in biomedicine. *Evaluation and the Health Professions, 22*(1), 33–43.

Petticrew, M., & Roberts, H. (2003). Evidence, hierarchies, and typologies: Horses for courses. *Journal of Epidemiology and Community Health, 57*, 527–529.

Reiss J. (2011). Empirical evidence: Its nature and sources. In I. C. Jarvie & J. Zamora-Bonilla (Eds.), *Handbook of philosophy of social science* (pp. 551–576). Thousand Oaks, CA: SAGE.

Rodwin, M. A. (2001). Commentary: The politics of evidence-based medicine. *Journal of Health Politics, 26*(2), 439–446.

Sackett, D. L., & Weinberg, J. E. (1997). Editorial: Choosing the best research design for each question. *British Medical Journal, 315*, 1636.

Thornton, T. (2006). Tacit knowledge as the unifying factor in evidence-based medicine and clinical judgment. *Philosophy, Ethics, and Humanities in Medicine, 1*(2). Retrieved April 18, 2014, from http://www.peh-med.com/content/1/1/2

Thouless, R. (1990). *Straight and crooked thinking* (revised edition). London, UK: Hodder Arnold H&S.

Toulmin, S. (1979). *An introduction to reasoning*. New York, NY: Macmillan.

Upshur, R. E. G. (2001). The ethics of alpha: Reflections on statistics, evidence and values in medicine. *Theoretical Medicine, 22*, 565–576.

Upshur, R. E. G. (2002). If not evidence, then what? Or does medicine really need an evidence base? *Journal of Evaluation in Clinical Practice, 8*(2), 113–119.

Upshur, R. E. G., & Colak, E. (2003). Argumentation and evidence. *Theoretical Medicine, 24,* 283–299.

Upshur, R. E. G., VanDenKerkhof, E. G., & Goel, V. (2001). Meaning and measurement: An inclusive model of evidence in health care. *Journal of Evaluation in Clinical Practice, 7*(2), 91–96.

Urquhart, B. (2006, May 11). The outlaw world. *New York Review of Books, 53*(8), 25–28.

Walton, D. (1998). *The new dialectic: Conversational contexts of argument*. Toronto, ON, Canada: University of Toronto Press.

13

Credible and Actionable Evidence

A Framework, Overview, and Suggestions for Future Practice and Research

Melvin M. Mark

pplied social research, including program and policy evaluation, is typically undertaken with the hope that it will have positive consequences. For instance, an evaluator may hope that her findings will lead to the selection and retention of more effective programs. Or an evaluator may hope that his evaluation, with its recommendations about possible changes, will lead to improved processes and outcomes in an ongoing program. Alternatively, an evaluator might hope to contribute in the long run by improving people's understandings of a social problem and its potential solutions or by increasing capacity within an organization.

In most cases, for an evaluation or for any applied social research to lead to any of these or other positive consequences, somebody has to think that the findings are believable and that they can and should be acted on. In other words, the study and its findings must be taken as credible and actionable. This book focuses on the nature and determinants of credibility and actionability as well as their possible role within broader views about the use of evidence. Choice of research methods, not surprisingly, is one of the potential determinants of credibility and actionability. Accordingly, many of the preceding chapters address the consequences of method choice on credibility and actionability.

Readers of these chapters will have seen that although there are areas of general agreement, complete consensus does not exist about what constitutes credible and actionable evidence. This chapter builds (largely) on ideas presented in previous chapters, with the hope of providing a model that might contribute to a greater sense of consensus where agreement exists and to a clearer understanding of why any disagreements remain. The chapter is not meant to be a comprehensive review or summary of the preceding chapters. Instead, I draw selectively on other chapters in this book in an attempt to sketch out a more comprehensive model. At times, I refer to chapters in the previous edition of this book (Donaldson, Christie, & Mark, 2009) as well as to other work. I begin with a brief discussion of credibility, actionability, and other attributes of evidence. I subsequently consider these attributes in the context of a broader general framework.

Christie and Fleischer (Chapter 2) ground contemporary debates about evaluation methods within different research traditions and paradigms. The current chapter aspires to contribute to moving those debates beyond matters of methods and paradigms. In service of this aspiration, credibility and the other attributes of evidence, along with the broader framework in which they reside, are used here as a lens for considering the reasons that underlie different method and practice preferences. My hope is that if we better understand *why* people disagree about method preferences, we might be able to have more productive discussions in the future. That is, we might move from relatively unproductive debates centered on methods to more productive discussions focusing more on the considerations that underlie diverging preferences for methods. At the end of chapter, some suggestions for practice are given. In addition, Appendix I includes a relatively detailed discussion of Michael Scriven's views about randomized experiments.

Credibility and Actionability in a General Framework of Evidence Use, Part 1

In addition to credibility, other characteristics of evidence can also affect whether people are inclined to see evaluation and other research findings as a worthy guide to action. Here I draw on, and expand, a framework that Schwandt (Chapter 12) provides. Specifically, in this section, I discuss credibility, inferential potency, relevance, comprehensiveness, and actionability as attributes of evidence. Explicitly or implicitly, people may make judgments about each of these attributes.

I believe that treating these characteristics separately is helpful for those who want to understand the use of evidence. But this formulation, with its five attributes, is not inevitable. (Indeed, many of the chapters in this volume combine characteristics I treat separately here, such as credibility and inferential potency.) Putting this and other possible caveats aside, I turn now to the five attributes.

Credibility refers, in general terms, to whether something is believed or, put differently, taken to be true or correct. In certain research traditions, the concept of validity has received more emphasis. Validity presumably is a determinant of credibility. However, how strongly a technical assessment of validity causes or predicts credibility judgments will vary. When will credibility judgments be based more on considerations other than validity? When the perceiver lacks the expertise in research methods to judge validity and when the perceiver relies more strongly on other possible cues to credibility (see Miller, Chapter 3). Whether credibility judgments are based on validity or not in a particular case, evidence will often need to be seen as credible if it is to be used, as many chapter authors have noted.

Schwandt identifies *probative* (or *inferential*) *force* as another important characteristic of evidence. Drawing on the philosopher Cartwright, high probative force would be evidence that essentially clenches an argument. If an evaluation has high probative force and indicates that a training program increases employment, this should settle the question about that effect. Probative force can be differentiated from credibility, however. In particular, a finding could be credible without having high probative force. That is, the finding is believable but not completely convincing with respect to the issue at hand. It does not clinch the point. Reichardt and Mark (1998) noted a kind of finding from quantitative research that illustrates the distinction: An experiment might be credible (and valid) but have a large confidence interval. Study results like this are believable (i.e., they are credible), but they leave a too-wide range of uncertainty to clinch the argument (i.e., they have lower probative force). I prefer the term *inferential potency* to *probative force* and will use it here.

Relevance is another criterion that Schwandt mentions. A given program evaluation might provide findings that are both credible and inferentially potent but nevertheless are of limited value—they address issues that are not strongly informative for the decision at hand. They clinch a point, but it's not the right point for the decision at hand. For instance, suppose that information is needed about the quality of program implementation. In that case, an estimate of program effectiveness, such as from a randomized controlled trial (RCT) comparing a treatment and control group, would not be relevant (Rallis, Chapter 7). Relevance is also an issue when one questions whether the findings from an RCT will apply to a new setting (Cartwright & Hardie, 2012). Thus Bickman and Reich's (Chapter 5) and others' discussion of external validity involves the criterion of relevance.

A fourth criterion, *comprehensiveness,* was not explicitly identified by Schwandt. *Comprehensiveness* refers to the extent to which the evidence at hand covers the full range of questions that are of interest. We can further distinguish between *specific comprehensiveness* and *global comprehensiveness.* Consider as an example early evaluations of alternative welfare arrangements, which estimated the effect of then-new welfare practices on employment and income. Those evaluations were lacking in specific comprehensiveness. Decision makers were interested in whether new welfare approaches affected outcomes other than employment and income, such as family configurations (and today, they would also be interested in effects on health and children's well-being). *Specific comprehensiveness*, then, refers to completeness within a particular evaluation task or question, such as, *What are the program's effects?* In contrast, *Global comprehensiveness* refers to completeness across the multiple evaluation questions that are of interest. For instance, imagine an evaluation that gives relatively comprehensive evidence about the relevant range of program effects. This evaluation could nevertheless lack global comprehensiveness if it does not provide information that stakeholders want about the relative cost of implementing the new program and the quality with which it would be implemented at varied locations.

Trade-offs in study planning often involve trade-offs among these four criteria. For example, assuming a given level of funding, efforts to increase comprehensiveness may come at a cost of credibility, inferential potency, or both. If more questions are to be addressed in a study, the quality of the answer to any single question may suffer. Trade-offs in study planning can, of course, also involve trade-offs between one or more of these criteria and the level of resources that are available. An evaluator might be able to increase comprehensiveness without a loss of credibility *if* the study budget and timeframe are increased.

As shown on Figure 13.1, credibility, inferential potency, relevance, and comprehensiveness presumably combine to determine judgments of actionability. *Actionability* refers to the perceived degree to which evidence is suitable as a guide to possible action. Little is known about the relative importance of the four criteria as precursors of actionability judgments. To take but one specific example, one might ask how important comprehensiveness is for perceived actionability relative to credibility and the other attributes. (As a speculative response, the importance of comprehensiveness may vary, depending on whether or not multiple evaluation questions are salient.) Nor is a great deal known about the extent to which the four criteria are related or affect each other. For example, if evidence is seen as credible, does that make it seem more relevant? Clarifying the relationships among the criteria in Figure 13.1 would be a potentially valuable research agenda. It could lead to improved understanding of the way people do or do not use research and evaluation evidence. (Note that arrows could be included in Figure 13.1 to represent possible interrelations among the four criteria to the left; these are omitted for the sake of simplicity.)

Figure 13.1   Credibility, Other Characteristics of Evidence, Actionability, and the Threshold for Action

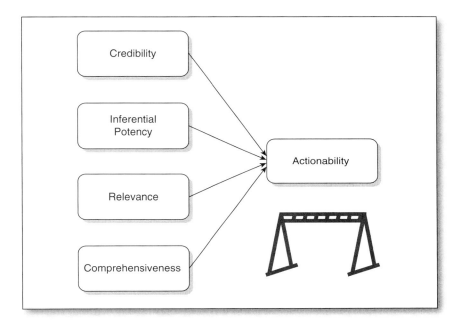

THE THRESHOLD FOR ACTIONABILITY

In principle, judgments about actionability could be conceptualized on a continuum, with multiple gradations ranging from very low to very high. In practice, however, the decision is more of a dichotomous, go/no-go, act/don't-act kind of choice. The image of a bar or hurdle under actionability in Figure 13.1 is meant to represent the threshold for deciding to act. The height of the bar almost certainly varies across circumstances. Sometimes the threshold is high, sometimes not.

Bickman and Reich (Chapter 5) allude to this idea when they refer to the cost of being wrong about a causal relationship. These costs are not uniform, as Bickman and Reich suggest with their example of drugs that vary in cost. Julnes and Rog (Chapter 11) also address the height of the metaphoric hurdle. They refer to the confidence required for a conclusion. In this regard, Julnes and Rog note that incremental program changes, such as the choice of activities for a one-day teacher in-service program, typically require less confidence than the choice between major program alternatives, such as the selection of an integrated K–12 math curriculum.

Taking Julnes and Rog's discussion a step further, thresholds for action may vary, even across instances of choosing between major program alternatives. When a mandate exists to implement *some* alternative program (e.g., when legislation requires schools to implement a substance abuse program), the only choice is *which* program to implement. Weaker or less-comprehensive evidence about a program may suffice, relative to what would be needed if instead there were no mandate and continuing without a substance abuse program was therefore an option.

More generally, the hurdle image in Figure 13.1 conveys the idea that the aggregate quality required for evidence to support action is not a constant. Action will be seen as justified in some circumstances by less impressive evidence, while in other instances, more impressive evidence may be required. At times, the height of the hurdle is implicit. At other times, it is the subject of intense, explicit debate. This was the case, for example, when advocates fought for lower evidence requirements for the approval of treatments for HIV/AIDS in the 1980s and 1990s.

ADDITIONAL FACTORS IN A BROADER FRAMEWORK

The criteria in Figure 13.1 can be seen as one part of a broader framework. Judgments about credibility, comprehensiveness, and the other criteria do not take place in a vacuum. Instead, they occur within, and are influenced by, multiple levels of context. Expanding on this general idea, Julnes and Rog (Chapter 11) provide a framework suggesting how method choices can be guided by thinking about five aspects of context: (a) alternative evaluation questions and tasks that might be addressed, (b) attributes of the phenomenon being investigated, such as whether change is likely to be easy and quick or difficult and slow, (c) characteristics of the program or policy to be investigated, (d) specific circumstances of the evaluation or study, and (e) more general characteristics of the context in which the program or policy operates.

In addition, judgments about credibility and the other criteria can be affected by a variety of processes. Some of these are individual and psychological in nature. Others are interpersonal and involve social interactions. Yet others involve social aggregates and may be political or organizational in nature. As one example of these kinds of processes, Miller (Chapter 3) reviews in considerable detail the individual psychological processes that can affect judgments of credibility and also have implications for the other criteria in Figure 13.1.

I return later to these additional aspects of a broader framework. Prior to that, I consider how the criteria listed in Figure 13.1 can clarify divergent views about method choice in evaluation.

The RCT Debate, Illuminated in Terms of Credibility and Other Criteria

As noted in Chapter 1 and many of the other chapters in this volume, the last dozen years or so have seen considerable debate about the role of randomized experiments in evaluation. One of the tripwires starting these skirmishes was a proposal, subsequently implemented, by the Department of Education through its Institute of Education Sciences (IES) to establish a priority for randomized trials for selected funding programs. In essence, this priority, when applied to a funding program, gives extra points to proposals that use randomized experiments when review panels discuss and score the proposals. Randomized experiments also receive special consideration in the review process at the What Works Clearinghouse (WWC), which was designed to identify educational interventions that have demonstrated effectiveness with credible evidence (Gersten & Hitchcock, 2009). In education, this relatively newfound emphasis on randomized experiments arose in a context that had led some observers to argue that the field of educational research had been underusing randomized trials relative to their potential benefits (e.g., Cook, 2003). Henry (Chapter 4) reviews the actual funding patterns since the IES priority was implemented—adding a dose of evidence to what has mostly been a data-free debate about evidence.

The move to give preference to randomized experiments (and the closest quasi-experimental approximations) has not been limited to education. This preference existed previously in medicine, where the term *RCT* (for *randomized clinical trial*) was popularized (users of term outside of medicine often refer to *control* or *controlled* rather than *clinical* trials). In other areas of practice, such as "development" evaluation (that is, the evaluation of international aid to developing countries), there have also been efforts to increase attention to RCTs. This includes the efforts of the International Initiative for Impact Evaluation or 3ie. 3ie, with support from multiple foundations and national development agencies, advocates for and funds impact evaluations and systematic reviews, with a preference for randomized experiments and strong quasi-experiments. More generally, evidence hierarchies are one of the ways that preferences for RCTs are expressed. An evidence hierarchy essentially rank orders methods from best to worst, and RCTs typically fall at or near the top.

There may currently be less heat than was initially the case around these and other instances of advocacy about RCTs and related methods. At the same time, there may not yet be the desired increase in light to illuminate the important task of choosing methods for evaluation and applied social research. By thinking about the various characteristics in Figure 13.1 and the different views held by advocates and opponents of a priority for RCT, we might find a way to more productive conversations.

METHOD CHOICES IN LIGHT OF RELEVANCE

The underlying differences that help motivate the two sides in the RCT debate can be clarified in terms of the factors listed in Figure 13.1. First, consider relevance. Advocates of more widespread use of RCTs presume that the findings from such studies are generally relevant for key decisions about programs and policies. Keep in mind that although RCTs can be expanded to address other questions, their basic contribution—if the experiment is successfully conducted—is an unbiased estimate of the average effect of the treatment (e.g., the mean difference in the outcome variable between the program group and the control/comparison group).

Advocates of RCTs hold the question of average program effects in high regard. They believe this question is commonly quite relevant in deliberations about programs and policies. Specifically, advocates of RCTs believe that a valuable form of use (if not *the most* valuable form) occurs if decision makers draw upon evidence of an intervention's average effects when they make choices about program or policy initiation, expansion, maintenance, or cessation. For example, Bickman and Reich (Chapter 5) make this point when talking about "the cost of making a wrong decision about causality." They state,

> We know that there are costs in making the wrong decision. To call a program effective when it is not means that valuable resources may be wasted and the search for other means to solve the problem will be hindered. Some programs may not only be ineffective but also harmful. In such cases, the costs of a wrong decision would be higher. On the other hand, falsely labeling a program as ineffective would mean that clients who would have benefited from the intervention would not have that benefit. (pp. 85–86)

Henry expands this position by explicitly locating it in the context of democratic decision making within representative democracies. The choice of better programs and policies, Henry argues, and especially the debunking of bad ideas are key needs within representative democracies. Henry states,

> Public policies and programs are intentional acts undertaken with the coercive force of government behind them. Authoritative bodies, such as legislatures and administrators, make public policy and program choices in most cases. The choices of these bodies are binding on the governed and therefore, to inform citizens' beliefs about public programs' positive, negative, or null results and potentially to influence voting decisions, democracies require that both the intended and unintended consequences of programs and policies be evaluated. (p. 70)

In short, Henry makes a case that findings from RCTs are highly relevant to major decisions in democracies.

At the same time, Henry does not see the RCT and the question it addresses as the only option for evaluation:

> It is possible for program administrators who also control evaluation funds to focus evaluations on questions of program coverage, studies of variations in implementation, single-case studies of a program or organization, descriptive studies of program participants, or subjective assessments of satisfaction. At a given time and in a specific situation, any of these could be the best choice for evaluation funding. (pp. 77–78)

Henry does, however, see a clear place for the RCT and its cousins: "But continually and indefinitely postponing addressing the public program effectiveness question cannot be in the interest of society."

In the earlier years of the debate about RCTs, it was easy to find statements from those opposed to the priority that were based (sometimes implicitly) on the claim that findings from RCTs usually were not relevant to the key questions that should be addressed. In the previous edition of this book, for example, Rallis (2009) expressed the view that evaluation should generally address questions other than the average effectiveness of programs or policies. In lauding evaluators who follow what she called *nonconsequentialist ethics*, Rallis stated that "[t]hese evaluators attend to the means and context more than to the outcome of a program. They ask, What does the experience mean to the individual?" (p. 218). Rallis further said, "The nonconsequentialist theories with which I am comfortable shape research ethics that turn away from experimental type of studies that seek to know outcomes and turn toward the qualitative approaches that inform process and meanings" (p. 218). For Rallis at that time, the findings from RCTs seemed generally less relevant than those from other methods. The same appeared to be true of Greene (2009):

> [Q]uestions about the causal effects of social interventions are characteristically those of policy and decision makers, while other stakeholders have other legitimate and important questions. . . . This privileging of the interests of the elite in evaluation and research is radically undemocratic. (p. 157)

Rallis's and Greene's positions on the relevance of findings from RCTs appear to be tempered in this edition relative to the previous one. At least, their positions as stated in this edition seem more open to the kind of evidence that comes from RCTs, under certain conditions. Rallis notes that the evaluations she does typically focus on program implementation, in which case findings from an RCT would not be relevant. However, she also states that if the question of interest is whether the program caused a change in outcomes, then a method such as an experiment would probably be chosen. Greene gives us a completely different chapter in this edition than in the previous one. In the current chapter, she describes practices that, in her view, increase credibility, which she illustrates in the context of a randomized experiment.

The two sides seem less polarized than in the past, at least with respect to the possible relevance of evidence from RCTs. Whether there is agreement about the conditions under which to use RCTs or other methods, however, is not clear. To the extent these disagreements continue, we may understand them better by thinking about them in the context of the criteria in Figure 13.1 and in a broader framework related to the use of evidence.

GENERALIZABILITY AS AN ASPECT OF RELEVANCE

Cartwright and Hardie (2012) emphasize that RCTs (and other forms of impact or outcome evaluation) answer a limited question: whether the program or policy "worked there." That is, in the ideal, the RCT gives an unbiased estimate of the effect of the specific way the program was implemented in the specific setting and time in which the RCT took place with the particular study participants. Cartwright and Hardie further emphasize that policy deliberations need to ask a different question—*Will it work here?*—that is, in the circumstances in which the policy or program may be implemented. Readers familiar with the earlier evaluation literature will recognize the *It worked there* versus *Will it work here?* formulation as an echo of Cronbach's (1982) critique of the limited reach of internal validity.

In their relatively detailed and thoughtful discussion of the limits of RCTs, Bickman and Reich point out that the "most often-cited criticism of this design is its reduced external validity." This refers to the possibility that you may not be able to generalize from the perhaps artificial circumstances that allow random assignment to other circumstances about which decisions are to be made. Bickman and Reich cite Berk (2005):

> It cannot be overemphasized that unless an experiment can be generalized at least a bit, time and resources have been wasted. One does not really care about the results of a study unless its conclusions can be used to guide future decisions. (p. 428)

Bickman and Reich applaud signs of possible increased attention to external validity in evaluation and applied social research. However, it is not yet clear how (and when) to give comfort to potential evidence users that the results of an RCT should indeed apply to future decisions.

Greene (Chapter 10) emphasizes the importance of relevance and suggests that relevance is required for credibility:

> The evaluation is directed toward issues, concerns, and questions of *contextual meaning and relevance;* the evaluation is designed to generate information of import and consequence to stakeholders *in the contexts* being evaluated. Evidence that is relevant only for remote stakeholders does not have the potential for credibility. (p. 208)

In contrast, the model in Figure 13.1 allows for the possibility that evidence could be credible but not relevant. Regardless of whether relevance is viewed as a separate characteristic or as an aspect (or precursor) of credibility, Bickman and Reich, Greene, and others in this volume see relevance as an important concern.

In her chapter in the previous edition of this book, Greene pointed to the power of contexts, including the possibility that relevant processes may be different at one point in history than another. Citing Berliner (2002), she noted that "it is because of the need to understand the particularities of each local context that 'qualitative inquiry has become so important in educational research'" (p. 160). One response to this point would be to emphasize the importance of mixed methods, melding qualitative and quantitative to seek both unbiased estimates of treatment effects and sensitivity to local context. Absent that, advocates of RCTs would be well advised to engage in work to improve our understanding of the conditions under which generalizations from such studies are successful. And those who wish to debate the value of alternative methods would be well advised to try to assess the *relative* capacity of different methods to provide findings that support conclusions across different contexts, or put differently, different settings, persons, and times. For instance, does a case study with, say, eight sites provide more support than an RCT for generalizing to new locations in the future?

Henry (Chapter 4) reminds us that there often are limits on how microscopic this attention to generalizability—and thus to relevance—needs to be. He notes that governments commonly take actions that apply across a wide scope of persons, settings, and times. A math curriculum is selected for an entire school district, not for a given child in a specific classroom with a particular teacher. Classroom size laws may be implemented at the state level, again cutting across a wide range of contexts. The challenges of generalizability presumably are greater if choices among alternative programs are to be made at the individual level than at the state level. That is not to say the challenges are absent for, say, state-level choices but only that they are lesser in magnitude.

METHOD CHOICES IN LIGHT OF CREDIBILITY

Preferences for methods are often framed in terms of credibility and its companion, inferential potency. For instance, Henry addresses credibility in the context of the view that a democracy needs to evaluate the consequences of the programs and policies that are binding for its citizens. Henry contends that to obtain findings about program consequences that are "as conclusive as possible," the "most conclusive and widely regarded as compelling means for producing findings that eliminate these alternative explanations are RCTs and FEs." In contrast, others, including Chelimsky, Rallis, Mathison, and Scriven, explicitly endorse the credibility of methods other than RCTs. These disparate views appear, at least in part, to be based on differing views about relevance. Even though these two criteria are listed separately in Figure 13.1, they may be linked in people's judgments.

Credibility assessments can be influenced by numerous factors, as discussed especially by Miller (Chapter 3) and as addressed later in this chapter in the context of a broader framework that includes Figure 13.1. The advocacy of RCTs that surrounded the IES priority, the creation of 3ie, and related initiatives can be seen in this light. These activities could be viewed as part of a social movement intended in part to enhance the credibility of RCTs as seen by government officials, foundation staff, and others.

METHOD CHOICES IN LIGHT OF INFERENTIAL POTENCY

Assume for the moment that an estimate of average program effects is relevant for an upcoming decision. Disagreements about the desirability of conducting an RCT can also rest on differing views about inferential potency. Note that, when considering a priority for one method over another, the real question is about *relative* inferential potency. Although not using such terminology, Henry contends that RCTs have more inferential potency than alternative methods. He bases this on the idea that random assignment experiments are superior in terms of eliminating alternative explanations.

Scriven (Chapter 6), in contrast, suggests that other methods are equally and sometimes better suited for estimating program effects. As a result, Scriven argues forcefully against giving a general priority to RCTs. Scriven's argument is considered in detail in Appendix I. In short, Scriven's position regarding RCTs is that "the usual claimed intrinsic advantage of the RCT design is only a theoretical advantage, and its actual achievements are frequently matched in practice by many other designs."

Bickman and Reich add another voice to this discussion. They consider a list of potential problems that can undermine the inferential potency of RCTs. To have a fair discussion about relative inferential potency, one would need to do that same kind of analysis for whatever method alternatives are under consideration. As Scriven's analysis reminds us, an analysis of the *general* inferential potency of any method in the abstract may not apply to a *specific* study. As an example, several of the problems that Bickman and Reich describe for RCTs may occur in one study, while another RCT may be free from these problems. Unfortunately, evaluators/researchers and funders often need to try to assess, *in advance,* whether a study with a particular design will be subject to flaws. To the extent this can be surmised in advance, review panels could make defensible judgments about the relative value of alternative research designs. However, if there is little ability to foresee the presence or potency of validity threats, then one might prefer to bet on the *general* inferential potency of a design.

Credibility and Actionability in a General Framework of Evidence Use, Part 2

Figure 13.1 provides a simplified model in which four characteristics of evidence—credibility, inferential potency, relevance, and comprehensiveness (both specific and general)—combine to result in judgments about actionability. As noted previously, one way that Figure 13.1 is simplified is that it ignores the possible interplay between the four characteristics on the left. For instance, perceived relevance may affect judgments of credibility, as suggested by Greene's quote about the two.

A second way in which Figure 13.1 is simplified is that it represents a limited slice of a larger, prior sequence. In particular, judgments about credibility, inferential potency, relevance, and comprehensiveness can be affected by a variety of factors. Accordingly, Figure 13.2 places the evidence attributes of Figure 13.1 within a broader framework with two additional sets of factors. On the left of Figure 13.2 are four of the aspects of context from Julnes and Rog. The fifth, *evaluation* or *study context*, sits slightly to the right of the other aspects of context, because the other four generally are present prior to the study. For example, information needs and characteristics of the problem exist before the evaluation begins in most cases. Indeed, one hopes that thoughtful analysis of the other contextual areas took place as part of the planning of the evaluation.

At the bottom of Figure 13.2, in bold, are three levels of processes that may influence judgments of credibility and the other attributes of evidence.

These are individual, interpersonal, and collective levels. Along with the areas of context, the three levels of process are discussed in the current section.* The arrows in Figure 13.2 from the processes are intended to show that processes at the three levels can affect, for example, the relationships between context and the perceived attributes of evidence. Figure 13.2 would be technically more accurate if there were arrows emanating from each of the areas

Figure 13.2   A Broader Framework With Five Aspects of Context, Three Levels of Process, Four Attributes of Evidence, and Judged Actionability

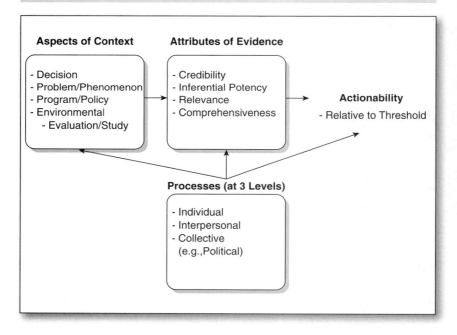

---

*A third way in which Figure 13.1 is simplified has not been addressed in Figure 13.2. Presumably, actionability judgments are not important in and of themselves. Instead, they—like credibility and other such judgments—are primarily important because they affect the likelihood of use. They presumably help determine whether evidence contributes to subsequent changes in action and understandings. Ultimately, the primary concern is even further downstream: Does the use of evidence help set in play a chain of events that results in improved outcomes for the intended program and policy beneficiaries? In terms of Figure 13.2, this means there are important potential additions that could be made on the right-hand side. However, given the focus of this book, the already ambitious Figure 13.2 will not be further elaborated here. (For one approach to the kind of additions that might be made, see Henry & Mark, 2003; Mark & Henry, 2004.)

of context and from each of the levels of processes. It would, however, also be less legible.

FIVE ASPECTS OF CONTEXT

As noted during the discussion of Figure 13.1, judgments about credibility, relevance, and the other characteristics of evidence generally do not take place in a vacuum. Rather, they take place in the context of, for example, a specific evaluation conducted of a particular program, which was implemented on a pilot basis to address a given social problem, in the face of the information needs of certain stakeholders, with all of this taking place within a broader social context.

Julnes and Rog (Chapter 11) employ a framework that specifies five areas of context: (a) decision context, which involves stakeholders' information needs and the alternative evaluation questions and tasks that might be addressed, such as formative versus summative evaluation purposes; (b) problem/phenomenon context, which involves key attributes of the phenomenon being investigated, such as whether change is likely to be easy and quick or difficult and slow; (c) program/policy intervention context, which includes characteristics of the program or policy, such as the level of program maturity; (d) evaluation context, which concerns specific circumstances of the evaluation or study, including funding and evaluation capacity; and (e) environmental context, that is, more general characteristics of the context in which the program or policy operates, which includes political constraints and ethical considerations. Four of these are represented on the left side of Figure 13.2, with the evaluation or study context placed slightly to the right of the others (which typically precede the study).

The Julnes and Rog model of alternative areas of context can be used to organize many points raised throughout this book and elsewhere. As one example, drawing on her experience leading a major unit of what is now called the Government Accountability Office (GAO), Chelimsky (Chapter 9) identifies different kinds of evaluation questions. According to Chelimsky, the questions that come to evaluators fall into four categories: management questions, knowledge questions, accountability questions, and development questions. This distinction could be incorporated within Julnes and Rog's decision context.

More important than its ability to incorporate others' conceptualization, Julnes and Rog's model of context can be useful in thinking about method choices. Julnes and Rog sensibly caution against the idea that any framework can effectively generate method choices automatically. But they also suggest that attention to relevant contextual factors can be useful when a preferred method is being selected. For example, in their Table 11.2 and thereabout, Julnes and Rog discuss a set of contextual factors that they see as making RCTs particularly valuable. These include information needs that center on the merit and worth of a program (such that an estimate of average program effects would be informative); the need for evidence that provides a high level of confidence about the program effects; a phenomenon that does not allow a confident estimation of effects with simpler methods; a program that is sufficiently mature; and adequate resources for an RCT, along with the absence of major ethical concerns.

It would be possible to engage in a similar exercise to try to identify the contextual factors that would make other methods particularly valuable. This includes methods that were discussed in this volume and ones that were not. Some readers might wish to take this on as an exercise (this might be a good exercise for graduate students, for example).

Returning to Figure 13.2, the specifics of context are likely to affect perceptions of credibility and the other attributes of evidence. For instance, the decision context should strongly affect judgments of relevance. Suppose the decision context is such that information is needed about a program's overall merit and worth. RCTs and related methods would then be more likely to be seen as relevant, while a study that provides descriptive information about implementation would be likely be viewed as less relevant.

Contextual factors could also affect the relative importance (or weighting) of the various criteria as precursors of actionability. Imagine, for example, a decision environment in which a high level of confidence is needed in the estimate of program effects. Inferential potency should be relatively more important in this context as a determinant of judged actionability. (For the sake of simplicity, Figure 13.2 does not have arrows showing all the possible effects of context on each of the perceived criteria of evidence.)

THREE LEVELS OF PROCESSES

Figure 13.2 expands on Figure 13.1 in another way—by including three levels of processes that may be involved in generating judgments about credibility and the other attributes from Figure 13.1. Mark and Henry (2004) used the same levels in discussing processes that lead to the use or influence of evaluation findings. In short, these three are the individual, interpersonal, and collective levels (the collective level could involve political process or other organizational processes, depending on the circumstances). Different distinctions could be made, either coarser or finer, but the three categories in Figure 13.2 appear to be useful without being too cumbersome. Contributors to this volume did not explicitly highlight the existence of these three levels. However, several authors focused on different levels, as noted in this section.

Individual level processes are, for the most part, psychological in nature. Miller's (Chapter 3) primary focus is on the individual psychological processes that can affect judgments of credibility. Although her emphasis is on credibility, the processes Miller reviews have implications for the other characteristics of evidence and potentially for the perception of the Julnes and Rog's aspects of context.

As Miller explains, the extent to which a potential user relies on the actual content of an evaluation depends on the user's ability and motivation to do so. Otherwise, various peripheral cues or heuristics may be employed. For example, the format and appearance of a report (or briefing) may matter. The prestige of the evaluator's affiliation, consistency of findings with deeply held beliefs, and various other factors (many reviewed by Miller) can affect perceived credibility and other perceived attributes of evidence at the individual level. Chelimsky makes a related point, drawing on her experience rather than the psychological literature on credibility. She shares the lesson that evaluators should attend to "the evidence of credibility" as well as the credibility of evidence. In this way, Chelimsky offers practice guidance that is conceptually related to Miller's research-based review. Chelimsky also calls for clear communication based on the actual strength of the evidence. Without careful attention to this, peripheral cues could lead to weak evidence being viewed as strong or vice versa. At the individual level, personally held values can also affect perceptions, for example, by making findings seem more credible if they agree with the person's values.

The *interpersonal level* involves processes by which one or more individuals influence another. For example, legislators' views of the credibility of evidence are often based on input from their staff or others. More generally, people with expertise and interest in a program or policy area often are among the first to become familiar with relevant evaluations or other studies; they may then engage in efforts to persuade others. Such intermediaries may undertake explicit efforts to shape others' views of the credibility and relevance of the evidence. Or their efforts may be more subtle.

Greene (Chapter 10) emphasizes the importance of interpersonal processes as determinants of credibility. Mathison makes a similar point, but in less detail. Like Mathison, Greene does not focus on congressional staff, experts, or other intermediaries. Instead, she focuses on the interactions between the evaluator and local stakeholders. Greene contends that, in addition to strong and appropriate methods, credibility depends on the evaluation questions (a) having "*contextual meaning and relevance*," that is, being of interest "to stakeholders *in the contexts* being evaluated" and, further, (b) being of interest "to a *diversity of stakeholders* in the contexts being evaluated, with special inclusion of the interests of stakeholders who are least well served in those contexts." To achieve this, Greene focuses on the cultivation of respectful relationships with local stakeholders and quality communication. She also emphasizes the inclusion of local stakeholders and their values in generating judgments of a program's value. For Greene, these aspects of interpersonal relations are key to achieving credibility.

The *collective level* involves processes that take place in identifiable and relatively stable social aggregates, such as private organizations and governments. I focus here on the political processes that operate in democratic governments. To be clear, the focus here is not on collective processes in the *use* of findings, such as the passage of a law that expands a pilot program to a national one. Rather, the focus here is on how collective (in this case, political) processes can affect relevant aspects of context and therefore influence the perceived characteristics of evidence, such as credibility. In particular, political deliberations frequently set the decision context, which in turn affects the judged relevance of different kinds of information. Political considerations also may affect the height of the hurdle required for a decision to act. For instance, if a program is well entrenched (think Social Security during much of its life), the threshold required to make a change is higher. Political processes do not fully determine judged relevance or other perceived attributes of evidence, however. Consider as an example the IES priority, which was established by appointed officials using standard procedures in response to legislation. The priority may have affected some people's view of what constituted relevant and credible evidence. But clearly, not all observers agreed.

Several contributors to this volume refer to political processes and their role in the evaluation of evidence. For example, Henry (Chapter 4) discusses political processes in a general sense. Chelimsky (Chapter 9) draws on her impressive experiences to describe the interactions between the GAO and Congress in several evaluation efforts involving synthesis of the available evidence.

The contrast between these two evaluators' typical work settings may point to an aspect of context that is not adequately appreciated relative to its importance. Sometimes evaluators work in circumstances that allow them to interact directly with key potential users of their work. Chelimsky at the GAO could engage in negotiations with members of congress and their staff about the scope of a synthesis or other evaluation. Greene presumes that the evaluator can interact with local stakeholders. In contrast, evaluators sometimes are several steps removed from the ultimate key potential users of their work. For instance, a national evaluation that could inform legislative action might be mandated by Congress but overseen by an agency in the executive branch. The number of steps between evaluation and evaluation users may alter the effectiveness of the use of various practices that an evaluator might undertake to try to increase credibility and actionability.

Selected Additional Issues Related to the Framework

The framework presented in Figure 13.2 can serve as background to thinking about several other issues raised, explicitly or implicitly, across the preceding chapters.

DIVERGENT VIEWS ABOUT DEMOCRACY AND EVALUATION

Greene (Chapter 10, 2009) and Henry (Chapter 4) both appeal to democratic values, but in support of rather different views of evaluation. Henry refers to contemporary theory about representative democracy. More specifically, Henry highlights the contribution that can occur when convincing information about program effects is available to democratically elected and appointed officials (and to voters who may be disappointed in their representatives' choices).

Greene (2009), in contrast, emphasized that stakeholders other than policy makers "have other legitimate and important questions" and that the "privileging of the interests of the elite in evaluation and research is radically undemocratic." In Chapter 10, Greene states, "Evidence that is relevant only for remote stakeholders does not have the potential for credibility." Thus Greene emphasizes direct, participatory democracy. Related to this, she highlights interpersonal processes by which the evaluator includes, communicates with, and respects local stakeholders, especially the least well-off. Because Henry emphasizes representative democracy, he instead seems willing to address the information needs of elite and remote stakeholders such as legislators, who may be interested in assessing the effects of a program they have funded.

Perhaps the difference between Henry and Greene is smaller than it appears. That is, the questions that interest legislators may be of interest not *only* to these remote decision makers but also to local stakeholders. Even so, Henry and Greene would seem to diverge at least in terms of assumptions and preferred procedures. Henry appears to assume, in general, the legitimacy of addressing the question about average program effects when policy makers request such information. In contrast, Greene seems not to assume the legitimacy of this question, unless respectful interactions with local stakeholders reveal their interest in it.

Perhaps an alternative approach is to recognize that in the U.S. and most modern democracies, a mixed model of democracy operates. The reality is a mix of representative democracy, direct participatory democracy, and probably other abstract models. From this vantage, evaluators can serve democracy by addressing either the information needs of elected and appointed officials or the information needs of local stakeholders. Indeed, it can be argued that both democracy and the field of evaluation benefit from having evaluators who emphasize and serve different audiences. Further, for both approaches, a persuasive argument can be made for the evaluator to try to ensure that multiple value positions are considered and the needs of the least well-off are represented. But, from this perspective, there is not a single pathway by which evaluation can serve democratic ends.

WHOSE VIEWS?

The issue raised by Henry and Greene of representative versus participatory democracy represents a more general concern: Whose views about credibility, actionability, and the like matter? The pragmatist is likely to say that the views that matter most are those of whoever is supposed to be influenced by the evaluation or applied social research and perhaps whoever else will influence them. So, for example, if the potential use of evaluation findings is by legislators voting on reauthorization of welfare, then for the pragmatist, the perceptions that matter most are those of the legislators as well as others who may affect their judgment, such as key legislative staff. Greene's (Chapter 10) comments indicate that not all researchers and evaluators would agree with this idea, however. Greene appears to give priority to the perspectives of various local stakeholders directly involved with the program, especially the disadvantaged.

The question of whose views matter reminds us of an additional consideration that overlays Figure 13.2: Whose judgments are we considering when we assess the decision context and other contextual considerations? Whose perceptions of credibility, relevance, and so on matter? Left unconstrained, these views may well vary, as shown for example by the contrast of Henry's and Bickman and Reich's views with those of either Scriven or Rallis and Mathison.

WITH WHAT SUPPORTS?

Drawing on the psychological literature on credibility, Miller (Chapter 3) reminds us that people often rely on peripheral cues, such as a researcher affiliation or an evaluation report's appearance. For people instead to do a thoughtful assessment of the quality of a report and its findings, they need to have both the ability and the motivation to do so. Many potential users of applied research and evaluation do not have the training required to pass technical judgment of the quality of the work. Many also have too much else to do in their jobs and lives. This shortage of ability and/or motivation is among the reasons why legislators often rely on staff for guidance as to how heavily to weigh evidence.

A variety of professional arrangements can be seen as offering support for the sensemaking efforts of decision makers and other stakeholders who may have to decide whether and how to weight evaluative or other evidence in their decisions. These include but are not limited to peer review panels that select studies for funding, expert advisory panels that help guide the project, meta-evaluators who offer judgments on the quality of the work, and the comments from scholarly and professional experts who praise or criticize the study.

In addition, efforts are sometimes undertaken to increase capacity to make sense of evidence. Professional associations may hold "boot camps" for reporters and other intermediaries. Professional evaluators have held briefings about using evidence for staffers and government officials. In Chapter 9, Chelimsky's advice about "evidence of credibility" offers a concise roadmap for evaluators to create a guide to evidence quality within an evaluation briefing or report.

The creation and dissemination of *evidence hierarchies*, which rate methods in terms of quality, can be seen as another attempt at capacity building. That is, in a sense, an evidence hierarchy is an effort to assist stakeholders who lack training in research methods but who need to decide whether one or more studies provide actionable guidance. The problem is that in practice, evidence hierarchies tend to be too broad and too general. Too often, they seem to suggest that a preferred method, such as the RCT, is *generally* preferable; it would be better to suggest that the method tends to be valuable for certain purposes in specific circumstances. Thus evidence hierarchies tend not to give adequate attention to the kind of analysis of a specific context that Julnes and Rog call for. Many evidence hierarchies also tend to give short shrift to the strengths and weaknesses of a study *as conducted*. Thus they tend not to give adequate attention to the kind of detailed inventory of validity threats and related weaknesses presented by Bickman and Reich. An important ongoing project for the future involves the construction of better forms of support for those who should consider research evidence in their decisions but do not have advanced training in the methods used.

GIVEN WHAT ASSUMPTIONS?

As noted previously, people with different method predilections probably start with different default assumptions. They may, for example, assume that different decision contexts generally exist. Consider the earlier discussion of Henry and Rallis, who make different default assumptions about relevance. Or people may have opposing assumptions about the extent to which the problem and program context enable causal inference with methods other than RCTs; this would create differing views about credibility and inferential potency. A case can be made that these different default assumptions often arise, at least in part, from differences in training and in adherence to the kind of traditions and paradigms that Christie and Fleischer (Chapter 2) describe.

A case can also be made that if one could create greater agreement about the nature of the context in which evidence is to be generated, then greater agreement would probably result about method choice, credibility, and so on. This notion was a major thrust of the Julnes and Rog chapter. In the absence of detailed information about context, different evaluators may have quite varied views about what kind of evidence is typically relevant. On the other hand, if a particular situation is detailed, with the various aspects of Julnes and Rog's five aspects of context spelled out, evaluators may agree more. (Put differently, we can ask evaluators to make *conditional judgments*, assessing the credibility, actionability, etc. of evidence conditional on certain detailed contexts.) If this is true, future discussion could focus more on the factors that underlie opinions about credible and actionable evidence rather than on the more superficial matter of method choice *per se*.

FUTURE RESEARCH

The framework in Figure 13.2 suggests a number of research questions that could be fruitfully addressed. Among the possible questions are the following: (1) One could investigate the interrelations among (and indeed, the construct validity of) credibility, inferential potency, relevance, and comprehensiveness. (2) The extent to which these four attributes affect judgments of actionability could also be investigated. (3) Another group of research questions involves the effects of the various aspects of context on judgments about credibility and the other judged attributes of evidence. (4) The effect of various individual, interpersonal, and collective processes on the other factors in the framework is another arena for research. A range of research methods could be employed, from reflective case studies of past evaluations to surveys measuring evaluators' and stakeholders' perceptions to simulations with random assignment to levels of a factor of interest.

CHOICES FOR INDIVIDUAL
STUDIES AND FOR PORTFOLIOS OF STUDIES

Scriven and Henry, in different ways, raise a very important consideration for a more general theory of credibility and value of evaluation and applied research. Scriven thoughtfully and explicitly raises the question of funding priorities not for individual studies but rather for broader portfolios of studies. He suggests that even if RCTs are preferable in general, one would likely be better off not putting all the investment eggs in the basket of RCTs: "the best single investment—better than every alternative—is not the best bet for the whole portfolio budget." This is a relatively compelling point, especially in light of the kind of external validity and other validity limits noted by Bickman and Reich. For example, RCTs might give the most internally valid, unbiased estimates of the effects of a program; nevertheless, because of the limited circumstances in which random assignment is feasible, RCTs might result in serious reservations about external validity. If true, funding a second RCT with the same external validity limits might purchase less of an increment in confidence relative to funding a strong quasi-experiment. Although the latter would allow less study-specific confidence about the program's effects, it could better facilitate generalization to policy-relevant settings. Recognition that the considerations that guide method choices for one study might be quite different than the considerations that guide method choices for a second, third, or subsequent study is quite consistent with the literature on critical multiplism (e.g., Cook, 1985), but this point has not been adequately recognized in contemporary debates about method preferences and credibility, such as the debates about RCTs in education, development evaluation, and elsewhere.

Henry reminds us that any single funding stream is part of a broader portfolio. He acknowledges the appropriateness of "program administrators who also control evaluation funds to focus evaluations on questions of program coverage, studies of variations in implementation, single-case studies of a program or organization, descriptive studies of program participants, or subjective assessments of satisfaction." But he also supports priorities at select agencies:

> This situation is likely to be best addressed by establishing and funding alternative institutions to provide priorities for evaluations of program effectiveness. It appears that independent or quasi-independent federal organizations such as IES, the National Institute of Justice, and the National Institutes of Health have rebalanced institutional priorities by providing resources for independent evaluations. While evaluations sponsored and conducted by the agencies administering the programs are likely to be biased toward questions that do not include an assessment of the program's consequences, these quasi-independent institutes can help to ensure that the resources needed to implement designs at the top of the hierarchy to evaluate the consequences of public policies and programs are available. (p. 78)

Expanding on this point, we can raise a question about what the conceptual boundary is for the portfolio of studies. Is it, for example, the particular funding program that uses the IES priority for random assignment? Or is it the broader array of Department of Education funding programs, some of which rarely, if ever, fund RCTs? Or is it the still broader set of educational research and evaluation with numerous funding sources? Advocates of the priority for RCTs may, like Henry, take the broader view and see the priority as a rebalancing. Critics of the priority may take the narrower view and see the priority as an unjustified unbalancing.

SELECTED SUGGESTIONS FOR PRACTICE

This chapter provides a framework combining (a) Julnes and Rog's five aspects of context with (b) four attributes of evidence (credibility, inferential potency, relevance, and comprehensiveness) believed to be precursors of judged actionability and (c) three levels of processes that can affect the judgments about credibility and the other factors in the model. Much of the chapter has focused on how the elements of this framework can help clarify why different views exist about method preferences. My hope is that if future debate can be focused on the underlying reasons, the resulting discussion may be more fruitful. Ideally, future discussion could lead to more contingent and consensual guidance statements, indicating which methods are preferable under which circumstances. The framework may also be useful in organizing and supporting suggestions for the planning of applied research and evaluation. The latter possibility is the focus of the current section.

When planning an upcoming evaluation or other applied study, the investigator should consider the areas of context described by Julnes and Rog, probably starting with the decision context. For example, are the issues of interest ones about the overall merit and worth of an intervention, and would these be addressed well by estimating the effects of an identifiable treatment? An example would be "Stakeholders want to know whether the new pre-algebra math curriculum actually leads to improved student performance and interest in math." If the upcoming research should estimate the effect of a specific intervention (e.g., the new math curriculum) on already identified outcomes (e.g., math performance and interest), then experiments, quasi-experiments, and other related cause-probing techniques would provide relevant evidence. In contrast, if the key question instead is "What variants in program implementation exist?" then experiments and their approximations would not be informative. As these examples suggest, the decision context should inform study design and should also inform subsequent judgments of the relevance of the resulting evidence.

Second, consider the other aspects of context. Assume for the moment that the decision context is such that the question of program effects is of interest. As Julnes and Rog discuss, the relative value of a method should be made in light of relevant aspects of context. Is the nature of the phenomenon and program such that effects should be large and quick and alternative explanations of change unlikely? If so, simpler methods, such as a simple pretest–posttest design should suffice. In contrast, if program effects are likely to be modest in size relative to the changes that are plausible from other factors (or validity threats), then an RCT has greater add-on value. Aspects of context will influence perceived credibility and the other attributes of evidence.

Third, be sure to think about comprehensiveness. If the question of program effects is of interest, for example, which outcomes need to be measured in order to meet stakeholder information needs (specific comprehensiveness)?

For instance, can action be taken if relevant stakeholders learn of an effect of a job training program on employment? Or do they need to know about a broader range of outcomes, such as effects on income, family composition, health, and children's well-being? Also, which (if any) other questions, such as ease of quality implementation across sites, need to be addressed (general comprehensiveness)? Even if the study design and budget have been set by others, the evaluator may be able to increase comprehensiveness, especially specific comprehensiveness, by adding other measures.

Fourth, think about generalizability (or external validity) as an aspect of relevance. The decisions that an evaluation are meant to inform may involve places and persons different than the ones examined in the study. At the least, the decisions will be about a future time. Thus practitioners should think about how to increase the presumed application to the settings that would be affected by the decision. For instance, if an RCT is planned, theory-based tests of moderation and mediation may be valuable, as would the sampling of different contexts and subgroups.

A fifth point of action—or an alternative starting point—involves thinking about whose views matter most in this case. For example, whose questions are given priority when assessing the decision context? Of course, the researcher sometimes comes to the scene after the funding agency or some other body has defined the scope of the study, effectively taking this kind of planning exercise out of the hands of the researcher. In other cases, the researcher or evaluator has considerable latitude to set, or at least influence, the key research questions and methods. Even when aspects of the study design are defined before the researcher is on the scene, there may be opportunities to modify or at least expand on the original plan. In those cases in which the researcher has more leeway, the pragmatic approach is to consider most strongly the views of the expected users of an evaluation, whether those are legislators, a local service delivery organization or school, a foundation, or others. As we have seen, some applied researchers and evaluators emphasize representative democracy (and, typically, providing information for elected and appointed officials), while others prefer to give voice to the least powerful. The evaluator or applied researcher should at least consider these alternatives. Depending on the answer, this issue may have important implications, including whether to engage deeply in the kind of stakeholder interactions described by Greene.

Sixth, consider the potential supports that will be provided to assist in relevant parties' assessments of credibility and inferential potency. If stakeholders lack the expertise or motivation to make technical judgments of credibility and inferential potency, they may not have strong initial preferences about design. But the practitioner should consider what judgments the stakeholders are likely to have after the researcher has undertaken an educative function with the stakeholders or what judgments would be made by intermediaries such as legislative staff. Chelimsky's points about the evidence of credibility apply.

Seventh, keep in mind that the goal is to facilitate the appropriate use of evidence, not to get all evidence used. Evaluators should not try to sell weak evidence as credible and actionable. Chelimsky reminds us of this in her discussion of telling policy makers what is *not* known. Related to this, the professional standards to which most researchers adhere commonly include statements about technical quality or accuracy—bad research is not justified, even if the relevant stakeholders would find it credible.

At the same time, the height of the threshold for a judgment of action should also be considered. Are high levels of credibility, relevance, inferential potency, and comprehensiveness needed to justify action? Or could action reasonably be guided by the evidence, even if credibility or inferential potency is somewhat lower? Even if the threshold for action is lower, the researcher ought to obtain the strongest evidence possible in light of the available resources. And if credibility, inferential potency, relevance, or comprehensiveness are low, this should be honestly communicated.

Thoughtfully consider trade-offs. As noted previously, trade-offs may exist among credibility, relevance, inferential potency, and comprehensiveness as well as between these and resource constraints. The thoughtful researcher keeps in mind the costs of various trade-offs and attempts to make the choices that will best support judgments of actionability in light of the specific constraints faced.

Think about the next study in context of a portfolio of studies, if more than one study has been or will be done. Much of the past debate about RCTs implies that one size fits all and, therefore, that the fifth study should aspire to the same gold standard as the first four. This is undesirable. For example, the fifth highly credible study about a program's average treatment effect may provide less value relative to a first study that examines another important question. As an another example, a fifth study that is less credible in terms of internal validity could add great value if it extends external validity by examining clients and settings not included in the previous four studies.

Take appropriate advantage especially of the individual and interpersonal processes that can affect judgments of credibility and other attributes of evidence. Examples at the individual level again include Chelimsky's recommendations for providing evidence of credibility. At the interpersonal level, Greene's recommendations about respectful communication and involvement seem valuable, regardless of one's views of democracy.

Conclusion

Frameworks such as those summarized in Figure 13.2 can seem like an academic exercise, of value only to ivory-tower types who care about nothing but abstractions such as *theory*. In the ideal, however, such frameworks will have value both for scholarship and for *practice*. I hope that readers will be able to find both kinds of values in the framework offered here. I would hope that the framework might contribute to more fruitful debate and discussion about method choices, including highlighting common ground where such can be found; guide future research to increase understanding; and support thoughtful practice in generating credible and actionable evidence in service of evidence-informed decision making that may lead to better outcomes for the intended beneficiaries of the programs, policies, and practices that we study.

References

Berk, R. A. (2005). Randomized experiments as the bronze standard. *Journal of Experimental Criminology, 1,* 417–433.

Berliner, D. C. (2002). Educational research: The hardest science of them all. *Educational Researcher, 31,* 18–20.

Cartwright, N., & Hardie, J. (2012). *Evidence-based policy: A practical guide to doing it better.* Oxford, England: Oxford University Press.

Cook, T. D. (1985). Post-positivist critical multiplism. In R. L. Shotland & M. M. Mark (Eds.), *Social science and social policy* (pp. 21–62). Beverly Hills, CA: SAGE.

Cook, T. D. (2003). Why have educational evaluators chosen not to do randomized experiments? *Annals of American Academy of Political and Social Science, 589,* 114–149.

Cronbach, L. J. (1982). *Designing evaluations of educational and social programs.* San Francisco, CA: Jossey-Bass.

Donaldson, S., Christie, T. C., & Mark, M. M. (2009). *What counts as credible evidence in applied research and evaluation practice?* Thousand Oaks, CA: SAGE.

Gersten, R., & Hitchcock, J. (2009). What is credible evidence in education? The role of the What Works Clearinghouse in informing the process. In S. Donaldson, T. C. Christie, & M. M. Mark (Eds.), *What counts as credible evidence in applied research and evaluation practice?* (pp. 78–95). Thousand Oaks, CA: SAGE.

Greene, J. C. (2009). Evidence as "proof" and evidence as "inkling." In S. Donaldson, T. C. Christie, & M. M. Mark (Eds.), *What counts as credible evidence in applied research and evaluation practice?* (pp. 153–167). Thousand Oaks, CA: SAGE.

Henry, G. T., & Mark, M. M. (2003). Beyond use: Understanding evaluation's influence on attitudes and actions. *American Journal of Evaluation, 24,* 293–314.

Mark, M. M., & Henry, G. T. (2004). The mechanisms and outcomes of evaluation influence. *Evaluation, 10,* 35–57.

Rallis, S. F. (2009). Reasoning with rigor and probity: Ethical premises for credible evidence. In S. Donaldson, T. C. Christie, & M. M. Mark (Eds.), *What counts as credible evidence in applied research and evaluation practice?* (pp. 168–180). Thousand Oaks, CA: SAGE.

Reichardt, C. S., & Mark, M. M. (1998). Quasi-experimentation. In L. Bickman & D. Rog (Eds.), *Handbook of applied social research* (pp.193–228). Newbury Park, CA: SAGE.

Appendix I

Scriven's Argument
Against the Superiority of RCTs for Estimating
Program Effects: Summary and Critique

S criven (Chapter 6) argues forcefully against giving a general priority to RCTs. In this Appendix, I go into Scriven's argument in relative (and perhaps not always reader-friendly) detail, because it is a potentially quite important and influential position articulated by a major figure and deserves serious consideration.

Scriven states, for example,

> One of the main attractions of the RCT approach is that it appears to provide a greater degree of certainty for its conclusions than the alternatives. There are circumstances in which this is true, but it is not true across the board for several reasons.

That is, Scriven suggests that any advantage RCTs have is not general but only applies in specific, in perhaps rare or unimportant cases for evaluation and applied social research. Moreover, Scriven indicates that "the highest relevant standards for scientific purposes are readily attainable by many alternative designs in many cases, including cases where RCTs cannot meet those standards."

Summarizing his position, Scriven states,

> It will be shown (i) that the usual claimed intrinsic advantage of the RCT design is only a theoretical advantage, and its actual achievements are

frequently matched in practice by many other designs; (ii) that even such a theoretical advantage is not present in the RCT designs currently being advocated because they are not in fact true RCT designs; and (iii) that, nevertheless, there are real advantages for a near-RCT approach in some circumstances, although they can only be determined by weighing its comparative merits on . . . the . . . considerations . . . that bear on the merit of a research design.

One way that Scriven makes his case (especially in relation to his point "(ii)") is by pointing out, quite rightly, that in social and educational evaluations (unlike good drug trials), "blindness" to conditions is rare. That is, participants and researchers typically know which condition participants are in. As a result, the Hawthorne effect (and other expectancy-based effects) can occur. One response from advocates of RCTs is to question the frequency or strength of Hawthorne effects in the kind of evaluations Scriven is addressing. If these effects were so powerful, an RCT advocate can suggest, then almost surely they would have been used to create powerful interventions. And if Hawthorne effects were frequent and large, previous evaluations would not have found so many treatments to be ineffective. In addition, blindness, also known as *masking*, is not common in evaluations that do not use RCTs, so their absence in RCTs is not a competitive disadvantage.

Scriven also supports his arguments that RCTs do not have a general advantage by giving a hypothetical example. The treatment in the example is a new instructional method, studied with a nonequivalent-groups pretest–posttest quasi-experimental design, using morning and afternoon college class sections as the nonequivalent groups. The morning class is assigned to the treatment group in the first semester, with a plan to replicate another semester with the afternoon class receiving the treatment. The same instructor teaches both sections, observers look for differences other than the intended ones (and do not find them), pretest scores are similar across groups, and the treatment group students show about two standard deviations more improvement in the comparison group.

I agree with Scriven that the study, as described, is reasonably compelling in terms of demonstrating the effectiveness of the new instructional procedure. More generally, without a doubt, Scriven is correct that under certain conditions, RCTs are not required for causal inference. As Scriven points out, children's learning about the world demonstrates that actionable causal inferences can be drawn without randomized trials. The question, however, is what (if any) implications this observation should have for the debate about the role of RCTs in evaluation. Do critics of the IES priority win the debate if they can point to a hypothetical or actual case in which some other method gives a compelling causal conclusion? I think not. I believe Scriven's argument falls

short in at least three interrelated ways when viewed in relation to arrangements such as the IES priority for randomized experiments.

First, Scriven's treatment of RCTs and their alternatives is asymmetrical.
That is, he allows assumptions in benefit of the alternative procedures that he
does not allow for RCTs. In particular, he discounts the desirability of RCTs and
educational and social evaluation because, absent blinding to conditions,
Hawthorne effects and the like are possible. But this same shortcoming does not
lead him to discount the hypothetical study using the pretest–posttest nonequivalent design, which would seem to be equally susceptible to expectancy effects.
He also builds into the hypothetical study design features such as the use of
independent observers who assess implementation of the intervention and do
not find other differences. However, a more symmetrical comparison would
build the same design ancillaries, such as quality implementation assessment,
into both RCTs and the alternatives with which they are being compared. Scriven
also builds into the example a set of characteristics that contribute greatly to the
strength of causal inference that the quasi-experimental design allows in this
case: pretest equivalence, replication, no apparent confounds in implementation,
a huge treatment effect, and no other apparent validity threats. What are the odds
that all of these will occur in practice? If the quasi-experiment is conducted but
pretest scores turn out to differ significantly between sections, for example, the
study results may be hard to interpret. More generally, wouldn't a fair comparison across method types endow RCTs with equally ideal circumstances (or at
least circumstances that are equally likely to arise in practice)?

Moreover, the critic could suggest potential threats to the quasi-experimental
design Scriven presents. These would include the possibility of an experimenter
or instructor expectancy effect that the observers did not see, initial differences
that were not identified by the pretest because of its low reliability with students
who are new to the course content, or selection effects that arise because of relevant factors other than those captured by the pretest (i.e., factors other than initial
course-related content knowledge). For example, selection bias might arise
because of the differential scheduling across semesters of another course that
must be taken by some but not all of the students in this class, specifically those in
a harder and highly competitive major (think pre-med). In practice, the quasi-
experimentalist would, of course, try to assess the plausibility of each threat (e.g.,
by looking for equivalence not only on pretest scores but also on other factors,
such as student's major) and then consider whether any remaining factors could
plausibly account for the observed treatment effect. But in Scriven's argument, he
uses the theoretical possibility of Hawthorne effects as a criticism of RCTs but
does not, in my view, apply a similar standard to alternatives. If he had, then the
theoretical possibility of selection biases due to factors other than pretest scores
would seem to lead to a poorer grade than he gives to the quasi-experiment in his
hypothetical example. In short, I believe that Scriven's comparison between RCTs

and their alternatives is asymmetrical. The argument is designed to show that alternatives *can* at least *at times* be equal or better, not that they *generally* are.

Second, then, the demonstration of at least occasional superiority of alternatives to RCTs is of questionable relevance to the controversies about RCTs, particularly for funding priorities such as that specified by IES. In this regard, the relevant considerations are somewhat different for the IES-type issue of the funding of proposed studies than for the WWC-type issue of screening studies after the fact. For IES-type funding decisions, the question must be about the *a priori* expectation of valid findings for the different kinds of designs under consideration in the sort of contexts covered by the funding program. For instance, before Scriven's hypothetical study was conducted, it would not be possible to know with confidence that the treatment and comparison groups would be equivalent at the pretest or that the treatment effect would be huge (relative to any likely selection effects or other validity threats). For funding decisions, it may be possible to know some general, likely characteristics of the research context (more on this momentarily), but one will not know the details of important things such as pretest equivalence in the absence of random assignment. Instead, for funding decisions, the relevant task is to assess the *expected* validity of inferences in light of certain assumptions about the causal context in which the study will occur. One makes one's bets on expectations. Thus Scriven's argument, at least the portion I have reviewed to this point, seems more applicable to the kind of after-the-fact screening done by the WWC, where, in a particular review, a nonrandom quasi-experiment could be rated more favorably than a (flawed) RCT. The WWC rating procedure can downgrade an RCT, for example, if there are unaddressed attrition problems. (One can still question whether the review protocol and reviewers do a good job of taking into account all the relevant factors for making such judgments in the context of individual studies.)

Third, and most importantly, Scriven's presuppositions about the causal field differ from those that I believe are assumed by thoughtful supporters of RCTs in educational and social evaluation. As already noted, Scriven presumes relatively large effects of the treatment in his hypothetical example. Moreover, in his discussion of everyday causal inference and direct observation of causation, his examples typically involve a relatively stable causal field. For example, the child's shaking of a rattle leads to a noise, but rattles do not become noisier over time as they mature with age. Nor are there are a myriad of forces in the world that lead rattles to make noise, other than shaking them.

In contrast, advocates of RCTs appear to presume a very different kind of causal background. They assume, for example, that children commonly will do better over time, and so the study of the effects of educational interventions requires comparison groups. They further assume that individual differences exist and that these are often are related to the amount of improvement over time and, further, that nonrandom groupings into conditions will often be con-founded with individual differences. Put somewhat differently, selection bias will often occur. The belief that selection biases are common drives the preference for random assignment in general. Advocates of RCTs also generally assume that a wide variety of forces (captured in a generic sense in the list of threats to internal validity popularized by Campbell and his colleagues) exist that can cause changes in the outcome variable of interest. In addition, most advocates of RCTs presume that it is worthwhile to identify much smaller effects than those assumed by Scriven in his hypothetical example. This issue of what effect size is of interest is important. If Scriven is correct that only huge effects are of interest, then designs other than RCTs will more often provide credible conclusions about whether the treatment was effective. In contrast, if small or modest effects are worth identify-ing, this reduces considerably the likelihood that other designs will allow confi-dent judgment about whether or not a treatment effect occurred.

Scriven addresses the idea of the expected or worthwhile effect size while presenting his hypothetical quasi-experiment. Scriven says "Clearly the size of the difference [between the treatment and comparison group] is crucial here, as is often the case." He asks the reader to reflect "on the fact that you are not very interested in small differences because they have a track record of not showing up on the replications at distant sites." He also indicates that the pretest–posttest nonequivalent-groups design should be preferred, "knowing that it's a net that will catch only big fish, but you don't want little fish." In contrast, I believe that many educational evaluators, taking into consideration the track record of edu-cational interventions (similar to other evaluators informed by meta-analyses in various program domains), presume that the typical fish is not a huge one. Moreover, many of these evaluators implicitly or explicitly assume that moderate effects, and perhaps even small ones, can make worthwhile contributions.

Perhaps we should consider two different debates. One debate focuses on whether all scientific evidence comes from RCTs and whether RCTs are required for all causal inference. If this is the debate, Scriven wins by a mile. Science benefits from a wide array of methods, including in areas in which RCTs are never conducted and are perhaps impossible. Likewise, causal infer-ence is often justified without RCTs. Scriven also wins if the debate is about the inevitability of any advantage RCTs have in general: RCTs are not bulletproof.

But is this the relevant debate? Or is the more important debate, at least for the IES-type issue of relative preference, about the expected quality of causal inference for RCTs versus other kinds of studies and for the specific kinds of circumstances expected in the kind of study being funded. In the case of educational interventions, one version of the debate would be, What is the *a priori* preferability of RCTs, relative to alternatives, when the research question involves the estimating the effects of a given treatment (such as an educational intervention); when even small to moderate effects are of interest; and when the causal field is such that the key outcome variables are likely to be affected by a range of other forces, such as maturation, history, and selection?

Perhaps the prior question for debate is, To what extent is the preceding framing of the debate the proper one? For example, is Scriven correct that the relevant method choices need only to be able to net "big fish—that is, very large effect sizes—or is it important to choose methods that have the potential for identifying moderate or even small effects? Credible evidence might be infused into the debate. What does the history of educational evaluation tell us about how big the fish usually are? In addition, more detailed arguments—rather than explicit claims or implicit assumptions—can be made about the relative value of small or moderate effects. Ideally, these would be made from the perspective of different stakeholder groups.

To be fair, there are reasons that Scriven tried to demonstrate that RCTs did not have a general advantage and that alternatives can give equally compelling causal inference at times. His focus appears to be a response, first, to unfortunate language that has been used in promulgating the IES priority and the WWC review process. At times, that language has seemed to equate *scientific research* with *randomized trials*. Thus critics of the IES priority and the WWC sometimes appear to think the debate is won simply by demonstrating that scientific procedures do not always involve random assignment (hence, for example, Scriven's reference to plate tectonics). It would have been preferable, from my perspective, if more advocates of RCTs themselves critiqued the unfortunate language that appears to equate science with random assignment studies. And it would have been beneficial if more critics of the IES priority had recognized that, in demonstrating the inaccuracy of such statements, you might not persuade those on the other side—those who think a different question is the relevant one for debate (i.e., the likely strength of different designs, judged prior to the conduct of the research, for estimating small or moderate program effects amidst many other factors in a complex causal field).

Scriven's emphasis on demonstrating that alternative designs can provide a causal inference at least as credible as an RCT may have also stemmed in part from a second source. That is, the IES priority gives extra points to grant proposals for *all* the proposals that include random assignment to conditions. The applicant does not have to demonstrate that RCTs are preferable in the particular case or that alternatives would not be equally or more effective. In other words, the priority appears to assume the preferability of RCTs across the board. Thus one might ask, wouldn't the logic of the priority be undercut if one demonstrates that RCTs do not have superiority across the board? Again, my view is that the more appropriate question has to do with the expected strength of inferences that will arise, in the expected causal context, if the question of a program's effect is of interest. In the particular case of the IES priority, one could ask, Do the circumstances that most call for an RCT actually hold in the kind of places where Department of Education–funded research takes place, or is it more similar to the circumstances Scriven posits? At the same time, the arguments Scriven makes about the desirability of varying the methods investments in a broader portfolio are persuasive, assuming the funding otherwise would go to multiple RCTs examining the same program.

This appendix has gone into detail about Scriven's argument about RCTs in the current volume. The Appendix is not presented in terms of the framework sketched out in Figure 13.2. Interested readers may find it a worthwhile exercise to translate and expand the ideas in the Appendix using the elements of that framework.

Author Index

Subject Index

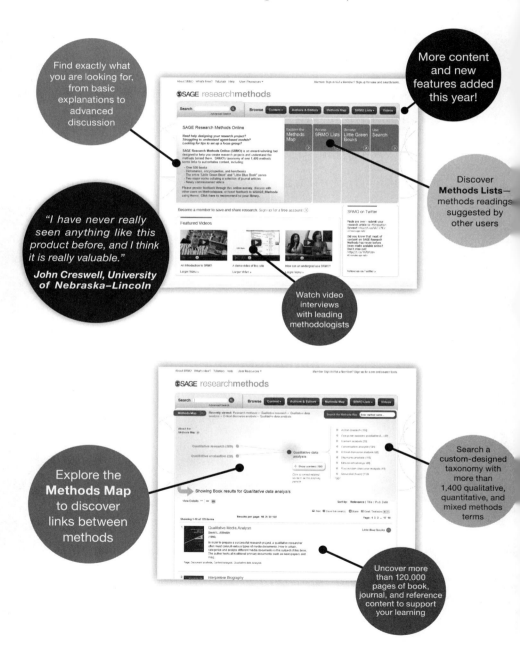